MEDIEVAL NARRATIVE SOURCES
A GATEWAY INTO THE MEDIEVAL MIND

MEDIAEVALIA LOVANIENSIA

Editorial Board

Carlos Steel
Jean Goossens
Geert Claassens
Werner Verbeke

SERIES I / STUDIA XXXIV

KATHOLIEKE UNIVERSITEIT LEUVEN
INSTITUUT VOOR MIDDELEEUWSE STUDIES
LEUVEN (BELGIUM)

MEDIEVAL NARRATIVE SOURCES
A GATEWAY INTO THE MEDIEVAL MIND

Edited by

Werner VERBEKE
Ludo MILIS
Jean GOOSSENS

LEUVEN UNIVERSITY PRESS
2005

© 2005 Leuven University Press / Presses Universitaires de Louvain / Universitaire Pers Leuven, Blijde-Inkomststraat 5, B-3000 Leuven/Louvain (Belgium).

All rights reserved. Except in those cases expressly determined by law, no part of this publication may be multiplied, saved in an automated data file or made public in any way whatsoever without the express prior written consent of the publishers.

ISBN 90 5867 398 7
D/2005/1869/33
NUR: 613-684

CONTENTS

Ludo MILIS
Medieval Narrative Sources: A Fascinating Gateway into the Medieval Mind — VII

Renée NIP
Changing Demands, Changing Tools: A Survey of Narrative Historical Sources Written during the Middle Ages in the Northern Low Countries — 1

Elisabeth van HOUTS
Gender, Memories and Prophecies in Medieval Europe — 21

Steven VANDERPUTTEN
From Sermon to Science: Monastic Prologues from the Southern Low Countries as Witnesses of Historical Consciousness (10th-15th Centuries) — 37

Paul BERTRAND
Réformes ecclésiastiques, luttes d'influence et hagiographie à l'abbaye de Maubeuge (IXe-XIe s.) — 55

Brigitte MEIJNS
The 'Life of Bishop John of Thérouanne' by Archdeacon Walter (1130) and the Bishop's Pastoral Activities — 77

Michael GOODICH
Microhistory and the Inquisitiones *into the Life and Miracles of Philip of Bourges and Thomas of Hereford* — 91

Werner VERBEKE
La 'Vie de saint Amand' par Gillis de Wevel et ses modèles — 107

Pieter-Jan DE GRIECK
L'image de la ville et l'identité monastique dans l'oeuvre de Gilles Li Muisis (1272-1353) — 139

Janick APPELMANS
The Abbey of Affligem and the Emergence of a Historiographic Tradition in Brabant (1268-1322) — 163

Thomas KOCH
Selbstvergewisserung und Memoria in der Devotio Moderna: Die Traditionscodices der brabantischen Augustiner-Chorherrenstifte   181

Rudi KÜNZEL
Oral and Written Traditions in the 'Versus de unibove'   205

Geert H.M. CLAASSENS
The 'Schale of Boendale': On Dealing with Fact and Fiction in Vernacular Mediaeval Literature   231

Steven VANDERPUTTEN
Une iconographie de l'historiographie monastique: réalité ou fiction?   251

Annex:
Jeroen DEPLOIGE
The Database Narrative Sources from the Medieval Low Countries: A short introduction followed by the User's Guide   271

Index codicum manu scriptorum   299

Index nominum   301

INTRODUCTION

Ludo MILIS

MEDIEVAL NARRATIVE SOURCES:
A FASCINATING GATEWAY INTO THE MEDIEVAL MIND

More than ten years ago, some medievalists of the Catholic University of Leuven and the University of Ghent joined together in order to create a repertory of medieval narrative sources focusing on the southern Low Countries. Since that very tentative beginning, this intellectual challenge has received generous support from the Fund for scientific Research – Flanders, officially the *Fonds voor Wetenschappelijk Onderzoek – Vlaanderen*. It gave us the necessary means, scholarly as well as financial, with which to proceed.

When we started, Werner Verbeke, Jean Goossens, and myself, were joined by some young, active, and bright collaborators. We did not know exactly where we would end up or if we would achieve anything at all. The collaboration between the two groups was excellent. I cannot say often enough how much I have appreciated the intellectual openness of my Leuven colleagues, their sound generosity, and their fruitful helpfulness throughout.

At that time, we did not know what form the final product would take. Would it, perhaps, be something akin to the unprecedented Carasso-Kok for the Northern Netherlands? The latter remains an excellent tool, even after so many years, complete in its contents and reliable in its information. Or, should we use the *Repertorium fontium*, the New Potthast, as our model? Reliable as well, it is slow in its rhythm as a result of its wide, pan-European scope. Finally, should our final product be published in a classical format – that is, printed – or would it be better to join the electronic highway which was then about to be developed? This solution promised to link speed to adaptability. Ultimately, what we called a pre-print – a draft, in other words – was published in a paper version and was soon followed by the electronic database entitled 'Narrative Sources'.

Since 1996, 'Narrative Sources' has been adapted, supplemented, and rearranged every year in the spring, the season of new life. The number of inventoried items have been increased to far more than 2150 titles.

The database itself is stored on the server of the Ghent University Library and is available free of charge through the Internet, courtesy of, among others, SilverPlatter Software. It is immediately apparent that its possibilities are, in all aspects, much greater than CD-ROM versions ever will be. They are usually prohibitively expensive and even if they were cheaper, their consultation remains dependent on the physical presence of the disk. We suggest that those who are interested add the address of 'Narrative sources' to the links they offer on their institutional web page or that they at least store it in their personal bookmark list.

Our intent from the start was to offer a system that was available and open to every form of enlargement. One could envisage a geographical extension, or a chronological, or a typological one. If users ask for supplementary information that we had yet to consider, fields could be added to the individual records. That is not a problem at all. Electronic systems are easily adaptable.

A repertory is, however, just a tool. It facilitates the preparatory work of the historian, or the philologist, or any other interested scholar. Thus, it must be reliable and brought up-to-date constantly. Nevertheless, the exploitation of the information remains the real goal.

What is the next step that we seriously have to consider? Immediate links from the 'Narrative Sources' repertory to the full text. The Ghent University Library has been working on such a system in which bibliographies, catalogues, and articles in reviews are interchangeably linked. Obviously, the availability of full texts in an electronic format and accessible through the Internet is an essential condition for us. Publishers who used to offer CD-ROMS with medieval texts are increasingly forced to work in the direction of on-line consultation, which is a great help. For the medievalist of tomorrow the link bibliography – catalogue – full text will only be hindered by the cost the information providers will continue to impose for every consultation.

The information present thus far in 'Narrative Sources' already allows and facilitates the study of the sources as such, individually or collectively, qualitatively or quantitatively. Thus it has led, in turn, to another project, our current project. This volume is, in fact, the result of this group effort, in which, once again, the universities of Leuven and Ghent are sharing their expertise, and are also assisted by the Royal Library and the General Archives, both in Brussels. In this project, the exploitation of the contents is the goal, with a specific focus on monastic historiography, its social setting, and self-image. In this proceedings, amidst the other highly esteemed scholars from abroad or from other parts of the country, who have been invited to collaborate, some of those working on this project will present their work, their methodology, and their results to-date.

The starting point of the project questionnaire is to determine how and to what extent medieval religious people paid attention to the world outside and how this attitude and mental scope were related to their life choice. This theme has been divided among the four centres involved according to their own areas of expertise. In Leuven, a selection of texts are being studied in depth; let us call it the qualitative approach. In Ghent, some hundreds of texts are being analysed statistically in order to provide a quantitative view. In the Manuscript Room of the Royal Library, miniatures are being compared with the texts they illustrate, a confrontation, thus, of visual and narrative representation. The task of the General Archives is to contrast a selection of narrative sources for specific religious houses with the totality of the records available. Those working at each of these four interdependent pillars will try to detect the criteria according to which religious individuals reduced global information. Their insights in these criteria will then facilitate the entry into the minds of medieval people.

We expect you to inform us of your, sometimes extensive, experience and to join us in the common exploration of medieval narrative sources and thus of medieval life and mental horizon.

Finally, I would like to extend my very warm thanks to the Katholieke Universiteit Leuven and the *Instituut voor Middeleeuwse Studies*, in particular, for being our hosts. Most people know the excellence with which Professor Verbeke organises meetings of this type and much larger ones as well. I greatly appreciate his and his colleagues' sincere and spontaneous friendship.

Renée NIP

CHANGING DEMANDS, CHANGING TOOLS: A SURVEY OF NARRATIVE HISTORICAL SOURCES, WRITTEN DURING THE MIDDLE AGES IN THE NORTHERN LOW COUNTRIES*

Recently, a new project on medieval historiography has received the go ahead at the Department of History of the University of Groningen, where traditionally medieval historiography and hagiography have been central research subjects. Its primary goal is to revise, correct and extend electronically the survey by Marijke Carasso-Kok, published in 1981 under the title *Repertorium van de verhalende historische bronnen uit de Middeleeuwen. Heiligenlevens, annalen, kronieken en andere in Nederland geschreven verhalende bronnen* (Survey of the narrative historical sources from the middle ages. Saint's Lives, annals, chronicles and other narrative sources written in the Low Countries).[1] Confronted with the choices that Carasso-Kok had to make two decades ago and the consequences of her decisions, we have to reconsider these for various reasons, for instance, the new scholarly demands of such a survey in the form of a database. New choices will have to be made. In this contribution I should like to discuss some of the problems most pressing and their possible solutions. But first I shall touch upon the history of the *Repertorium*.

SAMUEL MULLER FZN. (1848-1922)

It was W. Holzmann who first suggested that the *Repertorium Fontium Historiae Medii Aevi* (RFHMA) needed to be accompanied with national surveys of sources which could not be given the attention they deserved in the comprehensive survey known as the 'new Potthast'.[2] The Dutch

---
* I wish to thank dr Elisabeth Van Houts for correcting my English.
1. M. Carasso-Kok, *Repertorium van de verhalende historische bronnen uit de Middeleeuwen. Heiligenlevens, annalen, kronieken en andere in Nederland geschreven verhalende bronnen.* Bibliografische reeks van het Nederlands Historisch Genootschap, 2 (The Hague: Nijhoff, 1981).
2. Carasso-Kok, *Repertorium*, p. viii.

starting-point was the list of chronicles from the Northern Low Countries published by Samuel Muller in 1880.[3] This list in turn had been an answer to the call, frequently heard during the nineteenth century, for a survey of Dutch historiography. In fact, the very first such effort, De Wind's *Bibliotheek van Nederlandsche Geschiedschrijvers* (Library of Dutch historians), published in 1835, was judged quickly to be a failure.[4] Despite the creation of a chair for Dutch History at the University of Leiden in 1850, there was little interest to improve De Wind's work. Thirty years later Muller considered his own list insufficient as a result of the lack of cooperation he had experienced. His scheme had been ambitious and had been aimed at a full list of all Dutch chronicles including information on manuscripts, authors and contents. To that end, he sent out a circular to collect details of existing manuscripts and then asked individual scholars to research a particular chronicle. The list was meant to be a preparation to the *Scriptores rerum nederlandicarum medii aevi*, proposed by J. Bolhuis van Zeeburgh, who had already composed a similar survey on Frisian historiography.[5] Although Muller had the support of the *Nederlandsch Historisch Genootschap* (Historical Society) at Utrecht, only three scholars gave serious support. Nevertheless, he decided to publish the information that he had gathered to serve as a base for further research.[6] Muller did not clarify his geographical and chronological limits. Roughly speaking, he devided the works into three categories: saint's Lives, chronicles and biographies. The chronicles were divided geographically by province and thematically by town, monastery and dynasty. All works were ranked chronologically. Subdivisions listed the most important, edited chronicles, unpublished ones and the shorter ones. He would list, as far as available, the author's name, title, manuscripts, editions and literature, but only occasionaly details on authors or the textual genesis. In all, he listed 266 works.

---

3. S. Muller Fz., *Lijst van Noord-Nederlandse Kronijken, met opgave van bestaande handschriften en literatuur*, Werken van het Historisch Genootschap, 31 (Utrecht, 1880).
4. S. De Wind, *Bibliotheek van Nederlandsche Geschiedschrijvers, I: bevattende de inlandsche geschiedschrijvers der Nederlanden, van de vroegste tijden tot op den Münsterschen Vrede (970-1648)* (Middelburg, 1835); J. Romein, *Geschiedschrijving van de Noord-Nederlandsche geschiedschrijving in de middeleeuwen. Bijdrage tot de beschavingsgeschiedenis* (Haarlem, 1932), pp. xiii-xvii.
5. J. Bolhuis van Zeeburgh, *Kritiek der Friesche Geschiedschrijving* (The Hague, 1873; reprint Amsterdam, 1962).
6. Muller Fz., *Lijst van Noord-Nederlandse Kronijken*, pp. v-ix.

JAN ROMEIN (1893-1962)

It took a long time before another attempt was made to bring together all known information on Dutch medieval historiography. In the interval, several historians filled in the gap. In a brief account of the main sources for the period until 1559 P.J. Blok inserted a summary and characterization of the most important narrative historical sources concerning the Netherlands as an appendix to his history of the Dutch people, first published in 1893.[7] His aim, of course, differed from Muller's. Blok wished to account for his work and, at the same time, to show what historical information was available. He did not intend to provide an instrument to study these sources. Henri Pirenne included in his *Bibliographie de l'Histoire de Belgique* (1902) also the Northern Low Countries, but he gave only an incomplete and rather bare catalogue of narrative sources.[8] H.P. Coster's research on the chronicle of Beka and its sources meant an important step forward with regard to the knowledge of Dutch historiography, in that his introduction to his study, published in 1914, contained a survey of the historiography of Utrecht and Holland preceding Beka's chronicle.[9] Finally, Jan Romein was the first historian who collected systematically full information for his history of Dutch medieval historiography.[10] He planned to publish the book in five volumes, viewing Dutch historiography as a mirror of Dutch self-consciousness. However, he only completed the first volume on medieval historiography.[11] In his introduction he explained why there was so little interest in Dutch medieval historiography. Firstly, there was the undeniable fact that Dutch medieval historiography was second – or even third – rate. Secondly, in the Protestant Netherlands the interest in the past was, especially after the separation of Belgium in 1830, mainly focused on the Dutch Revolt and the Golden Age in the sixteenth and seventeenth century. Thirdly, most scholars were convinced that history could only be a scientific subject if

---

7. P.J. Blok, *Geschiedenis van het Nederlandsche Volk*, I (Leiden, 1923³), pp. 647-79.
8. H. Pirenne, *Bibliographie de l'Histoire de Belgique. Catalogue méthodique et chronologique des sources et des ouvrages principaux relatifs à l'histoire de tous les Pays-Bas jusqu'en 1598 et à l'histoire de Belgique jusqu'en 1830* (Brussels and Ghent, 1902).
9. H.P. Coster, *De kroniek van Johannes de Beka: haar bronnen en haar eerste redactie*, Bijdragen van het Instituut voor Middeleeuwsche Geschiedenis der Rijksuniversiteit te Utrecht, II (Utrecht, 1914).
10. J. Romein, *Geschiedschrijving van de Noord-Nederlandsche geschiedschrijving in de middeleeuwen. Bijdrage tot de beschavingsgeschiedenis* (Haarlem, 1932).
11. M. Carasso-Kok, 'Jan Romein en de Middeleeuwse geschiedschrijving in de Noordelijke Nederlanden', *Theoretische Geschiedenis*, 9 (1982), pp. 231-46, there 233-6.

it was based primarily on documentary sources which were considered to be more reliable. For Romein, however, historiography was the manifestation in which a culture expresses its understanding of the present. Therefore, modern historians should not mine these texts for factual information, but they should study their image of the past. For what reasons did the medieval authors write their history down and why in that way?[12] Nowadays, such questions are common place for all cultural historians or historians of mentalities, but in those days Romein had little followers.

Romein wanted to study historiography in relation to the history of civilization and for that purpose he also had to construct an useful apparatus.[13] Therefore he used a rather complicated structure. He grouped most of the works chronically in so-called cultural circles connected to certain regions, for example the Frisian circle, or institutions, such as the abbey of Egmond, or religious groups like the Modern Devouts. Neither the geographical origin of a text nor its author was significant, but the character of the work. For instance, he treated the late medieval historiography of Holland, that is to say the present provinces of North and South Holland (1350-1490), as separate entity from the Holland-Utrecht circle (1350-1480), eventhough both cover the same period and partly the same region. According to Romein, the typical late medieval historians differed so much from their more traditional colleagues in status and in focus, that they ought to be considered as the forerunners of the Renaissance.[14] Apart from the cultural circles, he also distinguished two types of chronicles, that of dynastic chronicles and of town chronicles. An introduction precedes each group, in which Romein gave a historical context, intertextual relationship, and a characterization. The works are ranged under the author's name, if known, or under their title. The text descriptions contain all available information about author, subject, manuscripts, editions, translations, dating and localization of the writing, commissioner, and, of course, scholarly discussions and literature; they conclude with an analysis of the contents and the author's methods. Romein's survey lists 94 works, but in fact includes more than one hundred works, since some authors wrote more than one work, all to be found under one number. Like Muller, Romein included also saint's Lives and biographies.

---

12. Romein, *Geschiedschrijving*, pp. xxii-xxiii.
13. *Ibid.*, pp. xix-xxiv.
14. *Ibid.*, pp. 95-100. Recently, a first move was made to revise Romein's history of Dutch historiography: J.W.J. Burgers, 'Geschiedschrijving in Holland tot omstreeks 1300', *Jaarboek voor Middeleeuwse Geschiedenis*, 3 (2000), pp. 92-131.

In view of his ideas on historiography his inclusion of hagiography is not surprising. He considered hagiography as a historiographical genre and especially the older Lives as extremely important to our knowledge of history, above all the history of civilization. He therefore considered Liudger's *Life of Saint Gregory* as the first Dutch example of historiography.[15] In this respect, he was far ahead of most of his fellow historians who regarded hagiography as a fictional genre, unreliable and totally useless to our knowledge of the past except, perhaps, that of religious history. Nowadays, most historians would agree with Romein.

In a way, Romein's study offers much more than Muller's list, but in another way it offers less. First of all, Romein applied stricter criteria in his selection of texts. For practical reasons he confined his research to works that were edited. He was not to happy about this, but the job was simply to big for one. He guessed that he would cover about 20% of all existing narrative historical sources. Furthermore, he included only works that were written by Dutch authors and within the frontiers of the modern Netherlands excluding the present provinces of Brabant and Limburg, because during the Middle Ages these were oriented southward. He justified this rather artificial construction on the ground that during the Middle Ages the regions in question did not form a political or cultural entity, while the frontiers were still rather flexible.[16] Still, his geographical choice is ambiguous. Muller ignored these boundaries and listed, for example, also the chronicle of Jever (East Friesland, Germany) and Alcuin's Life of Willibrord.[17] Chronologically, Romein ended in 1517 with Cornelis Aurelius's *Divisiekroniek*, which he considered to be the last medieval work, because he considered Reinier Snoy's *De rebus Batavicis*, published only two years later, in 1519, to belong to a new, humanistic area.[18] In contrast, Snoy can be found in Muller's list.[19]

For a long time, Romein's study had no follow-up other than the supplement which H. Bruch published in 1956 to Romein's work that was since long out of print.[20] The publisher, however, thought an updated reprint would not be profitable and therefore, Bruch decided to produce

---

15. *Ibid.*, p. 1.
16. *Ibid.*, pp. xxiv-xxix.
17. Muller, *Lijst*, p. 1 en 62.
18. Romein, *Geschiedschrijving*, p. xxx.
19. Muller, *Lijst*, p. 20.
20. H. Bruch, *Supplement bij de Geschiedenis van de Noord-Nederlandsche geschiedschrijving in de middeleeuwen van Dr. Jan Romein* (Haarlem, 1956).

a simple supplement that only is of use together with Romein's book.[21] Romein was also one of the editors of a history of the Low Countries in twelve volumes, of which the last volume, on 1914-1945, contains a chapter on Dutch historiography.[22] Following in Romein's footsteps, J.A. Kossmann-Putto produced in 1958 an overall view of the development of the medieval historiography in the Northern Low Countries, as did Ph. De Vries for the sixteenth century. In the mean time, H. Baudet had listed all Latin works that were written in the Northern Low Countries, and were available in print.[23] He constructed the list for the use of a new volume of the *Lexicon Latinitatis Medii Aevi* and therefore could be less informative. These were important steps further than Blok's summary of 1893. All did not result, however, in a growing interest in narrative historical works as Romein had hoped.

THE REPERTORIUM

At last, more than a century after Muller's list and almost fifty years after Romein's history, a proper *Repertorium* compiled by Carasso-Kok was published. The focus was on Dutch medieval narrative historical sources transmitted in manuscripts and, according to the preface and the introduction, this survey, indeed, was meant as a perfected version of Muller's list. Carasso-Kok intended to construct a tool to make narrative historical sources accessible, but emphatically not to study Dutch historiography as Romein did. She sought comprehensiveness as much as possible and, therefore, she had to define her task conscientiously. She set rather rigid criteria. First, she had to define her survey geographically and chronologically. Thus, she decided to enter only works written within the modern territory of the Netherlands, including the southern provinces of Brabant and Limburg, even though there had been no such political entity in the Middle Ages. This could be justified on the basis of the international division of tasks, as she understood it, between the RFHMA and the national states.[24] Already Raoul Van Caenegem had observed some

---

21. *Ibid.*, p. ix.
22. J.A. Van Houtte, J.F. Niermeyer, J. Presser, J. Romein, H. Van Werveke eds, *Algemene Geschiedenis der Nederlanden*, 12 vol. (Zeist etc., 1949-1958), there XII, pp. 440-58 and 458-63, see also the survey on sources and literature, pp. 509-11.
23. H. Baudet, 'Index scriptorum auctorumque latino-neerlandicorum medii aevi', *Archivum Latinitatis Medii Aevi* (Bulletin du Cange), XXIV,2 (1954), pp. 3-50.
24. Carasso-Kok, *Repertorium*, p. xii. See also: M. Carasso-Kok, 'Verhalende historische bronnen', *Holland*, 16 (1984), pp. 75-84.

problems this choice brought about, especially in relation to the southern part of the modern Low Countries, where it led to a somewhat artificial selection.[25] Carasso-Kok chose to incorporate only texts that certainly originated from the Dutch provinces. However, she listed also Altfried's *Life* of Saint Liudger, first bishop of Munster, although this probably was written in the German monastery of Werden (nr 60). Altfried was related to Liudger, who was born within the diocese of Utrecht. According to Carasso-Kok, Altfried wrote from a Utrecht view. Unlike Romein, she included also works of foreign authors who wrote during a short stay in the Northern Low Countries, for example the Frenchmen Jocundus and Thomas Basin. During his stay in Maastricht (1067-76), Jocundus collected his material and wrote a first draft of his *Life* of Saint Servaas, bishop of Tongeren (nr 81). Thomas Basin lived for a while in Utrecht (1477-90), where he composed a history of the reign of the French kings Charles VII and Louis XI, that included an account of the struggle between Holland and Utrecht (nr 369). The chronological limits concerned the period up to ca. 1515, which Johan Huizinga considered to be the turning point between the Middle Ages and the Renaissance. Moreover, by then, the production of texts had changed, and printing had become more common. Thus, unlike Romein, Carasso-Kok did not include Cornelis Aurelius and his *Divisiekroniek*. In this she followed H. Kampinga's view, expressed in his study on the ideas of sixteenth- and seventeenth-century historians on Dutch history, that Aurelius' work must be considered as product of the Early Modern Time. Furthermore, the *Divisiekroniek* was very soon printed.[26] Carasso-Kok understandably set her limits rather loosely in an attempt to present a rounded corpus of medieval historiographical works for the various Dutch territories.

Unlike Muller and Romein, Carasso-Kok felt the need to give a definition of what constitutes a narrative historical source. In this, she followed Van Caenegem, who defined narrative historical texts *stricto sensu* as texts, in prose as well as in verse, written with the intention to present

---

25. R.C. Van Caenegem, review of M. Carasso-Kok, *Repertorium van de verhalende historische bronnen uit de Middeleeuwen. Heiligenlevens, annalen, kronieken en andere in Nederland geschreven verhalende bronnen.* (Bibliografische reeks van het Nederlands Historisch Genootschap 2; Den Haag: Nijhoff, 1981), in *Bijdragen en Mededelingen betreffende de Geschiedenis der Nederlanden (BMGN),* 100 (1985), pp. 91-3, there 92.

26. Carasso-Kok, *Repertorium,* p. xiii; H. Kampinga, *De opvattingen over onze oudere vaderlandsche geschiedenis bij de Hollandsche historici van de XVIe en XVIIe eeuw* (The Hague, 1917, photographic reprint 1980).

the past in a narrative form.²⁷ Thus, Carasso-Kok included saint's Lives, annals, chronicles, gesta, histories, travel-stories, memoirs, (auto) biographies and historical poems and songs. For practical reasons, she left out correspondence, although she considered this to be a genre closely related to that of narrative historical texts. Equally she disregarded other categories, even though they often contain historical annotations, for example memorial books. These categories may also cause a problem of selection, for example, does one include the whole genre or only the exemplars that contain historical annotations?

Carasso-Kok divided the works into two groups: hagiographical writings (nrs 1-96) and narrative sources of non-hagiographical nature (nrs 97-412). To the hagiographical genre she reckoned saint's *Lives* and stories about relics and miracles.²⁸ Within the two sections, Carasso-Kok numbered the works not in chronological, but in alphabetical order, in the hagiographical section under the name of the saint, in the non-hagiographical section primarily under the name of the author, or, in the case of an anonymous writer, under the title.²⁹ I shall come back to this system later. Often, the works are provided with an introduction, that is to say, if there are, in the hagiographical section, more works on one saint or, in the historiographical section more works by a certain author, then the text description of the first work is preceded by an introduction. The introduction can contain all sorts of useful information that could not be inserted within the structure of the text descriptions, for instance on the subject, the author, historical context, sources and perception, scholarly disputes. They are also crossreferenced. The descriptions of a text have a more detailed structure than Romein's had. The title of the work is followed by an *incipit* and *explicit*. The mention of the subject is often amplified with information on the textual context, on the transmission or otherwise, while the identification of the author can lead to a short account of a scholarly dispute of his or her identity. The same can be the case in localizing and dating the work. Then, there is a summary of manuscripts, editions, translations and literature. Unlike Romein, Carasso-Kok does not characterize or appraise the works. Her information is primarily descriptive.

---

27. Carasso-Kok, *Repertorium*, p. x; R.C. Van Caenegem, *Encyclopedie van de Geschiedenis der Middeleeuwen. Inleiding tot de geschreven bronnen van de Geschiedenis der Westerse Middeleeuwen* (Gent, 1962), pp. 21-57 (English translation: 1978; French translation: 1997).
28. Carasso-Kok, *Repertorium*, pp. x-xi.
29. *Ibid.*, p. xv.

The Ordening Method

Scholars of Dutch history and language in the Middle Ages consider Carasso-Kok's survey as an indispensable tool. Recently, however, some criticism emerged. For instance, working on the relation between hagiography and historiography in the writings of medieval historians in the Northern Low Countries, Anja Petrakopoulos used the *Repertorium* as a primary reference tool. Analyzing the survey, she concluded that the structure of the *Repertorium* masks the textual relationship of the various works, especially those of hagiographical with historiographical texts.[30] The reason for this, so she argues, is the separation of hagiography from non-hagiography, as well as the difference in arrangement of the works within these two sections, but also the way Carasso-Kok handled the relation between works and manuscripts played an essential role in this.

The main argument put forward by Carasso-Kok for a division of the material into two sections is that hagiographical texts are a special kind of narrative sources.[31] Apparently, the other narrative sources have in common that they are not hagiographical. Of course, Carasso-Kok made the division for pragmatic reasons to be of assistance to the users of her survey. However, in what way hagiographical narrative sources differ from the non-hagiographical texts is not clarified, nor are the supposed similarities within each of the two sections explained. What is more, Carasso-Kok arranged the two sections in a different way.[32] This is not easily to understand. The lack of justification suggests that it was done for practical reasons. It seems that Carasso-Kok had sought for the most neutral order. Of course, for an encyclopedic reference book as she planned, an alphabetical order by author's name is the most obvious, but in this case not sufficient, because many medieval authors are anonymous and their works are usually known by the title. Less than 30% of the hagiographical works are contributed to an author, whom we know by name, and, besides, several of these contributions are uncertain. Consequently, the large majority of texts would have been listed under their title, *Life of...*, *Miracle of....* Besides, all the hagiographical works deal either with a saint or a relic, that could be used as an ordering category.

---

30. I want to thank Anja Petrakopoulos for sharing her findings with me. She presented her analysis in her paper 'Syncopated Pasts. Engendering the Missionary Position' at the 'Transmission of Knowledge and Problems of Gender Workshop', Medieval Institute and Netherlands Research School for Medieval Studies, October 22-23, 1999, Notre Dame.
31. Carasso-Kok, *Repertorium*, p. x.
32. *Ibid.*, p. xv

So, the first text in the hagiographical section is about saint Adalbert, while the last is about saint Wiro. In case of the non-hagiographical works a similar arrangement would have been more complicated, although possible, if, for instance, Muller's structure was followed. Another explanation for the arrangement chosen by Carasso-Kok may have been that she did not consider hagiographers to be historiographers. The former pursued, indeed, other goals in their writing, namely, not so much to describe the Dutch past, but to prove the holyness of their protagonists. At the same time, for us, their stories can function as historical sources, because the events toke place, at least partly, in the Netherlands and therefore contain Dutch information.

In the non-hagiographical part, the works were arranged under the name of the author, or, in the case of an anonymous writer, under the first noun of the title and/or a person's name or a geograhical notation taken from the title. This led to a rather artificial and inscrutable order. For instance, the first work *Aantekeningen uit Albergen* (Notes from Albergen, nr 97) is followed by the *Vriesche Aentyckeninge* (Frisian notes, nr 98) and *Aantekeningen uit Galilea Minor* (Notes from Galilea Minor, nr 99). Or, we find Gerard Suggerode, author of a chronicle titled *Chronicon* (nr 267) followed by the *Gesta Fresonum* (Deeds of the Frisians, nr 268). Under the C we find chronicles and, as a result of the various spellings (chronycke, cronijk, cronica, kroniek etc.), it is sometimes hard to find the logic in the order. Even more complicating is that Carasso-Kok treated one particular group of narrative sources, namely dynastic chronicles in a similar way as the hagiographical texts, namely by keeping the works on one family together. In that case, the name of the family is decisive and Carasso-Kok could confine herself to one introduction per family. Again, a pragmatic route was followed.

The consequence of this methodological inconsistency is that, on the one hand, the emphasis seems to be on the *subject* of the hagiographical texts, while, on the other hand, the focus is on the *author* or on the *genre* in chronicles and, in only the second instance, on the *subject*. As a result, there is a survey of all medieval historiographers in the Northern Low Countries listed by name, but not of the hagiographers. The same can be said of their writings. All historiographical works of one author are brought together under the author's name. However, hagiographical writings of one author are scattered within the section. Nor do we have at one glance a complete view of all historiographical and hagiographical writings by one author. For example, under the 'R' we find in the historiographical section Radbod, bishop of Utrecht (900-17), as the author of a vision, *Annotatio ad annum 900* (nr 352) and in the hagiographical section, also under the 'R', as the protagonist of the *Vita sancti Radbodi episcopi et confessoris* (nr 75), composed by an anonymous. In the latter he can also be found under the 'A', 'B', 'L', 'M' and 'S' as the (supposed) author of texts on Saint Amalberga (nr 8), Saint Boniface (nr 18), Saint Liafwin (nrs 52-53), Saint Martin (nr 62), Saint Gervase (nr 80), and Saint Suitbert (nrs 88-89). Still, all the necessary information can be found in the *Repertorium*, if we take pains to read Carasso-Kok's introduction on the historiographer Radbod, or by observing the conscientious cross-references and by using the excellent index.

COMPILATIONS

Finally, there is the problematic relationship of texts and manuscripts. The problem concerns primarily compilations. Only recently, scholars became aware of the importance of the study of compilations as individual works[33]. As a result, the edition of Dutch medieval compilations was initiated and in 1994 the first, the so-called 'Geraardsberg manuscript', was published[34]. Thus, it is understandable that Carasso-Kok did not handle compilations in a well-thought-out way. In the non-hagiographical section, two compilations can be found of dynastic chronicles, one in Latin (nr 148) and one in Dutch (nr 149). These compilations have been transmitted differently in a number of manuscripts. Carasso-Kok listed several of the texts included also separately, namely, when other chronicles on a certain family are available. The same goes for a compilation of texts of the Modern Devouts, the *Collectanea Devotionis Modernis* (nr 204), which contains mainly biographies. Some of the forty-eight texts are also listed elsewhere, although there are not always other text witnesses. The conclusion must be that Carasso-Kok considered these compilations to be individual works in agreement with the modern definition that a compilation is a work, when the composer or his commissioner intended to form a particular collection of texts[35]. We may assume that

---

33. P. Wackers, 'Het belang van de studie van verzamelhandschriften', in: Gerard Sonnemans, ed., *Middeleeuwse verzamelhandschriften uit de Nederlanden* (Hilversum: Verloren, 1996), pp. 23-38.
34. M.J. Govers e.a. eds, *Het Geraardsbergse handschrift. Hs. Brussel, Koninklijke Bibliotheek Albert I, 837-845*. Middeleeuwse verzamelhandschriften uit de Nederlanden, I (Hilversum: Verloren, 1994).
35. H. Kienhorst, 'Middelnederlandse verzamelhandschriften als codicologisch object', in: Sonnemans, *Middeleeuwse verzamelhandschriften*, pp. 39-61, there p. 40.

the dynastic chronicles were not an accidental hotchpotch, because there are several text witnesses. It is well known that the Modern Devouts collected these devout biographies in so-called broeder- en zusterboeken (brother books and sister books) as edifying literature. However, Carasso-Kok considered some texts included in these compilations also to be independent works. In the case of the Latin compilation of dynastic chronicles, this certainly is understandable, because the chronicles were written before 1480 and only afterwards brought together. The case of the *Collectanea*, however, is slightly different. Most of the texts are transcripts or translations in Latin of works of several authors, only a few of them are known by name. Not all are categorized as independent works. The reason for that is not always clear. For example, the *Life of Lutgert of Buderick* is not mentioned as a separate work, but only in the original version in Dutch, that is listed under the author Rudolf Dier of Muiden (nr 360). Thus, the translation in Latin is not considered as an independent work. Than, one must wonder what makes a text into an independent work. The *Life of Albert ter Achter* (nr 384), written anonymously and only available in the *Collectanea*, is also listed as a separate work. So is the *Life of Ysentrude of Mekeren* (nr 391), presumably, because there are reasons to assume that it is a translation of a lost work in Dutch. The Lives of Egbert ter Beek (nr 385) and Jan of Hattem (nr 390), that both can be found in another text collection, are too mentioned as independent works. So is Peter Hoorn's *Life of Geert Grote* (nr 347), although supposedly an autograph and only available in the *Collectanea*. This text, one of two works attributed to Peter Hoorn, certainly, is categorized separately, because author's names are used as the leading category in this part of the *Repertorium*. Wybren Scheepsma considers Carasso-Kok's method confusing, because by separately listing them it is suggested that they once functioned independently, which they did not.[36] However, Carasso-Kok mentions this clearly in her text descriptions. The question remains, though, to what extent texts which are part of a compilation must also be treated as independent works.

The question is even more acute within the hagiographical section. As Petrakopoulos observed, twelve works, included in the hagiographical

---

36. Wybren Scheepsma, 'Verzamelt de overgebleven brokken, opdat niets verloren ga: Over Latijnse en Middelnederlandse levensbeschrijvingen uit de sfeer van de Moderne Devotie', in: Paul Wackers e.a. ed., *Verraders en bruggebouwers. Verkenningen naar de relatie tussen Latinitas en de Middelnederlandse letterkunde,* Nederlandse literatuur en cultuur in de middeleeuwen, XV (Amsterdam: Prometheus, 1996), pp. 211-39, p. 340 n. 89.

section, can also be found in two manuscripts that are part of one collection of saint's *Lives* in three volumes.[37] The collection is known as the *Passionale* and was compiled by Zweder of Boecholt in the first quarter of the fifteenth century in the carthusian monastery of Nieuwlicht (Nova Lux) near Utrecht.[38] This compilation is not included as a work, nor is Zweder of Boecholt mentioned as an author. He even cannot be found in the index. Strictly speaking he was not an author, but a compiler or a copyist, though the distinction between these occupations is very hard to draw. In many a medieval work the so-called author had exercised all these activities. However, Zweder did not copy all texts to the letter, but abbreviated. Carasso-Kok did not distinguish Zweder's Lives as new versions of older works, but she just named the compilation as a text witness of the original works. Why is it not treated like the dynastic chronicles or the *Collectanea*? To understand that we have to turn to the selection of saint's Lives that Carasso-Kok made. The vast majority of surviving writings from the Middle Ages are hagiographical texts. In Carasso-Kok's survey, however, they form only one quarter of the total. Thus, the conclusion must be that this does not adequately reflect the true extent of Dutch medieval hagiography. Carasso-Kok's selection may clearify why she did not consider hagiography such an essential part of historiography. All saints whose Lives are listed lived at least for a while in the Netherlands. Some were born here, others came as missionaries, bishops or abbots. Miracle stories within these territories, regardless of the saints who performed them, were also inserted. These Lives as well as the miracle stories may reveal something about what happened in these regions and what people lived here. As said before, this was not the main purpose of the authors, but there it is, their protagonists were part of the Dutch world. For instance, we can find some stories, probably for the first time written down within the Nothern Low Countries, about miracles of saint Barbara that took place in these regions. Although St. Barbara was one of the most popular saints in the Netherlands of the Late Middle Ages, no *Life* of her is listed, even though the author was Dutch. What could Barbara's Life tell about the past of this country, since she lived in Nicomedia (Asia Minor)? Apparently, Carasso-Kok had in the first place factual history in mind. Or, was she just being wise? Carasso-Kok considered including miracle collections that can be found in miracle and

---

37. Nrs. 1, 11, 29, 33, 50, 67, 73, 75, 95, 36, 92, 93.
38. Utrecht, University Library nr 391. J.P. Gumbert, *Die Utrechter Kartäuser und Ihre Bücher* (Leiden: E.J. Brill 1974), pp. 80-90.

example books, but for practical reasons she left these out.[39] Most saint's Lives also are part of hagiographical collections or legendaries, for example, Dutch versions of Jacob de Voragine's *Golden Legend*. When Carasso-Kok compiled her *Repertorium*, studies on Dutch collections of saint's Lives were not available. Nowadays, Williams-Krapp's study, published in 1986, provides us with a sound base.[40] Nevertheless, in the case of an extension of the hagiographical section the complexity of the material, the number of manuscripts and the great variety in texts, will demand a pragmatic approach.

These objections against Carasso-Kok's *Repertorium* tell us more about the users of the survey than about the reference work in itself. The criticism results mainly from the change in demands of modern historians. They have developed new research questions that cannot be answered by such a survey. Nowadays, the emphasis has shifted from the wish to reconstruct the past and from events per se to cultural history, the history of ideas and mentalities or gender history. Therefore, historians search to inquire their sources in different ways. We are no longer mainly interested in the texts as sources for the factual history of the Low Countries. We want to know how these texts came into existence and how they were related to each other. Who wrote them and why, and for what public? What was the text's purpose and how was it read? How did the writing function, what sources were used and what was its influence? This new approach especially changes the ideas about hagiographical texts as historical sources. Our interest is no longer confined to local saints. Nowadays we would like to know the functioning of all saint's Lives in Dutch cultural and religious life. Why was saint Barbara so popular and what texts about her circulated? Who wrote about her and with what purpose? How did her cultus develop? Or, like Petrakopoulos, what is the relation between Dutch medieval hagiographical writings and historiography? Why did historiographers write also hagiography or insert hagiography in their histories?

NARRATIVE SOURCES

This brings us to the new project aimed to revise, correct and extend the twenty-year old survey by Carasso-Kok according to the latest developments and present this in an electronic way. It proceeds from and links

---

39. Carasso-Kok, *Repertorium*, pp. x-xi.
40. W. Williams-Krapp, *Die deutschen und niederländischen Legendare des Mittelalters. Texte und Textgeschichte*. Würzburger Forschungen, 20 (Tübingen 1986).

up with the Flemish project *Narrative Sources* that has resulted in the database of the same name, which since 1996 can be consulted on the Internet.[41] The database constructed under the auspices of the universities of Louvain (Jean Goossens, Erik van Mingroot, Werner Verbeke) and Gent (Ludo Milis) presents a survey of narrative texts that were written during the Middle Ages in the Southern Low Countries and were meant to describe the past. Carasso-Kok's *Repertorium* served as a model. A publication in the form of a database offers great advantages above a printed book. First of all there are the numerous search possibilities that enlarge the useful value of such a reference work substantially.[42] Also, an electronic database is more flexible than a conventionally printed book. Corrections and additions can be made at any time. Thus, a database can be put in use before it is 'complete', while at the same time, a database can be always up-to-date. More than a database does, a printed book imposes restrictions, for example, on size and format. Also, once printed, the book is static and suggests completeness. Therefore, the content must be complete in itself and the choices made by the composer must be clearly justified and consistently applied. Naturally, an electronic publication has disadvantages too. Firstly, there is the problem of securing copy-right. Then, in case of a publication on the Internet, technical problems may hinder the accessibility. There is also the question of the everlasting availability of the database in the light of maintenance and technological developments. Another point is that browsing through a book, one may find things that one was not looking for and that can lead unexpectedly to new ideas. A database does not invite always to browsing, and it functions best when the user knows what to look for. A similar difference can be found in the use of a open shelf library and a closed one. Nevertheless, the advantages win and the decision to publish a revision of Carasso-Kok's *Repertorium* incorporated in the Flemish database *Narrative Sources* became easier, because again the publisher thought an updated reprint not paying and was prepared to gave up all rights.

The composers of the electronic Flemish survey use also Van Caenegem's definition of these sources, but they give it a much broader interpretation. They intend to include also correspondence, diaries, fiction,

---

41. http://www.narrative-sources.be
42. See for some examples Ludo Milis, 'Narrative Sources: A Quantification of Culture and Religion', in: Franz J. Felten and Nikolas Jaspert ed., *Vita Religiosa im Mittelater. Festschrift für Kaspar Elm zum 70. Geburtstag*, Berliner Historische Studien, 31. Ordensstudien, XIII (Berlin: Duncker & Humblot, 1999), pp. 819-36.

circumstantial-literature or literature written for special occasions, genealogies, historical-notes, lists, history of literature, memorial books, obituaries and miscellanies. Their geographical defining is very pragmatic. They use neither modern nor medieval frontiers. In the north, they take as a starting point the medieval frontier and include also the Dutch provinces of Brabant and Limburg. In the south, as yet, Northern-France, in sofar this was part of the Southern Low Countries during the Middle Ages, is not systematically included, but the bishopric of Liege, then formally German, is. The survey covers the period 600-1500 and deals with many more works written in and transmitted in the Southern Low Countries. At this moment, *Narrative Sources* contains circa 2150 descriptions against Carasso-Kok's *Repertorium* of 412.

The Belgians apply the criteria loosely, because their method is in the first place pragmatic. The intention is to make available as soon as possible all known information on as many works as possible. New information can easily be added in a later stage to the database. The underlying idea is that, in that way, *Narrative Sources* also can profit from the expertise of researchers all over the world. The managers of *Narrative Sources*, therefore, invite expressly all users of the database in aid of the yearly update to supply corrections and additions, and even whole new text descriptions, which can be included under their authorship. As in Muller's case, this does not work in practice as well as was hoped for. Carasso-Kok's text descriptions are of an excellent quality, because they are based on primary research of manuscripts, but, at first, the Flemish compilers had to use another strategy. For practical reasons, like lack of time and money, most of their descriptions are based on editions and modern literature. Therefore, the quality of the text descriptions varies depending on the availability of a modern edition and recent literature.

In the Flemish-Dutch database the text descriptions are structured in twenty-three fields that all can be searched separately, in combinations or all together. The identification number is followed by a typology of the work and the language in which it is written. Then follows the name of the author, information on the author, title, incipit and explicit. Next we can find the size of the work and the a global dating, followed by information like place and year of writing, commissioner etc., an abstract, lists of manuscripts, editions and translations, information on used sources and influence of the work as a source in other works. There is a field desiderata, while the last two fields contain the name of the contributor and the update code. For a quick localization a field 'region' has been added.[43] The field 'context' contains extra information. In many cases, the descriptions contain blank fields, because the required information lacks to fill them in. This is, however, no reason to prevent the description from being presented. Perhaps, one day they all will be complete. This structure offers ample space to present all sorts of information. This is important, because we do not want to lose any of the information, now available in the printed *Repertorium*. On the other hand, this might cause problems in presenting the text discriptions. The fields in the database often contain too much text and the lay out is not very user friendly.

THE NEW PROJECT

The first fase of our project of updating Carasso-Kok's text descriptions and bringing them in the format of *Narrative Sources* is now in full operation. To put the contents of these descriptions into the fields of the database is not without problems, because only eleven of the search fields correspond with the headings in the *Repertorium*. This does not necessarily mean that the database offers more information than Carasso-Kok's book does. It simply is ordered in a different way. On the one hand, some of Carasso-Kok's information had to be reorganized. For example, her introductions must be split up and divided over several fields. Information on the author must be brought together in the 'status' field, and on the text genesis in the 'redaction' field. Under the heading 'subject', Carasso-Kok described shortly the subject of the work amplified with a lot of background information, while the 'abstract' field in *Narrative Sources* is meant to keep a summary of the content of the work. On the other hand, sometimes information must be added, for instance to fill in the 'source' and 'influence' field. The updating implies not only adding new literature, updating manuscript signatures and so on, but also incorporating new scholarly insights. All this often causes intervention in Carasso-Kok's original texts that now and then prick one's conscience. It is for sure that, when time goes on, the gap between the printed survey and the database only will grow.

The database rejects the division between hagiography and non-hagiography. In fact, the arrangement will be unimportant. When one wants to know all that Radbod, bishop of Utrecht, has written, one can search on the 'author' field. If one only wants to know his hagiographical works,

---

43. See Appendix 1.

than this search can be combined with one on the 'type' field. A combination of the 'type' field and the 'century' field could provide, for example, a survey of all twelfth-century hagiographers. In this way, all the problems about the division and difference in arrangement of the sources are solved. The 'typology' field has no corresponding paragraph in Carasso-Kok's survey. In this field in *Narrative Sources* the works are categorized according to Genicot's classification used in the series *Typologie des Sources*.[44] To meet modern scholarly demands, this categorization will, perhaps, need refinement. It might be useful to subdivide, for instance, hagiography into saint's Lives, miracle stories and other subgenres, and chronicles in universal, town, monastic and dynastic chronicles. The relationship between texts can be found by searching the 'source' and 'influence' field. A search on a manuscript signature can provide information on the textual context. This could be perfected if the database were to be linked to other databases that give full information on manuscripts like the databases of the *Bibliotheca Neerlandica Manuscripta* (University Library of Leiden), and the one of the *Bibliotheca Hagiographica Latina* (University of Namur), and electronic published catalogues.

During the second fase, we intend to refine the survey by making a distinction between different versions of texts, whenever relevant. Further research will be necessary concerning translations in Dutch of works included in Latin. Often Carasso-Kok has no other information on these than a short list of manuscripts, editions and literature. The third fase, we aim at expanding the survey. In the light of changing demands, explained above, it seems obvious to start expanding the hagiographical section, firstly with the miracle and example books that Carasso-Kok forced to omit. Then, legendaries and Lives of other than local saints could be added. However, this will confront us again with the problems, discussed earlier, about compilations and individual works. How do we define saint's *Lives* as narrative historical sources? Do we have to insert all hagiographical texts written within the chosen territorial frontiers? Or, can we apply certain criteria? Of course, this will not all be possible during the course of this project and, thus a practical solution has to be found. We aim to widen the geographical and chronological boundaries. We have decided to expand the eastern frontier and include in our research East Friesland, Munster, Cleves and Juliers, and the central Rhine-area.

---

44. L. Genicot, *Introduction. Typologie des sources*, 1 (Turnhout, 1972); see Appendix 2.

In the Middle Ages these regions formed a cultural and economical, and sometimes even a political entity with the eastern parts of the Northern Low Countries. This is especially important with regard to works originating from the circles of the *Devotio Moderna*. With regard to chronology we shall strive to improve the links to a survey of Dutch historians and their works from the period 1500-1800, published in 1990.[45] The composers of this survey listed only printed works. Therefore, several sixteenth-centuries writings, which were never printed, for example a number of interesting monastic chronicles, are included neither in this survey nor in Carasso-Kok's. Also all available information on *deperdita*, texts that now have been lost, will be gathered. If all is going well, we also shall start to include new text categories, first of all the so-called memorial books, following in this the composers of *Narrative Sources*. Hopefully, further extensions may be possible in the future.

CONCLUSION

I have sketched the development of an instrument to make available narrative historical sources, that were written during the Middle Ages within the Low Countries. Muller and Carasso-Kok had a tool in regard to Dutch history in mind, while Romein thought of civilization history, though confined to the Netherlands. Since the interest of historians has shifted from factual history to cultural history, the history of ideas and mentalities or gender history, the emphasis is no longer exclusively on Dutch past. The Dutch sources can be used to study these research fields in a Dutch perspective or in a more universal context. Therefore another tool is needed, namely a survey of narrative texts that were written during the Middle Ages in the Low Countries and were meant to describe the past. We are convinced that the adaptation of the *Repertorium* in that way, together with the use of all the profits of modern technology by the way of a electronic publication, will put new life into this reference tool. We also hope that the revised *Repertorium* will set off new research.

---

45. E.O.G. Haitsma Mulier, G.A.C. Van der Lem, withe the cooperation of P. Knevel, *Repertorium van Geschiedschrijvers in Nederland 1500-1800*. Bibliografische reeks van het Nederlands Historisch Genootschap, 7 (The Hague: Nederlands Historisch Genootschap, 1990), p. xi.

APPENDIX 1.

Fields in *Narrative Sources*

ID	Identification Number	**AB**	Abstract
TY	Type	**CO**	Context
LA	Language	**MS**	Manuscripts
AU	Author	**ED**	Editions
ST	Status of the author	**TL**	Translations
TI	Title	**SC**	Sources
IC	Incipit	**IF**	Influence
EX	Explicit	**LI**	Literature
SI	Size	**DS**	Desiderata
CE	Century	**NA**	Name of the Contributor
RG	Region	**UD**	Update code
RE	Redaction: Place, Date, Patron and Dedication		

APPENDIX 2.

Types of texts distinguished in the database *Narrative Sources*

- Annals
- Chronicles
- Circumstantial literature
- Correspondence
- Diaries – Memoirs
- Encyclopedia
- Exempla
- Fiction
- Genealogies
- Hagiography
- Histories – Gesta
- Historical notes
- History of literature
- Lists
- Memorial-books
- Pamphlets – Treaties
- Necrologia – Obituaries
- Poems
- Sermons
- Travel-stories

Elisabeth van HOUTS

GENDER, MEMORIES AND PROPHECIES IN MEDIEVAL EUROPE

Adeliza of Louvain

In January 1121 a teenage girl, perhaps as young as twelve, left her home in Louvain to become the young bride of King Henry I of England then aged 53.[1] Her name was Adeliza. Her attractions were her beauty and her childbearing age which hopefully would allow for a new heir to the English throne.[2] In the previous month of November Henry's only legitimate son William Adelin had drowned in the White Ship disaster off the coast of Normandy and his loss of life had left the court stunned and in despair.[3] As an act of penance for his sins that were seen as the cause of the shipwreck but at the same time as an omen for good fortune the king and the young queen founded Reading Abbey where a community of monks would pray for a new heir.[4] And for the next fourteen years Adeliza can be found in Normandy, Maine and England at her husband's side in the hope that she would become pregnant. The career of the girl from Louvain, is an appropriate starting point to illustrate the concerns with memory and prophecy of medieval aristocracy and royalty. Men and women shaped the knowledge of the past and both genders were preoccupied with the future. There are plenty of narrative and other sources to underline these concerns and the gendered responsibilities men and women took on.

---

1. *The Ecclesiastical history of Orderic Vitalis*, ed. and transl. M. Chibnall, 6 vols (Oxford, 1969-80) 6: 308-9; *The Chronicle of John of Worcester*, ed. and transl. P. McGurk, 2 vols [2 and 3], (Oxford, 1995-8) 3: 148-51.
2. L. Wertheimer, 'Adeliza of Louvain and Anglo-Norman queenship', *Haskins Society Journal. Studies in Medieval History*, 7 (1995), pp. 101-16.
3. Marjorie Chibnall has tentatively suggested that Empress Matilda may have had some involvement in the marriage negotiations which perhaps had started as early as 1119, the year of a possible meeting between the Empress and her father Henry I, see M. Chibnall, *The empress Matilda. Queen consort, Queen Mother and Lady of the English* (Oxford, 1991), pp. 37-38.
4. P. Stafford, '*Cherchez la femme*. Queens, queens' lands and nunneries: missing links in the foundation of Reading Abbey', *History. The Journal of the Historical Association*, 85 (2000), pp. 4-27.

GENDER AND MEMORIES

Family and small kin groups are the circles which feature most prominently in memories of the past.[5] Most of the source material is biased in favour of the aristocracy and it is amongst these circles that we find the most interesting evidence for the survival of memories and the ways in which they were preserved. It is becoming increasingly clear that from the early Middle Ages men and women passed on information about ancestors to their children and grandchildren. The gendered role for (aristocratic) women in this context has been known for some time but we owe it to the study of Regine Le Jan that this process is known to have been in place in the Merovingian period.[6] The interesting glimpses of genealogical information preserved by women foreshadows the much more abundant evidence of the later medieval periods. Le Jan argues that biological memory was responsible for knowledge about parents, grandparents and occasionally great-grandparents, that is the straightforward knowledge about the direct kin every noble person had. Political memory in contrast was the memory stretching back further in time or sideways in wider circles, which was determined by choice as to whom was remembered and why. The political memory would normally comprise stories concerning ancestors who were interesting or well-known for various reasons (status, memorable death) or whose inheritance had relevance for the present day. One very important conclusion is that the political memory comprised the male and the female line even though in time the agnatic (paternal) line mattered most. The position of (great) grandmothers too is singled out as of immense importance for the preservation of family knowledge.[7]

Aristocratic women were often educated at the homes of their fiancés, a situation that was especially demanded of future queens. As members of their new family they had to become accustomed to the language and customs of the country, knowledge they needed for the education of their children (sons in particular) and for themselves in case they needed to act as regents for their sons (or daughters in the case of heiresses). Thus a thorough grooming in new and foreign customs was necessary. The expectation that the woman could adapt herself and shape herself according

---

[5]. This section is based on my introduction to *Medieval Memories. Men, women and the past 700-1300*, ed. E. van Houts (Harlow, 2001), pp. 1-16.
[6]. R. Le Jan, *Famille et pouvoir dans le monde franc (VIIe – Xe siècle)* (Paris, 1995), pp. 31-58.
[7]. Le Jan, *Famille et pouvoir*, pp. 55-6.

to the demands of her new family had profound consequences for her memorial role. Two Norman examples, both from the monastery of Le Bec, illustrate this very well. Robert of Torigni, who wrote a biography of King Henry I as a sequel to William of Jumièges' *Gesta Normannorum Ducum*, relates how Henry I's daughter Matilda was sent to Germany as a young bride for Emperor Henry V. There 'she should be carefully educated until the appropriate time for the marriage and that she should learn the language and to behave according to the customs of the Germans.'[8] A similar sentiment is expressed by Robert's younger contemporary Milo Crispin, who wrote a family chronicle in which he recorded his aunt's experience: 'Eva [Crispin née de Montfort-L'Amaury] came from neighbouring France and took on her husband's family's preferences and love for the abbey of Le Bec'.[9] Both Empress Matilda and Eva Crispin were expected to adapt themselves to their husbands' families. In order to be a good wife and good mother they accepted their in-laws' affiliations in order, in due course, to pass them on to their children and grandchildren. In Empress Matilda's case, however, this had to wait until her second marriage to Geoffrey of Anjou, for her first (German) marriage remained childless. Were women then not concerned any longer with the memories of their birth families? The extent to which the in-laws' expectations in fact cancelled out the woman's own customs is an area that needs more investigation. The topic is important because the practicalities faced by aristocratic women involved in multiple marriages were enormous. Familiarisation with new ancestors, lines of inheritances, family mementos and so forth required not only a good memory, but also a skill to compartmentalise the past in portions according to the family to which these portions belonged.

That noble women had an important commemorative role to play is particularly clear in the case of women who were heiresses and thus had no brothers to pass on the information about the family and the estates. Where families for several generations survived only in the female line, a predominantly female chain of stories is all we have. Between the years 1000 and 1200 the county of Boulogne, for example, was handed down in the female line more often than in the male line.[10] The responsibility of the Boulogne women to pass on knowledge about the past thus rested

8. *The Gesta Normannorum Ducum of William of Jumièges, Orderic Vitalis and Robert of Torigni*, ed. and trans. E.M.C. van Houts, 2 vols (Oxford, 1992-5) 2: 218-9.
9. *Miraculum quo b. Mariae subvenit Guillelmo Crispino seniori; ubi de nobili Crispinorum genere agitur*, ed. J. P. Migne, PL 150: 741.
10. Van Houts, *Memory and Gender*, pp. 73-5.

solely on their shoulders. It is perhaps no surprise therefore that so many biographies of women or commissioned by the women in this family were produced.

A complicating factor in the commemorative role of women was the high rate of death in childbirth. Thus a lot of time and energy by older women had to be invested in the younger generation, some of whom would almost certainly die and with death lose their place in the commemorative chain. Thus for every woman who survived to tell the tale of ancestors, several others in the family had died. The fragile nature of the commemorative chain was known to all and may have been one of the reasons why the literate members of the families, male and female, stepped in to provide written records. It is in this field that we find the gendered roles of men and women as most distinctive and complementory. In many cases the stories told by women were passed on orally before they were ultimately written down by male members of the family. Where in this chain of family memories the male line intertwines and diverges from that of the women is a topic that needs more exploration. As has been observed recently, the relationship between uncles and nephews, especially in those cases where both were attached as ecclesiastical officers to the same cathedral of church, is a potentially fruitful area for such research.[11] They received (oral) information for their female kin which they incorporated into the documents of the institutions for which they worked.

CARE FOR THE DEAD

The area where class and gender determined memorial roles was that of funeral rites.[12] The actual care for the terminally ill, wounded and dead bodies was mostly in the hands of women. Aristocratic women had the responsibility of overseeing funeral arrangements and the collection of bodies from battlefields or foreign expeditions, but the actual washing and laying out of bodies was done by lower class people. Renée Nip reminds us of the role of women tending to the wounded and the dying in the streets of Bruges during the civil war following the murder of Count Charles the Good of Flanders in 1127.[13] While these women risked

---

11. Van Houts, *Memory and Gender*, p. 90.
12. P. Geary, *Phantoms of Remembrance: Memory and Oblivion at the End of the First Millennium* (Princeton, 1994), pp. 48-80.
13. R. Nip, 'Gendered memories from Flanders', *Medieval Memories*, ed. van Houts, pp. 113-31.

their lives removing bodies from the gutters, it was an abbess who delivered a ring from a dead man to his family. The role of abbess as messenger combined with the fact that the dead man possessed a ring suggests that he was of an aristocratic background. The lower class and distinctly unnoble connotations of the task for the care of dead bodies is also made clear in a well-known Norman example. During the siege of Alençon in c. 1050 William the Conqueror was taunted by the inhabitants, who had gathered on the battlements, having covered the walls with pelts (soaked with water they protected against arson attempts). Beating the animal skins they shouted insults at him referring to the fact that his kinsmen (on his mothers' side) were morticians. Not William's illegitimate birth but the low status of his mother Herleva was a cause of deep insult which was punished severely (all offenders had their hands and feet cut off).[14]

Before the mid-eleventh-century Church reform movement pagan rituals as part of Christian funeral arrangements were still common. Carl Watkins draws attention to William of Malmesbury's reminiscences, who had heard stories of people (women) dancing in German churchyards, an occasion witnessed by someone whose testimony was deemed impeccable. Churchyards were sites closely associated with ghosts of the dead and the dancing after burials was one way of appeasing the dead people's souls. The dancing was done by women, as Bishop Burchard of Worms (1000-25) reported, even though he did not specify the dancers' social backgound which presumably was that of servants.[15] In a recent book J. C. Schmitt discusses the fact that ghosts themselves came from all backgrounds and the stories about them circulated in lay circles as well as in monasteries, as witnessed by the historians Guibert of Nogent (d. c. 1130) and Orderic Vitalis (d. c. 1142), and in bishops' courts.[16] Burchard of Worms mentioned them frequently in his penitential handbook, but other sources are available as well.[17] A Latin poem, entitled *Semiramis,* formed part of a collection of poems some of which were dedicated to Archbishop Robert of Rouen (987-1037). In it the ghost of Semiramis (a former queen) comes back to haunt the life of her brother

---

14. *The Gesta Normannorum Ducum*, ed. and trans. van Houts, 2: 124-5.
15. C. Watkins, 'Memories of the marvellous in the Anglo-Norman realm', *Medieval Memories*, ed. van Houts, pp. 92-112.
16. J. C. Schmitt, *Ghosts in the Middle Ages. The Living and the Dead in Medieval Society* (Chicago, 1998).
17. *Medieval Handbooks of Penance. A Translation of the principal Libri Poenitentiales,* trans. J. T. McNeill and H. M. Gamer (New York, 1990), pp. 321-45.

the priest/ soothsayer Tollund, who reproaches him for having sided with the ghost's mother. Mother and daughter are said to have resembled each other closely. The poem may be a satire on Archbishop Robert (?Tollund), his sister Emma (the ghost Semiramis) and her mother Countess Gunnor who formed the aristocratic audience for this enigmatic literary piece on necromancy.[18] The poet takes Emma to task for having allowed herself to be captured and married by Cnut in London and at the expense of her sons Edward and Alfred in exile at the Norman court. The pagan setting of animal sacrifice and necromancy in order to know the future is the sort of background from which Emma emerges as saying to her brother: 'That you may believe my words, I'll shake the dragon's teeth – like a sorceress I'll scatter sybilline murmurs for you'. The poetic death of a daughter who has acted against her brother's and mother's wishes is a clever device to illustrate the seriousness with which the Norman court looked at Emma's defection to a second marriage, and potential second offspring, in England. Striking are the (poetic) roles of the women in the care and responsibility of the dead souls, while the archbishop is caricatured as a wimp, who is hopeless in keeping up contact with the dead.[19]

Another example concerns Emma's son Edward and her daughter-in-law Queen Edith. Edward's gift of prophecy is linked to his long exile in Normandy so touchingly described by his biographer the monk of Saint-Omer who had been commissioned by his wife Queen Edith. The prophecies concerned Edward's succession and thus the future of England facing uncertainty about the succession due the king's childlessness. Edward's wife Edith certainly believed in her husband's skill as prophet. While attended Edward's deathbed, Archbishop Stigand brushed aside the king's dying prophecy as an old man's rambling words, whereas Edith had them recorded and so salvaged the king's own gloomy prediction of the fate of England after his death.[20] Thus while church officials like Archbishop Robert of Rouen in the case of young Emma, Archbishop Stigand in the case of Queen Edith and Bishop Burchard of Worms in Germany were supposed to apply canon law and theological prescripts for

---

18. The text is edited and translated by P. Dronke, *Poetic Individuality in the Middle Ages. New Departures in Poetry, 1000-1500* (London, 1986), pp. 66-113 and for the Norman context, see E. van Houts, 'A note on *Jezebel* and *Semiramis*, two Latin Norman poems from the early eleventh century', *Journal of Medieval Latin*, 2 (1992), pp. 18-24.

19. P. Stafford, *Queen Emma and Queen Edith. Queenship and Women's Power in eleventh-century England* (Oxford, 1997), p. 12.

20. *The Life of King Edward who rests at Westminster*, ed. and trans. F. Barlow, 2nd edition (Oxford, 1992), pp. 116-21; Stafford, *Queen Emma*, p. 45.

the liturgy of the death and pastoral aftercare for the survivors, prophecies and unorthodox explanations remained part of the Christian mourning process in practice with women and men (priests) each providing their own explanations for manifestations of life after dead.

Memories of the dead, visions of the dead and other phenomenons linked to life after death are also the stuff of marvels discussed. Chroniclers (all male and all ecclesiastical men themselves) felt that if the reports had been filtered through the minds of men schooled in theology, and thence accepted, this constituted a guarantee that God was responsible for them. Unauthorized reports, as they would have been if they had been told exclusively by women, were unacceptable. The paradox of the clerics' attitude is surprising, for on the one hand they encouraged women's rapport with the dead (their prayers in particular were meant to be most efficacious according to the twelfth-century theologian Abelard), while on the other hand they underwrote the institutionalized disbelief in women's stories concerning contacts with the dead.[21] As Renée Nip has pointed out for Flanders and northern France, chroniclers reported visions by women (in some cases of dead relatives) only if sanctioned by their chaplains or other priests. Thus, while it was accepted that women were responsible for the rites of the dead (care for bodies, burials, mourning and commemorative prayers), any attempt to interpret what happened in afterlife (by visualising or communicating with dead relatives, ghosts, and resurrections) was deemed to be a (clergy)man's task. The line between these seemingly clear gendered roles was in fact a very thin one. The care for the dead and the commemoration of dead ancestors constituted in a sense the control over the family's past, which was a task at times shared and at times contested between men and women. The shared guardianship over the past did not stop in the present but also extended into the future.

Memory and Prophecy

Memory is present centred and the past, whether recent or long ago, is viewed from the perspective of the present day. Any story about the past is told because of its present day relevance.[22] Besides being a

---

21. M. Innes, 'Keeping it in the family: women and aristocratic memory, 700-1200', *Medieval Memories*, ed. van Houts, pp. 17-35 at pp. 25-6.
22. H. W. Goetz, *Geschichtsschreibung und Geschichtsbewusstsein im hohen Mittelalter*, Vorstellungswelten des Mittelalters, 1 (Berlin, 1999), pp. 243-310.

reflection of present day preoccupations, memory and commemoration also constitute attempts to control the future. Why remember ancestors and forebears if not to secure their everlasting life, that is a future from the present day perspective? The gendered tasks of men and women were clear. Men were expected to fight and die while protecting their lands and estates, while women were expected to remember their menfolks' deeds performed in this process and to pass on stories of those deeds to posterity. Thus women, as we have seen, kept in touch with the dead through funeral rituals, proper mourning, listing names of the dead and praying for them. Occasionally we find women conversing with the dead and communicating with forebears in much more physical ways (visions and physical trances). As part of the same process we find women prophesying, foretelling the future themselves or consulting others to do so for them.[23] Aristocratic women in particular were anxious to know what would happen to their family in years to come. Their concern for house and kin extended in the future as much as it extended into the past and both concerns were commemorative as well. Women, with the consent of their male kin, set aside large payments for the commemoration of souls in perpetuity. They laid down instructions for their granddaughters to do the same (Queen Matilda I of Germany handing the commemorative role of names to her granddaughter and namesake Matilda abbess of Quedlinburg).[24] They did every thing they could to ensure the permanency of their arrangements.

In c. 950 Queen Gerberga, wife of King Louis IV of France, became increasingly anxious about the prospects of her children. Like many aristocratic women of her time she had two sets of children from two marriages. The elder ones were due to inherit Lotharingia, the lands of their father Giselbert who had died in 939, while for the younger ones for a French inheritance would be waiting. Lotharingia, however, situated between Germany and France had become a bone of contention between Gerberga's brother King Otto I of Germany and her husband Louis IV. Torn between two ethnic loyalties, symbolizing her past and her present, and faced with her offspring's uncertain future Gerberga consulted a wise

---

23. H. Dienst, 'Zur Rolle von Frauen in magischen Vorstellungen und Praktiken nach ausgewählten mittelalterlichen Quellen', in W. Affeldt, ed., *Frauen in Spätantike und Frühmittelalter. Lebensbedingungen, Lebensnormen, Lebensformen* (Sigmaringen, 1990), pp. 173-94. The standard work on medieval prophecy, M. Reeves, *The influence of Prophecy in the later Middle Ages. A Study in Joachimism* (Oxford, 1969), pays no attention to gender.

24. *Vita Mahthildis reginae antiquior*, ed. R. Koepke, MGH SS, 10: 581.

abbot, Adso of Montier-en-Der, about the future. Faced with so much uncertainty she feared that the end of time was near and that the Antichrist, the source of all evil, was about to be defeated. If only she would be reassured by Adso what the Antichrist had in store for her two lots of children she could adjust the advice she would give to them. Adso, somewhat surprised, compiled a small treatise on the basis of the scraps of information about the Antichrist and other prophecies he could find about the end of the world and presented this to the queen.[25] Very early on in the textual transmission of Adso's text on the Antichrist, his treatise was joined the prophecy of the Tiburtine Sybil, the female seer immortalized by Virgil in his Fourth Eclogue, who according to St. Augustine foresaw the birth of Christ. Her prophecy of Christianity as the new religion gave the Sybil an unrivalled status as authority for knowledge about the future. The female gender of Sybil made her particularly attractive to women readers and her prophecies, as we shall see later on, were on demand by many queens and princesses. Fortunately for Adso, the Antichrist stories as well as Sibyl's prophecies regarding the future were conveniently vague for any interpretation to be possible. Though Gerberga's reaction to the work is not known, Adso's work cannot have satisfied her for very long because in 954 her husband died and the conflict she had dreaded did indeed ensue.

Why was Gerberga so keen on having the future mapped out for her and her children? One of the reasons, I suggest, is that knowing the future would help her to interpret past events and shape them into memories of the past order to make sense of the present. The great difficulty with thinking about the past is its amorphous mass of important and trivial incidents, full of people who only in hindsight can be signified as having had any influence or not. How to distinguish between the important and unimportant? For a queen, or indeed any other aristocratic woman, making precisely those distinctions was part of their commemorative task. These women had to decide whom among the many family members, and dependants on the estates, needed to be remembered and for what reason. Their main task was to remember the names of those who had left lands, rights or other property and to make sure that those who were in line to inherit them would not only know the ancestral names but also any information (legal or otherwise) attached to such an inheritance. Needless

---

25. *Adso Dervensis de ortu et tempore antichristi necnon et tractatus qui ab eo dependunt*, ed. D. Verhelst, Corpus Christianorum, Continuatio Mediaevalis, 45 (Turnhout, 1996), pp. 20-30; Reeves, *The Influence of Prophecy*, pp. 293-392.

to say life is fickle and the hand-over of property from one generation to the next fraught with difficulties and disputes. Amidst the chaos of violence and warfare, accompanying most disputes and executed by men, the women in the family had the unenviable task to select ancestors and ensure that their children and grandchildren would know them and pray that the rightful inheritance would reach them. The process of 'ancestor selection' was intimately tied up with knowing the future as well as the past.

QUEENS AND PROPHECIES

Interesting evidence for the influence of Adso's treatise on the Antichrist in conjunction with the sybilline prophecies comes from Normandy on the eve of the Normand Conquest. In 1066 Duchess Matilda, wife of William the Conqueror, was pregnant of a child due to be born probably early in 1067. Matilda would have consulted all her advisers: chaplains and other ecclesiastical officers as well as her maid servants on the significance of her pregnancy and on what line of action to take in order to ensure a positive result for her husband's undertaking. It is well known that during other critical periods in her life, and particularly during her husband's quarrels with their eldest son Robert Curthose, she consulted magicians, of whom one, said to be German, may have been Flemish.[26] From her homeland too originated a custom, recorded for the Flemish communities in southern Wales, of consulting the bones of a sheep's shoulder in order to know the future.[27] Matilda's pregnancy in particular may have made her especially sensitive to the need to try to influence God's will with the help of pagan gods; certain prophetical books may have been a comfort to her.[28] There is more convincing evidence that Duchess Matilda knew both Adso's work and the sybilline prophecies, for the oldest manuscript of Adso's book on the Antichrist, which is also one of the oldest manuscripts for the Tiburtine

---

26. *The Ecclesiastical history*, ed. Chibnall, 3: 104: His temporibus in Teutonica regione quidam anachorita uir bonus et sanctus erat, qui inter cetera uirtutum insignia spiritum propheticae habebat. Ad quem Mathildis regina legatos et xenia misit ac ut pro marito filioque suo Rodberto Deum oraret suppliciter rogauit, ac ut uaticinium quod eis in futurum contigeret sibi mandaret adiecit.

27. *Giraldi Cambrensis opera*, ed. J. F. Dimock, Rolls Series, 6 vols, (London, 1861-91), 6: 87-8. Gerald of Wales, *The Journey through Wales/ the Description of Wales*, trans. L. Thorpe (Harmondsworth, 1978), p. 145.

28. D. Lett, *L'enfant des miracles. Enfance et société au moyen Age, XIIe – XIIIe siècle* (Paris, 1997), p. 252-5.

prophecy of Sybil (Paris BN ms lat. 5390 ff. 230v-235v) was copied at the scriptorium of Fécamp at the time of Abbot John of Ravenna (1028-78).[29] To be more precise, copied in the period *c.* 1060-1070, the manuscript can be placed around the time of the Norman conquest of England and I would not be surprised if it actually owed its existence to that very event.[30] It seems extremely likely that Abbot John of Fécamp, famous for his spirituel guidance of aristocratic women,[31] requested that to the *Life of William of Volpiano*, the first abbot of Fécamp (d. 1031), be added a copy of the prophetical texts. Since William of Volpiano may have known Adso, and Adso in turn had known Queen Gerberga for whom he had written the book on the Antichrist, William's authority would have enhanced the value of the prophecies for a potential queen in the context of the conquest of England.[32] Duchess Matilda, like queen Gerberga, and her court would have wished to consult every prophecy in order to know the future. As a mother she was anxious to know the future for her children, as a pregnant woman the future of her unborn child, and as wife the future for her husband.[33] Knowledge of the future is directly linked to the memorial role of aristocratic women, whose responsibility it was to recall the past and the deceased members of the family in order to pass on their names to future generations.[34] Here I should like to underline that knowing the future was as important for the women surrounding kings (and other noble men) as it was to know the past. The knowledge of the future necessarily explains the dominance of women among references to magic, prophecy and witchcraft.[35]

29. *Adso Dervensis*, ed. Verhelst, p. 6-8; *Sibyllinische Texte und Forschungen*, ed. E. Sackur (Halle, 1898), p. 104.

30. *Rodulfus Glaber Opera*, ed. J. France, N. Bulst and P. Reynolds (Oxford, 1989), p. xciv-xcv. Paris BN Ms lat. 5390 also contains the oldest copy of the Life of William of Volpiano by Rodulfus Glaber (ff. 222r-230r). All three texts are by the same scribe. Neithard Bulst, however, has pointed out that the three texts were probably bound with a collection of homelies of Gregory the Great. On this basis he would be inclined to see the collection as a monastic one rather than that meant for a queen, see his 'Rodulfus Glabers Vita domni Willemi abbatis', *Deutsches Archiv für Erforschung des Mittelalters*, 30 (1974), 450-87 and personal communication.

31. J. Leclercq, J. P. Bonnes, *Un maître de la vie spirituelle au XIe siècle, Jean de Fécamp*, Études de théologie et d'histoire de la spiritualité, 11 (Paris, 1946), pp. 205-10 and 211-17.

32. N. Bulst, *Untersuchungen zu den Klostereformen Wilhelms von Dijon (962-1031)*, (Bonn, 1973), pp. 31-3.

33. S. Gouguenheim, *Les fausses terreurs de l'an mil* (Paris, 1999), pp. 87-8.

34. Le Jan, *Famille et pouvoir*, pp. 31-57; G. Duby, *Women of the Twelfth Century, vol. 2: Remembering the dead*, trans. J. Birrell (Oxford, 1998); E. van Houts, *Memory and Gender in Medieval Europe 900-1200* (Basingstoke, 1999).

35. Dienst, 'Zur Rolle von Frauen', pp. 173-94.

Another aspect of the conquest and Matilda's pregnancy is important in this respect namely Matilda's gift of the ship *Mora* to her husband William with its figure head in the form of gilded child. The figure head of the golden child might have been based on a classical source, namely the Fourth Eclogue of Virgil.[36] In the year 40 BC Virgil wrote a poem on the imminent birth of the child of Octavia and Antonius, who symbolised the beginning of a golden age and a new future. Virgil was inspired by the sybilline prophecies which he introduced in lines 4-5, where they are said to have prophecised the birth of the child and given a description of an imaginary fecund and happy country.[37] From the time of the Church Fathers and all through the Middle Ages this theme was interpreted as the birth of God and the arrival of Christianity, the true religion.[38] According to St. Augustin in his *City of God*, using the Virgilian passage, the prophetess Sybil had announced the birth of Jesus Christ.[39] The combination of the description of the child as a herald of a golden age and a land of gold links in with another Virgilian theme, namely that of the age of gold as presented in the *Aeneid*, vi. 792-3.[40] It is attractive to hypothesise that the combination of the Virgilian themes with the references to the precious metals and riches of England in Julius Cesar's *De bello Gallico*,[41] inspired the artist responsible for the figure head of the golden child of the ducal ship. William of Poitiers, chaplain and biographer of the Conqueror knew the classical texts very well.[42] In Normandy the monastery of Fécamp, the nerve centre of the logistical conquest operation, had a manuscript of Vergil, while Le Bec had one of Julius Cesar.[43] Virgil himself was known as a poet as well as a prophet

36. *Virgil, Eclogues*, ed. W. Clausen (Oxford, 1994), 11-13 and the commentary at pp. 119-50. P. Courcelle, 'Les exégèses chrétiennes de la quatrième églogue', *Revue des études anciennes*, 59 (1957), p. 294-319.
37. *Virgil*, p. 11: Vltima Cumaei uenit iam carminis ordo./ magnus ab integro saeclorum nascitur ordo./
38. *Ibid*, p. 127 et B. McGinn, '*Teste David cum Sibylla*: the significance of the Sibylline tradition in the Middle Ages', in *Women of the medieval World. Essays in honor of John H. Mundy*, ed. J. Kirschner and S.F. Wemple (Oxford, 1985), 7-35 at pp. 13-18.
39. *Sancti Aurelii Augustini episcopi de civitate dei libri xxii*, Lib. XVIII, c. 23, ed. B. Dombart and A. Kalb, 2 vols (Leipzig, 1928-9) 2: 285-8.
40. *Virgil in two volumes I. Eclogues. Georgics. Aeneid I-VI* (London-Cambridge, Mass, 1960), pp. 560-1, lines VI, 792-3: Augustus Caesar, Divi genus, aurea condet/ saecula qui rursus Latio regnata per arva/.
41. *C. Iulii caesaris commentarii reum gestarum, vol. 1: Bellum Gallicum*, Book V, chapter 12, ed. W. Hering (Leipzig, 1987), p. 72.
42. *The Gesta Guillelmi of William of Poitiers*, ed. R.H.C. Davis and M. Chibnall (Oxford, 1998), pp. xviii et 189-90.
43. G. Nortier, *Les bibliothèques médiévales des abbayes bénédictines de Normandie* (Paris, 1971), pp. 230 and 205.

and his prophetical role may have helped the introduction of the theme of the golden boy in the context of the conquest of England. If the hypothesis with regard to the original idea of the golden child is acceptable as a Virgilian theme, we may attempt to resolve the question of the meaning of the name Mora. I propose that Mora stands for the greek word 'Moira', which means Fates. The Fates were the goddesses Clotho, Lachesis and Atropos, who ruled birth, life and death. Medieval poets knew them very well as the classical goddesses and we find many references to them in the eleventh and twelfth centuries. Such literary usage, implying some belief in the goddesses, seemed to have been permissable amongst erudite clerks. In contrast, the practical usage of references to the Fates and an active belief in their workings was not allowed judging by the words of Bishop Burchard of Worms (1000-1025), who condemned all superstitious belief in them.[44] The combination of the classical tradition with the pagan and popular tradition of the Fates led to the myth of the good and bad Fairies, active around the birth of a child (think of Snow White). Here in the context of 1066 we find, perhaps, an early instance of belief in the Fates as Fairies at the eve of the birth of a ducal child.

The last glimpse of Matilda's interest in omens comes from the early 1080s on the occasion when she stood godmother to Matilda II, who unbeknown to her would in due course be her daughter-in-law, wife of her son Henry I. The moment is recorded through a chain of female witnesses down to the time of her granddaughter Empress Matilda. The written source, based on the Empress's information, is a letter of Gilbert Foliot to Brian fitz Count from 1139 which tells the following story: Queen Matilda I stood godmother to Matilda II, the baby daughter of Malcolm III and Margaret of Scotland.[45] During the christening the little girl got hold of her godmother's veil and drew it over her face. It was explained to the bystanders that this was a significant moment because it was an omen that the girl one day might become a queen herself. Gilbert Foliot extrapolates the story that the omen became true and that with a mother (Matilda II) and grandmother (Matilda I) as queen of England, the Empress had every right to become a queen herself. What Gilbert does not mention, of course, is that Matilda I and Matilda II were queen

---

44. Burchard de Worms, *Decretum*, XIX, c. 151, 153, ed. H. J. Schmitz, *Die Bussbücher*, 2 vols, (Graz, 1958), 2: 442; *Medieval Handbooks of Penance*, trans. McNeill and Gamer, p. 338.

45. *The Letters and Charters of Gilbert Foliot*, ed. A. Morey and C.N.L. Brooke (Cambridge, 1967), p. 66.

46. Hildebert of Lavardin, epistola 1.18, ed. J.P.Migne, PL 171: 189-91; P. von Moos, *Hildebert von Lavardin 1056-1133* (Stuttgart, 1965), p. 325.

consorts, whereas the Empress was aiming to become queen in her own right. The story about the omen, however, is very interesting as a glimpse not only of the symbolic interpretation of the veil's movement, which we might see as a perfectly harmless incident, but also as evidence for a woman's view of queenship transmitted through three generations.

ADELIZA OF LEUVEN

Foretelling the future became very popular during Henry I's reign in particular after the death of his son and successor William Adelin in the White Ship Disaster of 1120. The king married a second time, but his young wife Adeliza of Louvain failed to produce a male heir. Although she followed her husband everywhere and was never left behind in the hope that their frequent proximity would result in pregnancy, conception failed turning Adeliza and the king's advisers increasingly desperate. Adeliza took advice and though her own letters have not survivied, the responses of several bishops, e.g. from Hildebert of Lavardin, indicate the high level of anxiety.[46] The more illegitimate children Henry I produced, in all more than 20 are known, the more his masculinity and fertility were obvious and the greater the probability that the childlessness was all Adeliza's fault.[47] The future looked increasingly bleak and desperate, so recourse to prophecy and sorcery seemed an obvious answer to questions about the future. The *Brevis Relatio*, a short chronicle of William the Conqueror's reign written at Battle Abbey during Henry I's reign, contains the first version of the seven generation prophecy.[48] According to the story a stranger told his host with whom he stayed the night that he could look into the future. Sitting in front of the fire he kindled the wood, looked into the flames and then traced with a piece of wood a pattern in the ash. He identified the seven generations with the seven generations of Norman dukes from Rollo onwards. Henry I was seen as the seventh after whose time internal war and rebellion would reign. Robert of Torigni, as Henry I's biographer, not only copied this prophecy but he

---

47. *The Gesta Normannorum Ducum*, ed. and trans. Van Houts, 2: 247-9 and p. 249 n. 6.

48. E. van Houts, '*The Brevis Relatio de Guillelmo nobilissimo comite Normannorum* written by a monk of Battle Abbey, edited and translated with an historical commentary', in: E. M.C. van Houts, *History and Family Traditions in England and the Continent 1000-1200*, Variorum Collected Studies Series (Aldershot, 1999), no. vii, 1-48 at pp. 42-44.

went so far as to renumber the eight books of the *Gesta Normannorum Ducum* in order for the eighth on Henry I to be counted as the seventh.[49]

What is very interesting is that the first use of the seven generation prophecy in western Europe can be traced to a text datable to c. 1100 from the north west corner of France.[50] It has been associated with Ponthieu, Flanders and the Amiens area, in other words the very same place where Flemish peasants consulted animal shoulderblades for news about the future. From the same geographical area and time stems the interest in prophecies as far as the Flemish comital dynasty was concerned, judging by Hermann of Tournai's testimony.[51] Thus there is abundant evidence for an interest in dynastic prophecies from areas not too far away from where Queen Adeliza was brought up. We cannot positively link her or her courtiers with the seven generation prophecy, but some connection seems highly likely.

After her husband's death Adela commisioned his biography, probably in the vernacular and, thus, probably in verse from David the Scot. A work that is now lost but that was well known to contemporaries, and especially Gaimar. Adeliza had a splendid copy made of this work, the first part of which was set to music. Gaimar's patron, the Lincolnshire woman Constance, also had a copy.[52] As David's patron Adeliza stands in a long line of queens and other aristocratic women who commissioned biographies or chronicles of their fathers, brothers and husbands and sons.[53] She was also the dedicatee of other works. The *Voyage of St. Brendan*, originally dedicated to Queen Matilda II, was rededicated to Adeliza.[54] Perhaps in connection with her husband Henry's preference for exotic animals, he had a zoo at Woodstock,[55] she was the dedicatee

---

49. *The Gesta Normannorum Ducum*, ed. and trans. Van Houts, 2: 282-7 and 1: lxxxiv-lxxxv.

50. *Ex historia relationis corporis s. Walarici abbatis*, in: *Recueil des Historiens de France*, ed. M. Bouquet, 9: 147-8.

51. *Narratio restaurationis abbatiae sancti Martini Tornacensis*, ed. G. Waitz, MGH SS 14: 280; *Herman of Tournai, The restoration of the monastery of Saint-Martin of Tournai* trans. L. H. Nelson (Washington, D.C., 1996), pp. 28-9. For a commentary, see Nip, 'Gendered memories', p. 121.

52. *L'Estoire des Engleis by Geffrei Gaimar*, ed. A. Bell (Oxford, 1960), lines 6480-6484, p. 205.

53. Van Houts, *Memory and Gender*, 65-71.

54. Benedeit, *The Anglo-Norman voyage of St Brendan*, ed. I. Short and B. Merrilees (Manchester 1979), line 1, p. 30 and I. Short, 'Patrons and poluglots', *Anglo-Norman Studies XIV. Proceedings of the Battle Conference 1991*, ed. M. Chibnall (Woodbridge, 1992), 229-49 at p. 237.

55. William of Malmesbury, *Gesta Regum Anglorum*, ed. and trans. R.A.B. Mynors, R.M. Thomson and M. Winterbottom, 2 vols (Oxford, 1998-9) 1: 740-1.

of Philip of Thaon's vernacular Bestiary.[56] The same author may also have dedicated his French version of the *Livre de Sibyl* to her in the first place, before he later changed his appeal in line 1208-16 to Empress Matilda and later still to Eleanor of Aquitaine. As we have seen above in the case of Matilda I, knowledge of the Sibyl was available in the Anglo-Norman realm, though at that time only in Latin.[57] Though that did not detract from the Sibyl's role as 'fairy' in the context of childbirth. The topic was suitable for a queen who had not given up hope for a child. If so, the Sibyl's prophecy worked, but not as Adeliza expected. She survived her husband as a childless widow, but then married their butler William d'Aubigny by whom she had as far as we know at least two sons. One was their son and heir William d'Aubigny II and the younger was called Reiner.[58] Adeliza lived through most of the troubled reign of her husband's successor King Stephen, a period from which the oldest Anglo-Norman horoscopes have survived.[59] They form the ultimate evidence for a hankering for knowledge about the future during a time when two branches of William the Conqueror's descendants were fighting for power: Stephen, the son of William's daughter Adela versus Empress Matilda, the daughter of William's son Henry I. For unknown reasons in 1150 Adeliza retired to the nunnery of Afflighem in her home country where she died the following year.[60] She was, however, buried in Reading Abbey the monastery she and her first husband had founded in the year of their marriage thirty years ago.[61]

---

56. A.H. Krappe, 'The historical background of Philip de Thaun's "Bestiaire"', *Modern Language notes*, 69 (1944), 325-7; M. D. Legge, *Anglo-Norman Literature and its Background* (Oxford, 1963), pp. 23-6.

57. *Le livre de Sibile by Philippe de Thaon*, ed. H. Shields, Anglo-Norman Texts, 37 (London, 1979), pp. 23, 89-90, 111. The suggestion that the text may originally have contained an appeal to Adeliza is mine.

58. G. E. C [ockayne], *Complete Peerage of England, Scotland, Ireland, Great Britain...*, new ed. by G. H. White, 12 vols (London, 1901-59), 1: 233-5 and 9: 366-7. Another son Reiner is mentioned in *Reading Abbey Cartularies*, ed. B. Kemp, 2 vols, Camden 4th s., 31, 33 (London,1986-7), 1: 369. For the origin of the Aubigny family, see also *Charters of the Honour of Mowbray 1107-91*, ed D.E. Greenway (London, 1972), pp. xvii-xix.

59. J. D. North, 'Some Norman horoscopes', *Adelard of Bath, an English Scientist and Arabist of the early twelfth century* (London, 1987), pp. 147-61.

60. *Annales de Margam*, in *Annales monastici*, ed. H. R. Luard, 5 vols (London, 1884-9), 1: 14.

61. *The Reading Abbey Cartularies*, ed. Kemp, 1: 416. Note that C[ockayne], *Complete Peerage*, 1: 235 and Wertheimer, 'Adeliza of louvain', p. 115 are wrong to say that she was buried at Afflighem.

Steven VANDERPUTTEN

FROM SERMON TO SCIENCE:
MONASTIC PROLOGUES FROM
THE SOUTHERN LOW COUNTRIES AS WITNESSES
OF HISTORICAL CONSCIOUSNESS
(10th-15th CENTURIES)[1]

1. THE PROLOGUE AS CAPTATIO BENEVOLENTIAE:
IMPOSING THE OFFICIAL VIEW OF THE PAST ON THE MONKS

From the tenth century onward, monastic chronicles from the Southern Low countries often feature prologues that focus on the identity of the commissioner, on the targeted public, on the topic(s) discussed in the text and on the intentions at the basis of the latter's creation. These short but revelatory introductions have received very little attention from scholars, presumably because their contents are topical, demonstrative of highly developed literary skills and are filled with vacuous praise for the commissioner. Other scholars have demonstrated, however, that prologues are often the only direct sources for the medieval historian's vision of his own work. We can learn a great deal about *whom* he wrote the work for, what the intended public *consisted* of (an important observation for the interpretation of the narrative itself), what he had in mind when speaking of a proper historical work, and what *message* he intended to spread on a *conscious* level. Because there is, in fact, hardly any explicit evidence concerning these questions in the corpus of most historiographical narratives, the basic source for the analysis of the *explicit* discourse on the function of historiography is the prologue. The topical phrases in these introductions can thus be re-interpreted as being discursive elements with a continuously fluctuating function.

---

1. The present contribution is an expanded version of my lecture, presented at the congress 'Narrative sources', held in Leuven on March 28th 2000. I would like to express my sincere gratitude to Lieve de Mey, dr. Katrien Heene, prof. Thérèse de Hemptinne, prof. Ludo Milis and ms. Susie Sutch, with whom I was able to exchange some very stimulating ideas while correcting the first draft of this article. As usual, nothing of this would have happened were it not for Melissa Provijn.

Whereas historiography bases itself on a fairly contingent series of events, the prologues try to *persuade* the public with the aid of certain discursive strategies,[2] culled from a vast legacy, dating back to the Antiquity and the early Church Fathers. Historiographers often demonstrate a highly evolved stylistic feel and express interest for the *artes liberales* in general. In the space of a few lines, the historiographer has to elucidate the work's reason for existence, its intentions and its function for later generations. In the case of medieval monastic historiography, we often get to know the (*official*) motivation for an innumerable series of chronicles and *gesta*.[3] Prominent incentives were the fear of *oblivio* (forgetfulness), the necessity of *memoria* (remembrance of the past, embedded in a semi-liturgical context), the problems caused by the difficult access to important historical information (as was the case from the twelfth century onward, when the increasing number of histories and chronicles made it difficult for the reader to obtain a general overview of history) and the moral or exemplary value of the past for the benefit of present and future audiences. In order to make his arguments persuasive, the author made the public receptive with the topos of the *rustic* (i.e. boorish, uneducated) style and several other minimising *topoi* (like his own insignificance, the fact that he could not rival with the best of his predecessors and the fact that he could never compete with Biblical history). After that, he depersonalised his account: by minimising his personal impact, he would be able to bring the work under the patronage of an abbot, a bishop or a worldly leader, thus enhancing its unquestionable claim on veracity and validity.[4] In the following paragraphs, I will illustrate these observations with evidence taken from prologues dating from the tenth until the fifteenth century, especially with regard to the function the authors themselves attributed to their narratives. The article is concluded by the edition of a previously unpublished *Epistola contra eos qui dicunt cronicas inanes seu inutiles* from around 1300.

---

2. M. Sot, 'Rhétorique et technique dans les préfaces des *Gesta episcoporum* (IXe-XIIe s.)', *Cahiers de Civilisation Médiévale*, XXVIII (1985), p. 189-190 and 196-197.

3. '...tant qu'individu, il énonce et se porte garand, par l'écriture, d'une vérité collective, de ce qui se veut la mémoire officielle de sa communauté.', cf. C. Marchello-Nizia, 'L'historien et son prologue: forme littéraire et stratégies discursives', in D. Poirion, *La chronique et l'histoire du moyen âge. Texte du colloque des 24 et 25 mai 1982* (Paris, 1986), p. 24.

4. M. Sot, p. 182-186 and D.W.T.C. Vessey, 'William of Tyre and the art of historiography', *Mediaeval Studies*, XXXV (1973), p. 436.

2. HISTORY AS A SERMON?
Measuring the value of historical representation against rhetorical standards (from the earliest prologues to the middle of the twelfth century)

It is now commonly accepted that the antique conception of the function of history dominated the historiographical practise up to the twelfth century. The inheritance of Ciceronian thought, which stated that history is only a means to refine rhetorical techniques, was readily taken up by Christian authors, who found in history a factual basis for their moral and mystical aspirations. In other words, history was considered to represent the past as it happened, thus allowing the reader to extract the moral meaning of what had happened to mankind by himself.[5] In a world where few groups in society had access to a written past, this interpretation allowed historical texts to be propagated without encountering too much opposition.

The first elaborate introductions to monastic historical narratives in the Southern Low Countries coincide with the emergence of the earliest known *fundationes* and *gesta* during the second quarter of the tenth century. In the earliest known prologue, a tiny paragraph preceding the *Ratio fundationis* of the abbey of Saint Peter in Ghent (founded 650-674/5) from 941-944,[6] the author implicitly acknowledges the fact that the text does not have any *factual* value for the monastic community. Its strong hagiographical tendencies, however, show a definite inclination toward turning history into an example of moral conduct[7] and adoration of the founding saint, in this case the well-known missionary Amandus. This allows the author to call his work an *oracionis sermo*, a sermon for the monastic community, intended to make it benefit from the sanctity of its founder and the moral values and rules of conduct transmitted by the story. Its inclusion in the cartulary of the abbey is of course highly remarkable, as the spiritual intentions of the author prevail in

---

5. P. Defourny, 'Histoire et éloquence d'après Cicéron', *Les Études classiques*, XXI (1953), p. 158-161.
6. M. Gillissen and A.F.C. Koch ed., *Diplomata Belgica ante annum millesimum centesimum scripta. I. Teksten* (Brussel, 1950), p. 123-126. The prologue is printed on page 123. In the following paragraphs, I will refer to the on-line repertory *Narrative Sources* (http://www.narrative-sources.be). The codes, mentioned in the text, refer to the relevant pages in the database (in the case of the *Ratio fundationis*, it is F033).
7. H. Wolter, 'Geschichtliche Bildung im Rahmen der Artes Liberales', in J. Koch., *Artes Liberales von Antiken Bildung zur Wissenschaft des Mittelalters* (Leiden – Köln, 1959), p. 59 and 61.

the *fundatio*.⁸ Nonetheless, it becomes clear that the sanctity of the subject is commendable for the material claims, expressed in the remainder of the codex. A cunning mixture of opportunism and sermon-like rhetoric is created, acting as an indication of what is to come.

In Lobbes, Folcuin's *gesta* of the abbots (circa 980) are infused with even more didactic fervour, in the sense that the text explicitly features highly deterministic opinions on the influence of God on human history. According to Folcuin, it is clear that history and its sequencing of facts throughout time is controlled by a divinity that is not subject to temporality.⁹ Remarkably, he acknowledges the important role of human action: history appears to be the interactive field in which mankind can strive for its salvation, but does not relate to the transcendental aspirations of the monks.¹⁰ History, as it appears to Folcuin, does not represent the essence of human behaviour (which, in fact, is a constant repetition of the biblical drama and needs no further exemplification), but is there to express the continuity of the attempts to overcome the frustrating aspects of human time. Indeed, as the author expresses a vivid interest in secular power and the dynasties from the Roman Empire onward, the main point in expressing that aspect of history is to prove the legitimacy of the origins of Lobbes. As secular powers proved unable to introduce the Kingdom of God into the world, the Carolingian dynasty made way for a redistribution of power in favour of the clergy and the monasteries.¹¹ The real impetus to acquire transtemporal status no longer comes from a secular authority (from Constantine the Great onward, rulers had tried to impose a near-life reflection of the heavenly kingdom on earth, be it with very little success), but from a spiritual elite. The latter has dropped its outer-worldly status and emerges as a group of *virtuosi*, essential for the

---

8. The text is preserved in three versions: one fragment from 940-944 and two complete but slightly adapted versions from the first quarter of the eleventh century and from c. 1035 (see the record in *Narrative Sources*). Each was intended to precede a cartulary.

9. '...Deus est creator temporum, cum et ipse antiquior sit tempore cuius creator est, et cuncta creaverit in tempore...sola rerum causa voluntas Dei est.' (F013; ed. W. Arndt, in: *Monumenta Germaniae Historica. Scriptores*, IV, Hannoverae, 1869, p. 54-55. In the following footnotes the title of the series will be referred to as MGH SS). The twelfth-century author of the *Annales Cameracenses* (L017) expresses the same opinion: '...nec capillus hominis movetur absque Dei vultu.' (ed. G.H. Pertz, in: *MGH SS. XVI*, Hannoverae, 1859, p. 532). It is, therefore, highly commendable to thank God for his continuous dedication to mankind (*Historia monasterii Viconiensis*, H046, 12th century; ed. J. Heller, in: *MGH SS*, XXIV, Hannoverae, 1879, p. 294).

10. 'Ergo non potest quicquam ultra citrave progredi nisi cum voluntate Domini, salvo cum gratia Dei dono hominibus dato liberi arbitrii' (ed. W. Arndt, p. 55).

11. 'De regnorum quoque successionibus seu permutationibus, quas vel audivimus vel vidimus, non multum mirandum.' (*Ibidem*).

subsistence and the salvation of mankind.[12] Of course, God himself engendered this permutation.[13] This spectacular reasoning features obvious limitations: as the monastic community has not yet developed a clear historical concept of itself as a group, the author struggles with providing an answer to the crisis of secular authority and the dubious take-over by the spiritual elite.[14] This does not result in a firm statement regarding the identity of monasticism, and so the *gesta* of the abbots ultimately contradict the firm assertions of the author in the prologue by their structure, which relies heavily on an uncertain balance between wordly and ecclesiastical influences.[15]

Folcuin's awkward enthusiasm soon won out, however, as the historiographers from the second half of the eleventh century onward expressed a heightened self-awareness and an acute sense of their importance to society.[16] This evolution, heavily influenced by the struggles of the church and the monasteries to liberate themselves from the clutches of the local nobility and a general uneasiness about the sorry state of affairs in the Church, implied political, socio-economic and cultural shifts, which in turn influenced the themes and contents of contemporary historiography.[17] At first hesitantly, later on with more confidence, the monastic authors no longer defined the group they belonged to as opposed to the world, but rather an essential part of its social network.

At this point, we can see two rather different options emerging simultaneously in the prologues: on one hand, there are the highly elaborated *captationes benevolentiae*, dedications and other stylistic topoi, with a strong tendency to show off the author's level of education, whereas on the other hand there are strong indications of a heightened social awareness among the monks that occasionally pierces through the screen of

---

12. A. Angenendt, 'Deus, qui nullum peccatum impunitum dimittit. Ein "Grundsatz" der mittelalterlichen Bußgeschichte', in M. Lutz-Bachmann, *Und dennoch ist von Gott zu reden. Festschrift für Herbert Vorgrimler* (Freiburg – Basel – Wien, 1994), p. 147.

13. 'Et quare non maneret, quam sapientia Dei, quae ait: Per me reges regnant, fide firmabat, aequitate et iustitia roborabat? Testantur hoc episcopia vel monasteria ante id temporis diruta aut nulla, quae abhinc aut rediviva pullularunt aut novis auspiciis inchoarunt.' (ed. W. Arndt, p. 55).

14. O.G. Oexle, 'Les moines d'Occident et la vie politique et sociale dans le haut moyen âge', *Revue Bénédictine*, CIII (1993), p. 265-266.

15. The authors of the contemporary *Annales Lobienses* (A076; ed. G. Waitz, in *MGH SS*, XIII, Hannoverae, 1881, p. 226-235) still make every effort to align their dating system with the imperial succession line.

16. D. Iogna-Prat, 'La geste des origines dans l'historiographie clunisienne des XIe-XIIe siècles', *Revue Bénédictine*, CII (1992), p. 150-151.

17. T. Struve, 'Die Wende des 11. Jahrhunderts. Symptome eines Epochenwandels im Spiegel der Geschichtsschreibung', *Historisches Jahrbuch*, 112 (1992), p. 339.

formulaic discourse. In the *Historia monasterii Hasnoniensis* (written between 1070 and 1085), the anonymous author praises the good abbot Rolland for his virtuous conduct and his religious government, thereby making him the patron of the work (thus making it unquestionable), and lures the whole of the community into a net of responsibility. In a subtle manner, the author imposes on the others his responsibility as the creator of the work by imploring and later on simply stating their silent approval of the concept and the contents.[18] By anticipating all possible protests at the very start of the narrative, the writer ensures that everyone within the monastery who reads on or who does not protest while listening will become responsible for the claims expressed in this *historia*. The group as a whole is completely and consciously involved in the creation of a detailed narrativised past.[19] For similar reasons, some contemporary authors will also express their preference for local historiography instead of the efforts of universal chroniclers, such as Sigebert of Gembloux.[20]

At the start of the twelfth century, the words *utilitas*[21] and *memoria*[22] tend to feature with increasing frequence in the prologues. There is a

---

18. 'Exigis enim a me antiquam Hasnoniensis coenobii constructionem novo stylo cudere passimque in archivis divisam in unum volumen colligere, quantumque divae memoriae marchio Balduinus beneficum eiden loco nostra aetate indulserit, subscribere... Sed me sub fasce gradientem baculus tuae sustendabit sanctitatis, cumque extremam operi manum dedero, tui sit muneris, si placeo, tuae correctionis, si displiceo, dum unum auctoritate probes, alterum oratione robores. Succurrunt et labori meo orationes fratrum Hasnoniensium sub cura tua in castris Christi arma iustitiae gerentium, quibus in ore numquam dormitat oratio, in corde dilectio, in virtute numquam languescit operatio.' (H045/T041; ed. O. Holder-Egger, in *MGH SS*, XIV, Hannoverae, 1883, p. 149).

19. 'Dicturus fundationem Hasnoniensis loci, res postulat temporibus et personis loco accomodis uti; id enim grammaticis cum oratoribus commune est, locum, tempus, personam in cuncto adtendere negotiis.' (*Ibidem*).

20. '...domnus abbas illi, qui hec narrabat, mansueta voce dicit: "Magis hec enim scribere debuisse ad uitilitatem filiorum huius ecclesie, quam gesta regum et bella imperatorum in chronicis componere."' (*Chronicon Marchianense* (A057), end of the 12th – early 13th century; Douai, Bibliothèque Municipale, ms. 850, folio 103v°).

21. See also the *De fundatione abbatiae Ninivensis* (D013, final decades of the twelfth century): 'ad utilitatem posteriorum dignum...' and '...indecens videatur silentio deperire...' (ed. A.-J.-A. Bijsterveld and D. Van de Perre, *Het mirakelboek en de stichtingsgeschiedenis van de Ninoofse abdij: Liber miraculorum Sancti Cornelii Ninivensis – Historia fundationis ninivensis abbatiae*, Leuven, 2001, p. 134).

22. There is a severe selection in what ought to be remembered, what is *dignum memoriae* (Renier of Saint-Jacob, R034, between 1194 and 1230: 'Dignum esse memorie duximus...' (ed. L.C. Bethmann, in *MGH SS*, XVI, Hannoverae, 1859, p. 677)). The same goes for the *Annales Cameracenses* (L017; ed. G.H. Pertz, *o.c.*, p. 546) and the *Fundatio monasterii Arroasiensis* (G002, between 1180 and 1193; ed. B. Tock and L. Milis, *Momunenta Arroasiensia*, Turnhout, 2000, p. 49). Even in the thirteenth century, the author of the *De inchoatione monasterii Sancti Andree iuxta Brugis* (C009-D016) indicates that

strong tendency, especially in *gesta,* to emphasise the moral and utilitarian value of continuity through *imitatio.* No longer a sermon, the historical narrative is there to be used by both leaders and their subjects, to perpetuate the community and to keep up the moral standards, measured against and compared to situations in other periods. A painful fear of *oblivio,* which would lead to the ultimate demise of the group, begins to permeate the discourse. In Herimannus Tornacensis' *Liber de restauratione monasterii Sancti Martini Tornacensis* (around 1142-1147), one can easily sense the fear that, three generations after the facts, the crisis-related instalment of Benedictines in Tournai would be forgotten.[23] As remembrance formed an important part of the monastic liturgy,[24] the heightened group-related consciousness would not allow them to forget either individuals, or the group itself.[25] As the monastic community's self-awareness increased, the need for arguments for its existence also became more important: no longer could the author assume its position to be issued by God through a redistribution of power, as was the case with Folcuin.[26] The author of the *Chronica monasterii Guatinensis* (eleventh century) states that the past has a group-building potential, as families recall the future of their ancestors to relate better to the latter and to their actions.[27] The family-model takes shape at a time when theory also tended to stress the father-role of the abbot,[28] and a certain shift

'...posteris nostris id profuturum speramus...' as far as the actual story of the foundation is concerned (ed. C. Van den Haute, 'Une chronique inédite de l'abbaye bénédictine de Saint-André-lez-Bruges du XIIe-XIIIe siècles', *Annales de la Société d'Emulation de Bruges. Revue trimestrielle pour l'étude de l'histoire & des antiquités de la Flandre,* LIX, 1909, p. 280).

23. H030; Migne, J.P. ed., in *Patrologiae Latinae Tomus 180,* Turnholti (reprint), s.d., col. 39-42.

24. O.G. Oexle., 'Die Gegenwart der Lebenden und der Toten. Gedanken über Memoria', in K. Schmid ed., *Gedächtnis, das Gemeinschaft stiftet* (München – Zürich, 1985), p. 74-75.

25. The same can be said of the prologues of the twelfth-century *Fundatio monasterii Sancti Nicolai de Pratis Tornacensis* (F032, ed. O. Holder-Egger, in *MGH SS,* XV/2, Hannoverae, 1883, p. 1113) and the *Exordium seu fundatio monasterii Haffligeniensis* (C014, ed. V. Coosemans and C. Coppens, 'De eerste kroniek van Affligem', *Affligemensia. Bijdragen tot de geschiedenis van de abdij van Affligem tot 1794,* 4, 1947, p. 13).

26. That is why the author of the *Chronica monasterii Villariensis* (C010) wants to designate '...qualiter ordo ibidem viguit...' (ed. G. Waitz, in *MGH SS,* XXV, Hannoverae, 1880, p. 195).

27. 'Sed nos neminem latere volentes, tam nolentibus scire quam volentibus innotescere studeamus, ut, sicut quis, de qua sit oriundus linea, novit, ne itidem, cuius sit originis Guatinense coenobium, filii qui nascentur ignorent.' (C011; ed. O. Holder-Egger, in *MGH SS,* XIV, Hannoverae, 1883, p. 166).

28. *Regula Benedicti,* II, 3: '...Accepistis spiritum adoptionis filiorum in quo clamamus: abba, pater.'

in identities is to be seen here, from individual spiritualisation to group-related action in the world.[29] It would, however, be rather imprudent not to acknowledge a constant undercurrent of legitimisation of material possessions,[30] institutional continuity, and so on.[31]

A second level in the *utilitas*-idea is reserved to the spiritual interpretation: young, fervent communities like the one in Anchin had their *fundatio* written with many references to the exemplary function of the narrative: in the prologue of the *Fundatio monasterii Aquicintini* (about 1170), the monastic silence is referred to as an important identifying aspect of their lives, as opposed to other observations, like the then-emerging regular canons.[32] In a rare moment of candour, Rodulphus of Saint-Trond even acknowledges the value of abbatial misconduct and anarchy in order to reassess governmental and other issues in monastic life.[33] Elsewhere, the religious *fervor* is somewhat downplayed to the

---

29. Even in the fifteenth century, Joes van Dormael wrote his gesta of the community of Hertogendal '...tot eueghen kinnessen den nacomelinghen tsgodshuys van tsHertogendale...' (J178, ed. C. Vleeschouwers, 'Joes van Dormael's kroniek der hervorming binnen de Brabantse Cisterciënserinnenabdij Hertogendal (1468)', *Ons Geestelijk Erf. Driemaandelijks tijdschrift gewijd aan de studie der Nederlandse vroomheid vanaf de bekering tot circa 1750*, 47, 1973, p. 196).

30. E.g. the *Poleticum Marceniensis cenobii* (12th century; ed. B. Delmaire, *L'histoire-polyptique de l'abbaye de Marchiennes (1116/1121). Étude critique et édition*, Louvain-la-Neuve, 1985, p. 66-67).

31. *Chronica monasterii Guatinensis* (C011): 'Quae ita scire, ut supra posuimus, reor, non oberit, ymo et post ex illo die eandem possessionem solide et quiete nos tenuisse, apud memoriam posterorum multum nosse proderit.' (ed. O. Holder-Egger, in *MGH SS*, XIV, Hannoverae, p. 169). See also G. Simon, 'Untersuchungen zur Topik der Widmungsbriefe mittelalterlicher Geschichtsschreiber bis zum Ende des 12. Jahrhunderts. Erster Teil', *Archiv für Diplomatik, Schriftgeschichte, Siegel- und Wappenkunde*, 4 (1958), p. 83.

32. '...subit animum etiam de situ eiusdem loci, necnon a quibus et a quantis viris prima ipsius fundamenta iactata sint, aliqua perstringere eorumque exempla, quorum nimirum laus est in ecclesia, nomina vero in libro vitae, generationi omni quae ventura est tamquam decentissimam cui imprimant formam, silentio hactenus deformatam, litterarum utcumque figuris reformare.' (F030; ed. G. Waitz, G. ed., in *MGH SS*, XIV, Hannoverae, 1883, p. 579). See also Reinerus' continuation of the *Annales Sancti Jacobi* (R034): 'Huic operi pauca volo inserere, ut sciant fratres nostri futuri sibi cavere, quod damna, quod labores, quod iniurias, quod tribulationes sustinuerint a tribus abbatibus...' (ed. L.C. Bethmann, in *MGH SS*, XVI, Hannoverae, 1859, p. 662). The remarkable use of the word *fratri* indicates how futile the borders between the living and the dead must have been in the eyes of the historiographers.

33. 'Abbates et monachos post me futuros in hoc coenobio volo sollicitos inde reddere, quatenus in anteriorum suorum negligentiam ulterius non incidant, sed suis quoque posteris de predecessoribus suis plenum fidei monumentum scripto relinquant. In quo dum probitas seu improbitas singulorum frequenter legi poterit, probi piorum exemplo accensi, in melius et melius semper proficiant, improbi imaginata sibi vita sua confusi, a malis operibus suis vel sic saltem resipiscant.' (G056-R117; ed; R. Köpke, in *MGH SS*, X, p. 228). See also D.W.T.C. Vessey, *o.c.*, p. 453-455.

benefit of objective intentions, like assisting the reader in finding his way through the massive information provided by both archives and libraries in the monastery.[34] All of these arguments made the veracity of the narrative indispensable (*narratio verissima*),[35] even when the demand for continuity has forced the authors to fill some gaps with the aid of questionable sources.[36]

3. Prologues from the later part of the Middle Ages: marking the onset of scientific historiography?

In recent years, scholars have assumed that historical prologues underwent important changes at the end of the twelfth century. The emergence of science, Aristotelian and Thomistic thought and a general need for better educational tools at universities and other institutions inspired many historiographers to write in a somewhat more scientific style, with dry introductions instead of the vivid prologues of the past. More often than not, the prologue became a clear guide to the contents of the new compilation, thus

---

34. *De fundatione et lapsu monasterii Lobiensis* (D014, 12th century; edited by G. Waitz., in *MGH SS*, XIV, Hannoverae, 1883, p.548). See also H. Jedin, 'Zur Widmungsepistel des "Historia ecclesiastica" Hugos von Fleury', in C. Bauer, L. Boehm and M. Müller ed., *Speculum Historiale. Geschichte im Spiegel der Geschichtsschreibung und Geschichtsdeutung* (München, 1965), p. 562.

35. The explicit valorisation of veracity is underscored by the incessant references to *auctoritates* (e.g. *De antiquitate urbis Tornacensis* (D005, 12th century; ed. G. Waitz., in *MGH SS*, XIV, Hannoverae, 1883, p. 358) and the contemporary *Historiae Tornacenses* (H048, ed. J.J. De Smet, *Receuil des chroniques de Flandre. Tome II*, Bruxelles, 1894, p.481-483). Veracity is also a personal virtue: see the first continuation of the *Gesta abbatum Trudonensium* (G056-R114, 12th century): '...rem quam certissime scio fidelissime referam, ecce coram Deo, quia non mentior...' (ed. R. Köpke, in *MGH SS*, X, Hannoverae, 1852, p. 279) and Reinerus' continuation of the *Annales Sancti Jacobi* (R034): 'O crudele scriptum, set verum!' (ed. L.C. Bethmann, in *MGH SS*, XVI, Hannoverae, 1859, p. 661). 'De peregrinis et Acra multa sunt dicta, que vera non fuerunt probata' (*Ibidem*, p. 676). The dignity of the event is also an important element in the attribution of the epithet *memorabile dignum*: in the *Poleticum Marceniensis cenobii* (12th century), the author states that: '...nichil enim frivolum, nichi[l] fallaciter commentatum, nichil fictum digestum est hic nisi quod ex annalibus, ex chronicis, ex excerptione eorum quae in descriptionibus de vita quorundam sanctorum vel in gestis Cameracensium pontificum repperiuntur seu quod personarum fidelium idonea relatione et veraci assertione compertum est.' (ed. B. Delmaire, p. 65-66).

36. 'Quia vero nonnulli vestrum a me petierunt multoties ut modum constructionis, sive restaurationis ecclesiae nostrae litteris mandando tam futuris quam presentibus notificarem, ecce petitioni eorum libenter satisfacere volo, sciens priorum notitiam plerumque posteris profuisse, eorumque ignorantiam saepenumero non parvum detrimentum intulisse.' (H030, P.L. 180, col. 39-40). See also I. Guyot-Bachy, 'Les prologues du Memoriale Historiarum de Jean de Saint-Victor', *Journal des Savants*, (1993), p. 237.

avoiding the pitfalls of excessive rhetoricism.[37] Already in the course of the twelfth century, the *Continuatio Aquicinctina* of Sigebert's universal chronicle betrays a clear tendency toward compiling *reference works*.[38] Even annalists start to refer more explicitly to their sources: in the purely contingent *Annales Laubienses*, there are obvious references to the *Gesta* of Lobbes, when the author(s) indicates that the reason for an act involving the abbot (*causa*) is described elsewhere,[39] but that this type of story does not belong in the concised narrativity of the annals.

A second shift in monastic prologues is to be sought on the epistemological level: departing from a mixed pragmatic-spiritual vision of history, authors from the latter part of the Middle Ages tend more toward a rather antiquarian or paleo-journalistical style. Consequently, quite a few texts suffer from a lack of traditional legitimising tools, as personal or broader social interests enter the historiographic discourse.[40] Even when written from within a very definite monastic setting, the outdated motivations become superfluous stylistic displays, with little relation to actual situations.[41] They express their wish to discover the past of the clergy as a whole, more out of a gneral interest than out of a desire to propagate a group-related consciousness.[42]

37. M. Sot, p. 183-184 and 199.
38. 'Decreta ipsius concilii, quia multa sunt, et penes multos habentur, in hac cronice brevitate scribere non fuit utile.' (ed. L.C. Bethmann, in *MGH SS*, VI, Hannoverae, 1844, p. 417) and 'Omnis ab eis ibi facta constitutio non indiget penna vel pergameno' (*Ibidem*, p. 436).
39. 'Willelmus Remorum archiepiscopus, apostolicae sedis legatus, Lobbias venit, comitatus Cameracensi episcopo, et comite Haynoensi; causam adventus eorum alibi require.' (A073; ed. G.H. Pertz, in *MGH SS*, IV, Hannoverae, 1829, p. 25).
40. *Historia compendiosa de cladibus Leodiensium* (H020, 15th century; ed. P.F.X. De Ram, *Documents relatifs aux troubles du pays de Liège sous les princes-évêques Louis de Bourbon et Jean de Horne 1455-1505*, Bruxelles, 1844, p. 224); see also the *Annales Gandenses* (A071, 14th century): '...historias factaque autentica antiquorum libenter lego et audio...' (ed. F. Funck-Brentano, *Annales Gandenses. Nouvelle édition*, Paris, 1896, p. 1) and Adrianus de Budt's *Continuatio Chronodromis Brandonis et Bekae* (A017, 15th century): 'Quae res aliquando mihi dubia, sed cupienti plura noscere, ut moris est humano ingenio...' (ed. J. Kervyn de Lettenhove, *Chroniques relatives à l'histoire de la Belgique sous la domination des ducs de Bourgogne (Textes Latins). Chroniques des religieux des Dunes, Jean Brandon – Gilles de Roye – Adrien de But*, Bruxelles, 1870, p. 212).
41. *Annales Gandenses* (A071, 14th century): '...Movit etiam me communis utilitas ad hoc, quia, ut mihi videtur, quandoque, aliquis eventibus demergentibus, valde expediens est talia non ignorare.' (ed. F. Funck-Brentano, p. 1) and the [*Chronique de Floreffe*] (H022-S084, 15th century): '...celui qui desire de venir a la cognissance de sapience doit enquerir diligamment la vie, les cronicques, hystores et narracions des anchiens peres et vaillans hommes...' (ed. H. Peters, 'Über Sprache und Versbau der Chronik von Floreffe', *Zeitschrift für romanische Philologie*, XXI, 1897, p. 354), here, however, '...au bon edifiement...' of the audience (*Ibidem*, p. 357).
42. 'Quoniam scire gesta rerum, que priscis temporibus contigerunt, viris religiosis et ecclesiasticis pre ceteris quam plurimum expedit...' (ed. R. Köpke, in *MGH SS*, X, Hannoverae, 1852, p. 361).

It appears, however, that traditionally conceived prologues persisted longer in traditional environments, as was the case with Benedictine monasticism. As change here was very slow,[43] the prologues from these authors suffer very little from stylistic or rhetorical decline. Even the ancient urge to compile everything worth knowing in history in one volume (without genuinely operative references) would live on at least until the end of the thirteenth century. This, of course, had much to do with internal discussions regarding the function of chronicles. Compilers found it increasingly difficult to come up with viable conjectures to legitimise the monolithic character of their volumes. Hence the prologues' decreasing emphasis on moralisation and legitimisation.

In the course of the thirteenth century, a monk from the abbey of Marchiennes brought together a number of historiographic texts, starting with the so-called Ecclesiastical History of Eusebe of Caesarea and ending with its final continuation by Sigebert of Gembloers. As was the case with quite a few twelfth-century historiographic volumes with universal interests, Sigebert's final notes were complemented with contemporary texts of some importance, such as the *Historia Jherosolimitana abbreviata* by Jacobus de Vitriaco, a few texts on the counts of Flanders in the twelfth century[44] and some historical notes on the monastery of Marchiennes. The codex was obviously intended to serve as a general reference work for all things historical. The compiler(s) of the manuscript, however, supposedly underwent some criticism from moralists and those who preferred more immediate access to contemplation via other types of narratives (hagiography, prayers, and so on). That is probably why the manuscript, now preserved at the Bibliothèque Municipale of Douai,[45] features a general introduction, which has been given the title of *Epistola contra eos qui dicunt cronicas inanes seu inutiles*, obviously an admonition against those who were sceptical about the use of morally neutral and inexplicit historiography.[46] According to the anonymous author, there still

---

43. A.M. Piazzoni, *Guglielmo di Saint-Thierry. Il declino dell'ideale monastico nel secolo XII* (Roma, 1988), p. 69-70 and C. Proksch, *Klosterreform und Geschichtsschreibung im Spätmittelalter* (Köln – Weimar – Wien, 1994), p. 27.
44. *De Balduino VII comite Flandrensi* (D007) and *Epitaphium Balduini VII comitis Flandriae* (E023).
45. Douai, Bibliothèque Municipale, ms. 798, folio 2r° (*Catalogue général des manuscrits des bibliothèques publiques des départements. Tome VI. Douai*, Paris, 1878).
46. According to a (contemporary) marginal note on folio 2r°, the text of the second prologue to this manuscript was written during the lifetime of abbot Petrus I of Marchiennes (1296-1306), who appears to be the informal commissioner of this historical collection. If the *Epistola* was written by the same author as the *Prefacio*, which seems to be the case, then there can be no doubt that the text is to be dated in the years of Petrus' abbacy.

is a definitely negative feeling among some monks about historiography being a haphazard collection of irrelevant, ephemerous facts and events, with no additional information or interpretation of God's plan for mankind.

The compiler, who in fact is struggling with his own quasi-scientific or antiquarian conception of history, proposes some reasons for the legitimacy of his work. In the *Epistola*, one can discern two main arguments for the inclusion of historiography in monastic culture. On one hand, it cannot be questioned that the Bible features many passages that can definitely be categorised as histories. From the very beginning of the creation, all of God's actions can be placed on a time-line, where they relate to each other, not by their simultaneous presence, but by their contingency, perhaps even causality. The interpretation of Biblical events has to be performed on different levels: there is a literal meaning to everything said and done in the Holy Scripture, but in addition, there is a possibility to perform some of the interpretation models (like moral, anagogic and tropologic readings) on the texts. In fact, this epistemological argument includes the assumption that the literal reading of any kind of narrative necessarily precedes other levels of understanding, which belong to a greater extent to the domain of contemplation.

Secondly, and more explicitly, we can see how the author of the *Epistola* legitimises the use of secular history in a secluded environment like the monastery. Admittedly, spiritual history does not exist: only the institutional efforts of rulers and clerics or monks to gain access to an earthly City of God (or the lack thereof) can be included in linear history. As human history is essentially linear, chronology is indispensable, meaning that man as a race has to go through a set of different phases (*aetates*) before he can reach the end of time. This observation helps the reader to come up with an educated interpretation of the original and intentional placement of a certain event with moral or mystical potential in time, thus understanding its real meaning. Any event from the past has to be aligned on a time-line, in order to check its spiritual meaning by its situation in the history of salvation. This allows the monk to check the validity of spiritual and moral interpretations of events from the past. The best source to assemble a relevant time-line is not to be found in religious or ecclesiastical history, but in the succession of empires, kingdoms, rulers, and the like. An exact date is not always necessary or possible in the case of events of spiritual importance (there are many discrepancies in the dating methods and in the traditions of certain events). What really counts is its exact placement in man's continuous struggle to make an end to God's punishment, being linear time and mortality.[47] The end of the text features the most stunning fulmination against the critics: why should one hesitate to extract moral insights from hermetic texts, like historiography, when this can only increase the autonomous spiritual flexibility of the individual? One can only wonder whether these objections were likely to be accepted by the sceptic monks of Marchiennes.

The typical anachronism of Benedictine historiography continued to be operative at Saint Bavon in Ghent, where the extraordinarily confused *Chronicon Sancti Bavonis* by Johannes de Thielrode lays very little emphasis on the group-building impact of historiography. The prologue consists of topical references to the important role of *memoria* in monastic life and the means to engender its frequent use, which, of course, is a fundamental statement, but must have been fairly outdated in its claims to relevancy.[48] Remarkably, it appears that the author was aware of the new methods of his fellow-historiographers, as the table of contents clearly demonstrates:[49] sadly, this construction remains a fictional guide, as the text itself is chaotic. The intention to systematise access to the text can be found in a number of other narratives, such as the *Gesta* of the bishops of Liège by Gilles of Orval (A028, thirteenth century) and the

---

47. There are possible references to the prologue to Hugo of Fleury's first version of his *Historia Ecclesiastica* (ed. G.H. Pertz, in *MGH SS*, IX, Hannoverae, 1851, p. 350: 'Et Dominus quidem, qui cuncta de nihilo fecit, uno momento temporis potuisset omnia simul facere et universum genus humanum ad sui reverentiam cultumque perducere. Sed non fecit, immo secreto et inscrutabili sacramento non in mundi principio sed opportuno tempore disposuit nasci de virgine...'), although it appears that a genuine citation comes from the second version (see note 63).

48. 'Quoniam servare nunc in memoria cuncta que pretereunt non sunt ab homine ista provenientia, sed flamine divino humanitatem rationibus lucidis decorando, secundum quod dicitur: "Omnia in memoria habere pocius est divinitatis quam humanitatis." Igitur cum humana natura prorsus sit labilis necnon permutanda, oblivioni per tempora diversa se conferens facta precedentia minime recordando: hinc vox litteralis inventa est, modo debito inscripto protrahendo, ut ad id se prepararet, animum hominis labilem cognitione previa perlustrans, amnacca venturis hominibus lucide notificando; et quia Deus que fecerat cuncta videns quod essent valde bona, hominem inter illa sensualiter ad sui respectum illuminans, sensui suo utilia per ipsum conferendo, hecque ignorantibus spergere volentem eos imperfectam noticiam adducendo: nullus eidem invidere tenetur, factis et verbis nocumenta prebendo, sed eidem magis acquiescendo...' (J197; ed. J. Heller, in *MGH SS*, XXV, Hannoverae, 1880, p. 559).

49. The emergence of the functional table of contents can be closely related to the specialisation in contemporary scientific disciplines (A.D. Von den Brincken, 'Tabula alphabetica. Von den Anfängen alphabetischer Registerarbeiten zu Geschichtswerken (Vincenz von Beauvais OP, Johannes von Hautfuney, Paulinus Minorita OFM)', in *Festschrift für Hermann Heimpel zum 70. Geburtstag am 19. September 1971. Zweiter Band*, Göttingen, 1972, p. 901).

third continuation of the *Gesta abbatum Trudonensium* (G058/R116, fourteenth century), where a table of contents is already in functional use.[50]

Only at the start of the fifteenth century did historiography get a second wind, and a collection of chronicles and *gesta* with a dual purpose were newly conceived. Their authors obviously took notice of their predecessors' work, as quite a few prologues explicitly feature so-called 'scientific' tendencies as well as older, community-binding principles and a moralising undertone.[51] It is a fact that, by then, many of the chroniclers had become antiquarians, who saw it as their task to *report* important events of their own time or to *assemble* them from older sources. Nonetheless, the prologues keep to certain principles of morality and virtue, hardly ever to be encountered in the actual narratives.[52] According to Johannes Brando, in the prologue on his *Chronodromon* (J178, late fourteenth – early fifteenth centuries), and the anonymous author of the *Chronicon monasterii Aldenburgensis majus* (C015, fifteenth century), the purely scientific compilation of historical facts is senseless and repudiable:[53] only when set into a frame of mind, open to moral interpretation, does it become a genuine instrument of contemplation. Even if concrete textual reality demonstrates a nearly complete evolution toward strictly factual and scientific historiography, its intentions were encountered by a more spiritually ambitious frame of mind, which the monks obviously felt compelled to hold on to.[54]

---

50. It quickly became common usage to insert tables of contents before each separate chapter of the ever-expanding compilations (e.g. Johannes Iperius' *Chronicon Sancti Bertini* – J104, 13th century; ed. A. Martène and U. Durand, *Thesaurus novus anecdotorum. Tomus III...*, Lutetiae Parisiorum, 1717, col. 902)).

51. As appears to be the tone, set by the prologue to the *Chronicon* by Cornelius Menghers de Zantfliet (C053, 15th century): 'Quantae vero utilitatis fit verax historia, probari potest et ex his. Nam sive de bonis bona referat, ad imitandum bonum auditor sollicitus instigatur; si vero mala commemorat, de pravis nihilominus religiosus ac pius auditor sive lector devitando quod noxium est ac perversum, ipse sollicitus ad exequenda quae vera ac Deo digna esse cognoverit, accenditur indilate...praeterea omnes ad quos haec historia pervenire potuerit, legentes vel audientes suppliciter precor, ut pro meis infirmitatibus tam mentis quam corporis apud supernam clementiam quotidianis precibus interveniant, et hanc mihi remunerationis vicem pro laboribus impendant, ut quod de multis provinciis memoratu dignum excerpsi, apud omnes fructum piae intercessionis possit invenire. Amen.' (ed. A. Martène and U. Durand, *Veterum scriptorum et monumentorum...amplissima collectio. Tomus V*, Parisiis, 1729, col. 93).

52. *Chronicon* of Johannes de Loos (J194, 15th century; ed. P.F.X. De Ram, p. 3-4).

53. 'An oblitus es hominem nasci ad laborem?' (ed. P.L. 174, Turnholti (reprint), s.d., col. 1513).

54. '...singulisque regnorum titulis, annorum quoque numeris, veludi hucusque in sue dispositionis ordine, operis ut forma requirit asscriptis...' (*Chronicon Sancti Bertini* –

Other voices, however, express a severe scepticism with regard to this motivation of historiography and propose a definite goal.[55] This incites most monastic authors to bring up the marginalised moral implications of the story as an excuse for their relatively neutral interests.[56] The strongest appeals to this effect can be found in the comparatively rare works of younger observations, such as the congregation of Windesheim.[57] Even the outdated concept of the historical narrative as a genuine *sermo* emerges from the rare Cistercian historiography: the chronicle of Signy (thirteenth-fourteenth century) ends with a telling *Amen*.[58] Younger movements also emphasise the importance of identity-building narratives[59] and the necessity to praise God for his work on earth as well as to take lessons from the past. Here, teleology still works on the minds of the most determined monks.[60]

J104, 13th century; ed. A. Martène and U. Durand, *Thesaurus novus anecdotorum. Tomus III*, Lutetiae Parisiorum, 1717, col. 1514); prologue of the *Chronicon Flandriae* by Adrianus de Budt (A016, 15th century; ed. J.J. De Smet, I, Bruxelles, 1837, p. 261-262); Baudouin of Ninove (thirteenth century) refers to Norbertus' *vita* (*Chronicon*, B003; ed. O. Holder-Egger, in *MGH SS*, XXV, Hannoverae, 1880, p. 529). See also I. Guyot-Bachy, p. 238.

55. *Fundatio monasterii Arroasiensis* (G002): '...religiosi et Deo dediti viri qui mundum et ea que in mundo sunt pro Christi nomine relinquentes, et quicquid possederunt commune facientes, crucifixum Dominum crucem suam post ipsum baiulando sequuntur, temporalia cuncta non in affectu sed in usu necessitate habentes...' (ed. B. Tock and L. Milis, p. 49).

56. See the *Chronica domus virginis Mariae in Herne* (A107; 15th century): '...cum experientia sit rerum magistra.' (ed. E. Lamalle, *Arnold Beeltsens et Jean Ammonius. Chronique de la Chartreuse de la Chapelle à Hérinnes-lez-Enghien*, Louvain, 1932, p. 7).

57. See, for example, the *Cronyke van Nederlant* (C063, 15th century), where the author inserts an exemplum in a non-historical section of his work (ed. C. Piot, *Chroniques de Brabant et de Flandre*, Bruxelles, 1879, p. 3).

58. C022; ed. L. Delisle, 'Manuscrit légués à la Bibliothèque Nationale par Armand Durand', *Bibliothèque de l'école des chartes*, 55 (1894), p. 658. This might be a reference to the practise of liturgical *memoria*, with similar examples already being written in the tenth century, such as Witger's *Genealogia Arnulfi comitis Flandriae* (W037).

59. *De origine monasterii Viridisvallis* (H023, 15th century; edited by [J.B. De Leu], 'De origine monasterii Viridisvallis una cum vitis B. Joannis Rusborchii primi prioris hujus monasterii et aliquot coaetaneorum ejus', *Analecta Bollandiana*, 4 (1885), p. 264-265).

60. See, for example, Marcel Voet's *Liber fundationis* of the Carthusian monastery of Scheut, near Anderlecht (M001; circa 1480-1487): 'Ipsique successores antiquorum facta legentes et audientes occasionem sumant opera virtutum eorumdem commendandi, magnificandi ac imitandi...opera magnalia Dei et sanctorum magnificare et laudare honorificum est imitari autem...salutiferium. Ne igitur quis ex ignorantia historie predictorum labatur errore aut damno seu tedio aliquo afficiatur...' (Brussels, Royal Library, 5764, folio 9r°).

4. Conclusion

In the course of five hundred years, historiography underwent important changes involving different stylistic, epistemological, and functional options. As Benedictine historiographers had to respond in some manner to the shifting experience of time, history and society, their prologues to historical texts converged to the best interpretative model they could come up with. This resulted in a shifting discourse, which formed the avant-garde within historiography in the latter part of the eleventh century. During the Investiture crisis, the historian's discourse began to focus more on morality and the group-building potential of the narrative. This period was quickly followed by the decline of the traditional monastic orders, who lost their pre-eminence in the intellectual world to the Mendicant orders, universities and secular culture. As historiography began to live its own life and spread among the many groups of late medieval society, the monks and clerics also lost their virtual monopoly over the legitimisation of the genre and were no longer able to keep up their fairly ethereal allegations when authors began to rely more on the informative value of journalistic and compiled historiography. In the prologues of these texts, we can easily see how Benedictine authors struggled with the uneasy reconciliation of moralistic and 'scientific' history, thus illustrating the awkward social position of their order from the second half of the twelfth century onward. Through the ever-widening gap separating the theoretical reasoning and out-dated motivation embedded in the Benedictine prologues and the actual practise of historiography visible in the narratives, we can see a reflection of an ever-widening discrepancy between traditional monasticism and surrounding society. While the audience for historical narratives was expanding in general, the relative share of the audience for old-fashioned monastic historiography decreased dramatically. The relentless but rather senseless endeavours of the traditional historiographers to demonstrate their superiority effectively resulted in their reaching a considerably shrinking audience.

5. An *Epistola contra eos qui dicunt cronicas inanes seu inutiles* from the years 1296-1306 (?)
(Douai, Bibliothèque Municipale, ms. 798, folio 2r°)

Incipit epistola contra eos qui dicunt cronicas inanes seu inutiles, quoniam ea que in libris cronicorum continentur a multis altiora forte sentientibus tamquam inutilia et superflua reputantur, quia de regnis et bellis etceteris huiusmodi in eis enarrantur. Tamen attentius consideranti utilia satis esse probantur. Nam ex historie non solum gentilium, sed secundum Hebraicam veritatem primo et principaliter de operibus que fecit Deus in primis sex diebus. De dictis et operibus primorum parentum nostrorum seu de scientiis et artibus, quas cum magnis laboribus et studiis suis non solum sibi, sed etiam ad utilitatem posterorum suorum diligentius adinvenerunt. De causis diluvii et de perditione malorum. De causa etiam sive ortu regnorum in hiis duabus primis etatibus annotantur. Sed et insuper generationis linea ab Adam usquequo perveniatur ad Christum, qui postmodum pro nobis suspensus in cruce salvavit genus humanum. Que omnia secundum primorum patriarcharum seu imperatorum et regum tempora describuntur. Nempe ille res geste, ut dicit Hugo Floriacensis, que nulla regum ac temporum certitudine commendantur, nec pro historia recipiuntur, sed inter aniles fabulas deputantur.[61] Unde Lucas cum incarnationis dominice historiam texerit, in ipso evangelii sui principis de Herode rege et post penita de Augusto cesare mentionem fecit ut illa que minus nota erant hominibus ab hiis que pene apud omnes fama celebri ferebantur, confirmarentur et roborarentur. Valet itaque in hoc opere successionis temporum et annorum et imperatorum et regum necnon et Romanorum pontificum annotatio brevis non solum ad presentis historie, verum etiam ad cuiuslibet alterius nomen imperatoris, vel pape, vel regis sub quo gesta sit habentis confirmationem et elucidationem, ut scilicet si dubitetur de tempore hic, ad cathalogum regum illius terre in qua res illa gesta refertur recurri possit, ibique repperiatur quo temporis articulo rex ille regnaverit ac per hoc etiam quo tempore res illa gesta fit. Verumtamen quia de annorum numero multa est etiam inter historias dissonantia, nulli reor precise ac penitus adherendum maximeque numero cronicorum. Sed ad hoc tantum valet ut sciatur non quo anno, sed quo tempore vel sub quo imperatore queque res annotata acciderit. Denique ex diversis auctoribus hoc opus contextum est: ut sciatur quod cuius fit singulorum dictis eorum nomina annotavi. Verumptamen attendat legens que nimis adbreviata narratio legenti vel audienti minus sapiat. Hec moneat lectorem quod ex diversis auctoribus et diversis capitulis quedam ad eundem sensum pertinentibus demerim et in unum capitulum tam mordacius vel brevius attingendi materiam collegerim. Ut, quia dicit

---

61. Citation from Hugo of Fleury's *Historia Ecclesiastica* (ed. G.H. Pertz., in *MGH SS*, IX, Hannoverae, 1851, p. 355: 'Illae quippe res gestae quae nulla regum ac temporum certitudine commendantur, non per historiam recipiuntur, sed inter aniles fabulas deputantur.').

Augustinus, in apochriphis libris multa vera inveniuntur,[62] hinc est quod ego de quibusdam cronicis seu historiis, pre antiquitate sua approbatis que ullum auctorem nominabant, ea que huic operi congruere videbantur, collegi mihique idem auctori confidente intitulavi. Valet iterum ad expellendam accidiam sive otium, quia semper aliquid agendum est ne ager nostri pectoris manu cessante malarum cogitationum sentibus occupetur.[63] Omnium temptationum et cogitationum malarum sentina est otium. Quia[64] sicut punctiones muscarum vel spinarum iumentum discurrere faciunt, sic punctiones vitiorum animum instabilem reddunt, et monachum a cenobio sive claustro, etsi non corpore, mente tamen, expellunt. Quapropter non debet displicere litteratis, quia aliquando prodest simplicibus et ydiotis eos sepius revocando ab otiis seu pervagatione aut rumoribus vanis. Nam quosdam historia, alios allegoria, nonnullos vero edificat moralitas. Nec legenti debent esse honerosa si aliqua utilia que historie minus congruant, reppererint inserta. Et quia nullus, ut credo, delectatur fastidio, dabo pro posse operam ne fastidiosa sit lectio.[65] Explicit epistola.

---

62. The exact phrase the anonymous author refers to is impossible to determine. However, Augustine has expressed this opinion in at least two of his writings: 'De Origine autem quod rescribere dignatus es, iam sciebam non tantum in Ecclesiasticis litteris, sed in omnibus, recta et vera quae invenerimus, approbare atque laudere, falsa vero et prava improbare atque reprehendere.' (*Epistola LXVIII*; in P.L., 22, col. 650) and '...etiam liberales disciplinas usui veritatis aptiores [sunt], et quaedam morum praecepta utilissima continent, deque ipso uno Deo colendo nonnulla vera inveniuntur apud eos.' (*De doctrina Christiana* II, XL; ed. J. Martin, *Sancti Aurelii Augustini De Doctrina Christiana – De vera religione*, in *Corpus Christianorum. Series Latina*, XXXII, *Aurelii Augustini Opera*. IV,1, Turnholti, 1962, p. 74).

63. A few words, following the end of this sentence, were scrapped: '*Unde hec ad fratres de mente dei.*'

64. The words '*...otium. Quia...*' were erroneously scrapped.

65. The fragment from '... non debet ...' to '... set lectio ...' was almost literally quoted from the prologue to Andreas of Marchiennes' *Historia succincta* (see the edition by G. Waitz, MGH SS, XXVI, Hannoverae, 1882, p. 205).

Paul BERTRAND

RÉFORMES ECCLÉSIASTIQUES, LUTTES D'INFLUENCE ET HAGIOGRAPHIE À L'ABBAYE DE MAUBEUGE (IXe-XIe S.)

Le document hagiographique a acquis, depuis une cinquantaine d'années, ses lettres de noblesse au sein de la communauté des historiens. Trop longtemps, on a cru qu'il ne pouvait offrir aucune information historique digne de foi: tout semblait légende et seulement légende.[1] Ici ou là, quelques traces d'un évènement, d'un personnage historique, qu'il soit le sujet du texte ou non. Puis la Nouvelle Histoire s'est frayé un chemin à travers la forêt touffue et sombre de la littérature dite 'de dévotion'. Elle y a glané de quoi faire une histoire des 'mentalités', des mentalités religieuses surtout, mais pas seulement.[2] Ensuite, l'historien s'est attaché aux textes hagiographiques eux-mêmes, qui cessèrent alors d'être de simples réceptacles où on venait puiser des bribes d'information – à la source! La littérature hagiographique est donc devenue en soi objet d'Histoire, chaque texte étant témoin et acteur de son temps.[3] Enfin, les historiens se sont emparés des manuscrits hagiographiques, soit des états à un moment donné en un lieu donné d'un texte hagiographique. Chaque état

---

1. Voir les travaux pionniers des Bollandistes, depuis le XVIIe s dont l'œuvre fondamentale d'Hippolyte Delehaye S.J., notamment *Les légendes hagiographiques*, Subsidia Hagiographica, 18 (Bruxelles, 4e éd., 1973). Sur l'œuvre de Delehaye, on consultera surtout les travaux de Bernard Joassart S.J., dont *Hippolyte Delehaye: hagiographie critique et modernisme*, Subsidia hagiographica, 81, 2 vol. (Bruxelles, 2000).
2. On lira les travaux pionniers de E. Delaruelle, dont son recueil de travaux: *La piété populaire au Moyen Âge* (Turin, 1975). Comme publication récente dans cette optique, on lira: M. Lauwers, *La mémoire des ancêtres, le souci des morts. Morts, rites et société au Moyen Âge (diocèse de Liège, XIe-XIIIe siècles)*, Théologie Historique, 103 (Paris, 1997).
3. Voir, par exemple, les travaux du défunt SFB 231 de l'université de Münster i. Westf., traitant de la *Pragmatische Schriftlichkeit* comme le travail de St. Coué, *Hagiographie im Kontext: Schreibanlass und Funktion von Bischofsviten aus dem 11. und vom Anfang des 12. Jahrhunderts*, Arbeiten zur Frühmittelalterforschung, 24 (Berlin, 1997). Voir encore, dans un registre similaire: A.-M. Helvétius, *Abbayes, évêques et laïques. Une politique du pouvoir en Hainaut au Moyen Âge (VIIe-XIe siècle)*, Crédit Communal, collection Histoire, série in-8°, 92 (Bruxelles, 1994).

du texte est devenu à son tour témoin et acteur de l'Histoire.⁴ C'est à ces différents états évolutionnels de la recherche que ressortit le présent travail.

Un ensemble de crises économiques, religieuses, politiques dans une certaine mesure, jalonnent presque trois siècles, du IXe au XIe. La plupart des monastères du Hainaut belge et français les traversent; peu en sortiront sans séquelle. Je m'attacherai ici au sort du monastère de Maubeuge, un des plus importants de cette époque. C'est aussi un de ceux qui ont laissé le plus de traces historiques, s'agissant de ces périodes de troubles, sous la forme de textes hagiographiques principalement, du IXe au Xe s.⁵

A. Le Cycle de Maubeuge

Un nombre important de saints mérovingiens du Hainaut sont mis en relations les uns avec les autres, au sein des légendes qui les accompagnent, par des liens familiaux : ainsi sainte Aldegonde, présentée comme la fondatrice de l'abbaye de Maubeuge, est-elle la sœur de sainte Waudru? Celle-ci aurait décidé de rompre son mariage avec Madelgaire pour fonder une abbaye, celle de Mons. Tandis que Madelgaire aurait quitté le monde pour le monastère d'Hautmont et accédait à son tour à la sainteté, mais un peu plus tard, paré lui aussi à ce moment de la réputation de fondateur d'abbayes – Soignies, mais aussi Hautmont! Madelgaire et Waudru, avant de se retirer du monde, eurent des enfants, des filles – saintes, elles aussi – : Aldetrude, qui deviendra la seconde abbesse de Maubeuge, tandis que Madelberte lui succèdera comme troisième abbesse. Une tradition du XIe s. attribue aux saints parents deux autres enfants : Landry, que l'on fera évêque de Meltis Castellum (Meaux, Metz?) mais aussi abbé de Soignies et successeur de son père sur la cathèdre abbatiale et Dentelin, qui, bien que mort en bas âge, aurait eu le

---

4. Les travaux de G. Philippart sont ici pionniers. Rappelons ici *Légendiers latins et autres manuscrits hagiographiques*, Typologie des sources du moyen âge occidental, fasc. 24-25 (Turnhout, 1977) et sa *Mise à jour* (Turnhout, 1985). Ou encore, du même, 'Le manuscrit hagiographique latin comme gisement documentaire. Un parcours dans les *Analecta Bollandiana* de 1960 à 1989', in *Manuscrits hagiographiques et Travail des hagiographes,* éd. M. Heinzelmann, Beihefte der Francia, 24 (Sigmaringen, 1992), p. 17-48; 'Pour une histoire générale, problématique et sérielle, de la littérature et de l'édition hagiographiques latines de l'antiquité et du moyen âge', in *Cassiodorus. Rivista di studi sulla tarda antichità,* t. II (1996), p. 197-213.

5. La thèse d'Anne-Marie Helvétius, déjà citée plus haut, traite déjà de ces crises, mais nous pensons qu'il est possible de compléter voire nuancer ses profondes analyses.

temps de gagner de même sa sainteté. Ajoutons encore les heureux parents de Waudru et Aldegonde, Walbert et Bertille, dont la sainteté apparaît au Bas Moyen Âge. Autour de cette sainte famille, gravite un ensemble de personnages qui à un moment ou un autre de l'Histoire accèdent aux degrés ultimes de la sainteté: des conseillers comme saint Ghislain, des évêques comme saint Aubert, de lointains parents comme sainte Gertrude de Nivelles, etc. Le noyau de cette sainte famille est constitué par Aldegonde et Waudru. Bizarrement, la sainteté d'Aldegonde a éclipsé toutes les autres du VIIIe s. jusqu'au IXe voire au Xe s. Il faudra attendre le XIIe s. pour que le culte de Waudru prenne enfin l'essor qu'on lui connaît et qui en fait actuellement une des saintes les plus renommées en Hainaut – de même pour Vincent.[6]

Ce qui apparaît clairement à la lecture des différentes *Vitae* comme à l'analyse des phénomènes cultuels les concernant, c'est que, dans l'imaginaire hagiographique, ces saints ne peuvent pas vivre l'un sans l'autre. Dans les Vies de Vincent, on parle sans cesse de sa femme, dans celles d'Aldegonde, on parle de sa sœur et dans les *Vitae* de cette dernière, Waudru, le sort de l'abbesse de Maubeuge occupe quelques pages; tandis que dans la Vie d'Aldetrude comme dans celle de Madelberte, leur tante Aldegonde est omniprésente. Si on se penche sur l'iconographie tardo-médiévale, c'est la même chose: sainte Waudru est toujours représentée avec ses deux filles; saint Vincent avec ses deux fils.[7] De même, mis à part le cas de la première Vie d'Aldegonde, bon nombre des textes hagiographiques relatifs à ces personnages se retrouvent dans les mêmes manuscrits.[8] Comme si leur sainteté ne pouvait être que commune.

---

6. Outre le travail d'A.-M. Helvétius, on lira, sur la sainteté en Hainaut, les considérations de A. Dierkens, *Abbayes et Chapitres entre Sambre et Meuse (VIIe-XIe siècles). Contribution à l'histoire religieuse des campagnes du Haut Moyen Âge*, Beihefte der Francia, 14 (Sigmaringen, 1985). Pour une approche très générale, on consultera le petit ouvrage de L. van der Essen, *Le siècle des saints 625-739: Étude sur les origines de la Belgique chrétienne,* Notre Passé, I, 1 (Bruxelles, 1941), bien veilli, mais encore utile.

7. Voir, par exemple, L. Tondreau, 'Iconographie de sainte Waudru', in *Annales du Cercle Archéologique de Mons*, t. 70 (1976-1977), p. 207-282 et les considérations parfois sujettes à caution de E. Liénard, 'Manifestations du culte et iconographie de sainte Waudru', in J.-M. Cauchies (sous la dir. de), *Sainte Waudru devant l'Histoire et devant la Foi. Recueil d'études publié à l'occasion du treizième centenaire de sa mort* (Mons, 1989), p. 73-92, à partir de son mémoire de licence dactylographié inédit, *Sainte Waudru depuis le VIIe siècle. Le culte comme survie*, Mém. lic. dactyl., UCL, 1986.

8. Ce sont les mêmes manuscrits qui reviennent sans cesse au fil des articles de Fr. De Vriendt, 'Le dossier hagiographique de sainte Waudru, abbesse de Mons (IXème-XIIIème siècles)', in *Mémoires et publications de la société des sciences, des arts et des lettres du Hainaut*, t. 98 (1996), p. 1-37 et Idem, 'La tradition manuscrite de la *Vita Waldetrudis* (BHL 8776-8777). Les mécanismes de propagation d'un récit hagiographique régional

Comme s'ils ne pouvaient être vraiment saints qu'ensemble. La sainteté des uns rejaillissant sur celle des autres. C'est bien, selon moi, ce qui caractérise le culte de ces saints – pour le bas Moyen Âge, mais avec déjà de profondes racines ancrées dans le Moyen Âge des IXe et Xe s. – c'est une sainteté en famille, une *beata stirps*.

Cette *beata stirps*, on en trouve des traces jusqu'aux rapports intertextuels tissés entre les différentes *Vitae* relatives aux saints du groupe. C'est ce que Léon van der Essen a appelé le Cycle de Maubeuge.[9] Comme le rappelle heureusement François De Vriendt, 'les *Vitae* relatives aux différents saints de la famille forment en effet un véritable cycle littéraire, un réseau de récits étroitement liés entre eux par un jeu complexe d'influences, d'emprunts et de plagiats'.[10] Cinq à six Vies pour sainte Aldegonde, quatre vies pour sainte Waudru, deux vies pour Vincent, une vie pour Madelberte, une pour Landry, une pour Aldetrude, mais quatre pour saint Ghislain: si l'on s'en tient à la période du VIIIe-XIIIe s., c'est déjà impressionnant.

Le premier à avoir défriché le terrain, c'est Léon Van der Essen, dans son *Étude critique et littéraire des saints mérovingiens*, parue en 1907. Son travail, remarquable pour l'époque, n'est pas encore été remplacé en bien des aspects. Pionnier, il a le premier comparé chacun de ces textes, en a tiré des *stemma*, des groupes, a établi des datations, a proposé des hypothèses quant à leur rédaction voire leur a attribué des auteurs bien précis. Il est à l'origine de l'appellation toujours en usage: 'Cycle de Maubeuge'. Cependant, en ce qui concerne ce dernier cycle littéraire, nul ne peut plus s'attaquer à ces dossiers sans ouvrir la remarquable et récente thèse d'Anne-Marie Helvétius. Elle a complètement renouvelé la problématique, s'attaquant à tous les dossiers, redatant, proposant de nouvelles hypothèses.[11] L'objectif premier de sa thèse *stricto sensu* – les structures

---

(IXème-XVème siècles)', in *Analecta Bollandiana*, t. 117 (1999), p. 319-368, par rapport à notre travail sur 'La Vie de sainte Madelberte de Maubeuge (BHL 5129). Edition critique du texte', in *Analecta Bollandiana*, t. 113, fasc. 3-4 (1997), p. 39-76. Une consultation rapide de la *BHL Mss* est encore plus éclairante: http://bhlms.fltr.ucl.ac.be/.

9. L. Van der Essen, *Étude critique et littéraire sur les* Vitae *des saints mérovingiens de l'ancienne Belgique* (Louvain, 1907), *passim*.

10. Fr. De Vriendt, 'Les deux Vies latines de saint Vincent de Soignies (XIe-XIIe siècles). Un patrimoine littéraire sonégien?', in *Saint Vincent de Soignies. Regards du XXe siècle sur sa vie et son culte. Recueil d'études publié à l'occasion du quatrième centenaire de la confrérie Saint-Vincent 1599-1999*, éd. J. Deveseleer, Cahiers du chapitre, 7 (Soignies, 1999), p. 33-55, ici p. 36.

11. On lira une présentation critique des recherches sur l'hagiographie hainuyère dans P. Bertrand, 'Études d'hagiographie hainuyère. L'exemple du «cycle de Maubeuge»: un état de la question', in *Le Moyen Âge*, t. 3-4 (2001), p. 537-546 ainsi qu'une autre

politiques du Hainaut au haut Moyen Âge – a évidemment conditionné quelque peu son approche des motivations de rédaction et sa lecture des textes. Elle a en effet souvent lié ces sources à des situations politiques, voyant à leur genèse des manœuvres politiciennes, le reflet d'une soif du pouvoir toute cléricale. François de Vriendt a repris certains dossiers comme celui de saint Vincent ou celui de sainte Waudru; et ses résultats complètent fort heureusement les belles conclusions d'Anne-Marie Helvétius. Comme on le voit, l'étude de la sainteté hainuyère a encore de beaux jours devant elle et la *beata stirps* fait donc toujours recette – et je m'en voudrais de ne pas citer ici les récentes entreprises d'ouvertures de reliquaires à Mons (Waudru) et à Soignies (Vincent, Landry), en relation directe avec le monde scientifique et avec comme objectif parfaitement atteint une impressionnante publication de rapports scientifiques les concernant (pour Soignies, par exemple, entre autres la publication des authentiques conservés dans les châsses, des travaux sur les différentes *Vitae*...).[12]

Mais je voudrais donc approcher les cas spécifiques des textes hagiographiques liés de plus près au monde monastique de Maubeuge: Aldegonde, Aldetrude, Madelberte. Car, si les auteurs de ces textes ont rattaché nos saintes à la fameuse *beata stirps*, pour des raisons de stratégie cultuelle évidente, il serait naïf de s'en tenir là et de ne pas chercher plus avant d'autres motivations ayant pu guider les hagiographes dans leurs choix et leur présentation.

B. MAUBEUGE AVANT LE IXe S.:
LES PREMIERS PAS D'UNE GRANDE ABBAYE[13]

Une des principales sources pour les premiers temps de cette abbaye est la première vie d'Aldegonde, datée de 710-720.

Aldegonde dut naître vers 630, fonder Maubeuge vers 660-665 et mourir vers 684. Elle est la fille cadette de Walbert et Bertille, deux membres de l'aristocratie neustrienne, probablement bien possessionnés dans le

---

présentation parfois sévère par M. de Waha, 'Saint Vincent, Soignies, Lotharingie, Hainaut. Apports et questions de la recherche récente', in *Revue belge de philologie et d'histoire*, t. 80 (2002), p. 599-630.

12. *Saint Vincent de Soignies. Regards du XXe siècle sur sa vie et son culte. Recueil d'études publié à l'occasion du quatrième centenaire de la confrérie Saint-Vincent 1599-1999*, éd. J. Deveseleer, Cahiers du chapitre, 7 (Soignies, 1999); *Reliques et châsses de la collégiale de Soignies. Objets, cultes et traditions*, éd. J. Deveseleer, M. Maillard-Luypaert et Ph. Desmette, Cahiers du chapitre, 8 (Soignies, 2001), p. 191-202.

13. Les conclusions d'Anne-Marie Helvétius serviront ici à baliser le terrain.

Hainaut. Tandis que Waudru fonde son monastère dans ce qui deviendra Mons, après avoir quitté son mari, la cadette, elle, établit une abbaye sur un terrain qui pourrait avoir appartenu à ses parents, à Maubeuge. C'est une communauté double qui est fondée là, comme à Mons. Un 'Doppelklöster', avec un monastère de femmes et une communauté masculine.[14] Celle-ci est mise en place pour s'occuper des travaux manuels, protéger les religieuses, mais surtout pour effectuer le service liturgique à l'intention des religieuses. Soumise à l'abbesse, cette petite communauté d'hommes est réduite à un rôle secondaire. Ils sont probablement tous prêtres ou diacres, et leur règle de vie doit être légèrement différente de celle des moniales. La règle des sanctimoniales est, elle, au VIIIe s., une règle bénédictine plus que probablement aménagée, améliorée, adaptée par l'abbesse, comme c'en est l'usage à l'époque mérovingienne. 'L'impression qui se dégage de la lecture de la première Vie d'Aldegonde est que le monastère de Maubeuge était déjà, sous l'abbatiat d'Aldegonde, fort bien organisé et qu'il jouissait d'une certaine aisance matérielle, permettant à des jeunes filles souvent de bonne famille de mener une vie monastique irréprochable mais pas trop sévère, avec l'assistance d'un petit groupe de religieux', précise Anne-Marie Helvétius.[15] De leur côté, les moniales fréquentent d'abord l'église primitive du lieu, qui devait être l'église Saint-Pierre, puis, à la fin du IXe s. certainement, l'église Notre-Dame. L'église Saint-Pierre subsista, à l'usage de la communauté masculine – au Xe ou XIe s., les religieux ont tenté de lui donner le patronyme 'Saint-Quentin', pour des raisons encore obscures.

Aldegonde morte, on l'enterra non pas à Maubeuge, mais non loin de là, à Cousolre, avec ses parents. La première Vie d'Aldegonde dut être rédigée à ce moment, pour susciter un culte, une exhumation et une translation à Maubeuge.[16] Dans cette première biographie, énormément de

---

14. Sur les monastères doubles, voir *Doppelklöster und andere Formen der Symbiose männlicher und weiblicher Religiosen im Mittelalter*, éd. K. Elm et M. Parisse, Berliner historische Studien, 18 - Ordensstudien, 8 (Berlin, 1992), p. 203-211.

15. A.-M. Helvétius, *Abbayes, évêques et laïques. Une politique du pouvoir en Hainaut au Moyen Âge (VIIe-XIe siècle)*, Crédit Communal, collection Histoire, série in-8°, 92 (Bruxelles, 1994), p. 71.

16. *Vita Aldegundae prima*, BHL 244, éd. dans *Acta Sanctorum Belgii selecta*, éd. J. Ghesquière, C. Smet, t. 4 (Bruxelles, 1787), p. 315-326. Sur ce texte, on lira A.-M. Helvétius, *Abbayes, évêques et laïques*, passim, mais surtout p. 135-141 et 315-317 et son article 'Sainte Aldegonde et les origines du monastère de Maubeuge', dans *Revue du Nord*, t. 74 (1992), p. 221-237, résumé dans sa notice consacrée à la sainte dans la *Nouvelle Biographie Nationale*, t. 3 (1994), p. 19; A.-M. Helvétius, 'Le culte de sainte Aldegonde', in *De sainte Aldegonde à sainte Marie. 550 ans de service au jour d'Huy*, éd. Chr. Dury (Huy, 1995), p. 21-39 ainsi que notre 'Études d'hagiographie hainuyère. L'exemple du «cycle de Maubeuge»: un état de la question'.

visions, de miracles de son vivant, mais pas un mot sur son enterrement ou sur des miracles *post mortem*... C'est un texte qui présente une femme noble, instruite, autoritaire – le modèle de la sainte abbesse légitimant religieusement le pouvoir politique de sa famille, mais surtout une femme aux prises avec le surnaturel. Cependant, trente ou quarante ans après cette première biographie, probablement aussi à cause d'elle, un culte démarre à Maubeuge. Le corps d'Aldegonde a dû donc y être transférée peu après la publication de cette *Vita,* dans l'église saint-Pierre de Maubeuge. Notons ici qu'au début du VIIIe s., Aldetrude – l'autre fille de Waudru – comme Madelberte avaient été directement enterrées en l'église Saint-Pierre, l'église abbatiale Notre-Dame n'étant pas encore érigée.

Partout ailleurs en Hainaut, les séquences de fondation sont semblables pour le VIIIe s.: un saint personnage, souvent en relation avec le milieu aristocratique neustrien ou pippinide, fonde dans un domaine rural une communauté monastique, parfois double. Outre les sentiments religieux qui ont dû habiter ces hommes et ces femmes, ne faut-il pas voir également à l'origine de ces schémas le résultat d'une politique de consolidation de leur propre autorité, de leur pouvoir économique et politique, abstrayant celui-ci d'un contexte politique mérovingien très troublé et lui donnant une assise administrative plus stable voire sacrée, donc 'intouchable'.[17] L'hypothèse d'Anne-Marie Helvétius, selon laquelle Waudru et Vincent auraient quitté le siècle pour échapper à une tourmente politique liée à l'éviction temporaire des Pippinides en 656, même si elle est audacieuse, se trouve ici confortée.[18]

C. Les crises des IXe-Xe s.

Ces crises sont multiformes (économiques, politiques, religieuses) et, comme bon nombre de crises, ont un impact sur l'ensemble de la vie de ces institutions religieuses. Une des premières causes est la politique de sécularisation menée par les souverains carolingiens, mais aussi les princes ou de grands laïcs. En effet, à l'époque carolingienne, bien des abbayes sont des 'Eigenklöster' – les Pippinides auraient d'ailleurs fait main basse sur le *dominium* d'un grand nombre de monastères pour faire pièce aux puissants évêques. Une série d'abbayes deviennent donc royales – et le potentat peut alors en aliéner les propriétés ou en céder l'abbatiat à un de ses fidèles, en bénéfice. D'autres abbayes sont 'privées', possédées par

---

17. A.-M. Helvétius, *Abbayes, évêques et laïques...*, *op. cit.*, p. 127-141.
18. *Ibidem*, p. 135-140.

des grands laïques, mais leur sort risque d'être le même. Certaines abbayes, dirigées par des abbés laïques, ne peuvent donc que vivre une crise structurelle profonde: entraînant déclin économique (par la vente des biens ou la dilapidation des revenus) et déclin spirituel (par les agissements de ces abbés laiques). Les invasions normandes ont eu, elles aussi, un impact sur la vie économique de ces communautés, même s'il fut moins grand que ce que l'on a cru jusqu'il y a peu.[19]

Une autre cause est, elle, d'ordre monastique: au début du IXe s., une réorganisation du monde monastique s'impose, dans le cadre des grandes restructurations carolingiennes. Jusqu'alors, les règles suivies étaient mixtes: au départ, on trouvait souvent la *Regula Benedicti*, mais plus ou moins mitigée par des *consuetudines* propres à chaque abbaye. Cependant, les décrets de Louis le Pieux, en 816-817, imposent un choix pour les religieux, mettant un terme à cette gênante confusion: choix entre l'*ordo monasticus*, bénédictin, et l'*ordo canonicus*, la règle canoniale telle que proposée par Chrodegang de Metz. Les religieuses aussi sont confrontées au même moment à un choix similaire: la *Regula Benedicti* ou un décalque de cette règle des chanoines, promulgué en 816, le *De institutione sanctimonialium*.[20] Dans les monastères doubles, les religieux et les moniales ne réagiront pas de la même façon, semble-t-il. Les hommes se rallieront rapidement au système canonial, plus avantageux pour ces petites communautés, mieux adapté à leur fonction et à leur sacerdoce, ne les contraignant pas ou plus à l'obéissance à l'abbesse selon le mode bénédictin, leur donnant libre disposition de leurs biens. Mais dans les couvents féminins, l'adoption de l'un ou l'autre des modes de vie est moins claire. On cherche à conserver la règle mitigée d'avant.[21]

L'imposition de l'une ou l'autre *regula* conduit donc à la crise. Crise au sein des communautés elles-mêmes, tiraillées entre les deux plans de vie, fort différents et porteurs d'avantages bien spécifiques à l'un ou à l'autre, tandis qu'elles continuent, dans les faits, à suivre une règle mixte, mitigée, participant des deux systèmes. Crise aussi entre les communautés masculines et féminines, au cœur de ces monastères doubles: les

---

19. Voir les remarques de J. Nazet, 'Crises et réformes monastiques dans les abbayes hainuyères du IXe au début du XIIe siècle', in *Recueil d'études d'histoire hainuyère offertes à M.-A. Arnould*, dir. J.-M. Cauchies – J.-M. Duvosquel, t. 1, Analectes d'Histoire du Hainaut (Mons, 1983), p. 461-496 (p. 471 notamment).
20. T. Schilp, *Norm und Wirklichkeit religiöser Frauengemeinschaften im Frühmittelalter. Die* Institutio sanctimonialium Aquisgranensis *des Jahres 816 und die Problematik der Verfassung von Frauenkommunitäten*, Veröffentlichungen der Max-Planck-Instituts für Geschichte, 137 - Studien zur Germania Sacra, 21 (Göttingen, 1998).
21. T. Schilp, *Op. cit.*, p. 113-116 et 144-161 notamment.

communautés masculines préférant d'emblée l'ordre canonial, tandis que les religieuses, elles, hésitent et hésitent encore. En définitive, ces crises aboutiront à la transformation en communauté canoniale de la plupart des abbayes hainuyères (sauf l'ancienne et puissante Lobbes) au cours du Xe et XIe s. Certaines vivront temporairement au cours du XIe s. une restauration monastique, mais elle sera de courte durée, puisqu'au cours du XIIe et du XIIIe s., la transformation en chapitres de chanoines ou de chanoinesses sera définitivement accomplie.[22]

1. La Vie d'Aldetrude

Revenons aux IXe et Xe s., à Maubeuge et voyons comment l'abbaye a vécu ces crises. Selon moi, elles sont bien visibles au creux des textes hagiographiques.

Un premier texte daté habituellement du IXe s., et plus particulièrement de la première moitié du IXe s. par Anne-Marie Helvétius, est la *Vita Aldetrudis*.[23] Aldetrude, la sœur de Madelberte, seconde abbesse de Maubeuge, mourut probablement vers 696. L'auteur de ce document, qui ne semble rien savoir d'elle, s'inspire de la première Vie d'Aldegonde, en en attribuant des miracles et des visions à Aldetrude, tout en en inventant quelques autres. 'Oeuvre de valeur médiocre, tant au point de vue historique que littéraire',[24] mais surtout œuvre de rédaction locale, dont la rédaction peu soignée traduit une certaine hâte: sinon, aurait-on laissé un auteur plagier aussi maladroitement la seule Vie de la sainte patronne, plus que probablement toujours lue sur place (même si elle était

---

22. Sur les crises, on lira, outre les travaux de J. Nazet, dont 'La transformation d'abbayes en chapitres à la fin de l'époque carolingienne. Le cas de Saint-*Vincent de Soignies*', in *Revue du Nord*, t. 49 (1967), p. 257-280; J. Nazet, 'Crises et réformes monastiques ...', *op. cit.* et surtout son ouvrage *Les chapitres de chanoines séculiers en Hainaut du XIIe au début du XVe siècle*, Académie royale de Belgique. Classe des lettres, mémoires in-8°, 3e série, 7 (Bruxelles, 1993), ainsi que celui de A.-M. Helvétius, *Abbayes, évêques et laïques... op. cit.*, p. 204-209 et p. 284-310. Dernièrement paru: A.-M. Helvétius, 'Du monastère double au chapitre noble: moniales et chanoinesses en Basse-Lotharingie', in *Les chapitres de dames nobles entre France et Empire*, éd. M. Parisse et P. Heili (Paris, 1998), p. 34-45. Pour une pertinente étude des crises qui secouent les monastères à l'époque ottonienne et salienne et leurs implications hagiographiques, voir St. Patzold, *Konflikte im Kloster. Studien zu Auseinandersetzungen im monastischen Gemeinschaften des ottonisch-salischen Reichs*, Historische Studien, 463 (Husum, 2000). On y insiste notamment sur la longueur de ces crises, qui se compte en mois voire en années: *ibidem*, p. 220-223.

23. *Vita Aldetrudis*, BHL 253-254, éd. dans *AA.SS., Feb.*, 3 (Anvers, 1658), p. 510-511 et *Catalogus codicum hagiographicorum Bibliotecae Regiae Bruxellensis*, pars. 1. *Codices latini membranei*, 2 (Bruxelles, 1889), p. 379-381.

24. A.-M. Helvétius, *Abbayes, évêques et laïques...*, *op. cit.*, p. 317.

probablement déjà mal comprise)? N'aurait-on pas demandé à un scribe plus doué de se charger de cette rédaction, quitte à en prendre un hors de Maubeuge?

Mais la lecture attentive de la *Vita Aldetrudis* permet d'éclairer quelque peu la situation: après avoir replacé Aldetrude, *genere nobilis sed nobilior fide et operibus*, au sein de sa sainte famille. On y explique qu'Aldetrude fut placée à Maubeuge par Waudru *ad erudiendum ac sanctam regulam edocendum; cuius sectans exempla ad vitam pervenit beatam.*[25] L'auteur ajoute, pour justifier son propos: '*Si dicere aut narrare quis cupit, vitam [nutriendum] eius, exemplis ostenditur evidenter, quod cuius imitata est vestigia, ipsam post secuta est in caelis*'. L'auteur insiste sans arrêt sur le fait que suivre Aldetrude, c'est suivre Aldegonde, et faire partie de la cohorte des soeurs qui seront sauvées et connaîtront les noces célestes. La question qui se pose: quelle est la règle suivie et prônée? Il s'agit bien évidemment d'une règle dérivée de la *Regula Benedicti*, l'antique règle de sainte Aldegonde – c'est bien sur cette parenté que le texte insiste sans arrêt, jusqu'à attribuer les mêmes visions aux deux saintes, comme pour forcer l'assimilation. Par deux fois dans le texte, l'auteur décrit la traditionnelle litanie des actes pieux posés par la sainte et nécessaires pour gagner son paradis – et ce sont la pauvreté, les veilles, les jeûnes..., soit des exigences bien monastiques. Ce n'est donc pas l'idéal canonial.[26]

Dans cette *Vita* aux accents monastiques semblent apparaître des traces de conflit interne: celle qui suivra les recommandations d'Aldegonde gagnera les noces suprêmes: '*quatenus veniente sponso, non cum stultis virginibus pulsans et clamans, remaneret foris ad ianuam, sed cum electis coronaretur in gloriam*'.[27] Mais les autres, les vierges folles, perdront tout. Cette insistance sur le fait qu'Aldegonde puis Aldetrude et celles qui les suivront gagneront le ciel se retrouve ici et là dans cette Vita, comme on la retrouve dans une vision tout à la fin du texte, dont bénéficie un des prêtres religieux de la communauté masculine.[28] Celui-ci voit Aldetrude dans une maison céleste somptueuse entourée d'un grand nombre de *virgines* autour d'elles; il interroge une de ces soeurs sur la signification de cette vision. Elle répond: '*Est mansio ista caelestis Iherusalem, in qua domina vestra cum his lucifluis virginibus in aeternum permanebit cum*

---

25. *AA.SS., Feb.*, 3 (Anvers, 1658), p. 510.
26. *AA.SS., Feb.*, 3 (Anvers, 1658), p. 510-511.
27. *AA.SS., Feb.*, 3 (Anvers, 1658), p. 510.
28. *Catalogus codicum hagiographicorum Bibliotecae Regiae Bruxellensis*, pars. 1. *Codices latini membranei*, 2 (Bruxelles, 1889), p. 380-381.

Domino'.²⁹ Le fait qu'un des membres de la communauté masculine soit témoin de cela est significatif. En effet: au moment de la rédaction de ce texte, il s'avère très probable que les fameux décrets de Louis le Pieux aient été promulgués, que la règle canoniale soit déjà proposée avec insistance aux religieux. On pourrait donc y voir comme une mise en garde et en même temps une caution: quelque soit la règle que choisiront ces prêtres, ils doivent laisser leurs consœurs suivre la seule vraie règle, celle de sainte Aldegonde et de sainte Aldetrude, celle de leurs mères, qui ont accédé par la sainteté grâce à elle et ont entraîné à leur suite dans les cieux bon nombre de moniales. Et les autres religieuses, qui entendent ce texte, doivent bien comprendre aussi ce message: pas question de jouer aux vierges folles et de quitter la voie que tracent les deux premières abbesses. Pour conclure: la rédaction de ce texte n'aurait-elle pas été décidée après 817, afin de mettre un terme à des hésitations voire d'éventuels troubles, des dissensions face au choix plus ou moins imposé de ces nouvelles règles? L'urgence expliquerait le caractère un peu fruste de ce texte, tandis qu'on comprendrait mieux la confusion entre Aldegonde et Aldetrude, à la fois dans les textes et dans les actes, confusion volontairement entretenue, à la fois pour donner de l'importance à Aldetrude et pour montrer qu'une fidèle suivante d'Aldegonde peut devenir Aldegonde elle-même, une autre sainte. Et puis, s'il fallait donner en exemple les deux saintes, il valait mieux le faire par ce nouveau texte que par l'ancienne Vie d'Aldegonde, probablement déjà difficile à comprendre à cette époque, comme le prouve la rédaction, quelques années plus tard, d'une nouvelle Vie d'Aldegonde, dans laquelle l'auteur reprend et tente avec difficulté d'expliquer plus clairement le contenu de certaines visions de la première Vie.³⁰

2 La deuxième vie d'Aldegonde

Ainsi une deuxième *Vita Aldegundis* apparaît à la fin du IXe s, remaniement soigné de la *Vita Aldegundis* I. Le plan en est conservé; mais tout en est récrit. L'auteur – un religieux de Saint-Pierre de Maubeuge d'après A.-M. Helvétius – aurait ajouté ici et là des éléments recueillis de la tradition orale, plus une *clausula* finale insistant sur les reliques d'Aldegonde bien présentes à Maubeuge.³¹ Il a donc essayé de comprendre et

---

29. *Ibidem*, p. 381.
30. Sur la création d'un culte et d'une hagiographie dans le cadre d'un conflit monastique, voir les exemples de St. Patzold, *Konflikte im Kloster...*, *op. cit.*, p. 163-173.
31. *Vita Aldegundis secunda*, BHL 245, éd. *AA.SS., Ian.*, 2 (Anvers, 1643), p. 1035-1040. La *clausula* est éditée par W. Levison, dans *M.G.H., SS. Rerum Merov.*, 6 (Hanovre, 1913), p. 90. Voir aussi les commentaires de A.-M. Helvétius, *Op. cit.*, p. 159-160, 318-320.

d'expliquer les passages confus de la première Vie. Il s'est inspiré aussi quelque peu de la Vie d'Aldetrude. Ici, Aldegonde est davantage présentée comme fondatrice que comme une noble puissante, comme c'est le cas dans la *Vita Aldegundis* I. Mais c'est aussi un texte bien différent de la Vie d'Aldetrude! Construit, clair, il insiste très peu sur la sainte règle monastique, sur la nécessité pour les religieuses de suivre cette règle. Mais la règle bénédictine prévaut toujours chez les *sanctimoniales* – comme en témoigne l'insistance sur la pauvreté, sur le dénuement, sur la vente des biens...[32] Cette *Vita* est davantage un texte à plus large portée, pas seulement destiné aux soeurs ou aux religieux de Maubeuge. Les miracles sont mis en avant – c'est d'ailleurs un miracle qui constitue le seul emprunt important fait à la Vie d'Aldetrude.[33] Il semble évident que ce texte ait été rédigé pour soutenir un culte, pour le relancer, peut-être comme le pense Anne-Marie Helvétius, à la fin du IXe s., à l'occasion de la construction d'une nouvelle abbatiale, dédiée à Notre-Dame, dans laquelle les saints restes d'Aldegonde seront translatés. Rien ne s'oppose à cette hypothèse... et rien dans le texte ne permet de l'étayer concrètement, sinon l'insistance dans le dernier chapitre, la *clausula*, sur les reliques d'Aldegonde, concluant sur l'efficacité miraculeuse de ces restes sacrés.[34]

3. La fausse donation d'Aldegonde

Au même moment, un document très particulier est produit par les moniales de Maubeuge. Il s'agit de ce qu'on a appelé par la suite, improprement, le testament de sainte Aldegonde, soit un document sous une forme diplomatique, qui cherche à passer pour une charte d'Aldegonde elle-même, qui donnerait par là une série de biens fonciers à son monastère de Maubeuge.[35] Un faux grossier, de toute évidence, mais qui remonterait à la seconde moitié du IXe s. – l'auteur de la deuxième Vie d'Aldegonde paraît connaître ce document. Ce document a pour but de revendiquer une série de biens fonciers, dont la propriété est réclamée par les *sorores*. En effet, ce document s'inscrit probablement dans le

---

32. *AA.SS., Ian.*, 2, p. 1036, 1038-1039.
33. Les miracles font presque la moitié du texte, et même plus si on y ajoute les visions: *AA.SS., Ian.*, 2, p. 1036, 1038-1041.
34. *M.G.H., SS. Rerum Merov.*, 6, p. 90.
35. Voir l'excellente analyse de A.-M. Helvétius, *Op. cit.*, p. 161-168. Édition de ce texte dans J. Daris, 'Vie de S. Aldegonde. Charte de dotation de l'abbaye de Maubeuge. Revenus de ses terres', in *Analectes pour servir à l'Histoire Ecclésiastique de la Belgique*, t. 2 (1865), p. 36-47, éd. p. 42-44.

contexte des troubles liés à l'apparition d'un abbatiat laïque et de contestations quant à l'existence d'une mense conventuelle, aux IXe et Xe s. Crise, une fois de plus: avec d'une part, la sécularisation des abbayes, l'apparition de ces abbés laïques imposés sur le siège abbatial par le roi ou par un grand, recevant en bénéfice cet abbatiat – crise aussi, avec par ailleurs, pour sauver de quoi survivre, l'exigence par les membres des communautés religieuses à la merci de ces abbés pilleurs, de la création d'une mense conventuelle, d'un ensemble de biens déterminés dont l'usage est réservé à la vie de la communauté.[36] Ce faux pourrait donc faire l'énumération des biens réclamés par les *sorores,* contre les prétentions d'une abbesse laïque. Aldegonde y donne elle-même aux dites soeurs les biens réclamés – y a-t-il meilleure justification?

> '*ut sorores in predicto monasterio degentes iam dictas villas cum omnibus ad illas pertinentibus ad suas speciales usus habere debeant vel quidquid exinde facere voluerint, liberam in omnibus habeant potestatem faciendi, ut neque aliquis neque ex abbatissis et rectricibus ejusdem monasterii ulla aliquo in tempore quippiam inmutare et convellere atque a presenti ordinatione, quam pro amore Christi feci, alienare praesumat, sed ita omni tempore inviolatamque permaneat*'.[37]

Le but est clair, l'adresse aux *abbatissae* ou *rectrices* l'est aussi – on vise l'abbesse laïque.

Ainsi, à la fin du IXe s., le monastère de Maubeuge est-il sujet à des tensions internes évidentes. Des tensions religieuses et structurelles ont dû d'abord se faire jour – la Vie d'Aldetrude a dû être rédigée en réponse à celles-ci, pour rassurer les moniales quant à leur règle et pour leur donner un nouveau modèle à l'aune d'Aldegonde. D'autre part, des tensions économiques ont dû suivre: un abbé ou une abbesse laïque – on ne peut savoir de qui il s'agit – et une sécularisation dangereuse; des difficultés économiques liées à cette sécularisation, mais aussi liées à l'érection d'une nouvelle abbatiale. Ces difficultés auraient engendré de la part des religieuses la rédaction de deux textes: l'un, le faux testament, de la plume d'Aldegonde elle-même, accompagnée de ses fidèles abbesses et saints amis, justifiant la possession d'une mense conventuelle. L'autre, la seconde vie d'Aldegonde, outre qu'elle devrait permettre une relance du

---

36. Sur ces crises, voir par ex. A.-M. Helvétius, 'L'abbatiat laïque comme relais du pouvoir royal aux frontières du royaume: Le cas du nord de la Neustrie au IXème siècle', in *La royauté et les élites dans l'Europe carolingienne (du début du IXème aux environs de 920),* éd. R. Le Jan, Centre d'Histoire de l'Europe du Nord-Ouest, 17 (Villeneuve-d'Ascq, 1998), p. 285-299.

37. J. Daris (éd.), *Op. cit.,* p. 43.

culte d'Aldegonde dans la nouvelle église Notre-Dame, imposerait une fois de plus aux regards de tous les fidèles et pèlerins la stature de la fondatrice, sainte Aldegonde elle-même.

4. La Vie de Madelberte

C'est alors qu'apparaît un nouveau texte hagiographique, né à Maubeuge.

Parmi les signataires du faux testament d'Aldegonde, on retrouve, aux côtés d'Aldegonde et d'Aldetrude, une abbesse Madelberte. Cette Madelberte, les religieuses de Maubeuge ont plus que probablement voulu en lancer le culte alors. La *Vita Madelbertae* naît donc à ce moment.[38] Que connaît l'auteur de Madelberte, mis à part qu'elle est la troisième abbesse de Maubeuge, qu'elle a dirigé le monastère neuf ans et qu'elle serait la fille de sainte Waudru? Rien. Absolument rien. L'auteur ne semble pas plus créatif, en apparence, que celui de la *Vita Aldetrudis*. Il copie, emprunte, plagie deux *vitae*: la première Vie d'Aldegonde et la Vie d'Aldetrude. Pas d'autre texte. Il ne cite pas la seconde Vie d'Aldegonde, pourtant rédigée il y a peu. Même les citations bibliques qu'il fait sont tirées de ces deux dernières Vies. Peut-être a-t-il connu la *Vita Rictrudis* d'Hucbald de Saint-Amand, comme le pense Anne-Marie Helvétius, mais il n'y en a aucune preuve tangible.[39] L'hagiographe se débat dans un style complexe, enchevêtré, parfois incompréhensible, maltraitant des passages empruntés à ses modèles. Son vocabulaire, recherché, 'fleuri', a fait dire de cette Vie qu'elle était poétique.[40] Quant au contenu de ce texte, il fait penser, indiscutablement, à celui de la Vie d'Aldetrude. Mais l'insistance sur la *regula*, la sainte règle monastique y est encore plus marquée: pauvreté, dénuement, ascèse monastiques sont des qualités martelées. La moitié de l'ouvrage est consacré à la sainteté d'Aldegonde, une fois de plus. Et une fois de plus, la fusion 'Aldegonde et ses suivantes' est mise en exergue: Madelberte devient, à la suite d'Aldegonde, une autre Aldegonde. Une autre caractéristique de ce texte, que l'on retrouvait déjà dans la *Vita Aldetrudis*, mais de façon moindre, réside dans l'insistance sur la lutte contre les embûches, les difficultés rencontrées sur cette terre. A ce

---

38. *Vita Madelbertae*, *BHL* 5129, nouvelle édition par P. Bertrand, 'La Vie de sainte Madelberte de Maubeuge (BHL 5129). Edition critique du texte', in *Analecta Bollandiana*, t. 113, fasc. 3-4 (1997), p. 39-76 (texte édité et traduit p. 55-76). Outre ce travail, on verra aussi A.-M. Helvétius, *Abbayes, évêques et laïques...*, *op. cit.*, *passim* et surtout p. 322-325.
39. A.-M. Helvétius, *Op. cit.*, p. 324-325.
40. L. van der Essen, *Étude critique*, *op. cit.*, p. 243.

propos, le prologue est édifiant.[41] A sa lecture, les sanctimoniales ont le choix: être des vierges folles ou des vierges sages, *'cum prudentibus virginibus amissis stolidis'*. Le propos est martelé: suivre Madelberte, c'est gagner son ciel, puisque *'Mira virtute floruit vivens, animas sanctarum virginum lucratas secum duxit ad gloriam'*.[42].

Une autre particularité de cette Vie: une fois Madelberte décédée, son corps est enterré dans l'église Saint-Pierre (abandonnée par les religieuses à l'époque de la rédaction de la *Vita Madelbertae*, cette église devait servir à la communauté masculine). Deux miracles *ad sepulchrum* s'ensuivent, impliquant des dévots de la région.[43] C'est ce qui a fait dire à Anne-Marie Helvétius que ce texte avait été rédigé pour relancer un culte dans l'église Saint-Pierre, alors dépossédée de corps saints (Aldegonde reposant, probablement avec Aldetrude, dans la nouvelle abbatiale Notre-Dame) – ce culte de sainte aurait été lancé à l'instigation de la communauté masculine pour bénéficier de reliques prestigieuses, attirant pèlerins et considération. Mais, si la volonté de lancer un culte est claire, s'il est possible que ce soit pour relancer une dynamique culturelle en l'église Saint-Pierre, il est peu probable que ce soit, on l'a clairement vu, à l'instigation d'une communauté masculine qui n'a même pas été entr'aperçue au fil de ce texte.

Il est bien plus probable que ce texte ait aussi été rédigé dans le même esprit que la Vie d'Aldetrude: pour apaiser des conflits au sein du monastère, entre tenants de l'antique Règle d'Aldegonde, d'Aldetrude et maintenant de Madelberte et les partisans d'une règle canoniale, très

---

41. P. Bertrand (éd.), *Op. cit.*, p. 56-57: 'En faisant revenir avec empressement les fêtes des saintes vierges au fil des cycles annuels, nous renouvelons d'immenses louanges à l'unique Seigneur pour les vertus données. Eclairés par leurs exemples, nous tentons de nous hâter vers l'amour de la patrie céleste afin de pouvoir nous puissions rencontrer le véritable et insaisissable l'époux et parvenir à la maison de la beauté éternelle, où brille la lumière de la plus éclatante clarté, avec l'aide du tout-puissant créateur, par le chemin étroit qui conduit à la vie, au prix d'incessants efforts, ensemble avec les vierges prudentes *et* débarrassés des folles et portant dans les vases l'huile la plus limpide; et nous pourrons entendre cette voix désirable qui dit: «Venez les bénis de mon Père, recevez ce royaume qui vous a été préparé depuis le début du monde, en raison des peines que vous avez endurées au combat». Et là, nous recevrons les couronnes inflétrissables de celui-là qui dit: «Venez à moi, tous qui peinez et qui êtes accablés et je referai vos forces. Mon joug est doux, en effet, et mon fardeau léger». Et l'apôtre l'a appris: «Qui nous séparera de la charité du Christ? Le glaive, la faim, le froid, le danger, la mort, la vie? Et à nouveau le Seigneur lui-même dit dans son évangile: «Je suis venu mettre le feu sur terre, je veux qu'il brûle». Affermis grâce à ces appuis sacrés, nous foulerons au pied les embûches de l'antique ennemi pour parvenir au séjour fleuri'.
42. P. Bertrand (éd.), *Op. cit., passim*, notamment p. 56 et 68.
43. P. Bertrand (éd.), *Op. cit.*, p. 68-70.

certainement en vigueur dans la communauté masculine à l'époque de la rédaction de la *Vita Madelbertae*. Pour résumer les choses: il faut suivre l'exemple monastique des vierges sages, suivre Madelberte, sa sœur et sa tante, pour accéder aux félicités éternelles.

Ceci nous amène à la datation de ce texte. La rédaction de cette *Vita* a été située entre 870 et 956. Plus probablement au début Xe s., disait Anne-Marie Helvétius, se basant sur une hypothétique utilisation de la *Vita Rictrudis* (907) par l'auteur de la *Vita Madelbertae*.[44] C'est possible. Mais la comparaison de ce texte avec la *Vita Aldetrudis* apporte un autre éclairage et suscite d'autres hypothèses. Les méthodes d'écriture sont similaires. Ainsi, dans la *Vita Aldetrudis,* on lit:

> *Nam quos omnipotens Deus, inquit, sui desiderii amore videt accensos, eos per multa argumenta attrahere non desistit, ut magis ac magis exonerati animo ad calorem fidei inardescant, quatenus ad destinata praemia tenaciter festinent, ac mundi illecebras perhorrescant, et calcando per angustum callem, ad illum perveniant, coram quo se credunt in ampla beatitudinis sede permanere,*[45]

comparé à un passage similaire dans la *Vita Madelbertae*:

> *Earum exemplis illuminati, ad amorem caelestis patriae properare conamur, quatinus ad mansionem perpetui decoris, ubi lux summae claritatis refulget, auctore summo iuvante, per angustum callem qui ducit ad vitam perpetuis [...].*[46]

L'auteur n'utilise pas la seconde Vie d'Aldegonde, contemporaine pourtant. Il utilise les mêmes modèles que dans la Vie d'Aldetrude, celle-ci comprise. Son style est plus 'fleuri'. Soit ces deux textes ont été rédigés par le même auteur, soit par deux différents, mais dans tous les cas, chacun des auteurs ne peut être qu'une moniale de Maubeuge. Ces textes ont dû être de toute façon conçus à peu de temps d'intervalle – et si l'on considère qu'il s'agit ici de deux auteurs, deux moniales, alors celle qui s'est chargée de la *Vita Madelbertae* a voulu prendre la *Vita Aldetrudis* comme modèle, probablement pour montrer une continuité spirituelle. Ceci expliquerait dans les deux textes la même insistance sur l'époux spirituel, la même insistance sur les joies (quasi sexuelles?) de l'union mystique au Christ,[47] la même insistance sur la communauté des soeurs et

---

44. Cf. note 45.
45. *AA.SS., Feb.*, 3, p. 510.
46. P. Bertrand (éd.), *Op. cit.*, p. 56.
47. Ainsi dans la Vie de Madelberte, on lit: '*Quae iam paradysi florigera introspexit nemora, flammigero vibrantique gladio perforata viscera, iam Christi manavit amor in praecordiis*', 'l'amour du Christ se déversa dans le cœur de celle qui avait déjà aperçu l'intérieur des bois fleuris du paradis, et dont les entrailles avaient été transpercées par un vibrant glaive de feu'.

rien qu'elle, les mêmes insinuations à propos des difficultés rencontrées. Deux textes commandés à trente, quarante ou cinquante ans d'intervalle à la même sœur ou à deux sœurs de Maubeuge, par les religieuses du clan des fidèles d'Aldegonde. C'est ce qui expliquerait le mieux, selon moi, la particularité de ces deux textes, l'un de la première moitié du IXe s., l'autre de peu après 870.[48]

5. La troisième Vie d'Aldegonde

A la fin du IXe s., à l'aube du Xe s., où en sommes-nous? Du côté de la communauté masculine, il est certain qu'elle a adopté la *regula canonialis*. Mais du côté féminin? Les crises se poursuivront au cours du Xe s., mais les moniales cèderont le pas aux partisans de la règle des chanoines. Un autre exemple parfait de l'évolution de cette crise est représenté par la troisième vie d'Aldegonde, de la seconde moitié du Xe s., selon Anne-Marie Helvétius – mais je pense, vu la redéfinition de la date de rédaction de la Vie de Madelberte, qu'il n'y a pas de raison pour préférer la première moitié du Xe s. à la seconde: pour rester cohérent, je dirai qu'il s'agit d'un texte du Xe s.[49] Cette troisième Vie d'Aldegonde est un centon hagiographique, rédigé dans le seul but de revendiquer la possession de certains biens censés appartenir à la communauté féminine de Maubeuge. L'auteur, probablement un religieux du cru, avait pour seul but d'intégrer dans une vie d'Aldegonde une version de la fausse donation de celle-ci. Outre cela, tout le reste est tiré au mot à mot de la *Vita*

---

48. Pour en revenir aux arguments de datation proposés par Anne-Marie Helvétius (*Op. cit.*, p. 322-325) et leur faire un sort...: 'et si c'était Hucbald de Saint-Amand, rédigeant la *Vita Rictrudis* (907), qui avait lu la Vie de Madelberte et s'en était inspiré pour l'un ou l'autre détail, et non l'inverse, cela expliquerait les hésitations quant aux sources de la *Vita Madelbertae*'. Une série de passages litigieux dans la *Vita Madelbertae* fait tenir à Anne-Marie Hélvétius le discours suivant: 'comme l'auteur montre Aldegonde distribuant en cachette l'argent de ses parents de leur vivant et fuyant des châtiments corporels pour fonder Maubeuge, cela signifierait qu'il n'est pas très élogieux à l'égard de Maubeuge et donc qu'il n'est pas de la région': ce me semble un peu forcé, ce sont là des *topoi*. Par ailleurs, un autre passage trouble et difficile à traduire fait dire à Anne-Marie Helvétius que, selon l'auteur, Aldegonde se serait installée sur une terre qui ne lui appartenait pas. Encore un signe d'un mépris pour Maubeuge, pour Anne-Marie Helvétius. Il est quand même peu probable que les religieuses commandent un texte à un scribe extérieur, dans lequel celui-ci se permettrait ou de contredire la tradition ou d'apporter des éléments nouveaux clairement néfastes à la bonne marche du culte d'Aldegonde, sans que les religieuses le lui fassent remarquer. Il me semble plus adéquat de rendre responsable de ces imprécisions et indélicatesses les errements littéraires d'une moniale de Maubeuge – car si elle prend pour modèle la *Vita Aldetrudis*, n'est-ce pas aussi certainement pour masquer d'éventuelles incompétences (ce que soulèvent les nombreux problèmes stylistiques et grammaticaux de ce texte)?
49. *Vita Aldegundis tertia*, BHL 247b, J. Daris (éd.), *Op. Cit.*, p. 37-41. Voir A.-M. Helvétius, *Op. cit.*, p. 330-331.

Aldegundis secunda et de la *Vita Madelbertae*. On y insiste cependant lourdement sur le caractère canonial des religieuses: celles-ci ont bien sauté le pas et choisi de vivre selon la règle des chanoines.[50] Au cours du texte, l'un ou l'autre passage fait bien comprendre que la transformation a eu lieu, mieux, que les religieuses ont toujours été des chanoinesses – que les fondatrices étaient profondément imprégnées de l'esprit de la règle canoniale. Aldegonde elle-même transmettra cette règle canoniale à ses nièces qui lui succèderont: '*neptasque suas venerabiles Aldedrudem ac Madelbertam canonicae tradidit vitae*', explique l'auteur, reprenant ici, en la manipulant à bon escient, une phrase de la *Vita Madelbertae*: '*Neptasque suas venerabiles, Aldedrudem ac Madelbertam, monasticae tradidit vitae*', modifiant donc avec une conscience aigüe de son geste le mot *monasticae*, remplacé par le significatif *canonicae*.[51]

Tout cela est porteur de sens. Voir dans ce texte seulement une construction littéraire pour appuyer la revendication des biens déjà réclamés dans la fausse donation d'Aldegonde, cinquante ou cent ans plus tôt, me semble un peu court. Certes, c'est bien un des objectifs de ce texte. Mais ne pourrait-on y voir aussi ou plutôt une tentative de reprendre et d'éradiquer tous les textes sacrés antérieurs et relatifs à Aldegonde et ses deux nièces? L'auteur reprendrait bon nombre d'informations de ces textes – surtout ceux qui martelaient l'importance de la règle monastique, rédigés pour soutenir les tenants de la tradition, comme la *Vita Aldetrudis* ou la *Vita Madelbertae* – en un pot-pourri où, subtilement, l'idéal canonial se mêlerait à l'idéal monastique, jusqu'à l'effacer. Certes, il reste de nombreuses traces héritées du 'monachisme', comme l'insistance sur la pauvreté volontaire, l'ascèse.[52] Mais, on l'a déjà souligné, il serait absurde d'attendre de ces *regulae* qu'elles soient strictes et étanches: souvent, elles sont mitigées,[53] même au Xe s., même au XIe s. La seule différence: ici, la donne a changé, c'est l'idéal canonial qui a pris le dessus. Ce texte est donc un autre instrument créé au service d'une cause, d'un groupe de religieux et de religieuses. En supprimant la nécessité liturgique et spirituelle de retourner aux textes hagiographiques antérieurs par leur reprise 'améliorée' en une anthologie savamment construite, au sein de la *Vita Aldegundis tertia*, les chanoines et chanoinesses de Maubeuge tentent d'effacer les derniers et les plus puissants arguments des

---

50. Notamment J. Daris (éd.), *Op. cit.*, p. 39.
51. J. Daris (éd.), *Op. cit.*, p. 40, par rapport à la *Vita Madelbertae*, P. Bertrand (éd.), *Op. cit.*, p. 62.
52. Par ex. J. Daris (éd.), *Op. cit.*, p. 38-39.
53. Cf. *supra*, p. 62.

partisans de la règle monastique – les arguments d'autorité. Refaire l'histoire pour mieux contrôler le présent et faire accepter la nouvelle donne politique et religieuse.

En ce sens, la présence d'une grande partie de la fameuse donation d'Aldegonde dans cette troisième Vie de sainte Aldegonde s'explique. Elle n'est peut-être pas nécessairement liée à des réclamations foncières. Mais, comme c'est une autre de ces traces importantes attribuées à sainte Aldegonde elle-même, il est logique de la voir reprise ici, mise à la 'sauce canoniale'.

6. *La fausse confirmation royale de la donation d'Aldegonde*

Ensuite, ce sont les chanoines de Saint-Pierre de Maubeuge qui usent de l'écrit comme d'un instrument politique. Ou plutôt les chanoines de Saint-Quentin, puisque telle sera leur titulature à partir du Xe s.[54]. Au Xe s. (et plus précisément, pendant la seconde moitié?), ils font rédiger une fausse confirmation royale de la donation d'Aldegonde, dans laquelle les dons semblent faits en faveur des chanoines de l'église de Maubeuge, dite de Saint-Quentin.[55] Ici, je me rallie aux déductions d'Anne-Marie Helvétius: ce faux dut être réalisé pour donner au chapitre de chanoines un titre de propriété remontant à l'époque d'Aldegonde et justifier, contre toute critique venue de l'extérieur, le titre de Saint-Quentin bien que l'église soit dite de Saint-Pierre.

7. *Les quatrième et cinquième Vies d'Aldegonde*

Puis au XIe s., c'est la réforme, avec l'abbesse Ansoalde, qui impose, avec l'accord de l'évêque de Cambrai et du comte Regnier V de Hainaut, la restauration de l'*ordo monasticus* à Maubeuge. Dans la *Vita* de Thierry de Saint-Hubert, frère d'Ansoalde, oblat à Maubeuge durant son enfance, on laisse entendre que l'observance monastique n'a jamais été complètement abandonnée – ce que confirme la précédente mise en vigueur d'une règle canoniale mais 'mitigée', telle qu'elle est attestée dans la

---

54. Pourquoi Saint-Quentin? La question reste posée. Anne-Marie Helvétius pense que le bénéficiaire laïque de Maubeuge était le comte de Vermandois, que ce dernier aurait pu remplacer les clercs au service des religieuses par des chanoines de l'abbaye Saint-Quentin de Vermandois; que ces chanoines auraient gardé leur titulature: A.-M. Helvétius, *Op. cit.*, p. 247-249.

55. P. Bonenfant (éd.), 'Note critique sur le prétendu testament de sainte Aldegonde', in *Bulletin de la Commission Royale d'Histoire*, t. 98 (1934), p. 219-238, ici p. 235-238. Voir aussi les commentaires de A.-M. Helvétius, *Op. cit.*, p. 250-252.

troisième vie d'Aldegonde.[56] Seulement, avec Ansoalde, c'est le retour de balancier et la reprise officielle de la règle bénédictine – la cinquième Vie d'Aldegonde, peut-être rédigée par Thierry de Saint-Hubert entre 1030 et 1040, insiste à nouveau sur l'idéal de saint Benoît.[57] Tandis qu'une quatrième vie d'Aldegonde, qui consiste en une reprise de la seconde avec quelques additions maladroites, semble insister sur le culte d'Aldegonde à Cousolre, probablement en relation, pendant la première moitié du XIe s., avec l'oratoire récemment fondé sur place.[58] Un texte rédigé pour promouvoir le culte dans cette 'fondation fille' de l'abbaye de Maubeuge? A moins qu'à Cousolre, comme le propose en hypothèse Anne-Marie Helvétius, ne se retrouvent que les anciennes chanoinesses de Maubeuge, celles qui n'auraient pas voulu se joindre à l'observance monastique, chassées par Ansoalde et reléguées en ce lieu?[59]

Résumons ces trois siècles de vie religieuse mouvementée: une crise structurelle, religieuse semble poindre dès le IXe s., au travers de la *Vita Aldetrudis*, éclatant dans la *Vita Madelbertae*. Tandis que, dans la deuxième Vie d'Aldegonde, rédigée pour induire un renouveau cultuel et probablement une relance économique, on lit en filigrane une autre crise structurelle, peut-être liée à la sécularisation, à l'apparition d'un abbatiat laïque, ou, pour dire simplement les choses, à des difficultés économiques. Ce filigrane s'imprime noir sur blanc dans la fausse donation d'Aldegonde. Tout bascule au Xe s., avec l'arrivée au pouvoir des tenants de la *regula* canoniale, comme cela apparaît à la lecture de la troisième Vie d'Aldegonde. Tandis que les revendications identitaires des chanoines de Saint-Quentin œuvrant en l'église Saint-Pierre se font jour dans leur 'fausse confirmation de la fausse donation' d'Aldegonde. Enfin, le XIe s.: c'est la restauration monastique avec Ansoalde, une nouvelle Vie d'Aldegonde adaptée aux exigences d'allure bénédictine. Mais le retour à l'ordre de saint Benoît sera de courte durée: à partir de 1200/1250, les religieuses deviendront définitivement, cette fois, des chanoinesses.

---

56. *Vita Theoderici ab. Andaginensis*, BHL 8050, W. Wattenbach (éd.), dans *M.G.H., SS.*, 12, p. 37-57 et A.-M. Helvétius, *Op. cit.*, p. 252-253.
57. *Vita Aldegundis quinta*, BHL 247, éd. dans *AA.SS., Ian.*, 2 (Anvers, 1643), p. 1040-1047. Voir aussi A.-M. Helvétius, *Op. cit.*, p. 340-342.
58. *Vita Aldegundis quarta*, BHL 246, éd. dans *Catalogus codicum hagiographicorum Bibliotecae Regiae Bruxellensis*, pars. 1. *Codices latini membranei*, 2 (Bruxelles, 1889), p. 133-135. Voir aussi A.-M. Helvétius, *Op. cit.*, p. 253-254 et 334-335.
59. A.-M. Helvétius, *Op. cit.*, p. 308-309.

N'est-il pas abusif de lire ces différents textes avec cette grille de lecture? Je ne le pense pas: toute démarche historienne se nourrit du risque de l'hypothèse. Il ne faut évidemment pas oublier que la grande force de l'abbaye de Maubeuge à l'époque mérovingienne, c'est la présence des restes sacrés d'Aldegonde. Jouissant d'un culte en pleine expansion dès cette époque, sans commune mesure avec aucun autre culte dans cette partie du Hainaut alors, l'abbaye a fait des reliques d'Aldegonde son étendard, et de sa Vie son chant de triomphe. Supportant relativement mal l'émergence d'autres cultes – notamment au Xe s., avec, par exemple, l'efflorescence de la dévotion à saint Ghislain, dont les Maubeugeois voleront les reliques –, la communauté des religieuses de Maubeuge tentera de préserver sa toute-puissance sacrée (et donc aussi économique) par l'établissement de cultes de pseudo-Aldegonde, comme Aldetrude et Madelberte, par des translations des restes d'Aldegonde elle-même, par de nouvelles biographies. On le voit, les cultes des saintes de Maubeuge et les textes hagiographiques les concernant ont une réelle importance stratégique, voire tactique.[60] Mais il serait restrictif d'y voir seulement des instruments de politique extérieure. Ce sont aussi, pour un bon nombre d'entre eux, des instruments de régulation interne, des armes au service de la stabilité et de l'ordre d'une communauté, touchée de plein fouet par des crises multiples dont l'intrication n'a d'égale que la complexité. Les reliques et l'hagiographie malbodienne ne sont donc ici pas seulement les témoins d'une époque révolue et d'un lieu dont seul le clair de lune est resté célèbre. Ils sont aussi et surtout les acteurs inattendus et étonnamment loquaces d'un temps de crises.

---

60. Ces conflits vus comme 'occasions d'écriture' ont déjà été étudiés dans ce sens par quelques chercheurs, comme le montre St. Patzold, *Konflikte im Kloster...*, *op. cit.*, p. 163-173 avec le remarquable cas de textes hagiographiques à l'abbaye de Saint-Trond à la fin du XIe et au début du XIIe s. Voir aussi *ibidem*, p. 239-246. Un autre exemple, pour une période plus tardive et pour d'autres familles religieuses: Th. Füser, *Mönche im Konflikt. Zum Spannungsfeld von Norm, Devianz und Sanktionen bei den Cisterciensern und Cluniazensern (12. bis frühes 14. Jahrhundert)*, Vita regularis, 9 (Münster, 2000).

Brigitte MEIJNS

THE 'LIFE OF BISHOP JOHN OF THÉROUANNE' BY ARCHDEACON WALTER (1130) AND THE BISHOP'S PASTORAL ACTIVITIES*

The 'Life of Bishop John of Thérouanne' is one of the few biographies of eleventh- or twelfth-century bishops that were written immediately after the death of the protagonist.[1] A glance at the output of episcopal hagiography in the surrounding dioceses reveals that only the brief *Epistola* about the life of bishop Odo of Cambrai (†1113) by Amand du Chastel was also composed relatively shortly after his death.[2] Usually, there is a period of time of about twenty or thirty years, as is the case for the biographies of Lietbert of Cambrai[3] (†1076), Arnulph of Soissons[4]

---

* B. Meijns is postdoctoral Research Fellow of the Fund of Scientific Research-Flanders (F.W.O-Vlaanderen, Belgium).
1. Walter of Thérouanne, *Vita Iohannis episcopi Teruanensis*, O. Holder-Egger ed., *Monumenta Germaniae Historica* (MGH), *Scriptores* XV, 2 (Stuttgart-New York, 1963), p. 1136-1150; *Narrative Sources from the Medieval Low Countries* (www.narrativesources.be), nr. G009; BHL 4439; I. van 't Spijker, 'Gallia du Nord et de l'Ouest. Les provinces ecclésiastiques de Tours, Rouen, Reims (950-1130)', in: *Hagiographies. International History of the Latin and Vernacular Hagiographical Literature in the West from its Origins to 1550*, G. Philippart, red., II (Turnhout, 1996), p. 269; J. Deploige, 'Intériorisation religieuse et propagande hagiographique dans les Pays-Bas méridionaux du 11e au 13e siècle', *Revue d'Histoire ecclésiastique*, XCIV (1999), p. 808-831.
2. Amandus de Castello, *De Odonis episcopi Cameracensis vita vel moribus*, O. Holder-Egger ed., MGH Scriptores XV, 2, p. 942-945; *Narrative Sources*, nr. A051; BHL 6287; van 't Spijker, 'Gallia du nord', p. 271-272; S. Haarländer, *Vitae episcoporum. Eine Quellengattung zwischen Hagiographie und Historiographie, untersucht an Lebensbeschreibungen von Bischöfen des Regnum Teutonicum im Zeitalter der Ottonen und Salier* (Stuttgart, 2000), p. 526-527.
3. Written between 1092 and 1133 (probably c. 1100) by Rodulph, a monk of Saint-Sépulcre in Cambrai. Rodulph of Saint-Sépulcre, *Vita Lietberti*, A. Hofmeister ed., MGH Scriptores XXX, 2 (Hannover, 1915), p. 838-866; BHL 4929; van 't Spijker, 'Gallia du nord', p. 271; Haarländer, *Vitae episcoporum*, p. 521-522.
4. In 1114 abbot Hariulph of Oudenburg completed the first two books, which were based on a Life of Saint Arnulph by Lisiard, bishop of Soissons, c. 1108 (BHL 703). *De S. Arnulfo confessore*, G. Cuperus, ed., *Acta Sanctorum Augusti* III (Paris and Rome, 1867), p. 221-259; R. Nip, *Arnulfus van Soissons, bisschop van Soissons (†1087), mens en model: een bronnenstudie*. Ph.D. Dissertation. Rijksuniversiteit Groningen, 1995, (www.ub.rug.nl/eldoc/dis/arts/r.i.a.nip); *Narrative Sources* nr. H009; BHL 704.

(†1087) or Godfrey of Amiens[5] (†1115). But its speedy composition is not the only reason why the 'Life of John of Thérouanne' qualifies as a first-rate source; the identity of its biographer also contributes. For thirteen years, Walter was archdeacon of Thérouanne and, hence, one of the bishop's closest assistants and a privileged witness of his activities.[6] Ever since John had taken young Walter into his entourage, a close personal friendship had developed between them, a friendship that ended only when the bishop died in 1130. From the prologue, we learn that it was precisely this level of intimacy that was offered by the *fratres* as an argument in their effort to persuade Walter to write a *vita*.[7]

Apart from the *vita*, several other sources offer insights into the episcopacy of John of Thérouanne, which lasted for thirty years. I will only mention the most important. The second book of the 'Deeds of the Abbots of Saint-Bertin' in Saint-Omer gives interesting information concerning the bishop's personality and his deeds.[8] These *Gesta Abbatum Sancti Bertini Sithiensium* were recorded during the period 1136-1145 by Simon, a former abbot. Simon was well-informed about the relationships that existed between his abbey – the oldest and most powerful ecclesiastical institution of the whole diocese – and the bishop. Furthermore, nearly forty charters with John of Thérouanne himself as issuer, still exist.[9] They offer a survey of the very diverse activities of the bishop, who is known to have been a fervent supporter of the Gregorian Reform in Flanders.[10]

---

5. Composed between 1136 and 1138 by Nicolas, a monk of Saint-Crépin-le-Grand of Soissons. *De Sancto Godefrido episcopo Ambianensi*, A. Poncelet, ed., *Acta Sanctorum Novembris* III (Brussels, 1910), p. 905-944; BHL 3573; Cf. L. Morelle, 'Un "grégorien" au miroir de ses chartes: Geoffroy, évêque d'Amiens (1104-1115)', in: *A propos des actes d'évêques. Hommage à Lucie Fossier*, M. Parisse, red. (Nancy, 1991), p. 177-218.

6. N. Huyghebaert, 'Gautier de Thérouanne', *Dictionnaire d'histoire et de géographie ecclésiastiques* (DHGE), XX (1984) col. 115-116.

7. 'Aiebant enim nemini competentius hoc iniungi valere, eo quod tanto cum eo tempore moratus ...': Walter, *Vita Iohannis*, MGH Scriptores XV, 2, p. 1139.

8. Simon of Saint-Bertin, *Gesta Abbatum Sancti Bertini Sithiensium*. O. Holder-Egger, ed., MGH Scriptores XIII (Hannover, 1881), p. 635-663; *Narrative Sources* nr. S091.

9. Cf. O. Bled, *Régestes des évêques de Thérouanne 500-1553* (Saint-Omer, 1904-1907), I, p. 96-119: nrs. 351, 354, 356, 358, 369, 371, 372, 405, 408, 412, 419, 423, 426, 429, 436, 438, 449, 453, 454, 455, 461, 462, 465, 466, 474, 483, 491, 492, 493, 497, 499, 502, 503, 504, 506, 507, 510.

10. Cf. J.M. De Smet, *De Heilige Jan van Waasten en de Gregoriaansche hervorming in het bisdom Terwaan*. Dissertation, Katholieke Universiteit Leuven, 1943; W. Simons, 'Jan van Waasten en de Gregoriaanse hervorming', *De Franse Nederlanden. Les Pays-Bas Français*, XI (1986), p. 191-213; W. Simons, 'Jean de Warneton et la Réforme grégorienne', *Memoires de la Societé d'Histoire de Comines-Warneton et de la région*, XVII (1987), p. 35-54; H. Platelle, 'Jean de Warneton', DHGE, XXVII (1999), col. 796-798; B. Meijns, *Aken of Jeruzalem? Het ontstaan en de hervorming van de kanonikale instellingen in Vlaanderen tot circa 1155* (Leuven, 2000), II, p. 748-769.

Moreover, some of these charters contain interesting preambles and elaborate *narrationes* in which the bishop explained and justified his acts. There also still exist several diplomatic sources, composed by another issuer, but complete with explicit episcopal confirmation.[11] Finally, there are several letters addressed to John of Thérouanne.[12]

In this article, I would like to examine how the pastoral activities of John of Thérouanne were presented by his biographer, Walter, and to what degree this representation agrees with the facts as we have found them in the other sources concerning this episcopacy. Since a bishop had extensive pastoral duties, I will focus on one aspect, viz. the attitude of the bishop towards the clergy, whose purity he had to protect, and towards the numerous religious institutions in his diocese. There are two reasons for this choice. First of all, Walter, the biographer, himself strongly emphasizes this aspect of pastoral care. Indeed, John of Thérouanne is represented as a good pastor (*bonus pastor*),[13] but even so, it is mainly his concern for a pure clergy, stripped of the impurities of simony, and living according to the spirit of Church reform, which attracts the attention.[14] Only sporadically, references to pastoral care for the faithful are to be found. A pastoral tour is mentioned,[15] as well as the consecration of a cemetery and a confirmation,[16] but these elements are mentioned only in passing, in the margin of the description of a miracle. The bishop

---

11. Bled, *Régestes*, nrs. 379, 381, 388, 389, 392, 425, 446, 459.

12. Bled, *Régestes*, nrs. 414, 433, 441 (Pope Paschal II), nr. 505 (archbishop Rainald of Rheims); *Wolfenbüttler Fragmente. Analekten zur Kirchengeschichte des Mittelalter aus den Wolfenbüttler Handschriften*, M. Sdralek, ed. (Münster, 1891), p. 55-59: nrs. 5 (archbishop Rainald of Rheims), 14, 15, 22, 24, 28 and 31 (Pope Paschal II), 18 (cardinaldeacon John), 32 (archbishop R. of Rheims).

13. On the bishop as a 'good pastor' and his *sollicitudo*, cf. B. Guillemain, 'L'action pastorale des évêques en France aux XIe et XIIe siècles', in: *Le Istituzioni ecclesiastiche della 'Societas Christiana' dei secoli XI-XII. Atti della Settimana internazionale di Studio. Milano 1-7 settembre 1974* (Milan, 1977), p. 117-135; I. van 't Spijker, *Als door een speciaal stempel. Traditie en vernieuwing in heiligenlevens uit Noordwest-Frankrijk (1050-1150)* (Hilversum, 1990), p. 106-135; F. Dolbeau, 'Hagiographie latine et prose rimée: Deux exemples de Vies épiscopales rédigées au XIIe siècle', *Sacris Erudiri*, XXXII (1991), p. 223-268.

14. Walter, *Vita Iohannis*, MGH Scriptores, XV, 2, p. 1145 § 10; cf. *infra*.

15. 'Cum ante 15 fere quam decederet annos sollicitudine pastorali diocesim suam ex more lustraret...': Walter, *Vita Iohannis*, MGH Scriptores, XV, 2, p. 1146 § 12.

16. 'In huiusmodi ergo asylo pontifice cum suo illo frequenti et reverendo comitatu hospitaturo cum ingentem populi turbam tam in ecclesia quam in atrio eius manus impositione et sacri crismatis unctione confirmasset, ut vestimenta mutaret, eo quod cimiterium humandis fidelium corporibus benedicere statuisset, ad hospicium regressus est.': Walter, *Vita Iohannis*, MGH Scriptores, XV, 2, p. 1147 § 12.

is not represented as an zealous preacher,[17] and even when he holds a sermon about despizing worldly goods and longing for heaven while lying on his death bed, his public is limited to a select group of clerics, among whom Walter.[18] Occasionaly, Walter refers to preaching activity. When doing so, he always combines the *predicatio* (*verbum*) with the *actio* or performance of good works (*exemplum*), thus repeatedly mentioning that John was a shining example to all.[19] However, the episcopal *sollicitudo* mainly seems to be aimed at the improvement of the persons responsible for the spread of the faith on a local level. Secondly, the *Gesta* as well as the diplomatic sources focus almost exclusively on John's relationship with the abbeys, collegiate churches and nunneries of his diocese. Here also, scant attention is being paid to the *cura animarum* among ordinary people.

This article consists of three parts. In a first part, I will succinctly situate the passages in which pastoral activities have been described, within the source as a whole. Afterwards, I will analyze the relevant passages, and confront them with the data from the other sources. Finally, I will attempt to explain Walter's choice of presenting things. My final goal will be to discover the biographer's motivation for writing this saint's life.

*
* *

The 'Life of Bishop John of Thérouanne' was recorded in the Fall of 1130, nine months after the bishop had died.[20] This was not the first

---

17. In contrast with the *Gesta Abbatum Sancti Bertini Sithiensium*. This source contains a sermon of bishop John, addressing the monks of Saint-Vaast in Arras and exhorting them to welcome cluniac monks from Saint-Bertin: Simon, *Gesta Abbatum*, MHG Scriptores, XIII, p. 651-652 § 84.

18. 'Totus autem idem sermo de contemptu terrestrium et appetitu caelestium in auribus paucorum religiosorum et spiritualium virorum contextus est. Ubi et me peccatorem, non quidem ex meo merito, sed ut consuetae familiaritatis beneficio, loquenti sibi assidere passus est.': Walter, *Vita Iohannis*, MGH Scriptores, XV, 2, p. 1148 § 13.

19. Regarding his stay in the monastery of regular canons in Mont-Saint-Eloi: '... talis fuit ipsius in monasterio conversatio, ut omnibus prodesse posset et verbo pariter et exemplo.'; About his relationship with the *abbates religiosi*: 'Etenim quaecumque alios ut facerent bona, verbis exhortando monebat, in suis primum operibus faciens realiter ostendebat, quatenus ab eo quod lingua sonabat in predicatione vita non discreparet in actione.'; and concerning the improvement of the clergy of his diocese: 'Alios quoque dioceseos illius clericos latas seculi vias et carnis desideria multis retro temporibus sectatos ad normam recte vivendi reducere laboravit, tam exemplo quam verbo invitatos.': Walter, *Vita Iohannis*, MGH Scriptores, XV, 2, p. 1141 § 3, 1144 § 9 and 1145 §10.

20. 'Sed quoniam in huiusmodi coniectatione novem iam mensibus post eius transitum evolutis neminem eruditorum, vel quia non licuit, vel quia non libuit, id studere cognovi.': Walter, *Vita Iohannis*, MGH Scriptores, XV, 2, p. 1139, prologue.

sample of archdeacon Walter's penmanship. Two years earlier, he had written a saint's life about Count Charles the Good, who had been murdered in the Spring of 1127.[21] However, the 'Life of John of Thérouanne' is approximately only half as long as the *Vita Karoli*. In the edition of the *Monumenta Germaniae Historica*, the text of more than 6600 words has been split up into a prologue and nineteen paragraphs. All the traditional parts of a bishop's biography are present:[22] birth, social descent and youth of the protagonist, education and studies, life and – if any – functions held previously to the appointment to bishop, the actual appointment, the ordination and enthronement in the episcopal see, the prelate's relationship with the Pope, with the metropolitan bishop, with the other bishops and with the clergy of his diocese, and, to conclude, a description of his decease and his funeral. Only four of the nineteen paragraphs (viz. paragraphs 8, 10 and 11 entirely and 9 partly) contain information about pastoral activities. All put together, they comprise only a fourth of the *vita*. This is as much as all passages devoted to the bishop's last days and his funeral.

Apart from the prologue and the final paragraphs, Walter's story is very matter-of-fact, and he pays great attention to the situation within the dioceses of Arras and Thérouanne with regard to Church politics. After having discussed John's appointment to archdeacon of Arras, the biographer goes into the creation of this diocese in 1093, and into the election of its first bishop, Lambert.[23] John's appointment to bishop of Thérouanne, which was fraught with difficulties, is preceded by a description of the deplorable state of the diocese during the previous quarter of a century.[24] Strikingly, the miraculous barely enters into the story. Indeed, there is a miracle story about a collapsing bridge in which everybody, including the bishop, remains unscathed, but Walter spends almost as many words on the description of the local motte-and-bailey castle, as on the accident and its fortuitous ending.[25] The account of an attempt on the life of John of Thérouanne, an attempt that was miraculously foiled, is only the background against which the bishop's appeal to grant the perpetrator forgiveness, resounds.[26] As is the case in so many other saint's

---

21. Walter of Thérouanne, *Vita Karoli comitis Flandriae*, R. Köpke, ed., MGH Scriptores XII (Hannover, 1856), p. 531-561; *Narrative Sources* nr. G010; BHL 1573.
22. Haarländer, *Vitae episcoporum*, p. 465.
23. Walter, *Vita Iohannis*, MGH Scriptores, XV, 2, p. 1141 § 4.
24. Walter, *Vita Iohannis*, MGH Scriptores, XV, 2, p. 1141-1142 § 5.
25. Walter, *Vita Iohannis*, MGH Scriptores, XV, 2, p. 1146-1147 § 12.
26. Walter, *Vita Iohannis*, MGH Scriptores, XV, 2, p. 1146 § 11.

lives, some miracles also occur during the funeral.²⁷ John's face is wonderfully lustrous, and the coffin, a sarcophagus, which first seemed to be too small, afterwards appears to be spacious enough to contain not just one, but three persons.²⁸ Even rarer than references to the miraculous, are references to the laity. Apart from two exceptions,²⁹ no mention is made of the Counts of Flanders, of their spouses or of members of the nobility. This is rather curious, since it becomes clear from the *Gesta Abbatum Sancti Bertini Sithiensium* that the Countess Clementia played an important role in John's appointment to bishop.³⁰ Ordinary people are present only in the miracle story concerning the collapsed bridge, around the bishop's deathbed, and during the funeral.³¹

Let us now have a closer look at the passages devoted to actual pastoral activities. First, Walter sketches the image of a bishop who, right from the beginning of his episcopacy, carefully selects his fellow workers and assigns to them important 'executive' functions.³² The persons whose names Walter mentions are all regular canons, as was the bishop himself; some of them came from other dioceses, like, for instance, Acard from the abbey of Arrouaise in the diocese of Arras and Gerard from the abbey of Saint-Aubert in Cambrai. Some of them, the bishop invests with the dignity of archdeacon, others he put at the head of communities of regular canons in the diocese of Thérouanne. From these communities, John also chooses new 'staff members', such as Herbert and Walter, both of whom are made archdeacon. According to his own words, Walter had spent only thirteen months in the company of the bishop, and he was still very young, when John asked him to succeed to Arnulph as archdeacon.³³ Also according to Walter, the dynamic atmosphere emanating from the

---

27. Cf. P. George, 'Un moine est mort: sa vie commence. Anno 1048 obiit Poppo abbas Stabulensis', *Le Moyen Age. Revue d'Histoire et de Philologie*, CVIII (2002), p. 500.

28. Walter, *Vita Iohannis*, MGH Scriptores, XV, 2, p. 1149 § 14.

29. Count Baldwin V (1035-1067) is mentioned as the founder of the house of secular canons at Lille and his son, Robert I (1071-193), is described as one of the 'persecutors' of the Church of Thérouanne: Walter, *Vita Iohannis*, MGH Scriptores, XV, 2, p. 1140 § 2 and p. 1141 § 5 (Robert).

30. Simon, *Gesta Abbatum*, MGH Scriptores, XV, 2, p. 646-647 § 57.

31. Walter, *Vita Iohannis*, MGH Scriptores, XV, 2, p. 1147 § 12; p. 1148 § 13 and p. 1149 § 14.

32. Walter, *Vita Iohannis*, MGH Scriptores, XV, 2, p., 1143 § 8; Simons, 'Jan van Waasten', p. 202.

33. '... me quoque vere quasi abortivum sibi ascivit, et tredecim fere mensibus secum detento post decessum domni Arnulphi archidiaconi eius curam officii, cum admodum iuvenis essem, contra spem certe meam et omnium fere volutatem, in hoc forte, si dicere audeam, reprehendendus, imposuit.': Walter, *Vita Iohannis*, MGH Scriptores, XV, 2, p. 1144 § 8.

bishop's environment was so intense, that every community of regular canons that lost its abbot, promptly requested that he be replaced by someone from that episcopal entourage.[34]

Walter tells us that John of Thérouanne could also count on the support of many *abbates religiosi*.[35] He mentions abbots of regular chapters, such as Cono of Arrouaise – who became a papal legate – and Bernold of Watten – the oldest foundation of regular canons in the diocese of Thérouanne[36] –, as well as some abbots of Benedictine abbeys, among whom Lambert of Saint-Bertin. They were all zealous advocates of the Gregorian Reform, regardless of their monastic or canonical background. According to the *Gesta Abbatum Sancti Bertini Sithiensium*, John of Thérouanne owed his appointment to bishop to Lambert of Saint-Bertin and to two abbots who are not named (probably the abbots of Ham and Watten).[37] Walter, on the other hand, does mention the intervention of *abbates religiosi* in the selection procedure, but he does not give any names.[38] He suggests that the abbots imitated the pious lifestyle of the bishop.[39] In reality, John rather was a protégé of these abbots, all of whom had to have been older than he was.[40] Fact is, that the *Gesta* as well as the numerous charters contain information that they regularly spent time in each other's company, and that they all supported the reform. Since Walter – in these passages, but also elsewhere – attaches much importance to John's web of personal relationships, cultivated through the years, the entire saint's life more or less reads like a *Who's Who* in reform-minded Flanders and elsewhere.[41]

---

34. 'Sic omnis fere regularium fratrum congregatio, quae illis forte in locis pastore fuisset orbata proprio, de illius precipue domo sibi patrem ordinari optabat.': Walter, *Vita Iohannis*, MGH Scriptores, XV, 2, p. 1144 § 8.
35. Walter, *Vita Iohannis*, MGH Scriptores, XV, 2, p. 1144 § 9.
36. B. Meijns, 'De *pauperes Christi* van Watten. De moeizame beginjaren van de eerste gemeenschap van reguliere kanunniken in Vlaanderen (voor 1072-ca. 1100)', in: *Jaarboek voor middeleeuwse geschiedenis*, III (2000), p. 44-91.
37. Simon, *Gesta Abbatum*, MGH Scripters, XIII, p. 646-647 § 56.
38. 'Sed abbates religiosi cum nulli duarum electionum prebuissent assensum, domui Dei, cuius aestuabant zelo, dispensatorem ordinari cupientes idoneum...': Walter, *Vita Iohannis*, MGH Scriptores, XV, 2, p. 1142 § 5.
39. 'Preterea multi abbates religiosi ei frequentissime adherebant, qui zelum Dei habentes, ex ipsius imitatione proficere gestiebant.': Walter, *Vita Iohannis*, MGH Scriptores, XV, 2, p. 1144 § 9.
40. Simons, 'Jan van Waasten', 202 and 211.
41. Walter, *Vita Iohannis*, MGH Scriptores, XV, 2, p. 140 § 1 (Lambert of Utrecht and Ivo, later bishop of Chartres, the *magistri* of John); p. 1141 § 4 (the archdeacons of Arras who also became bishops: Clarembald of Senlis and Robert of Arras); p. 1142 § 5 (Pope Urban II), p. 1143 § 6 (John's colleagues on the (arch)episcopal sees: archbishops

After having praised John for his puntual presence at the canonical hours, Walter finally pays some attention to the clergy and religious institutions.[42] First of all, he discusses the reconstruction of the cathedral of Thérouanne, an activity which is confirmed by the *Gesta* of Simon of Saint-Bertin.[43] John's resolute refusal to levy certain taxes which bishops usually imposed is also mentioned in Simon's *Gesta*.[44] However, the lionshare of Walter's attention in that particular paragraph goes to the world of the canons. Apparently, John helped clerics of irreproachable character who held no fixed appointment in a church to obtain a prebend, at the cathedral's expense. Those who had strayed from the straight and narrow and who did not respect celibacy, were inspired by his word as well as by his example to mend their ways. Wherever he encountered clerics who had been tainted by 'the pest of simony', he made great effort to remedy the situation. Walter offers two examples, viz. the abbeys of Saint-Martin at Ypres and Notre-Dame at Voormezele. Both times, the bishop reformed a secular collegiate church into a community of regular canons.[45] The bishop's course of action was completely in keeping with the contents of the charters which the prelate had drafted at those occasions.[46] Usually, recalcitrant canons were dispersed and sent to different houses, and reform-minded clerics were sent for to populate the new community.[47] It is no coincidence that the reformation of the abbey of Saint-Martin at Ypres is discussed at great length, since Walter probably originated from this abbey, and since the local abbot, Gerard, was one of the

---

Hugo of Lyon, Manasses of Rheims, bishops Ivo of Chartres, Lambert of Arras, Odo of Cambrai, Walo of Paris and Godfrey of Amiens); 1144 § 8 (the bishop's fellow workers: Acard and Richard from Arrouaise, Gerard from Saint-Aubert in Cambrai, canon Herbert from Voormezele, abbot Gerard of Lo and, of course, archdeacon Walter) p. 1144 § 9 (the *abbates religiosi*: Cono of Preneste, abbot of Arrouaise who became papal legate, Lambert from Saint-Bertin, Bernard of Watten, Gerard of Ham, Hugo, abbot of Reading and later bishop of Rouen), p. 1146 § 11 (Pope Paschal II).

42. Walter, *Vita Iohannis*, MGH Scriptores, XV, 2, p. 1144-145 § 9-10.
43. 'Cuius memoriam in benedictione licet commendandam non suscepimus, illa illum in reaedificanda propria ecclesia...': Simon, *Gesta Abbatum*, MGH Scriptores, XIII, p. 647 § 58.
44. 'Bannos vel emendationes de forisfacturis vix aliquando suscepit, cum alii prelati ambiant, anxie petant, extorqueant et, cum non datur quantum volunt, insaniant.': Simon, *Gesta Abbatum*, MGH Scriptores, XIII, p. 647 § 57.
45. 'Testatur quod loquor ecclesia Iprensis, testatur Formosellensis, illas videlicet de manibus pervasorum, huius hereseos canonico iudicio convictorum, ereptas; illis enim de ecclesia, quam per simoniam sibi comparaverant, eliminatis, vineam dominicam aliis locavit agricolis.': Walter, *Vita Iohannis*, MGH Scriptores, XV, 2, p. 1145 § 10.
46. Meijns, *Aken of Jeruzalem*, p. 751-753 (Voormezele) and p. 756-762 (Ypres).
47. Meijns, *Aken of Jeruzalem*, p. 767-769.

bishop's closest co-workers.[48] However, Walter apparently 'forgot' how much effort it had taken to reform the Ypres abbey, and how vehemently the secular canons had opposed its reform, since he does not mention the pope's intervention at all, even though the matter could not have been resolved without it.[49] Walter, furthermore, emphasizes the lasting results of the episcopal activities: the regular canons there were still living as a community according to the Rule of Saint Augustine. The paragraph ends with a general reference to seven or more communities of monks or regular canons founded by John of Thérouanne.[50] In the next paragraph, he adds to this piece of information by mentioning how hard the bishop worked to have each of his foundations confirmed by the pope.[51] This posed no problem, since – according to Walter – John was a very close friend of Pope Paschal II, so that he received from the pope everything he asked for.

The reference to the speedy obtaining of a papal confirmation bull may fit the surviving charters,[52] but this does not alter the fact that Walter offers us an incomplete and one-sided view of John's relationship with the religious communities within his diocese. However, Walter is right when he talks about the crucial part the bishop played in creating communities of regular canons. It is John's merit that Thérouanne became one of the leading dioceses with regard to canonical reform in Flanders.[53] Indeed, it becomes clear from several charters to what degree the bishop exerted himself to reform collegiate churches, where secular canons lived moderate lives, into communities of regular canons who vowed to lead

---

48. Walter calls abbot Gerard from Saint-Martin in Ypres his *magister*: '... domnus quoque Gerardus, vir per omnia religiosus, ecclesiae sancti Autberti Cameracensis canonicus, ab ipso postea in monasterio Iprensi primus abbas ordinatus, magister meus...': Walter, *Vita Iohannis*, MGH Scriptores, XV, 2, p. 1144 § 8.

49. Meijns, *Aken of Jeruzalem*, p. 756-762; M. Carnier, 'Jan van Waasten en de hervorming van het Ieperse kapittel', in: W. Verbeke, M. Haverals, R. De Keyser en J. Goossens, red., *Serta devota in memoriam Guillelmi Lourdaux. Pars posterior: cultura mediaevalis*, Mediaevalia Lovaniensia, I, 16 (Leuven, 1995), p. 57-64.

50. 'Alia subinde septem vel eo amplius monasteria diversis locis instituit et congregationes monachorum sive clericorum secundum regulam apostolorum vivere proponentium per singula disposuit.': Walter, *Vita Iohannis*, MGH Scriptores, XV, 2, p. 1145 § 10.

51. 'Sane apud beatae memoriae Paschalem papam tantam obtinuerat familiaritatem, ut eum inter carissimos semper habuerit. Itaque toto papatus eius tempore, quicquid ab illa petisset sede, sine aliqua obtinuit difficultate. Privilegia ergo monasteriis, quae ipse fundaverat, idem papa eius interventu largitus est.': Walter, *Vita Iohannis*, MGH Scriptores, XV, 2, p. 1145 § 11.

52. Meijns, *Aken of Jeruzalem*, p. 769.

53. Meijns, *Aken of Jeruzalem*, p. 914-915; Meijns, 'L'ordre canonial dans le comté de Flandre depuis l'époque mérovingienne jusqu'à 1155', *Revue d'Histoire ecclésiastique*, XCVII (2002), p. 55.

lives of personal poverty, chastity and community.⁵⁴ In total, the bishop was personally involved in the reformation of eight houses of canons in his own diocese, viz. Notre-Dame at Voormezele (1100), Saint-Pierre at Lo (1100), Saint-Martin at Ypres (1102), Saint-Wulmer in Boulogne (c.1108-1113), Notre-Dame at Chocques (1120), Saint-Nicolas at Furnes (1120), Notre-Dame in Ruisseauville (1127) and Notre-Dame in Boulogne (1129), and of the secular chapter of Saint-Christophe at Phalempin in the neighbouring diocese of Tournai (1108). But the charters and Simon's *Gesta* furthermore show that John of Thérouanne was also favourably disposed towards the Benedictines. During the first decennia of the twelfth century, four nunneries were founded in his diocese, by – amongst others – the Countess Clementia of Flanders (Bourbourg, 1103) and the Counts of Guînes (Guînes, 1117). Each time, the bishop was involved.⁵⁵ Moreover, he was a zealous advocate of reform within the Benedictine abbeys through the introduction of Cluniac customs, without completely incorporating the abbeys in question within the Cluny congregation.⁵⁶ The Countess Clementia and abbot Lambert of Saint-Bertin supported him in this endeavour. As a result, Cluniac practices were introduced into the Saint-Bertin abbey, in the abbeys of Bergues-Saint-Winoc and Auchy in his own diocese and into the abbeys of Saint-Vaast in Arras and Saint-Pierre in Ghent. The more eremitical movement within monasticism also enjoyed his support, witness the dedication of the little church of Ten Duinen on the Flemish coastal plain, which would join the order of Cîteaux after the bishop had died.⁵⁷ Moreover, it becomes clear from the nearly forty episcopal charters how strongly the religious institutions of his diocese – regardless of their belonging to the canonical or the monastic order – could count on the generosity of the

---

54. For instance his charter in favour of the house of Voormezele (1103): *Chronicon Vormeselense*, F. Van de Putte en C. Carton, eds. (Bruges, 1900), p. 31 nr. IX or his confirmation of the regular canons at Lo (1100): *Cartulaire de l'abbaye de Saint-Pierre de Loo de l'ordre de Saint-Augustin (1093-1794)*, L. Van Hollebeke, ed. (Brussels, 1870), p. 1-2 nr. I.

55. Cf. N. Huyghebaert, 'Abbaye de Saint-Pierre et de Notre-Dame à Merkem' and 'Abbaye de Sainte-Marie à Nonnenbossche', in: *Monasticon Belge III. Province de Flandre occidentale*, I (Liège, 1960), p. 284-285 and 273-274; G. Michels, 'Guines', DHGE, XXII (1988), col. 1099-1100; P. Schmitz, 'Bourbourg', DHGE, X (1938), col. 137-141.

56. L. Milis, 'De Kerk tussen de Gregoriaanse hervorming en Avignon', in: *Algemene Geschiedenis der Nederlanden* (Haarlem, 1982), II, p. 177-178; Simons, 'Jan van Waasten', p. 203-205.

57. Milis, 'De Kerk', p. 181; Simons, 'Jan van Waasten', p. 205; M. Dubuisson, J.-B. Lefèvre and J.-Fr. Nieus, 'Une lecture nouvelle des sources relatives aux origines précisterciennes et cisterciennes de l'abbaye des Dunes (1107-1138)', *Revue d'Histoire ecclésiastique*, XCVII (2002), p. 59-88 and 457-494.

bishop or on his intervention as *ordinarius*.⁵⁸ Also Simon, in his *Gesta Abbatum Sancti Bertini Sithiensium*, had an eye for the varied relationships between the bishop and the communities of canons, monks or nuns.⁵⁹ Archdeacon Walter, however, dismisses the matter exceptionally fast by summarizing the varied pastoral activities in one short sentence mentioning the foundation of 'seven or more' monasteries.⁶⁰

How can we explain this overemphasis on the role of regular canons and the striking underexposure of the monastic in Walter's account? The fact that the author was restricted in his movements to a certain area undoubtedly played an important role. Walter himself was a regular canon from one of the collegiate churches which were reformed by John of Thérouanne. From the moment of his appointment to archdeacon in 1117, he worked with the bishop for years, and with the other regular canons in his entourage. It was from this environment that the impulses to reform canonical life came. Moreover, canons incited Walter to write the *vita*. The *fratres* to whom Walter repeatedly refers can probably be identified with the cathedral canons.⁶¹ These canons and their dean Gozlin had asked Walter to write a *Vita Karoli* two years before,⁶² a work which he dedicated to John of Thérouanne.⁶³ Even though these were traditional,

---

58. Beneficiaries of episcopal charters are the following religious institutions in the diocese of Thérouanne. Houses of regular canons: Lo (2), Watten (1), Ypres (2), Saint-Nicolas at Furnes (1), Chocques (1), Voormezele (2), Saint-Wulmer in Boulogne (1), Notre-Dame in Boulogne (1), Ruisseauville (1); Secular collegiate churches: Saint-Walburge at Furnes (3), Nunneries: Bourbourg (1), Nonnenbossche (1); Benedictine abbeys: Saint-Bertin and its priories (11), Anchin and its priory at Hesdin (1), Samer (2), Auchy (4), Andres (3), Bergues-Saint-Winoc (1).

59. 'Nam apud Lo, Eversham, Ypres regulares constituit [canonicos], et suo tempore apud Broburg, Gisnes, Merchem sanctimoniales constitutae sunt. Nobis [the monks of Saint-Bertin] vero altare de Merchem, de Eggafridicapella, de Warnestun, de Haveskerke sub cartarum allegatione et multa alia bona contulit': Simon, *Gesta Abbatum*, MGH Scriptores, XV, 2, p. 647 § 58.

60. Cf. *supra*, n. 50; There is no mention at all of the foundation of nunneries.

61. 'Quod quidem ut aggrediar opus, tum ille, quo eundem Dei servum ardentissime dilexi, suasit caritatis affectus, tum etiam nonnulli ex fratribus importunis admodum precibus et innumeris me impulerunt hortatibus.' and 'Quod certe ideo quam maxime facio, quatenus et in presenti pio fratrum meorum paream desiderio...': Walter, *Vita Iohannis*, MGH Scriptores, XV, 2, p. 1139, prologue.

62. 'Accessit etiam vestre iussioni domni Gozelini decani et fratrum nostrorum amica mihi et omni cum honore semper suscipienda peticio, cui in cunctis Deo placitis optemperare ferventi opto desiderio.': Walter, *Vita Karoli*, MGH Scriptores, XII, p. 538, prologue.

63. 'Domino suo et patri merito sanctitatis totius reverentia devotionis excolendo, Iohanni, sancte Teruanensis ecclesie episcopo, frater Walterus, dignationis eius inutilis servus, debitum omnimode subiectionis obsequium.': Walter, *Vita Karoli*, MGH Scriptores, XII, p. 537, prologue.

secular canons, we can assume that John of Thérouanne paid close attention to the way they lived and to whether or not they were familiar with the *vita apostolica* of their regular colleagues. Even so, Walter had to have been perfectly acquainted with the many contacts John of Thérouanne had with the non-canonical institutions within his diocese. Indeed, while being archdeacon, Walter signed numerous charters destined for Benedictine monasteries and nunneries.[64] Supposedly, he even actively took part in bringing about the juridical transactions confirmed in the charters. Moreover, Walter twice mentions that there was much more he could have told us about John of Thérouanne.[65] However, instead of actually doing so, he purposely selects some of the bishop's diverse activities. In all probability, this selection was made on the basis of his intentions in writing this *vita*.

Judging by the stresses laid by Walter, I assume that the 'Life of Bishop John of Thérouanne' was intended to underscore the ideals of the regular canons.[66] The angle offered in the life of bishop John was ideal for this purpose. Not only was the bishop responsible for the large-scale introduction of the canonical reform in his diocese and even outside of it, but he himself had been a regular canon in the abbey of Mont-Saint-Eloi near Arras.[67] Moreover, he had remained a regular canon during his episcopacy, as becomes abundantly clear from different passages in the *vita*. John remained resolutely constant to the ideals of apostolic poverty, celibacy and renunciation of the world, even though this ascetic mentality occasionally clashed with his duties as a bishop. In the *vita*, some inarticulate tensions become visible between the *sollicitudo* of the

---

64. Walter, *Vita Iohannis*, MGH Scriptores, XV, 2, p. 1136 n. 8 and 9.

65. 'Quas provincias ob studium peregrinando perlustraverit, quas urbes adierit, quos preceptores audierit, esuriendo, sitiendo, algendo, dies et noctes plerumque vigiliis continuando, dum videlicet diebus legeret et noctibus scriberet, non est nostrae facultatis evolvere.' and 'Vellem autem diutius immorari tantarum contemplationi virtutum, sed vereor, ne lectio, si prolixa fuerit, nimium lectori, ut assolet, pariat fastidium.': Walter, *Vita Iohannis*, MGH Scriptores, XV, 2, p. 1140 § 1 and p. 1146 § 13.

66. In contrast with the opinion of Deploige, 'Intériorisation religieuse', 825: 'Sa vie de Jean apparaît alors comme une dernière tentative pour restaurer l'influence de son maître regretté.' On the way of life of the regular canons: C. Dereine, 'Chanoines', DHGE, XII (1951), col. 375-395; C.W. Bynum, 'The spirituality of the Regular Canons in the Twelfth Century', in: *Jesus as Mother: Studies in the Spirituality of the High Middle Ages* (Berkeley-Los Angeles-London, 1982), p. 21-58; L. Milis, 'Van vrije kluizenaars tot georganiseerde kanunniken. Een spirituele evolutie in de Hoge Middeleeuwen', *Trajecta. Tijdschrift voor de geschiedenis van het katholiek leven in de Nederlanden*, VI (1997), p. 305-317.

67. Walter, *Vita Iohannis*, MGH Scriptores, XV, 2, p. 1140 § 3; On the house of regular canons of Mont-Saint-Eloi: Meijns, *Aken of Jeruzalem*, p. 719-728.

energetic bishop who does not shrink hard work, and the *renunciatio* of the regular canon. Three years before his death, the prelate's ascetic way of life had weakened him to the point that he could hardly walk, let alone celebrate mass.[68] A papal legate who visited him ordered him to, henceforth, eat meat once in a while. Walter tells us how John's time-consuming duties as a bishop did never prevent him to faithfully attend all canonical hours, even those celebrated in the dead of night.[69] Many canons could pattern themselves on their bishop, if only in this respect. This imitation was precisely what Walter's narrative was all about, a fact which he mentions repeatedly in its prologue, as well as at the end.[70] I suppose that the *vita* was primarily intended for a canonical public: the cathedral canons of Thérouanne, whose duty it was to watch over the memory of the bishop who lay buried in their church, but also the numerous canons who had come to the diocese of Thérouanne thanks to John. Walter's account emphasizes those aspects of bishop John's life that were important to regular canons: apostolic poverty, communal life, a puntual attendance at choral prayer and the renunciation of all worldly pleasures.[71] Indeed, as Walter's description of the worldly canons of the comital chapter of Lille indicates, these were not activities in which secular canons excelled.[72] John had been a canon there for a while, but he quickly traded this kind of existence for the asceticism of Augustine's rule in Mont-Saint-Eloi.[73] That the *vita* was intended for a canonical public also becomes clear, to some extent, from Simon's *Gesta Abbatum Sancti Bertini Sithiensium*. Simon describes how the memory of that

---

68. Walter, *Vita Iohannis*, MGH Scriptores, XV, 2, p. 1143 § 7.
69. Walter, *Vita Iohannis*, MGH Scriptores, XV, 2, p. 1444-1145 § 9.
70. '... si vitam viri venerandi, et qui merito censeatur imitandus, describendo ad multorum profectum in medio protulero.' and 'Expectet autem mercedem a Deo, non quicumque legendo scrutatus, sed quicumque agendo ea fuerit imitatus.': Walter, *Vita Iohannis*, MGH Scriptores, XV, 2, p. 1139 prologue. '... ipsa docente satis clareret talem virum non tam lamentatione quam imitatione prosequendum, qui dum sic coram nobis ambulavit, quod eum sequi debeamus, manifeste monstravit.': Walter, *Vita Iohannis*, MGH Scriptores, XV, 2, p. 1150 § 19.
71. Walter, *Vita Iohannis*, MGH Scriptores, XV, 2, p. 1140-1141 § 2-3 (renunciation of worldly pleasures, Rule of Saint-Augustine), p. 1143 (abstinence), p. 1145 § 9 (choral prayer), p. 1147 § 13 (imitation of Christ, apostolic poverty).
72. 'Cum enim illi vanitates intenderent et spectacula vel ludicra spectarent vel aliis ipsi ludendo spectanda preberent, ipse caelestibus magis quam intentus terrenis, lectioni vel orationi vacans, in conclavi residebat et nusquam [nisi], cum ad ecclesiam foret prodeundum, procedebat.': Walter, *Vita Iohannis*, MGH Scriptores, XV, 2, p. 1140 § 2.
73. 'Nam, quia beati Augustini regulam ipse in eodem monasterio observabat suisque imposuerat observandam, eius religionem et prudentiam non mediocriter sibi in hoc opere arbitratus est necessariam.': Walter, *Vita Iohannis*, MGH Scriptores, XV, 2, p. 1140 § 3.

extraordinary bishop was kept alive through his works (*viva operum testimonia*) because documents (*littera*) were absent.⁷⁴ A few years after the composition of the *vita* by Walter, the monks of the abbey of Saint-Omer, barely six miles from Thérouanne, apparently had not yet heard about it.

*
* *

In his 'Deeds of the Abbots of Saint-Bertin', Simon tells us the following story.⁷⁵ One day, the regular canons of Watten built a mill between their abbey and Vieux Monastère, property of Saint-Bertin. Since the construction seriously prejudiced the abbey's interests, abbot Lambert decided to broach the subject with John of Thérouanne. But the abbot sensed that the bishop would hardly be favourably inclined towards him, because the prelate was a regular canon, as were the brothers of Watten.⁷⁶ Because of this, Lambert appealed to the Count of Flanders, who did favour the monks of Saint-Bertin, and, eventually, the count ordered the construction of the mill to be stopped. There is no doubt at all that the regular canons were very near to John of Thérouanne's heart, he himself being a regular canon. Notwithstanding this, it becomes clear from his activities as a bishop, that this sympathy for the canons was not at the expense of the monks or the nuns in his diocese. Indeed, Simon most likely was mistaken to represent John of Thérouanne as being prejudiced. This characterization could probably better be applied to Walter, John's biographer. As archdeacon, he must have been familiar with the diverse pastoral activities of his bishop. Nevertheless, his attention almost exclusively goes to the episcopal efforts in favour of regular canons. Most probably, the latter were the intended public for the saint's life. The *vita* not only offered them an explanation for their existence in Thérouanne, but also gave them a spiritual footing. Now that their great patron had passed away and now that the institutions had to continue without his watchful eye, the canons could draw courage and inspiration from the 'Life of Bishop John of Thérouanne'.

74. 'In qua quem qualemque se per continuos 30 annos exhibuerit, littera non docet, sed viva operum testimonia hodieque probant.': Simon, *Gesta Abbatum*, MGH Scriptores, XIII, p. 647 § 58.
75. Simon, *Gesta Abbatum*, MGH Scriptores, XIII, p. 650 § 75.
76. 'Quod audiens pater Lambertus ... illosque constanter Taruennae coram episcopo Iohanne aggrediens, dum sensit eundem presulem egre sibi favere, quia eiusdem ordinis erant ipse et ipsi, ad comitem se convertit eiusque auctoritate inceptum opus cessare fecit...': Simon, *Gesta Abbatum*, MGH Scriptores, XIII, 2, p. 650 § 75.

Michael GOODICH

MICROHISTORY AND THE *INQUISITIONES* INTO THE LIFE AND MIRACLES OF PHILIP OF BOURGES AND THOMAS OF HEREFORD

In recent years, due to the greater availability of electronic databases and sets of machine readable sources, medievalists have begun to follow their colleagues in modern history by employing quantitative data as the underpinnings of historical inquiry. Such economic and social historians as Herlihy, Razi, and Klapisch, for example, have led the way through the study of tax, court and parish records.[1] Even a theme such as medieval suicide, recently studied by Alexander Murray, has rendered itself accessible to quantification.[2] Back in the halcyon sixties, when the use of computers for historical research was still in its infancy and a bent, spindled, mutilated or misplaced punch card could endanger days of research, I myself hesitatingly used quantification for the study of over five hundred thirteenth century saints.[3] With the creation of the *Patrologia Latina* and the forthcoming *Acta Sanctorum* databases, other students of medieval hagiography may be about to move away from the study of a few select sources in order to understand prevailing mentalities in the history of Christianity in favor of inquiries based on the search of key terms in such databases. For example, a search under the key words *puer*, *adolescentia* and *infans* may enhance our understanding of the affective history of childhood. Furthermore, the publication of critical editions from manuscripts may be greatly assisted through the greater ease in identifying sources. For example, I have recently been slowly undertaking a critical edition of the thus far unpublished treatise by the Austrian scholastic Engelbert of Admont (d. 1331), *De miraculis Christi* (ca. 1287), which attempts to provide a rational Aristotelian explanation for the miraculous.[4] The new

---

1. David Herlihy and Christiane Klapisch, *Les toscanes et leurs familles* (Paris, 1978); Zvi Razi, *Life, Marriage and Death in a Medieval Parish* (Cambridge, 1980).
2. Alexander Murray, *Suicide in the Middle Ages. Volume I. The Violent against Themselves* (Oxford, 1999), 348-422.
3. Michael Goodich, *Vita Perfecta: the Ideal of Sainthood in the Thirteenth Century*, in *Monographien zur Geschichte des Mittelalters*, 25 (Stuttgart, 1982).
4. Michael Goodich, 'A Chapter in the History of the Christian Theology of Miracle: Engelbert of Admont's (ca. 1250-1331) *Expositio super Psalmum 118* and *De miraculis*

Patrologia database has greatly facilitated identifying Engelbert's citations of Augustine, Ambrose, Hugh of St. Victor and others; although considerable textual variants and the author's apparent tendency to quote from memory, especially Scripture, does not always make use of the *Patrologia* edition practical.

Nevertheless, at the very moment when such new tools may considerably ease the task of the cliometrician or prosopographer, more historians are becoming disillusioned with the ongoing romance our discipline has carried out with the social sciences. The drop in the enrollment of students in traditional departments of history in favor of sociology, communications and computer science, may have also encouraged us to rethink the nature of our discipline and our unique access to the past. The baffling abstraction, quantification and attachment to theory with which we have been confronted have led to a genuine longing for a more personal relationship with persons in the past. Some of us, like Natalie Davis and Carlo Ginzburg, have therefore begun to prefer the microhistorical study of one family or community and the close observation of one individual instead of the accumulation of raw data as a more authentic way of appreciating the past.[5] Despite our ideological doubts about overstressing the impact of one person in history, Eileen Power's classic *Medieval People*, which relied largely on narrative rather than diplomatic sources, still remains the kind of volume that can bring the middle ages alive to students through its elegant style and focus on the individual.[6] But rather than focusing on the Carlylean great man or woman in history, those of us who call ourselves social historians (following the call by Lucien Febvre and Marc Bloch to write 'history from below') prefer to chronicle the traumas, life changes, and personal prejudices of formerly anonymous folk drawn from the urban and peasant classes, who had been marginalized in earlier works, rather than the careers of members of the nobility or clerical hierarchy.

Christi', in Michael Goodich et al., eds., *Cross-Cultural Convergences in the Crusader Period. Essays Presented to Aryeh Grabois on his Sixty-Fifth Birthday* (New York, 1995), 89-110 for an edition of part of this source.

5. Edward Muir and Guido Ruggiero, eds., *Microhistory and the Lost Peoples of Europe*, trans. Eren Branch (Baltimore, 1991) contains articles taken from the *Quaderni storici* written by microhistorians, along with a valuable introduction by Muir entitled 'Observing Trifles' (pp. vii-xxviii); see also Carlo Ginzburg, *The Cheese and the Worms*, trans. John and Anne Tedeschi (London, 1980); Natalie Z. Davis, *Women on the Margins* (Cambridge, Mass., 1995); Jacques Revel, 'Micro-analyse et construction du social', in Jacques Revel, ed., *Jeux d'échelles. La micro-analyse à l'expérience* (Paris, 1996), 15-36.

6. Eileen Power, *Medieval People*, 10th ed. (New York, 1963).

CANONIZATION INQUISITIONES

This contribution proposes to focus on two miracles found in canonization *inquisitiones*, a form of judicial inquiry that assists in the reconstruction of the spiritual world of such otherwise inaccessible folk. Such legal sources often served as the foundation for narrative biography and hagiography. These documents give voice to the experiences of the members of all social classes, male and female, rural and urban. As Edward Muir has remarked:

> 'If documents generated by the forces of authority systematically distort the social reality of the subaltern classes, then an exceptional document, especially one that records the exact words of a lower-class witness or defendant, could be much more revealing than a stereotypical source.'[7]

Narrative hagiography in the middle ages is filled with stereotypical *topoi*, typically drawn from Scripture, early Christian hagiography, and even pagan sources. Nevertheless, in the absence of sources produced by the 'subaltern classes', saints' lives and miracle collections are often the sole documentation which may inform us about the lives of the unlettered; and following the introduction of papal canonization, such narrative sources were often based on such judicial material.[8]

Medieval biographies and miracle stories often contain both direct and indirect quotation of the words of persons who had experienced the supernatural. These words were not always the invention of the author. Jolles and Boureau, among others, have noted a direct textual link between the testimony at canonization hearings and the narrative biographies they produced, in addition to the summarized *legendae* and even the *Sermones de sanctis* which brought the saints' lives to a wider public.[9] The Dominican Bernard Gui (d. 1331), for example, in his unpublished *Sanctorale* relied directly on the canonization protocols of Louis IX and Thomas Aquinas.[10] This well-known inquisitor and author of a guide for inquisitors, was himself a witness at Thomas Aquinas' canonization trial. He

---

7. Muir, *op. cit.*, xvi.
8. Early examples are the *Vita Stephani* by Stephan de Liciaco and the *De revelatione beati Stephani*, dealing with Stephen of Grandmont (d. 1124), canonized in 1189. See Jean Becquet, ed., *Scriptores ordinis Grandimontensis*, in *Corpus christianorum. Continuatio mediaevalis*, 7 (Turnhout, 1968).
9. André Jolles, *Einfache Formen* (Halle, 1930), 19-49; Alain Boureau, *La legende dorée. Le système narratif de Jacques de Voragine* (Paris, 1984), 4, 213-4.
10. Bernard Gui, *Sanctorale*, in MS *Bibliothèque Nationale* (hereafter *BN*) *Lat.* 5406, 46^r-55^r, 152^r-155^v, *BN Lat.* 5407, 48^v-58^v, 152^r-155^v, 132ra-144vb.

then composed a biography of the saint, which was followed by the summarized life and miracles found in his *Sanctorale*.[11] Likewise the *Collationes* of Pope Clement VI (d. 1352) cite directly from the protocols of Aquinas, Louis of Toulouse, Louis IX and Yves of Tréguier.[12] The narrative life of Bishop Richard of Chichester (d. 1253) by the Dominican Ralph Bocking clearly quotes the canonization trial directly, although the original hearing is not extant.[13] It may even be possible to partially reconstruct the hearing on the basis of the narrative biography. By imposing the standard questions raised at a canonization inquiry onto the text of the biography, one may break down the life into the answers provided to this series of questions, thereby laying the groundwork for the trial's partial reconstruction.

The inquisitorial procedure was applied to the investigation of heresy and canonization in the late twelfth century, and appears to have attained its permanent form under Innocent III.[14] This parallels its use in the post mortem investigation of suspicious death by the English coroner. A series of standard questions was posed to the witnesses, attempting to determine the 'who, what, why, when, where and how' of the event, the so-called *articuli interrogatorii*.[15] In the face of doubts concerning Christian miracles voiced by heretics, Jews, some scholastic philosophers, and

---

11. For Gui's work as a historian and hagiographer see Bernhard Schimmelpfennig, 'Bernard Gui: Hagiograph und verhinderter Heiliger', in Dieter R. Bauer and Klaus Herbers, eds., *Hagiographie im Kontext. Wirkungsweisen und Möglichkeiten historischer Auswertung* (Stuttgart, 2000), 257-65; Bernard Guenée, 'Bernard Gui', in *Entre l'Église et l'État. Quatre vies de prélats français à la fin du Moyen Âge (xiie-xve siècle)* (Paris, 1987), 49-85; Anne-Marie Lamarrigue, *Bernard Gui (1261-1331), un historien et sa méthode*, Etudes d'histoire médiévale, 5 (Paris, 2000).

12. *Sermones Clementi VII*, in MS Bibliothèque Ste. Geneviève 240, 397^v-403^v, 201^v-271^v, 26^r-41^v, 193^r-201^v; see Philibert Schmitz, 'Les sermons et discours de Clément VI, O.S.B.', *Revue bénédictine*, 41 (1929), 15-34; G. Mollat, 'L'oeuvre oratoire de Clément VI', *Archives d'histoire doctrinale et littéraire du moyen âge*, 3 (1928), 239-74.

13. Ralph Bocking, *Vita et Miracula S. Ricardi*, in *Acta sanctorum*, ed. Socii Bollandiani, 68 vols. to date (Paris, 1863-1940), 3 April I: 282-315; David Jones, ed., *Saint Richard of Chichester. The Sources for his Life*, in *Sussex Record Society*, 79 (1993). There are two recensions, MS *Royal Library in Brussels* 2057-63, on which the Bollandist edition is based, and a British Library manuscript (*Sloane* 1772).

14. Raoul Naz, 'Inquisitio', in *Dictionnaire de droit canonique*, 7 vols. (Paris, 1935-65), V, 1418-26; André Vauchez, *La sainteté en occident aux derniers siècles du moyen âge d'après les procès de canonisation et les documents hagiographiques* (Rome, 1981), 42-7; R. Klauser, 'Zur Entwicklung des Heiligsprechungverfahrens bis zum 13. Jahrhundert', *Zeitschrift der Savigny-Stiftung für Rechtsgeschichte. Kanonistische Abteilung*, 40 (1954), 101.

15. Ludwig Hertling, 'Materiali per la storia del processo di canonizazzione', *Gregorianum*, 16 (1935), 170-195 for the early use of the *articuli* in the case of Hildegard of Bingen in 1233 under Gregory IX.

wavering Christians, the central issue raised by the investigators was whether magical means had been employed and whether the faith had been strengthened in the performance of the miracle. As contemporary theologians such as Albertus Magnus, Thomas Aquinas and Engelbert of Admont argued, the performance of such miracles by proven pious believers was regarded as the firmest guarantee of the truth of the faith. The presence of trained theologians in the commission of inquiry insured that orthodoxy would be guarded; and the use of notaries and canon lawyers trained in the rules of evidence would guarantee that reliable court procedure would be applied.

Two cases drawn from the dossiers of Bishop Thomas of Hereford (d. 1282) and Archbishop Philip Berruyer of Bourges (d. 1261) will be treated here. Both took place after the procedures in the conduct of such inquiries had been perfected in the mid-thirteenth century, following Gregory IX's codification of canon law and its application to such inquiries. Thomas's canonization trial was conducted in London and Hereford in 1307 under Clement V by the influential theologian William Durand, bishop of Mende (in southern France), the papal nuncio in England William of Festa, and Ralph Baldock, bishop of London.[16] In Philip of Bourges' case, King Louis IX and the French bishops petitioned the pope for its opening.[17] It was heard in 1265/6 under Popes Urban IV and Clement IV at Beaugency (where Philip had served as archdeacon), Bourges and Orléans (where he had served as bishop) by Peter de Minci, bishop of Chartres and Robert de Marzy, bishop of Nevers and the Dominican prior of Paris, assisted by the Dominican prior of Bourges.[18]

Although Philip's case was re-examined on several occasions, the first to undertake a thorough review of the case was Odo of Châteauroux, cardinal-bishop of Tusculum, at the order of Clement IV. In Philip's dossier, forty-three miracles were recorded. In Thomas's case the postulator or his chief 'defender' was Henry de Schorne, a canon of Hereford cathedral and Oxford doctor of canon law. Thomas of Hereford's dossier, which is the fullest to survive from the medieval period and is supported by a large number of corroborating documents, encompasses over three hundred

---

16. *Processus canonizationis Thomae de Cantilupo*, in *Acta sanctorum*, 2 October I: 582-696.

17. On Philip, see *Bibliotheca sanctorum*, 12 vols. (Rome, 1980), 3: 87-88; A. Baudrillart, ed., *Dictionnaire d'histoire et de géographie éccésiastiques*, 27 vols. to date (Paris, 1912-1999), 8: 92-98.

18. The history of the procedure is recounted in MS *Vat. Lat.* 4019, 1^r-11^v.

miracles.[19] Two miracles will be examined which were performed on persons of middling or lower social status rather than aristocrats or clergy. In the absence of supporting material, a full life history of the participants is not always possible. The person experiencing the miracle (the *miraculé*), his or her family and neighbors must often remain rather fleeting actors in the drama of medieval piety whose lives are only revealed through the canonization sources; although through the agency of hagiography they are given a historical voice.

Nevertheless, a microhistorical analysis of these miracles represents one way of personalizing the facile generalizations that historians make and allows us to glimpse how such trends find local expression. Formerly anonymous persons, whose lives have often been subsumed under the undifferentiated broad remarks so often made by historians, may be given a face no less complex than those who, because of their literacy or social status have been granted a privileged position. We must however remain aware that the words of the participants reach us through the prejudicial and legalistic intervention of the notaries, theologians, inquisitors, and other persons charged with preparing the dossier. The witnesses did not speak spontaneously, but were rather responding to a series of fixed questions aimed at establishing the reliability of their testimony and supporting the candidate's sanctity. For example, one of the clerks who summarized Philip's case provided a checklist of the contradictions among witnesses to each miracle, attempting to eliminate those cases in which the facts could not be fully verified. Thomas's dossier likewise includes a detailed discussion of twenty-six selected miracles that reflect the curia's effort to find a scientific explanation for each miracle.[20] The gulf that separated the witnesses from the officers of the court is reflected in the fact that in Thomas's dossier, two Franciscans were employed to translate the testimony from Welsh into Latin; while other witnesses spoke French or English, which required translation. The dossier is filled with English words – like wheelbarrow – which are explained for the benefit of the participants.[21]

---

19. These documents are gathered together in MS *Vat. Lat.* 4015, 4016 and 4017.
20. For text see Vauchez, *op. cit.*, 633-47, which is taken from MS *BN Lat.* 5373A, ff. 66^r-69^v.
21. See Christian Krötzl, 'Zur Prozessführung und Zeugeneinvernahmen bei Kanonisationsprozessen', in Bauer and Herbers, *op. cit.*, 84-95.

JEANNE DE CROSSES

The first miracle concerns the demoniac Jeanne Laboysans de Crosses. It is recorded in the Vatican manuscript, Vat. Lat. 4019, a copy of the original non-extant dossier, made at the curia in 1329/31, and also found in B. N. Lat 5373A, fols. 1-65.[22] Regarding this particular miracle, minor differences distinguish the two manuscripts. The miracle occurred on a Monday in January 1263 and was supported through the testimony of twelve persons who testified in late April and late June 1266 at Bourges. These included Jeanne Laboysans, the *miraculée* of the village of Crosses, situated about ten kilometers south of Bourges, her husband Geoffrey, her mother Isabelle, the local curate Robert, and the Benedictine prior Pierre, along with eight others. Pierre took advantage of the opportunity afforded by his appearance in court to report his own miraculous cure from quartan fever. In brief, Jeanne, about thirty at the time of her testimony in 1265, testified that she had suffered from insanity ('alienata a sensa') for seven years, and was paralyzed and unable to walk except with assistance for three years. In order to effect a cure, her mother had taken her to the shrine of St. Étienne at Bourges, where several drops of the first Christian martyr's blood were to be found; and to St. Vrain (Veranus) at Jargeau near Orléans, over a hundred kilometers from Crosses, but without success. Jeanne testified that after this Philip of Bourges appeared to her in a dream ('in sompniis') ordering her to visit his tomb. After her husband and mother each made a vow, she was taken to the tomb, where she made an offering and prayed and, as a result, was cured of her diseases. On the journey home by cart, Jeanne realized for the first time that she was pregnant and became quite distressed. At home she again heard Philip's voice telling her that she would give birth to a daughter without pain. In the course of her labor, she beseeched Philip's aid and gave birth without suffering. As in her earlier cure, Jeanne cites the saint's precise words to her.

Other witnesses provided further information. Unlike the others, however, her husband Geoffrey claimed that her insanity had in fact lasted for ten years and she was unable to walk for seven. When Philip had

---

22. MS *Vat. Lat.* 4019, 56ᵛ-63ᵛ, MS *BN Lat.* 5373A, *Processus supra vita et miraculis domini Philippi archiepiscopi Biturcensis* 16ʳ-19ʳ. In the *BN* manuscript Jeanne's miracle is fully reported. All the others are given in abbreviated form. The *Vat. Lat.* ms. contains a full dossier of all the material. Although it is a copy of the original hearing, it also notes the pagination of the original text.

appeared to Jeanne in a dream, he was identifiable because of his episcopal robes. Geoffrey noted that a year had elapsed between her pregnancy and the complete cure of her lameness. Afterwards she undertook a pilgrimage to the popular shrines of Notre-Dame de Rocamadour and St.-Gilles-du-Gard, near Nîmes. Both were quite a long distance from Bourges, 350 and 500 kilometers respectively. Her mother Isabelle noted that when Jeanne was 'out of her mind' she looked and spoke like a child. She also added that the cures for insanity and lameness each required a separate visit to Philip's tomb. In the course of the vision concerning Jeanne's pregnancy, Philip had been dressed in clerical garb and had said that she would not need a midwife to give birth. The other witnesses essentially corroborate these accounts. The major area of disagreement concerns how long the victim had been ill prior to her cure.

This report of multiple miracles somewhat parallels the testimony of the notary Berardo Apillaterre during the canonization hearing of Nicholas of Tolentino in 1325.[23] Here also, many miracles are reported within one family, largely dealing with children. The saint has been transformed into the patron of a particular family. Papal canonization and the establishment of a cult would certainly lend great prestige to those who had been touched by a miracle, and sometimes might even entail financial gain. Since Philip's cult had not yet been established, older saints such as Vrain and Étienne were preferred at first, and even after a cure was effected, pilgrimages were undertaken to the competing shrines of Rocamadour and St.Gilles, whose widely distributed relics were regarded as especially effective against mental disorders. Jeanne and her family employed several therapeutic tools. This included prayer, the invocation of a saint, pilgrimage and incubation, which would normally last nine days. In the absence of direct personal contact with the saint, the vision of Philip speaking directly to Jeanne would serve as a substitute and as a good foundation for demands for his canonization. A similar vision of the saint had allegedly contributed substantially to the canonization of Philip's uncle William of Bourges by Honorius III in 1218.[24] Both Philip's words and Jeanne's invocation are cited verbatim, reflecting the court's desire to guarantee that a true miracle rather than the Devil's machinations was at work.

---

23. Nicola Occhioni, ed., *Il processo per la canonizzazione di S. Nicola da Tolentino* (Rome, 1984), 116-130.

24. 'Sancti Gulielmi archiepiscopi Biturcensis Vita, miracula post mortem et canonizatio', *Analecta Bollandiana*, 3 (1884), 350-6. For canonization bull see Pietro Pressuti, ed., *Regesta Honorii papae III*, 2 vols. (Rome, 1888-95), 1: 223, nos. 1343-45.

Jeanne's case was extensively summarized in Philip's later *Vita et miracula*, which further illustrates the dependence of narrative hagiography on judicial sources, particularly following the establishment of proper guidelines for papal canonization.[25] Completely absent from this narrative account, however, is any reference to her visits to the shrines of St. Étienne, St. Vrain, St.-Gilles-du-Gard and Rocamadour. Philip's biographer clearly feared that the mention of other shrines might undermine the saint's reputation. In addition, direct quotation from the *miraculée's* words is also lacking. In the contemporary case of Richard of Chichester noted above, in which Odo of Châteauroux was also involved and which was heard around the same time, the Dominican biographer is less cautious and direct quotation appears with respect to miracles which appear in the papal bull of canonization. Since Philip's case was not yet complete, his biographer was forced to exercise greater caution.

Edith of Hereford

The second miracle to be summarized is taken from the hearings in the case of Thomas of Hereford held in 1307. The most accurate version is found in Vat. Lat. 4015.[26] The Bollandists preferred to rewrite the text in narrative form and some information is lacking from their account. The case concerns the miraculous exorcism of Edith, the wife of an iron merchant of Hereford, and is supported by twelve witnesses. It is the first posthumous public miracle recorded in Thomas's extensive dossier, and took place rather fortuitously on March 28, 1287, the Friday just before Palm Sunday. This was about a week before the planned translation of Thomas's relics and at a time when a large number of pilgrims and spectators would be in Hereford. Thomas's relics were to be transferred to the chapel of St. Catherine on Maundy Thursday, April 4, 1287 in the northwest transept. It should be noted that, like Bourges cathedral, Here-

---

25. *Vita sancti Philippi archiepiscopi Biturcensis*, in Edmond Martène and Ursin Durand, eds., *Thesaurus novus anecdotorum*, 5 vols. (Paris, 1717-26), 3: 1927-46; here 1942-3, 'xii: De alienatis a sensu, intellectu, memoria et loquela liberatis'. As in the *BN* manuscript, Jeanne's miracle is given the greatest prominence of all the miracles, which suggests that this ms. may represent the raw material from which the author of the *Vita* worked.

26. MS *Vat. Lat.* 4015, fol. 211^r-219^v. For the Bollandist summary, see *Processus Thomae, op. cit.*, 632-3. For a more thorough study of this particular miracle by me see: 'Liturgy and the Foundation of cults, in the Thirteenth and Fourteenth Centuries', in *De Sion exibit lex et verbum domini de Hierusalem*: Essays... in Honour of Amnon Linder, ed. Yitzhak Hen (Turnhout, 2001), 145-157.

ford was just completing a period of extensive renovation, and the public performance of miracles would draw further attention and visitors.[27] A twenty-year old demoniac named Edith, the wife of Robert, an iron merchant and citizen of Hereford, had been brought to Thomas's temporary tomb and was cured. Gilbert, the procurator of the church of Hereford, testified that she had been brought to the site of Thomas's bones in the Ladychapel because her behavior would disturb the choir, which was some distance away. Just after sunrise and after prime, the chaplain was celebrating mass on the altar of the cross, beside the bishop's temporary tomb. In the course of the celebration all the candles and lamps suddenly lit up around the altar, and were just as quickly extinguished, although none of the witnesses had discerned a breeze. All were stunned and heard the unusual sound of rushing water. The only light that could be seen came from the ex-voto candle, whose wick had been measured to Edith's body by her friends in accordance with English tradition. The victim herself lay prostrate before the altar with her hands and feet bound together, a common practice in the 'treatment' of demoniacs. The candle lit up miraculously at three focal points, top, middle and bottom, with what witnesses called 'a celestial fire'. The moment this candle began to burn, the others in the church were suddenly ignited. Edith was freed of her bonds, stood up, and cried out repeatedly, 'St. Thomas has restored my sanity to me.' She turned to the woman who was holding her and said, 'Let go of me,' approached the altar, placed the lighted candle above it, and praised both God and Thomas of Hereford for her recovery. When the mass was over, Edith visited Thomas's bones in the Ladychapel unaided.

The witnesses to this miraculous exorcism were already anticipating the festivities which were to take place within a few days in Thomas's honor. They may have been part of the constituency that had arrived to support the burgeoning cult, which was still in need of a public miracle in order to enhance its chances of approval. Several of those who testified at the canonization trial on Edith's behalf appear to have come from the parish of Marden, the site of other miracles. After the participants prayed at the site of Thomas's temporary tomb, they returned to the altar of the cross, where Gilbert celebrated mass. Edith fully participated in the

---

27. Robert Gaudery, *Saint-Etienne de Bourges* (Paris, 1959); Camille-Louis Balland, *Saint-Etienne de Bourges* (Paris, 1964); Tanya Bayard, *Bourges Cathedral* (New York, 1976); Amédée Boinet, *La cathedrale de Bourges*, rev. ed. (Paris, 1952); Robert Branner, *The Cathedral of Bourges and Its Place in Gothic Architecture* (New York, 1989); Arthur Thomas Bannister, *The Cathedral Church of Hereford* (London, 1924); Nicholas Pevsner, *Hereford. History and Guide* (Harmondsworth, 1963).

offertory, kissed his hand, and gave an offering of one penny, remaining until the mass had ended. Gilbert then called together the four canons who were to be found in the city. Edith remained in the church until nones, the church bells were rung in praise, the people and clergy joined the procession, and all heard reports of the great miracle. Gilbert was joined by others enthusiastically reciting the *Te Deum*.

Despite the great public support given this miracle, as in the case of Jeanne of Crosses, the attribution to Thomas of Hereford was not unanimous. One of those who heard of Edith's liberation argued that the miracle was more likely to have occurred due to the merits of another former bishop of Hereford, Robert de Beton (d. 1147), who was also buried in the cathedral. Gilbert also testified that when Thomas of St. Omer, a canon of Hereford and member of the household of Thomas's opponent Archbishop John Pecham of Canterbury visited the town in order to deal with problems of the vacant Welsh see of Llandaff, he severely reprimanded Gilbert for publicizing Edith's exorcism. He was suspended for seven days, a suspension that was soon revoked by Master William de Montfort, dean of London and precentor of the church of Hereford. Edith herself also rejected any suggestion that another saint had intervened on her behalf, insisting that Thomas had appeared to her in a vision in the course of the cure, looking just as she had seen him when he was serving as bishop. The appearance of the saint to the *miraculée* dressed in ecclesiastical garb as a means of identification occurs elsewhere in Thomas's case. In the course of a very public miracle in 1289 at Swansea, when the Welsh rebel William Cragh of Llanridian was miraculously saved from hanging, Thomas was seen posthumously by the victim.[28] Although he claimed never to have seen Thomas during his lifetime, William easily identified him in his vision. This may perhaps be the result of rumors that had already spread concerning his miracle-making powers, undoubtedly accompanied by descriptions of the dead bishop. Frequent church-going and exposure to the religious images found in sculpture, stained glass, fresco or the minor arts, played an important role in the education of the laity. Such common exposure within the same community created a shared treasury of symbols and images that drew believers together and reinforced religious discourse.

Several witnesses reported that Edith had been married for two years before her affliction first appeared at the beginning of Lent, i.e. February 23, 1287. One night, in bed after dinner, she had begun to gesticulate and

---

28. MS *Vat. Lat.* 4015, fol. 220^r-222^r.

blasphemously attack her neighbors. Because of this behavior she was tied down and guarded by two neighbor women until a week before Palm Sunday. During this time, she was often delirious, barely ate or drank, and was severely weakened. In accordance with English custom she was measured and two ex-voto candles were made out of a quarter of a pound of wax, one for the Holy Cross at Wistanton, the other for the Holy Cross at Hereford. Two neighbors brought her to Hereford cathedral to incubate for five or six days, and at vespers on the Thursday just before Palm Sunday Edith was moved on the advice of an unnamed cleric to the Ladychapel, where, we have seen, Thomas's bones were interred. After her cure, she returned home on the same litter with which she had come to Hereford, and reportedly died two months later, on June 29, 1287. Unlike Jeanne, she was unable to testify at the hearing into her experience and we must thus rely on the testimony of others. The apothecary's wife testified in 1307 that Edith may well have been pregnant. At first this saddened her, and afterwards she became mentally deranged. This parallels the case of Jeanne of Crosses. In both cases, the rituals in which they partook may have helped to diminish their anxieties at a time of great physiological change. The cathartic effects of ritual may help to relieve the uncertainty and unpleasant emotions born of an unwanted pregnancy or other emotional stress.

Summary

The preceding miracle stories are based on the testimony of several witnesses before they had passed through the filter of a hagiographer or biographer, who would remove extraneous or problematic material. These episodes provide a bird's eye view of the lives of persons being drawn into the net of a burgeoning religious cult and whose experiences could serve as effective propaganda for its dissemination. Nevertheless, such close observation requires the contextualization that can be provided by comparison with other sources. The microhistorian begins with a close reading of the life experience of an individual or community, frequently through the prism of judicial documents. An effort is made to separate the 'directives' and aims of the inquisitor, judge, lawyer and other court officials from the authentic voice of the witnesses. This is then modified and understood through the comparative use of other contemporary documents and the application of analytical tools, often drawn from anthropology, psychology or other 'ancillary' disciplines. If we compare the cases of Edith and Jeanne, the problems that drove them and their families to seek supernatural assistance are characteristic of other cases found in contemporary miracle collections. In Sigal's statistical survey of miracles at French shrines in the eleventh and twelfth centuries, mental illness consists of 8.8% of the cures, with a higher rate for women. It ranks fourth in number, after neurological problems such as paralysis and epilepsy, which account for 40% of the cases.[29] In Vauchez's summary of miracles found in thirteenth century canonization trials, which covers all of Europe, 10.7% of the cures refer to mental problems, including what was diagnosed as epilepsy, possession and madness. Paralysis and other motor difficulties account for 28.8% of the cures, and in the early thirteenth century at least 40%. Difficult births and sterility constitute 1.2% of the cases, rising to 3.3% in the fourteenth century.[30] Of the miracles reported in Thomas of Hereford's canonization bull, the majority deal with women and children.

The link between Jeanne's and Edith's mental state and pregnancy is not unusual and sheds light on the pressures exerted on women to bear children. It was commonly believed that the failure to give birth could be the product of sin and the Devil's interference, made easier if the victim is of a melancholic nature.[31] The symptoms identified with mental disorder most commonly included cursing, loss of appetite, sleeplessness, and aggressive behavior. Women's weakness and sinfulness, rather than male sterility, were held responsible for their failure to conceive and this could bring disgrace on one's self and family. In one of Thomas of Hereford's miracles dating from 1300, a woman believed she was sterile and felt disgraced as a result. After prayers and pilgrimage, she gave birth to twins.[32] With the rise of the theory of the four humors in the thirteenth century, theologians, philosophers, natural scientists and physicians attributed the mental illness associated with melancholia particularly to those women suffering from a loss of humoral equilibrium and an excess of black bile. In Jeanne's case, all of the witnesses stated that she only became aware of her pregnancy (about which she was clearly worried) after she had been cured of mental derangement. Her mother's testimony states that her disturbed mental state had in fact appeared seven years earlier in the course of a previous pregnancy. In Edith's case, the pregnancy may have preceded the mental breakdown and may well have been

---

29. Pierre André Sigal, *L'homme et le miracle dans la France médiévale (xie-xiie siècles)* (Paris, 1985), 255-64.
30. Vauchez, *op. cit.*, 540-58.
31. Muriel Laharie, *La folie au moyen âge: xie-xiiie siècles* (Paris, 1991), 30 ff.
32. MS *Exeter College* [Oxford] 158, fol. 31^{rv}.

a causal factor. This suggests a possible link between unwanted sexual relations, childbirth, and her mental condition.

If we apply contemporary judicial and theological standards to judging the veracity of a miracle, neither Jeanne's nor Edith's case could pass examination by the papal curia and appear in a bull of canonization. In neither case does there appear to have been any effort to effect a cure through natural means, which might be confirmed in a physician's testimony, as is found in other cases. While both victims attempt to provide corroborating evidence concerning which saint had performed the miracle by referring to the ecclesiastical garb in which the saint had appeared, other saints and shrines are also noted and the visionary claims of the victims cannot be corroborated. For example, Pope Innocent III had himself experienced confirmatory visions prior to the canonization of several saints whose cases had not yet been resolved at the curia. He nevertheless warned that since the Devil might appear in the guise of a benevolent angel, caution should be exercised and a suitable judicial inquiry should be undertaken in order to determine sanctity and divine intervention, since 'simplici' may otherwise be easily led astray by false miracles.[33]

At the same time, women such as Jeanne and Edith, whose unwillingness or inability to bear children would have placed them outside the prevailing consensus and were subjected to the anger of their family and community, could be empowered through the agency of the dream or vision. The appearance of the saint legitimated the disease, possession or infertility that preceded it, and at the same time provided a resolution of the problem, the inevitable consequence of any miracle. Although the witnesses had apparently been well rehearsed and prompted before giving their testimony, it was still clearly necessary to provide evidence from members of the noble or clerical classes; in Jeanne's case a curate and Benedictine prior testified; in Edith's case several clergy appeared. Although the church might make use of these reports in order to forward a new cult, they nevertheless contain an air of authenticity as the personal testimony of members of the non-governing classes. The testimony of the victims themselves and members of their families, perhaps because of their occasional contradictions, possess a ring of truth.

It is difficult to judge whether the elements of popular piety that appear in these canonization inquiries were imposed by ecclesiastical authorities

---

33. Michael Goodich, 'Vision, Dream and Canonization Policy under Innocent III', in John C. Moore, ed., *Pope Innocent III and his World* (Aldershot, 1999), 151-64.

or accurately reflect public norms. Particularly in Edith's case, orchestration and manipulation by interested parties in the bishop's *familia* cannot be ruled out. Nevertheless, the wide involvement of family and community in the vows and pilgrimage surrounding the miracle point up the communal nature of the saint's cult as a means of bringing together quarrelsome spouses or contentious neighbors.[34] In the aforementioned case of the Welsh rebel William Cragh saved from execution, the local lord – who had himself apprehended the rebel and had vigorously persecuted the Welsh – along with his wife and their *familia* were to join the victim on a pilgrimage to Hereford.[35] They would also testify at the 1307 hearing. This particular case also illustrates the appeal to religion as a mediator in a time of conquest and colonization. The new cult of Thomas of Hereford could thus create a community of faith binding devotees of diverse backgrounds in a traditional patron-client relationship common to other cults. Likewise, the stereotypical features of the miracle clearly appear in our two examples – namely, a victim in distress, a saint able to provide assistance, a vow, its fulfillment, supernatural intervention, and an audience whose faith is strengthened. Theologians took note of the therapeutic role of the miracle and the value of prayer, confession, pilgrimage, incubation, the sign of the cross, the invocation of saints and contact with relics as effective agencies in driving away the Devil and curing mental diseases. These tools clearly served the clerical goal of insuring the church's exclusive position in the 'cure of souls'.

The theme of the vision that precedes the performance of a miracle also reflects clerical expectations, although this in and of itself does not deny the likelihood that both Jeanne and Edith would naturally be inclined to such an auto-suggestive experience. Long ago, William James in his classic *Varieties of Religious Experience* posited that the predisposition of the recipient and his or her audience to experience spiritual phenomena is the single most important causal factor in the occurrence of such events. Despite Innocent III's caution, the widespread appearance of visions in hagiographical narrative sources suggests that both learned and popular culture shared a common faith in their providential nature.[36] The vision

---

34. For example, Hans Conrad Peyer, *Stadt und Stadtpatron in mittelalterlichen Italien* (Zurich, 1955) on the urban saint.

35. *Exeter College* 158, fol. 27ᵛ.

36. The literature is considerable. I might just cite Peter Dinzelbacher, *Vision and Visionsliteratur im Mittelalter*, in *Monographien zur Geschichte des Mittelalters*, 23 (Stuttgart, 1981). A brief, but still useful study is Peter Burke, 'The Cultural History of Dreams', in *Varieties of Cultural History* (Cambridge, 1997), 23-42, first published in 1973.

may appear in a variety of contexts as a means of calling the recipient to act in pursuit of the fulfillment of a long contemplated goal: for example, prior to the liberation of a prisoner from captivity; as a means of identifying the site of long-buried relics or the place to establish a church or monastery. In the lives of Jeanne and Edith, such a vision serves both as private and public role: as a reflection of the victim's desire to undertake a pilgrimage to the shrine of a popular and politically important miracle worker in pursuit of a cure; and as confirmatory evidence of the saint's supernatural powers and claims to sainthood. Both of these themes could be exploited by ecclesiastical authorities in order to create a new cult. In order to spread support of the cult, as I have tried to suggest, the raw material of the canonization testimony was transformed into a narrative biography, which includes miracles which conform to a stereotypical literary genre. This in turn might be summarized into a brief legend, or serve as the foundation of a sermon, to be followed by a liturgical office, and, in some cases, a fresco or other illustrated source.[37]

---

37. The use of a biography as the foundation for a cycle of frescoes is illustrated in the cult of Giovanna da Signa. See Saturnino Mencherini, ed., 'Vita e miracoli della Beata Giovanna da Signa', *Archivum fratrum historicum*, 10 (1917), 367-86; Daniel Russo, 'Jeanne da Signa ou l'iconographie au féminin. Études sur les fresques de l'église paroissale de Signa (milieu du xve siècle)', *Mélanges de l'École française de Rome. Moyen âge*, 98 (1986), 201-18.

Werner VERBEKE

LA 'VIE DE SAINT AMAND' PAR GILLIS DE WEVEL ET SES MODÈLES

> Au Professeur Guy Philippart,
> pour son soutien aux
> 'The Narrative Sources from the Medieval Low Countries'

Gillis de Wevel n'a guère suscité l'intérêt des spécialistes de la littérature en moyen néerlandais, malgré ses précieuses informations à propos de la rédaction de 'La Vie de saint Amand' – *Leven van Sinte Amand* –, l'unique poème qu'il nous a laissé.[1] Dans l'épilogue, le poète révèle – 'à la demande d'un ami', comme il se doit – son nom et surnom au moyen de leur valeur numérique, ce qui amène le lecteur attentif au nombre de 667 (= gILLIs De VVeVeL), tout près de l'énigmatique 666.[2] Il aurait écrit les derniers vers à Bruges, le 27 janvier 1366 (1367 n.s.), soit à peine quelques jours avant le 6 février, fête de saint Amand, ce qui pourrait suggérer l'existence d'un lien entre certains Brugeois intéressés par son culte et le texte.

Le poème de taille moyenne (12.450 vers) a été repris dans un seul manuscrit, qui remonte, selon les codicologues, aux environs de 1440.[3] Il repose aujourd'hui à la bibliothèque de l'Université de Gand (n° 542); il contient également la traduction en moyen néerlandais de la *Visio Tnugdali* et un bref poème anonyme dédié à la Vierge Marie.[4] Le

---

1. Le poème a été édité par le juriste gantois Philippe Blommaert, *Leven van Sinte Amand, Patroon der Nederlanden, dichtstuk der XIVde eeuw*, Maetschappy der Vlaemsche Bibliophilen, I, 4, 2 tomes (Gand, 1842-43). Littérature: *Les sources narratives des Pays-Bas médiévaux, 1996-2004*, n° G085 (répertoire électronique publié par les universités de Gand, de Louvain et de Groningue: http://www.Narrative-Sources.be).
Pour le saint Amand 'historique', mort ca. 675, voir *Bibliotheca Sanctorum*, I (1961), col. 918-923 et la littérature récente concernant l'évangélisation de nos régions (A. Angenendt, A. Dierkens, N. Gauthier, L. Milis, F. Prinz, G. Scheibelreiter, M. Werner etc.).
2. *Amand*, II, 6348-6406.
3. W. de Vreese, *Bouwstoffen*, dans *Middelnederlandsch Woordenboek*, t. X (1927-41), p. 8, n° 19 (cf. Briquet, n° 11087 et 14179).
4. Gand, Universiteitsbibliotheek, n° 542, f. 1-237v. Littérature: J. de Saint-Genois, *Catalogue méthodique et raisonné des manuscrits de la bibliothèque de la ville et de l'Université de Gand* (Gand, 1849-52), p. 178 (n° 163); R. Verdeyen et H.J.E. Endepols, *Tondalus' visioen en St. Patricius' vagevuur*, Koninklijke Vlaemsche Academie voor taal- en

manuscrit mérite une attention toute particulière en raison de la technique utilisée lors de sa composition, comme l'a signalé Pieter Obbema.[5]

Éduard De Moreau, connaisseur par excellence du saint Amand historique, 'apôtre de la Belgique et du Nord de la France', n'a nullement apprécié 'l'originalité' du poème de Gillis: 'Laissons cette oeuvre poétique, ou qui prétend l'être'.[6] L'éminent spécialiste de l'histoire de l'Église en Belgique ne disposait manifestement pas d'une sensibilité qui convient à l'approche de l'hagiographie vernaculaire. Comme en témoigne la 'Leven van Sinte Amand', celle-ci s'éloigne souvent de la tradition latine pour s'enrichir des techniques et des thèmes propres à la littérature romanesque de l'époque,

Une première lecture de la 'Leven van Sinte Amand', permet déjà de mieux comprendre le jugement du Père De Moreau car on y retrouve difficilement le fil conducteur des *Vitae Amandi* qui circulaient depuis des siècles.[7] De nos jours, la suppression de plusieurs miracles dans les remaniements, les réécritures ou les traductions ne surprend plus le médiéviste; et le grand nombre de nouveaux exploits l'intrigue. Dans les pages qui suivent, je me hasarderai à démontrer la part de quelques témoins importants de l'hagiographie médiévale dans le montage complexe de Gillis de Wevel. Malgré ses innovations surprenantes et l'indéniable

---

letterkunde, 3ᵉ série, 20, t. I (Gand, 1914), p. 159-161; A. Derolez, *Inventaris van de handschriften in de Universiteitsbibliotheek te Gent* (Gand, 1977), p. 46; N.F. Palmer, *Visio Tnugdali. The German and Dutch Translations and their Circulation in the Later Middle Ages,* Münchener Texte und Untersuchungen zur deutschen Literatur des Mittelalters, 76 (München-Zürich, 1982), p. 345-346; J. Reynaert, *Catalogus van de Middelnederlandse handschriften in de bibliotheek van de Rijksuniversiteit te Gent,* t. I: *De handschriften verworven voor 1852* (Gand, 1984), p. 120-122; id., *Pretiosa Neerlandica: Schatten uit de Nederlandse Taal- en Letterkunde in de Gentse Universiteit* (Gand, 1988), n° 39, p. 74-75.

5. P.F.J. Obbema,'Writing on Uncut Sheets', *Quaerendo,* VIII, 4 (1978), 337-354 (p. 342).

6. E. de Moreau, *Saint Amand: Apôtre de la Belgique et du Nord de la France* (Louvain, 1927), p. 302; id., *Saint Amand: Le principal évangélisateur de la Belgique* (Bruxelles, 1942).

7. Il s'agit de la *Vita Amandi* mérovingienne (BHL 332; éd. AASS, Febr. I, Parisiis, 1863³, p. 859-865 et B. Krusch dans MGH SRM, V, 1910, p. 395-449), la versification par Milo de Saint-Amand (9ᵉ s.; *Narrative-Sources.be* M035, BHL 333; éd. L. Traube dans MGH *Poetae Latini Medii Aevi,* III, 1896, p. 561-609) et la réécriture en prose par Philippus de Eleemosyna (12ᵉ s.; *Narrative-Sources.be* P033, BHL 334; éd. AASS, Febr. I, Parisiis, 1863³, p. 867-882). Récemment on a retrouvé la trace d'une *vita antiqua,* cf. A. Verhulst - G. Declercq,'L'action et le souvenir de saint Amand en Europe centrale: À propos de la découverte d'une *Vita Amandi antiqua*', dans *Aevum inter utrumque: Mélanges offerts à Gabriel Sanders,* éds. M. Van Uytfanghe et R. Demeulenaere, Instrumenta Patristica, XXIII (Steenbrugge-Den Haag, 1991), p. 503-526.

influence de la littérature vernaculaire profane, Gillis s'inscrit néanmoins, me semble-t-il, dans la grande tradition hagiographique de l'Occident. Le choix intelligent de ses modèles décèle même une appréciation et une connaissance hors du commun de cette littérature.

Il est superflu d'insister préalablement sur l'importance de la synthèse réalisée par Vincent de Beauvais et ses collaborateurs dans le domaine de l'hagiographie. Le résultat s'en trouve reflété dans le *Speculum historiale*, le dernier volume de la gigantesque entreprise encyclopédique qu'a été le *Speculum maius*. C'est ce *Speculum historiale* qui a été traduit en moyen néerlandais – et en même temps remanié avec de nombreuses coupures et ajouts – à partir d'environ 1285 par le poète flamand Jacob van Maerlant.[8] Par la variété, la qualité et l'ampleur de son œuvre, ce poète compte parmi les auteurs les plus illustres de la littérature vernaculaire médiévale en Occident.[9] À la fin de sa carrière littéraire, il entreprit à Damme, tout près de Bruges, ce travail laborieux destiné au comte de Hollande, son mécène depuis le début de son activité littéraire. Pour des raisons inconnues, Maerlant n'a pas pu mener à bien son projet historique – à savoir, une histoire universelle, comme Vincent de Beauvais – étalé sur quatre volumes. La deuxième partie, principalement composée des vies de martyrs, a été réalisée seulement vers 1300 par Philip Utenbroeke. Ce poète quasi inconnu est localisé lui aussi à Damme, où Maerlant avait commencé la traduction du *Speculum*.[10] Il ne reste de la contribution d'Utenbroeke qu'un seul manuscrit, fort incomplet, conservé aujourd'hui à Vienne.[11] Le copiste brabançon anonyme a cru rendre service à sa communauté en éliminant des passages importants des vies des martyrs dont les faits marquants étaient déjà narrés dans d'autres textes conservés dans sa bibliothèque locale. La fin de la quatrième partie est

---

8. Éds.: M. de Vries et E. Verwijs, *Jacob van Maerlant's Spiegel Historiael, met de fragmenten der later toegevoegde gedeelten bewerkt door Philip Utenbroeke en Lodewijc van Velthem*, Maatschappij der Nederlandsche Letterkunde te Leiden, 3 t. (Leiden, 1863); lit.: *Narrative-Sources.be* J007.
9. F. P. van Oostrom, *Maerlants wereld* (Amsterdam, 1966).
10. F. Von Hellwald, M. de Vries et E. Verwijs, *Jacob van Maerlant's Spiegel Historiael: Tweede Partie, bewerkt door Philip Utenbroeke*, Maatschappij der Nederlandsche Letterkunde (Leiden, 1879); lit.: *Narrative-Sources.be* R002.
11. Vienne, Österreichische Nationalbibliothek, Ms. 13.708. Cf. J. Deschamps, *The Vienna Manuscript of the Second Part of the Spiegel Historiael* (Copenhague, 1971); J.A.A.M. Biemans, *Onsen Speghele Ystoriale in Vlaemsche: Codicologisch onderzoek naar de overlevering van de Spiegel historiael van Jacob van Maerlant, Philip Utenbroeke en Lodewijk van Velthem, met een beschrijving van de handschriften en fragmenten* (Louvain, 1997), p. 450-452.

issue de la plume d'un prêtre brabançon, Lodewijk van Velthem.[12] Lodewijk a aussi continué l'œuvre de Maerlant en y ajoutant un cinquième volume consacré à l'histoire contemporaine et à la fin des temps. Historien, mais aussi grand collectionneur des récits arthurièns, Lodewijk a, semble-t-il, travaillé pour le même milieu hollandais qui avait soutenu son prédécesseur, Jacob van Maerlant.

C'est dans le *Spiegel historiael,* commencé par Jacob van Maerlant et poursuivi par Philip Utenbroeke et Lodewijk van Velthem, que Gillis de Wevel a puisé les modèles, entre autres les 'classiques' de l'hagiographie médiévale, qui ont facilité la transformation substantielle de la 'biographie' traditionnelle de saint Amand.

– le dossier de saint Martin de Tours

Le premier 'signe' de l'élection divine du jeune Amand – il vient d'atteindre l'âge symbolique de sept ans – se manifeste lors de la guérison d'un serviteur de son père. Douloureusement piqué par un animal vénéneux, le malheureux est sauvé grâce à un simple attouchement de la part du – futur – saint.[13]

Le récit remonte aux *Dialogues* de Sulpice Sévère.[14] Gallus, le disciple de saint Martin, y relate une intervention similaire de la part du saint en faveur d'un travailleur de son oncle, un nommé Évantius. Les expressions identiques – ici en italique – ne laissent aucun doute: Gillis de Wevel a consulté les chapitres concernant Martin dans le *Spiegel Historiael* pendant la rédaction même d'une guérison qui ne connaît pas d'analogue dans les *Vitae Amandi.*

Spiegel Historiael, IIIe Partie, Livre IV, ch. XL, v. 21-54 (p. 256-257)[15]

...
21 Ende hier binnen so gesciede,
Dat een van sinen [= Evantius] mayseniede,

---

12. Lit.: *Narratives-Sources.be* L028.
13. *Amand*, I, 107-143.
14. PL 20, c. 202 D.
15. Maerlant suit de près Vincentius Bellovacensis, *Speculum Historiale* (Douai, 1624; reprint Graz, 1965), Lib. XVIII, c. XXI (p. 700): *Ex secundo libro dialogorum.*'...cum interim unum de familia puerum laethali ictu serpens perculit; quem iam exanimem vi veneni ipse Evantius suis humeris illatum, ante pedes sancti viri, nihil illi impossibile confisus, exposuit. Iamque se malum serpentis per omnia membra diffuderat; cernens omnibus venis inflatam cutem, et ad utris instar tensa vitalia. Martinus porrecta manu universa pueri membra pertractans, digitum prope ipsum vulnusculum, quo bestia virus infuderat, fixit. Tum vero (mira sum dicturus,) vidimus venenum ex omni parte revocatum, ad Martini digitum cucurrisse; deinde per illud ulceris foramen, exiguum, ita virus stipasse

```
                Een knecht, wart gevenijnt sciere
        24      Van enen ghevenijnden diere.
                Euantius hevet selve den knecht
                Up sine scouderen gerecht,
                Ende leidene bina recht al doot
        28      Voer die voete des heren groot;
                Want sijn gelove seidem daer,
                Dattem en gene dinc ware swaer.
                Gheent venijn dat haddem mede
        32      Ghespreet over alle sine lede.
                Sente Martijn diene anesach
                Dat hi al te blasen lach,
                Alse ene blase vul van winde,
        36      Die lede van ghenen kinde
                Betasti al omme tier stonde;
                Ende alse hi quam ter wonde,
                Daer in comen was tfenijn,
        40      Daer sette hi den vinger sijn.
                Ic sal u seggen wonder groot:
                Wi sagen metten ogen bloot
                Dat venijn van alle die leden
        44      Comen lopende tier steden,
                Aldaer Martijns vinger stont,
                Ende vor dat clene gaetkijn ront
                Versamet hem met bloede daer
        48      Inder gelike, wet vorwaer,
                Alse melc vor beesten spene.
                Doe so volghet uut al reene
                Inder gebaren, alsemen ziet,
        52      Datmen melc uut te melkene pliet.
                Die knecht stont up al gesont.
                Wonder hadden wijs alle tier stont.
```

Leven van Sinte Amand, I, 107-143

Eene miracle die god [dede] door sente Amande te sinen .vij. jaeren van eenen knecht die hi ghenas

```
        107     Dit scone kint, dese jonghe Amand,
                Wart tsinen .vii. jaeren becant
                Ouer die vroetste van sinnen daghen
        110     Daer men of hoorde ghewaghen
                Ende daer toe vul duechden mede.
                Nv hoort wat onse heere dede
```

cum sanguine, ut solet ex uberibus caprarum, aut ovium, pastorum manu pressis, longa linea copiosi lactis effluere. Puer surrexit incolumis: Nos stupefacti tantae rei miraculo, id quod cogebat ipsa veritas, fatebamur, non esse sub caelo, qui Martinum posset imitari.'

```
              Door tkint alst hout was .vij. jaer.
        114   Baland, sijn vader, ha[d]de voorwaer
              Groot goet ende beesten echt
              So dat hi hadde eenen knecht
              Die sijn vee te wachtene plach.
        118   So dat gheuiel up eenen dach
              Dat die knecht slapen soude
              Up tvelt, ende hi wert also houde
              Ghefenijnt van eenen diere quaet,
        122   So dat die knecht, dat uerstaet,
              Swal so groot dat elken man
              Of grees diene daer sach an.
              Maer eenighe hebben upghenomen
        126   Ende sinre mede inden casteel comen
              Daer Amand ende sijn vader was,
              Die zeere drouue worden das
              Dat die knecht hadde sulc grief.
        130   Ende Amand, die met gode lief
              Was ende uercoren mede,
              Dede an Xpristum sijn ghebede
              Ende daerna in corten *stonden*
        134   Taste hi die felle *wonden*
              *Daerin commen was tfenijn.*
              Ende als quam *den vingher sijn*
              Daer die felle bete *stond,*
        138   Waet daer een *gaetkin cleene ende ront*
              Ende dat fenijn liep al duere,
              Dies die knecht up die huere
              Wart ghenesen ende *al ghesont*
        142   Wient te voren so nouwe *stont*
              Ende wel na was up die doot.
```

Saint Amand remplace Martin et le père de saint Amand, un nommé 'Balland',[16] est substitué à Évantius, l'oncle du narrateur Gallus. Gillis s'intéresse non seulement aux grandes lignes de l'intervention miraculeuse,

---

16. Le nom de 'Balland' au lieu du traditionnel 'Serenus' est un mystère de plus. S'agit-il d'influences romanesques où les 'Balland' sont nombreux? Cf. E. Langlois, *Table des noms propres de toute nature compris dans les chansons de geste* (Paris, 1904, reprint New York, 1971), p. 65 ; L.-F. Flutre, *Table des noms propres avec toutes leurs variantes figurant dans les romans du Moyen Âge écrits en français ou en provençal et actuellement publiés ou analysés* (Poitiers, 1962), p. 24; A. Moisan, *Répertoire des noms propres de personnes et de lieux cités dans les chansons de geste françaises et les oeuvres étrangères dérivées*, Publications romanes et françaises, 173 (Genève, 1986), I, 1, p. 203-204 et II, 3, p. 136; II, 4, p. 110; II, 5, p. 892. Jean d'Outremeuse, contemporain de Gillis de Wevel, a même inventé toute une nouvelle 'famille' pour le saint. Cf. *Ly Mireur des histors,* éds. A. Borgnet et S. Bormans, Commission royale d'Histoire, Publications en 4° (Bruxelles, 1864-80), t. II, p. 289 (*Narrative-Sources.be* J083).

mais aussi à l'expression verbale, telle que la succession de rimes. Par contre, la comparaison (*Sp. Hist.*, 48-52) du venin au lait animal n'apparaît plus.[17]

Le séjour à Tours, haut lieu de la dévotion à saint Martin, joue un rôle prépondérant dans la vie – et les *vitae* – de saint Amand.[18] C'est à cet endroit précis qu'il prend la décision de rompre définitivement les liens familiaux pour devenir un *peregrinus* dans ce monde. La présentation vernaculaire du saint transmet cette tradition.

Par contre, en attribuant les multiples guérisons attestées à Tours à la seule intervention de son propre héros, Gillis exagère pour les besoins de sa cause. Un fait particulier mérite toutefois que l'on s'y attarde. Un évêque anonyme de Tours rend visite au saint homme pour obtenir la guérison d'un ami qui se trouve entre la vie et la mort.[19] Avant le retour de l'évêque auprès du malade, celui-ci a déjà complètement retrouvé la santé.

Le dossier hagiographique de saint Martin contient une anecdote fort similaire, localisée, elle aussi, dans la ville de Tours.[20] Le miracle fut repris par Jacob van Maerlant par le biais de Vincent de Beauvais.[21] Le dénommé Évantius déjà mentionné invita saint Martin chez lui pour qu'il favorise sa propre guérison. Gallus, le fidèle disciple de saint Martin, raconte comment Évantius a recouvré toutes ses forces avant même l'arrivée de Martin. Cette fois-ci, le lien probable entre les deux *mirabilia*, l'un dans la *Leven van Sinte Amand*, l'autre dans le *Spiegel Historiael*, ne se confirme pas par quelques tournures dans le texte de Gillis de Wevel. Néanmoins, on ne peut ignorer que la guérison 'à distance' obtenue par Martin précède immédiatement, dans le *Spiegel Historiael*, la guérison d'une piqûre vénéneuse que nous avons évoquée ci-dessus.

Selon De Wevel saint Amand a dû subir, dans la ville de Tours, de nombreuses attaques farouches de la part du diable. Un jour, Satan s'est présenté à lui sous l'apparence du Christ en personne.[22] Mais le saint homme, bien inspiré par le Saint-Esprit, a fermé ses yeux car il ne voulait pas voir le Christ dans ce monde de ses propres yeux.

---

17. Déjà Maerlant était moins précis à ce propos que Vincent de Beauvais.
18. *Vita S. Amandi*, c. 5, p. 860.
19. *Amand*, I, 718-768.
20. Sulpicius Severus, *Dialogi*, in PL 20, c. 202 C.
21. *Sp. Hist.*, IIIe Partie, Livre IV, ch. XL, v. 1-17 ; cf. Vincentius, Lib. XVIII, c. XXI, p. 700.
22. *Amand*, I, 618-643.

Le dossier de saint Martin – et le *Spiegel Historiael* ne fait pas exception –, contient une scène comparable.[23] La ressemblance entre les deux apparitions du diable laisse peu de doute quant à l'inspiration du poète flamand. L'absence de vers ou de rimes identiques dans le passage correspondant de Gillis, ainsi que dans la guérison à distance déjà mentionnée, s'explique entre autres par le fait indiscutable que l'auteur a feuilleté son exemplaire du *Spiegel Historiael* dans l'intervalle entre l'imitation du travailleur piqué et le remaniement des deux autres miracles de Martin cités. À ce moment précis de son travail, le poète a consulté dans une autre 'partie' du *Spiegel Historiael*, c'est-à-dire en dehors du dossier de saint Martin, le chapitre à propos des rois mages. Un extrait a été inséré littéralement dans une prière.[24] Est-ce une indication que Gillis rencontrait, malgré sa connaissance profonde du *Spiegel Historiael*, certaines difficultés à retrouver 'sur place' ses modèles dans un manuscrit volumineux?

– L'œuvre de Grégoire le Grand

Parmi les événements dignes de mention pendant l'épiscopat de saint Amand à Maastricht, De Wevel expose en détail un exemple de charité qui n'est rapporté nulle part ailleurs.[25] Selon sa 'biographie' vernaculaire, le saint recevait quotidiennement douze pauvres à sa table. Un jour, il est surpris par la présence d'un treizième, un inconnu qui disparaît soudain quand l'évêque s'approche pour lui laver les mains. Dans la nuit, il apprend dans un rêve que c'est Jésus Christ en personne qui s'est présenté à sa table.

Cette anecdote remonte à une homélie de Grégoire le Grand qui a fasciné plusieurs auteurs.[26] Le pape y raconte l'apparition du Christ à un

---

23. *Sp. Hist.*, IIIe Partie, Livre II, ch. XXXVI, v. 1-44; cf. Vincentius, Lib. XVII, c. XVIII, p. 659 et Sulpicius Severus, *Vita S. Martini*, c. 24 (PL 20, c. 147 B; J. Fontaine, *Sulpice Sévère, Vie de saint Martin,* Sources chrétiennes, 133, Paris, 1967, c. 24,4, p. 307-8).

24. *Amand*, I, 371-409 = *Sp. Hist.*, I^e Partie, Livre VI, ch. XLV, v. 1-32, cf. W. Verbeke,'*Ave vinculum caritatis*: Gillis de Wevel in de ban van Jacob van Maerlant', dans *In de voetsporen van Jacob van Maerlant,* éds. R. Bauer e.a., Symbolae Facultatis Litterarum Lovaniensis, A 30 (Louvain, 2002), p. 244-257.

25. *Amand*, II, 111-1194.

26. PL 76, c. 1183 C. Johannes Diaconus (9e s.) a interpolé cette histoire du pater familias dans sa vie de saint Grégoire (Lib. II, c. 22 cf. PL 75, c. 95). Jacques de Voragine raconte le même miracle dans la *Légende dorée*, c. XLVI (*Legenda aurea*, éd. Graesse, p. 194; ed. G.P. Maggioni, Firenze, 1998, p. 293). Voici la version de Vincent de Beauvais (Lib. XXII, c. 103, p. 895): *Idem in homelia 23:* 'Quidam Paterfamilias cum tota

'pater familias' qui donnait chaque jour à manger à des pauvres – sans préciser leur nombre –. Un jour, il se présente un inconnu... Le reste du récit est identique à celui de Gillis de Wevel.

Jacob van Maerlant n'a retenu dans les extraits des homélies de Grégoire qu'il a pu trouver dans le *Speculum historiale*, que précisément l'exemple du pater familias charitable.[27] À tort, Maerlant le présente comme un passage qui remonte aux *Dialogues* de Grégoire.[28] Je m'imagine mal que Gillis de Wevel ait pu se rendre compte de cette référence erronée.

Spiegel Historiael, IIIe Partie, Livre VII, ch. LI, v. 67-88 (p. 48)

67	Een huusman die vroede liede
	Gherne ontfinc ende sine meyseniede,
	Ende alle daghe ontfinc mede
	Aerme ten male, dat was sine zede.
71	Eens quam onder der aermer scare
	Een aerm mensche tetene dare.
	Die huusman, naer sine zede
	Ende naer sine omoedichede,
75	*Nam water* na, alsemen *ginc dwaen*,
	Ende wille water gheven *saen*.
	Ende teersten dat hi twater *ghiet*,
	Sone *can* hi *vinden niet*
79	No den ghenen scouwen na dien,
	Dien hi waende hebben gesien.
	Hier omme hi wonderen began.
	Ter naester nacht so quam hem an
83	Onsen Here, *aldaer hi lach,*
	Ende seide: '*Over menegen dach*
	Hevestu mi ende mine lede
	Ontfaen in grotre hoveschede,
87	*Maer ghistren* hadstu mi ontfaen

---

domo sua magno hospitalitatis studio serviebat. Cumque quotidie ad mensam suam peregrinos susciperet, quadam die peregrinus quidam inter alios venit, et ad mensam ductus est. Dumque Paterfamilias ex humilitatis consuetudine aquam vellet in eius manibus fundere, conversus urceum accepit, sed repente cum in eius manibus aquam fundere voluerat, non invenit. Cumque hoc factum secum ipse miraretur, eadem nocte ei Dominus per visionem dixit: "Caeteris diebus me in membra meis, hesterno autem die me in memetipso suscepisti".'

27. *Sp. Hist.*, IIIe Partie, Livre VII, ch. LI, v. 67-88 (p. 48). Cf. W. Verbeke,'Gregorius de Grote in de *Spiegel Historiael* van Jacob van Maerlant', dans *Pascua Mediaevalia*, éds. R. Lievens e.a., Mediaevalia Lovaniensia, I, 10 (Louvain, 1983), p. 369-397 (p. 374).

28. *Sp. Hist.*, IIIe Partie, Livre VII, ch. LI, v. 98-100.

          In mi selven, sonder waen.'
          ...
          Hier laten wi die bispele bliven,
          Die sente Gregorius wilde bescriven
100   In Dyalogus sinen boec...

Leven van Sinte Amand, II, 1113-1194

Hoe Amant alle daghe .xij. aerme lieden tetene gaf ende wat daer af gheuiel

1113   Het gheviel dat alle daghe
        Amand plach in aelmoesenen, sonder saghe,
        Te biddene met ootmoedichden
        .xii. die aermste vander stede
1117   Te siere maeltijt, ende die dedi
        Nevens hem sitten ter tafelen vry
        Daer hi selue te sittene plach.
        So dat gheuiel vp eenen dach
1121   Dat hiere .xij. hadde ghebeden,
        Ende als si quamen te siere stede
        So heeft hiere .xiij. voorzien.
        Ter tafelen dedi hise sitten mettien
1125   Ende ghinc selue dienen daer
        Voor hemlieden in teekene maer
        Dat Xpristus hem dertierster sat
        Vp den wittendonderdach ende at
1129   Daer hi sijn laetste mael dede.
        Ende in exemplen der waerheden
        So ne wilde selue sitten niet
        Omdat hi die siegye uervullet siet.
1133   Ne maer alser maer .xij. en waren
        So sat hi inde middele daer.
        Nv hoort van Amande, den heere.
        Hi bat hem allen harde seere
1137   Datsi alle wel te ghemake daden
        Ende troostese seere ter gods ghenaden
        Met scoonen woorden ende met soeten,
        So datsi haten met goeder moeten,
1141   Sonder die aermste die daer sat,
        Die dochte hem dat hi niet en hadt.
        Ende als hi dies wert gheware,
        So bat hi hem ootmoedelike dare
1145   Dat hi hate ende in dancke name,
        Ende begheerdi yet anders dander quame,
        Dat hijt seide, men sout hem bringhen
        Vp datmen conste bi eenighe dinghen.
1149   Die meinsche sat in de midelwaert
        Daer Amant toe sprac ter vaert

Ende hi andwoorde hem harde saen:
'Menich waerf hebdi mi ontfaen
1153 Vriendelike, met grooten ootmoede,
Dat sal hu ghelden gode, die goede.
Ende nv hebbic te deser stont
Wel ghehadt, dat si hu cont,
1157 Wat miere herten begheeren mach.
Du hu moete bliuen vp elken dach
Gods gracie meersende talre tijt,
Want ghi van gode sijt ghebenedijt.'
1161 Dus bleef tusschen hem beeden de tale
Ende men ontdiende altemale,
So dat die tafele al bloot lach.
Ende als Amand dat ghesach
1165 *Nam* hi dbat metten *watre saen*
Ende *ghinc* die aerme helpen *dwaen*
So als die twaleue hadden ghedweghen.
Ende vp den dertiensten ghelegen,
1169 Was die ghebuerte, wats ghes*ciet*,
Ne *conste* hi den armen *vinden niet*.
Dies haddi vremde int tghedochte
Wat dat wonder bedieden mochte.
1173 Ooc so waest selsene hem allen
Die dit voor hooghen saghen gheuallen,
Maer Amande bleeft meest inden moet.
Tsnachts so lach die heere goed
1177 Daer hi rustens soude plien.
Daer heefti groote claerheit voorzien
Ende Xpristus sprac tote hem *daer hi lach*:
'Amand, vriend, *ouer menighen dach*
1181 *Hebstu mi ende minen* boden
Wel *ontfaen* ende ghetroost in nooden.
Dies dijn loon wert sonder ghetal
Daer die blijscepe eewelike ghedueren sal.
1185 *Maer ghisteren* inden daghe, doe ic hu weten,
Was ic te diere tafelen gheseten
Ende sprac selue ieghen di,
Daer du vriendelike ontfincs mi
1189 Ende tooghdet mi ootmoedicheit groot.
Dat salic di ghelden voor dine doot
In wat saken dat ghi begheert
Ende na dit lijf werddi gheheert
1194 Daer bouen int soete rijke scoone
Met minen vader inden troone.'

Malgré la forte amplification, De Wevel a conservé – heureusement pour le chercheur moderne – quelques rimes de son exemple immédiat. Le récit lui rappelle évidemment les événements du Jeudi saint. Il précise le nombre exact de pauvres – douze – et se rapproche ainsi d'une série d'apparitions et d'activités charitables similaires, dont un exemple précède dans le dossier hagiographique de Grégoire précisément l'histoire du pater familias.[29]

– *La légende de Barlaam et Josaphat*

Deux épisodes de la *Leven van Sinte Amand* illustrent le succès inouï de *Barlaam et Josaphat,* légende d'origine orientale qui s'est répandue dans le monde occidental à partir du Xe siècle. Elle fut reprise par Philip Utenbroeke dans la deuxième partie du *Spiegel Historiael*.[30]

La conversion de Bavon, dont le nom reste étroitement lié à l'histoire de Gand, n'apparaît dans l'hagiographie concernant saint Amand qu'à partir du *Carmen* carolingien que lui a dédié Milo de Saint-Amand.[31] L'épisode a d'ailleurs inspiré Rubens pour un tableau monumental qui décore encore aujourd'hui la cathédrale Saint-Bavon à Gand. Pour évoquer ce moment décisif, Gillis de Wevel reproduit littéralement la conversion de Nachor, fils d'un roi indien, soumis à l'influence de l'ermite Josaphat. Il suit à la lettre la traduction par Philip Utenbroeke du passage correspondant chez Vincent de Beauvais et se borne à changer les noms des personnages. Est-ce le charme oriental de *Barlaam et Josaphat* qui a amené De Wevel à ce type de réécriture? Travaillait-il sous la pression d'un contrat de livraison? Considérait-il que Philip Utenbroeke avait atteint une telle perfection littéraire dans sa traduction? Ou bien Gillis ne veut-il pas toucher à un passage qui exprime parfaitement le message de son oeuvre, à savoir: Dieu ne requiert pas la perdition de l'homme; il n'est jamais trop tard pour se convertir.

---

29. Il s'agit de l'apparition d'un ange à une table de douze invités: cf. Verbeke, 'Gregorius de Grote in de Spiegel Historiael', p. 379-380. L'apparition similaire du dossier de Grégoire (*Vita*: PL 75, c. 95) manque dans le *Spiegel Historiael* mais se retrouve dans la *Legenda aurea* (éd. Graesse, p. 194 ou éd. G.P. Maggioni, p. 293-294). À propos des soins pour douze pauvres en général, voir par exemple: W. Witters,'Pauvres et pauvreté dans les coutumiers monastiques du moyen âge', dans *Études sur l'histoire de la pauvreté (Moyen Âge – XVIe siècle),* sous la direction de M. Mollat, Publications de la Sorbonne, Études, 8, t. I (Paris, 1974), p. 177-215 (p. 187, n° 28, p. 200, 201 et 214).
30. Cf. *Sp. Hist.*, IIe Partie, Livre VII, ch. I-XXXIX.
31. MGH *Poetae Latini Medii Aevi*, III (1896), p. 586 (Lib. II, v. 351-384).

Spiegel Historiael, IIe Partie, Livre VII, ch. XXIII, v. 35-52 et ch. XXIV, v. 1-34 (p. 468-469)

ch. XXIII[32]

...

35   Die danc es, dat *ic* [Josaphat] *di* [Nachor] *wille toegen*
       Van *den wegen daer du in bedrogen*
       Lange wetende in heefs gesijn,
       Ende ic wille *di wisen dat padekijn,*
       Dat di ter salecheit leiden sal.
40   Nu, Nachor, *hieromme vore al*
       Radic di *ane Christum cleven,*
       Die di dewelijc leven sal geven;
       Ende laet dese lidende dinge *quaet,*
       Want di niet ewelike en *staet*
45   Te levene, wanttu *stervelijc best,*
       Dat ons allen es ane gevest.
       Ende wee si di tallen *stonden,*
       *Comt*stu met bordennen van *sonden,*
       Ten vonnesse rechte *geladen,*
50   Daer men loenen sal die daden,
       Du en *werps* dine *bordene van di,*
       Want het licht te doene si.'

ch. XXIV[33]

1   Doe Nachor *horde dese tale,*
     Wert hi in *berouwe wale,*

---

32. Vincentius, Lib. XV, c. 37 (p. 594): 'Sed quae est retributio? Ista scilicet ut ostendam tibi declinare a via mala et lubrica, per quam hactenus incessisti, et ut ambules per rectam et salutarem semitam, quam non ignoranter, sed scienter et sponte male agendo effugisti; barathris ac praecipitiis teipsum committendo. Intellige ergo Nachor intellectualis existens, et prae omnibus solum desidera Christum, ut apud ipsum absconditam vitam lucreris, fluxa ista et corruptibilia despiciens: non enim per omne vives saeculum, sed cum sis mortalis, discedes hinc post modicum, sicut et omnes alij, qui ante nos fuerunt; et ne tibi sit grave, peccati onus baiulans, cum ieris illuc, ubi iudicium iustum et retributio operum est, et non abieceris prius illud, cum facilis eius sit depositio.'

33. Vincentius, Lib. XV, c. 38 (p. 594): 'Haec ut audivit filius Regis, mox Spiritu sancto inflammatus intrinsecus in corde concaluit, et cogitationem Nachor ad desperationem inclinatam relevare caepit, et ad stabilitatem fidei Christi erigere, dicens: Nulla ô Nachor, nulla tibi dubitatio sit. Scriptum est enim: Possibile est Deo de lapidibus istis excitare filios Abrahae, qui propter summam benignitatis eminentiam, omnibus ad se conversis caelestem aperuit ianuam, nulli salutis denegans introitum sed misericorditer paenitentes recipit. Nam ideo prima et tertia et sexta et nona et .11. hora aequalis omnibus merces redditur, sicut sacrum refert evangelium. Itaque licet hactenus in peccatis consenseris, si flagranti corde accesseris, eorum qui a iuventute pondus diei et aestus portaverunt, consortio dignus efficieris. Haec et alia multa de paenitentia sanctissimus locutus iuvenis, in malis inveterato Nachor, et pollicitus remissionem peccatorum, promittensque Christum fore propitium, et plurimis exemplis certificans, quia paratus est semper

Maer hi gaf weder selke woerde,
Dat die jongelinc *wel hoerde*
5 *Dat hem wanhope dede wee.*
Doe sprac *hi:* 'Nachor, nemmer*mee*
En moechstu in wanhopen sneven,
Want daer *staet aldus bescreven:*
"Hets Gode mogelijc van den steene
10 *Te makene Abrahams kindere reene,"*
Die om sijn goedertierenheit groet
Hen allen die hemelsche dore ontsloet,
Die hen willen te hem bekeeren.
Also dewangelsiten ons leeren,
15 Dat *gelijc loen* wert gegeven,
Daer dwerc al wert wel voldreven,
Te priemen, tierdchen, te noenen noch,
Ja die te *vespertide comt doch.*
Al bestu comen te dijnre ouden,
20 *Wilstu beteren dine scouden,*
Du souds *met hen loen ontfaen,*
Die den dach al dore *hebben gedaen*
Haren erenst ten *labure.'*
Als dit ende deser gelike *cure*
25 Josaphat hem hadde *geseit,*
Antwerdde Nachor *wel gereit:*
'*O* edele siele ende *lichame,*
Vol van leeringen bequame,
Blive in dit woert toten endde,
30 Dat di geen dinc af en wende.
Ic wille gaen *sueken mine salechede,*
Penitentie doen, daer ic mede
Saechte *Gode, dien ic vergramt*
Met dinge hebbe dic*wile on*bekant.

Leven van Sinte Amand, I, 4314-4365

4314 Het es tijt ende *ic [Amand] wille di [Bavo] tooghen*
Den wech daer du in bedrooghen
Langhe onwetende hebs ghesijn
Ende ic sal di wisen dat padelkin
4318 Dat hu *ter salicheit leeden sal.*
Hieromme, hedel graue, *voor al*

ad suscipiendam paenitentiam; languidam illius animam velut quibusdam medelis refocillans plene restituit sanitati. Ait enim confestim Nachor ad illum: Tu quidem, ô nobilissime anima pariter et corpore, bene instructus his mirabilibus mysteriis, persevera in bona confessione usque ad finem, et nullus modus, vel tempus hanc de tuo corde amputet: Ego vero vadam salutem meam quaerere, et per paenitentiam Deum placare iratum, non ego ulterius Regis videbo faciem, nisi tu tantummodo volueris.'

Radic hu *an Xpristum* te voughene hu *leuen*
Die hu *teewelike* lijf mach *gheuen*,
4322 *Ende laet dese* weerelt *quaet*,
Want di hier onlanghe *staed*
Te leuene, du die *steruelic best*,
Ende dat es ons allen an gheuest.
4326 *Ende wee* sal hem sijn ten *stonden*
Die comt gheladen met *sonden*
Ten hutersten daghe, daer god sal
Doemen dese weerelt al.
4330 Nv *werpt* dese *bordine van di*,
Want het licht te doene sij
Vp dat ghiere hu toe wilt uoughen
Ende ghi sult gode te bedt ghenoughen.'
4334 Als Baue *hoorde dese tale*
Wert hem een *berouwen wale*,
Maer hi gaf weder sulke woorde
Dat die helighe *man wel hoorde*
4338 *Dat hem wanhope dede wee.*
Dus seide *hi* Bauen: 'Nem*mee*, nem*mee*,
Ne moetti in wanhopen leuen,
Want het *staed aldus bescreven*:
4342 "*Hets moghelic gode vanden steene*
Te makene Abrahams kinder reene".
Ia, die hem willen te hem bekeeren
Als ons de ewangelien leeren,
4346 *Si sullen gheliken loon* ontfaen,
Al eist dat si spade te werke gaen,
Te priemen, te tierschen, te noenen noch,
Ia, te vesperen comen doch.
4350 *Al bestu commen te diere houden,*
Wiltu beteren dine scouden,
Du sult met hem loon ontfaen
*Die alden dach hebben gh*estaen
4354 *In haren* neersteghen *labuere.'*
Die graue uerstond wel ter *cuere*
Wat dat hem die helighe uader *seide*
Ende hi *andwoorde hem wel ghereyde*:
4358 '*O* helich man, uwen *lichame*
Es *vul van leeringhen bequame.*
Dies *willic souken mine salichede*
Ende *penitencie doen, daer ic mede*
4364 *Gode* ghenoughen *dien ic uergraemt*
Hebbe dicke met saken *on*betaemt,
Ende werken altoos bi uwen rade,
Tallen tiden, vrouch ende spade.

Dès sa première apparition au confluent de l'Escaut et de la Lys, Amand essaie de convaincre les Gantois de renoncer à leurs idoles païennes impuissantes.[34] Le vrai créateur leur est resté inconnu jusqu'aujourd'hui. C'est ainsi qu'ils se distinguent des juifs qui reconnaissent Dieu, mais nient la venue du Christ au monde.

Pour expliquer la différence entre juifs et chrétiens, De Wevel se réfère de nouveau à la légende de *Barlaam et Josaphat*. Dans la *disputatio* à la cour royale indienne, il reprend les mots de Nachor.

Spiegel Historiael, IIe Partie, Livre VII, ch. XXI, v. 1-58 (p. 466-467)[35]

```
1    Ten Joden sien wi nu vort,
     Wat van Gode es hare acort.
     Dese sijn van Abrahams geslachte,
4    Die God wilen leidde met machte
     Ute Egypten, ende nochtan
     So vielen si afgoden an.
     Doe sendde hen God propheten wijs,
8    Diese castiden; maer onprijs
     Daden si hen, ende namen hen dleven.
     Hier na, alst God wilde geven,
     Sende hi hen sinen enegen sone
12   Omme te bekeerne; maer die gone
     Ontseidenne ende gavenne in handen
     Pylate, den baeliu, met scanden
```

---

34. *Amand*, I, 2845-2920.
35. Vincentius, Lib. XV, c. 35 (p. 593): *De errore Iudaeorum, et vera fide christianorum.*'Veniamus ergo rex ad Iudaeos, ut videamus quid et ipsi sentiant de Deo. Hi namque existentes de stirpe Abrahae, Isaac, et Jacob, habitaverunt in Aegypto. Eduxit autem illos Deus inde in manu forti; nam saepius Dijs gentium servierunt, et missos ad se prophetas et iustos interfecerunt. Deinde postquam complacuit filio Dei ut veniret in terram, negantes eum, tradiderunt eum Pilato praesidi Romanorum et crucifixerunt eum, immemores beneficiorum eius, et innumerabilium miraculorum, quae inter eos operatus est, et perierunt propria iniquitate. Colunt etiam nunc solum Deum omnipotentem, sed non secundum scientiam, nam Christum negant filium Dei, et sunt similes gentibus licet approquinquare aliquo modo veritati videantur, a qua se ipsos elongaverunt. Ista vero de Iudaeis sufficient. Christiani autem a Christo dicuntur: sic etenim filius Dei altissimi vocatur, qui de caelo descendens propter salutem hominum, de Spiritu sancto ex Maria virgine absque virili semine, et salva matris integritate carnem suscepit, et hominibus apparuit, ut a multorum Deorum errore ipsos revocaret. Qui mirabili sua dispositione per crucem morte gustata spontanea voluntate, post tres dies resurgens per 40 dies cum eis conversatus, caelos ascendit. 12 Apostolos habuit, qui post eius in caelum reditum exierunt et in omnes orbis provincias, et docuerunt illius magnificentiam: unde qui adhuc ministrant iustitiae praedicationis illius Christiani vocantur; et hi sunt qui super omnes gentes terrae invenerunt veritatem. Cognoscunt enim Deum creatorum, et auctorem omnium in filio unigenito et spiritu sancto. Veraciter enim est haec via veritatis, quae ambulantes per eam in regnum ducit aeternum promissum a Christo in futura vita. Et ut noveris Rex...'

           Tontlivene ende pinen groot,
16   Ende hebbenne an tcruce gedoodt,
       Ende *daden* al *uut haren moede*
       Wat hi hen hadde gedaen te *goede*.
       Doch houden si hen ane *enen God*,
20   *Maer niet rechte na* Gods *gebod*;
       Want Christum loechenen si, den Gods sone,
       Ende *sijn* wel na *als die gone*
       Die de afgode anebeden.
24   Al hebbensi van der waerheden
       Ene gelike, si sijn *verwerret*
       Ende van der waerheit *sere ververret*.
       De *Kerstene hebben* van Kerste den *name*:
28   Die name was *den Gods sone* betame,
       Die van den hemele *quam beneden*
       Omme alle der liede *salecheden.*
       Van den *Heilegen Geest geboren*
32   *Uut Marien, der maecht vercoren*,
       Sonder enech mannes saet,
       Onbesmet des magedoems staet,
       Nam hi vleesch an, ende quam so vort
36   *Van den lieden gesien, gehort,*
       Om dat hise wilde bringen
       Gheloevende ane warachtegen dingen
       Ende van dolingen der *afgode*;
40   Ende sijns danx sonder *enige node*
       Aen tcruce die doot heeft gesmaect,
       Ende also hijt *cont* vore hadde *gemaect*,
       Es hi ten derden dage verresen.
44   XL *dage wandelde hi na desen*
       Met sinen jongeren hier *op deerde;*
       Te hemele voer hi doe siere veerde.
       XII *apostele sende hi uut,*
48   De werelt te leerne, wies luut
       Al die werelt *es doregaen.*
       Ende die noch na dat leeren staen,
       Heeten Kerstene bi namen,
52   Ende dese vore al te samen
       Hebben die rechte waerheit vonden.
       Ende si hebben *dien God in conden*,
       Die alle dinge *heeft gemaect.*
56   Dits de wech daer niemen in en wert *ontraect:*
       Diere in wandelen vroedelike
       Hi comt ten eweliken *rike*,
       O coninc...

Leven van Sinte Amand, I, 2842-2921

2842 Nv hoorter na, groot ende cleene,
Ende uerstaed tgrosse vanden bediede
Dat hi [Amand] seide voor dheydene lieden:
'Broeders, hu ghelooue es seere fel.
2846 Dit willic hu segghen bi redenen wel,
Want al uw gheloouelike saken
Moeste een god selue maken.
Want Mamet ende Appolijn,
2850 Teruogant ende Jupetijn,
Ende al dat ghi gode heet sijn hier,
Staen, ende bernen int helsche vier
Ende waren lieden also ghi.
2854 Hierbi so moghen weten wi
Datsi hem seluen niet ghemaect
Hebben, al sisi so ongheraect.
Dat ghi an hem lieden ghelooft.
2858 Hedt doet de duuel dat ghi so dooft.
Want een god es bouen al
Diet maecte ende ontmaken sal
Al dat yet lijf ontfinc,
2862 Ende desen kennen in warer dinc
Die jueden ende ghelouen in hem.
Maer si hebben een groot lem
Bi datsi *sijn van Abrahams gheslachte*
2866 Dat *wilen gode leedde* bi *machte*
Huut Egypten, door die roode see,
Sodat si leeden al sonder wee.
Ende hi *sende hem propheten wijs*
2870 *Diese* leerde; *maer* mes*prijs*
Daden si hem ende namen hem tleuen.
Hiernaer, alst god wilde gheuen,
Sende god *sinen eenighen sone*
2874 *Omme te bekeerne, maer de ghone*
Ne kendene niet, maer dadene vaen,
Ggheeselen, ende an een cruce slaen.
Hier daden si *huut haeren moede*
2878 *Al dat hem god hye dede in goede.*
Doch bekennen sij eenen god,
Maer niet te rechte na sijn *ghebod.*
Want Xpristus loochenen si, den gods sone.
2882 Hierbi so *sijn* si *als dieghone*
Die de afgoden anebeden.
Al hebben si vander waerheden
Een ghelike, si bliuen *uerwerret*
2886 *Ende van* gode *seere ontverret.*
Maer *kerstine hebben* desen *name*

Van Kerste, *den gods sone bequame*,
Die van bouen *quam beneden*
2890 *Om alder* weerelt *salichede*.
Biden *helighen gheest gheboren*
Hute der maghet Marien uercoren,
Sonder eenichs mans saed,
2894 *Onbesmet der magheden staed*,
Nam hi vleeschs ende quam dus *voort*
Vanden lieden ghesien, ghehoort,
Om dat hise wilde bringhen
2898 *Gheloouende an waeracteghe dinghen*
Ende sceeden souden vanden *afgoden*.
Ende sijns dancs, sonder sine *noode*,
Wilde hi ant cruce die dood smaken;
2902 *Ende also hijt* wilde *cont maken*
Es hi ten derde daghe uerresen,
Ende wandelde .xl. daghe na desen
Met sinen jonghers vp eerderijke.
2906 Ende *doe voor hi te hemelrijke*
Ende *sende sine apostelen huut*
Die weerelt te leerne wies luut
Ouer algader *es doorgaen*.
2910 *Ende die noch na dit leeren staen*
Hebben die rechte waerheit vonden
Ende den sekeren god in conden
Die alle saken *heeft ghemaecht*.
2914 *Dit es die wech daer niement ontraect*
Van *diere in wandelen vroedelike*,
*Want siere om hebben them*el*rijke.*
Hier bi biddic hu, broeders alle,
2918 Wilt Xpristus te ghenaden uallen.
Hi sal hu vriendelike ontfaen
Ende uergheven dat hi hebt mesdaen.'
Als Amand dese woorden hende
...

Dans le *Spiegel Historiael* une vive critique du culte païen précède le passage emprunté; le commencement du sermon de saint Amand reprend le même thème, un parallélisme de plus.[36] Au moment précis où Nachor s'adresse directement au roi (*Sp. Hist.*, v. 59), Gillis se distancie de son modèle au moyen d'une apostrophe (*Amand*, I, 2917-20) adressée aux Gantois. L'apostrophe servant à couvrir des changements dans l'inspiration du poète est un procédé rhétorique que Gillis domine

36. *Amand*, I, 2845-47.

parfaitement.[37] Il réduit les détails à propos de la mort du Christ (*Amand*, I, 2875-76) et évite de répéter l'explication du terme 'chrétien'.[38] La tradition manuscrite des deux textes est, je suppose, à l'origine des différences mineures.

– *La 'disputatio judeorum' des 'Gesta Silvestri'*

J. van Mierlo, l'auteur de la dernière grande synthèse de la littérature néerlandaise médiévale, estimait que la discussion entre saint Amand et quatre érudits juifs était l'un des passages les plus attrayants du poème de Gillis.[39] Déjà au 19ᵉ siècle, les éditeurs du *Spiegel Historael* avaient constaté le lien entre De Wevel et la traduction par Utenbroeke de la célèbre disputatio entre le pape Silvestre (314-335) et douze intellectuels juifs à la cour de Constantin.[40] En plus, ils signalaient que dans son récit de la vie du pape Silvestre le traducteur ne s'était pas contenté des seuls chapitres du *Speculum historiale* qui remontent aux *Gesta Silvestri*.[41] Pour une fois, Utenbroeke a remplacé le texte fort abrégé de Vincent de Beauvais par une version plus étoffée.

Par sa reprise du débat, Gillis de Wevel met en évidence son intérêt pour la question juive, thème complètement neuf dans le contexte de l'hagiographie concernant saint Amand. Le poète y parvient au moyen d'une technique bien connue: une réflexion sur le verset 9 du Psaume 31: '*Nolite fieri sicut equus et mulus, quibus non est intellectus*' (*Amand*, II, 1421-22).

---

37. Autres exemples: *Amand*, I, 169, 329, 333, 339, 367, 410, 437, 669, 825, 838, 1782, 1892, 1902, cf. W. Verbeke, 'O soete cruce...: een berijmd gebed in handschrift Brussel, K.B., 19588', dans *Serta devota in memoriam Guillelmi Lourdaux, Pars Posterior: Cultura Mediaevalis*, Mediaevalia Lovaniensia, Series I, Studia XXI (Leuven, 1995), p. 297-313 (p. 305) en id., 'Ave vinculum caritatis', p. 256. Le domaine de la rhétorique médiévale ne m'est pas suffisamment familier pour pouvoir évaluer la diffusion de cette technique.
38. *Amand*, I, 2887-88; *Sp. Hist.*, IIᵉ Partie, Livre VII, ch. XXI, v. 27-28 et 51-52.
39. *Amand*, II, 1421-2690; J. Van Mierlo, *De letterkunde van de Middeleeuwen*, t. I, p. 399. Voir aussi W. Bunte, *Juden und Judentum in der mittelniederländische Literatur (1100-1600)*, Judentum im Umwelt, 24 (Frankfurt am Main, 1989), p. 516-518 et 538-544 et id., *Religionsgespräche zwischen Christen und Juden in den Niederlanden (1100-1500)*, Judentum und Umwelt, 27 (Frankfurt a. M., 1990), 543-584. Bunte cite la discussion de Gillis de Wevel et traduit même plusieurs passages en allemand, mais il n'a pas remarqué le lien étroit avec Utenbroeke.
40. F. Von Hellwald, M. de Vries et E. Verwijs, *Jacob van Maerlant's Spiegel Historiael: Tweede Partie, bewerkt door Philip Utenbroeke*, Maatschappij der Nederlandsche Letterkunde (Leiden, 1879), p. XXVI-XXVII.
41. F. Von Hellwald e.a., p. XIV-XXIV; Vincentius, Lib. XIII, c. 50-52.

Un narrateur expérimenté comme Gillis de Wevel exploite pleinement les avantages du style direct: les dialogues, les sermons, les prières et les débats abondent. Aussi son 'contrefact' d'un 'Jeu du roi qui ne ment' est significatif à ce propos.[42] Ce jeu profane qui éveillait parfois des soupçons en raison de questions piquantes relatives à l'amour humain, sert de cadre au développement de différents aspects de l'amour divin. Ainsi la mise-en-scène de la polémique entre chrétiens et juifs a-t-elle certainement favorisé l'aspect didactique et littéraire de son poème, sans oublier les effets d'une présentation orale vivante.

La discussion est localisée 'en Pévèle'. La victoire du camp chrétien se concrétisera par la fondation de l'abbaye de Saint-Amand-les-Eaux (Elnon) avec l'aide financière de la communauté juive perdante, curieuse présentation des origines d'une abbaye bénédictine fondée selon la tradition par saint Amand et qui porte son nom.

Gillis réduit le nombre de participants juifs de douze à quatre, probablement pour des raisons techniques, entre autres la longueur de son modèle. Leurs noms – Abyachar, Godolyas, Bonoym etc. – sont remplacés par des noms à résonance biblique: Élie, Simon, Abraham, Moïse. La défense chrétienne ne se compose que de quatre personnes:

1° un mystérieux évêque de Wasmens (ou Wazemens), qui soulève pas mal de questions;[43]

2° saint Arnould, évêque de Metz (+ 640/1), qui a pris l'initiative de la discussion publique et en assure l'organisation. Dans sa présentation du saint mérovingien, comtemporain de saint Amand et membre de la cour royale, l'auteur le confond avec son homonyme Arnould, évêque de

---

42. *Amand*, I, 5082-5370; lit.: W. E. Hegman,'Het conincspel in de Middelnederlandse letterkunde', *Handelingen van de Koninklijke Zuidnederlandse Maatschappij voor Taal- en Letterkunde en Geschiedenis*, 20 (1966), p. 183-228; U. Peeters,'Cour d'amour – Minnehof: Ein Beitrag zum Verhältnis der französischen und deutschen Minnedichtung zu den Unterhaltungsformen ihres Publikums', *Zeitschrift für deutsches Altertum und deutsche Literatur*, 101 (1972), 117-133; Dieuwke E. van der Poel,'Minnevragen in de Middelnederlandse letterkunde', dans Frank Willaert e.a., *Een zoet akkoord: Middeleeuwse lyriek in de Lage Landen* (Amsterdam, 1992), p. 207-218 (p. 212); L. de Wachter, thèse de doctorat sous la direction de J.D. Janssens, *'Een literair-historisch onderzoek naar de effecten van ontleningen op de compositie en de zingeving van de Roman van Heinric en Margriete van Limborch'* (Bruxelles, 1998), p. 285-352.

43. Dans son *Gallo-Flandria sacra et profana* (Douai, 1628), Johannes Buzelinus a annoté à propos de 'Wazenna', faubourg de Lille, 'Qui litteris mandavere primam illic eorundem Tornacensium Episcoporum sedem fuisse Liderici Buccensis aetate, turpissimum errorem invehunt...' (p. 128). Je n'ai pas encore pu identifier ceux qui sont visés par 'qui litteris mandavere'.

Soissons et mort à Oudenburg en 1087, certainement mieux connu en Flandre.[44]

3° saint Amand, le champion incontournable des débats, qui est invité à y participer en tant qu'évêque de Maastricht. La proposition facilite son départ des bords de la Meuse, lieu traditionnellement hostile au saint homme, et aide ainsi à dissimuler les incidents entre l'évêque et ses fidèles mentionnés dans les *vitae*.

4° et finalement, il reste toujours le support divin...

Le roi Dagobert, qui apparaît dans toutes les *Vitae Amandi*, tient le rôle de modérateur, remplaçant ainsi l'empereur Constantin présent dans le modèle direct. Ses interventions contribuent à une composition harmonieuse selon un schéma précis: question juive – réponse de saint Amand – réaction juive – avertissement de la part du camp chrétien – intervention de Dagobert. Si les questions posées rapellent les interpellations des quatre premiers juifs dans le *Spiegel Historiael*, les réponses par contre ont été renouvelées. Ils reprennent souvent des thèmes développés dans *Scolastica* (ou *Rijmbijbel*), la bible rimée de Jacob van Maerlant composée vers 1271 selon le modèle de l'*Historia scolastica* de Petrus Comestor.[45] Seules les prophéties à propos de la naissance et la passion du Christ se trouvent dans le modèle du *Spiegel Historiael*. Bien qu'amplifiées et en partie renouvelées par De Wevel, leur origine n'a pas échappé à l'œil attentif des philologues du 19e siècle qui scrutaient partout les sources des textes médiévaux.

Spiegel Historiael, IIe Partie, Livre V, ch. XXIII, v. 174-213 (p. 296)[46]

174   Silvester hi *heeft geseit*:
        'Dit selen wi *bi uwen propheten*

---

44. Cf. *Bibliotheca Sanctorum*, II, 446-447 (Arnould de Metz) et II, 449 (Arnould de Tiegem ou d'Oudenburg). Certes, Gillis n'est pas l'inventeur de cette confusion. Voir R. Nip, *Arnulfus van Oudenburg, bisschop van Soissons († 1087)*, (Leuven, 2004), (avec résumé français).

45. À propos de *Scolastica* (ou *Rijmbijbel*) voir *Narrative-Sources* J004; éditions: J. B. David, *Rymbijbel van Jacob van Maerlant* (Bruxelles, 1858-59) et M. Gysseling, *Corpus van Middelnederlandse teksten (tot en met het jaar 1300)*, 2e série: Literaire handschriften, 3-4 (Leiden, 1983). Pour les parallèles voir: *Amand*, II, 2147-2173 versus *Rijmbijbel*, 2523-2540; *Amand*, II, 2193-2229 versus *Rijmbijbel*, 2017-2044; *Amand*, II, 2259-2294 versus *Rijmbijbel*, 3641-3660; *Amand*, II, 2295-2339 versus *Rijmbijbel*, 1806-1830; *Amand*, II, 2409-2436 versus *Rijmbijbel*, 123-141; *Amand*, II, 2467-2502 versus *Rijmbijbel*, 1675-1700.

46. Le passage n'a pas d'équivalent chez Vincentius, Lib. XIII, c. LI. Les *Gesta Silvestri* publiés par B. Mombritius dans *Sanctuarium seu Vitae Sanctorum*, II (Paris, 1910, reprint 1978), p. 508-531 contiennent le passage suivant (p. 519-520):'Ad haec Sylvester respondit: Haec omnia praedicta esse de Christo vestris hodie scriptis docebimus.

Proeven, dat al tevoren *was beheten:*
*Da*ttene de *Maget soude dragen*
178 Hort men *Ysayam gewagen,*
Ende *dat hi onder tfolc soude wanderen*
Vort sprac *Baruch metten anderen,*
*Da*ttene die viant prouven soude
182 Vort sprac *Zacharias die oude,*
*Da*tmenne verraden soude ende vaen
Vort sprac *Salomon, sonder waen,*
Dat hi Judase soude gescien,
186 Ende menne ontcleeden soude na dien
Ende dattene die valsche souden bedragen
Hort men *David gewagen.*
Dat menne bespotten soude onscone,
190 Ende oec van der dornecrone,
Ende dat menne groef, *wiltu dies lyen,*
Dat vintstu in Jeremien.
Moechstu, Jode, *redene geven,*
194 *Dat* dijne *propheten* dit *niet en screven,*
So doedt, *ende* en constuut *niet volbringhen,*
So geloef doch dinen *dingen.'*
Die keyser sprac ...
...
Die vierde sprac, die hiet Aman:
205 'Die propheten seident al*waer*;

– Nam nasci eum ex virgine sanctus Isaias hoc ordine praedixit: Ecce virgo in utero concipiet: et pariet filium: et vocabitur nomen eius Emanuel;
– quod vero inter homines conversatus sit: audi tuum prophetam dicentem: hic deus noster: et non estimabitur praeter eum: qui ostendit viam salutis Iacob puero suo et Israel dilecto suo. Post haec in terris visus est: et cum hominibus conversatus est:
– nam quod temptandus esset a diabolo: et vinceret diabolum: sanctus Zacharias propheta dicit: Vidi: Iesum magnum sacerdotem: et stabat diabolus a dextris eius: et dixit ad eum: imperat tibi deus diabole : qui redemit Israel, quod autem compraehendendus esset: sapientia dei per Salomonem loquitur: Dixerunt inquit impii compraehendamus iustum: quia inutilis est nobis:
– Nam quod a discipulo tradendus esset: dicit psalmigraphus: qui edebat panes meos: adampliavit adversum me supplantationem.
– Et quod expoliandus esset : et ros eius in sorte caderet: praedixit sanctus David propheta dicens: diviserunt sibi vestimenta mea: et super vestem meam miserunt sortem:
– Nam quod a falsis testibus accusandus esset: praedixit propheta dicens: insurreserunt in me testes iniqui:
– quod spinis quidem coronandus esset: praedixit sanctus Hieremias propheta Spinis peccatorum suorum circondederunt me populus hic. ...
– haec si potueris tu Iudaee probare: quia non a vestris prophetis prophetata sunt: quasi mendacem superabis me ...
Aunan dixit: vera esse omnia quae prophetae dixerunt omnes scimus: et nullus ignorat: sed tu ad alia dicta alia doces. Cui Sylvester: ergo dabis alium quem virgo concepit: et peperit: dabis alium qui gentes ad tuam legem spiritaliter intelligendam adduxit: dabis alium ...'

Maer du en toens ons niet al claer,
Dat hi dit selve wesen soude,
Christus, die dit al doegen woude.'
Silvester sprac: *'Toech enen anderen*
210 *Maech den Sone, die wilde wanderen*
Ende miraclen doen onder liede
Ende die selke dinc gesciede.'
Die keyser sprac...

Leven van Sinte Amand, II, 2591-2658

Hier spreect Moyses, de .iiij. juede:

2591 Moyses begonste vraghen dus:
'Ghi segghet uele van uwen Jhesus
Dat hi de gods sone was.
Twij liet hi danne ghescien das,
2595 Dat hi ter weerelt wert gheuanghen,
Ghepijnt ende an eene cruce ghehanghen?
Want ons ghelooue es van dien
Dat hijt niet hadde laten ghescien
2599 Hadde hij gods sone gheweesen.
Vander doot ware hi ghenesen
Bleuen, ende hadde met eenen woorde
Al tfolc brocht te sinen acoorde.'

Hier spreect Amand:

2603 Amand die *heuet* aldus *gheseit*:
'Te anderen tiden hebbic voor oghen gheleyt,
Noch salict *bi uwen propheten*
Hu *prouuen* dat dus *was beheten*.
2607 *Dat* eene *maghet soude draghen,*
Dit *hoorde* di *Ysayen ghewaghen*;
Een kint dat dalen souden huten troone,
Dat spreken sine boucken scoone.
2611 *Dat hi onder tfolc soude wanderen*
*Voor*seide *Baruch metten anderen,*
Ende ootmoedicheit tooghen groot
Dat vindi in scriftueren al bloot.
2615 *Dattene de viand prouuen soude*
*Voors*prac *Sakaryas, die oude,*
Ende ouerwonnen soude wesen,
Dit moghdi proper selue lesen.
2619 *Dat menne uerraden soude ende vaen*
*Voor*seide hu *Salmoen, sonder waen,*
Ende dat door onsen wille moeste sijn,
Dit tooght hij mede bij redenen fijn.

2623 *Dat* het bi *Judase soude ghescien*
     Ende dat *menne ontcleden soude nadien,*
     Ende dattene de valsche souden bedraghen,
     Dit *hoordi* wel *Dauitte ghewaghen.*
2627 *Dat menne bespotten soude onscoone*
     Ende ooc vander doornine croone,
     Ia, vander calumne, *wildijs lyen,*
     Dit vindi in boucken *Ieremien.*
2631 Vander crucen daer hi an hinc
     Ende van dat hij ter hellen ghinc,
     Ende sine vrienden loste daer huut,
     Maken Abrahams boucken gheluut.
2635 Van dat hi ten derden daghe es uerresen
     Ende wandelde .xl. daghe na desen
     Met sinen jongers vp eerderijke
     Seghet hu Josophus properlijke.
2639 Dat hi ten xlsten daghe vpvoer
     In midden staende, vp den berch van Thaboer,
     Van sinen discipulen menicheen
     Voorwijst ons Baruch ende Ysaac onder hem tween.
2643 Dat hi den helighen gheest sende neder
     Tote sinen jonghers voort, ende weder
     Predickende ende gauen ghesonde,
     Dat voorseide hu Dauid te menigher stonde.
2647 *Mooghdi* hier ieghen *redene gheuen*
     Dat uwe *profeten niet en screuen,*
     So segghet, *ende* moghdijt *niet vulbringhen,*
     So ghelooft doch waerachteghe *dinghen.*'

Noch spreect hier Moyses:

2651 Moyses seide: 'Dattu segghes dats *waer,*
     Maer du ne tooghes ons niet claer
     Vp *dat* die *selue wesen woude*
     Xpristus die dit ghedooghen soude.'

Noch spreect hier Amand:

2655 Doe seide Amant: *'Tooght eenen anderen*
     Maeghdensone die wilde wanderen
     Ende die de pine heuet leden
     Na dat die propheten vorseiden.'

Ce tour d'horizon des réminiscences à l'hagiographie transmise par le *Spiegel Historiael* de Jacob van Maerlant et son continuateur Utenbroeke serait incomplet sans la mention d'un combat avec un diable et du récit de la libération de prisonniers.

– *La vie de Marguerite d'Antioche*

Le combat violent d'Amand avec un diable qui est obligé d'admettre ses efforts pour tromper les fidèles, remonte à un épisode bien connue de la vie de sainte Marguerite d'Antioche.[47] Les tournures et rimes empruntées indiquent clairement la source du poète flamand.

Spiegel Historiael, IIe Partie, Livre V, ch. XIV, v. 92-126 (p. 279)[48]

92	Die duvel, die omme der lieder scende
	Altoes poghet, quam vor hare [Marguerite]
	Als een drake, omme met vare
	Te bringhene dat maghedijn
96	An die gode, ende voer te haer aenscijn
	Of hise al verslinden soude;
	Ende metten cruce also houde
	Heiftsoe verjaghet den viant.
100	Maer hi verkeerde hem te hant,
	Ende quam vor hare in mans gedane,
	Omme quaetheit haer te leeghene ane.
	Dat die duvel was soe *verstoet*,
104	Ende *waerpene onder* haren *voet*;
	Dat hi dat seeghe heiftsoene *ghedwonghen*,
	Dat *hi ghereet es tallen* spronghen
	Te bedrieghene die kerstine:
108	*Het* ware *die nature* sine
	Te *hatene alle doeghet*. Hi spr*ac*,
	Al waest dat menne dicken verspr*ac*
	Daer hi den mensce wilde *bedrieghen*,
112	So ware sijn ghere altoes dat *lieghen*,
	In hopen of hi *tenegher* stonde
	Den *mensce* niet *bedrieghen conde*,
	Want hi den mensce ofjan altoes
116	Die salicheit die hi verloes.
	Ende al weet hi wel nocht*an*,
	Dat hise niet weder ghecrighen *can*,

---

47. La *Bibliotheca Sanctorum* (VIII, 1150-1165) souligne le succès de ce passage, et particulièrement dans la littérature vernaculaire et les représentations artistiques.

48. Vincentius, Lib. XIII, c. 27 (p. 515): '...sed diabulus, ut eam terreret, subito ei in Draconem mutatus apparet, qui cum eam quasi devoraturus impeteret, signo crucis opposito protinus evanuit. Sed tamen ille adhuc, ut ei quoque modo suaderet, in hominem se mutavit. At illa Daemonem esse intelligens, eum per caput apprehendit, et sub se ad terram deijcens, coegit ut diceret, cur Christianos tam multipliciter attentaret? Qui respondit, naturale sibi esse odium contra virtutum viros, et quamvis saepe repellatur ab eis, spe tamen, et desiderio seducendi, semper infestus existit, et quia invidet nobis faelicitatem quam perdidit; etsi hanc recuperare non potest, eam aliis auferre contendit. Et his dictis dum virgo pedem sublevavit, ille statim velut fumus evanuit.'

So es hi nochtan pogende sere
120 Hoe hise elken mensce ontkere.
Als *hi dit ende andre dinghe*
Hadde *hare geseit ende sonderlinghe*,
Bat *hi* hare dat soene gaen *liete*.
124 Want soene hadde *in swaren verdriete*,
Ende haer tijt dochte, *heiftsoene gelaten*
Varen, ende hi voer *sire straten*.

Leven van Sinte Amand, I, 1232-1279

Hoe de viant lien moeste wie hi was ende waeromme datti die kerstine so gheerne tempteerde

Als dit uerhoorde die goede Amand,
Besach hi seere den viand
Ende mercte wel an sijn wesen
1235 Ende Jhesus Xpristus sende hem te desen
Sulc lijcteeken daer hi mede
Den viant kende te dier stede.
Daer scoet hi hem an metter *spoet*
Ende heeftene *gheworpen onder voet*
1240 Ende slouchene so zeere ende *dwanc*
Dat hi moeste sonder danc
Lien selue metter mont
Twi *hi ghereet es taller* stond
Te bedrieghene de kerstine.
1245 Hi seide: '*Hets die natuere* mine
Dat ic *uerhate alle duecht.*
Die redene waer bi ghi kennen muecht:
Het es om dat mi god uerst*ac*
Also ic hu hier voren uertr*ac*
1250 Ende warp mi in grooter aermoeden.
Enten kerstinen menschen goede
Heeft hi ter salicheit uercoren
Die ic bi houeerden hebbe uerloren.
Hieromme so es altoos *lieghen*
1255 Mine natuere ende *bedrieghen*,
In hopen of ic *teenighen stonden*
Eenighe *mensche bedrieghen conde*
Die helich ware ende uercoren *dan*
Ende ter blijscip gheroupen *an*
1260 Daer ic hute ben ghesteken.
Nochtan so moet mi ghebreken
Dat ic nemmermeer mach comen
Ter bliscip die mi es ghenomen.
Voort bi dat ic kende hu leven
1265 Haddic gheerne an hu bedreuen
Dat ghi sout sijn te onsen ghebode

                    Ende uerontweert van uwe gode
                    Ende uerloren hadt die scoen stede
                    Daer ic wilen was in de moghenthede.'
    1270   Hoe *hi dit seide ende ander dinghen*
                    Bat hi daer naer *sonderlinghe*
                    Amande dat hine varen *liete*
                    Want hi laghe *in zwaren uerdriete.*
                    Die helighe man heeft hem beuolen
    1275   Dat sijn gaen ware in de oolen
                    Van der hellen ende nemmeer
                    Faelgieren soude sijn bitter seer.
                    Ende hier mede *heeft hine ghelaten*
                    Henen loopen *siere straten.*

À la bataille de Marguerite Gillis a ajouté quelques éléments du dossier médiéval concernant les diables, par exemple l'accentuation de leur orgueil.

– *La vie de Julien du Mans*

Pour la libération de prisonniers, thème largement répandu dans l'hagiographie médiévale – et présent également dans toutes les *Vitae Amandi*[49] – Gilles avait l'exemple de Julien du Mans en tête – et en main –.[50]

Spiegel Historiael, IIe Partie, Livre I, ch. LXXXII, v. 34-44 (p. 58)[51]

    34   Vort dede hi menege nuttelijchede:
                    Te Sans quam hi weder hier naer,
                    Om die gevane bat hi daer,
                    Die men *hem al wederseide,*
    38   *Hi* ginc thuus ende sonder beide
                    Es dat gevangenesse onttaen allene,

---

49. C. 9 (MGH SRM V, p. 435).

50. Dans le poème de Gillis de Wevel le récit cadre dans un pèlerinage à Rome. De là il n'est pas exclu que le poète a confondu Julien, patron des pèlerins (Julianus Hospitator) avec Julien du Mans. Ce ne serait d'ailleurs pas un cas isolé (cf. *Dictionnaire des lettres françaises: Le Moyen Age,* Paris, 1992, p. 1343).

51. Vincentius, Lib. IX, c. 113 (p. 362):'Cum autem urbis a Domino sibi commendatae portam subiret, carcerali custodiae mancipati, clamantes, ut sui misereretur, exorabant: et ille benignissimus ad eos, quibus id officii commissum erat, supplex accessit precans, ut adventus sui gratia redderent absolutos, quos iniquitas propria fecerat reos. Spretis vero precibus, proprio hospitio se recepit, et tacitus ac gemens, Dei misericordiam praestolari caepit. Mox Angelico ministerio ostia carceris aperta sunt, et illi egredientes sancti viri conspectibus se obtulerunt. At ille gaudens in domino iam laetus cibum accepit, et quos merito solverat, sancti etiam convivii participatione donavit.'

>   Ende si *gingen uut al gemeene,*
>   Ende tot Juliane si gingen
> 42 Die God lovede van dien dingen
>   Ende dede hen allen tetene geven.
>   Al vol doegden was sijn leven.

Leven van Sinte Amand, I, 2102-2112

Hoe alle die gheuanghene uerlost waeren vander stede bi Amands bede ende hoe dinghel Amande uerloste

> 2102 Amand, die gode heeft ghebeden,
>   Den moghensten van alder stede,
>   Datsi hem die gheuanghene gauen
>   Daer vant hise onghewillich aue
> 2106 Want sijt *hem al weder seiden.*
>   *Hi* dede te gode sijn ghebede,
>   Entie gheuanghene *ghinghen huut ghemeene*
>   Ende quamen toet hem ende dancten hem seere.
> 2110 Maer hi seide: 'Danct onsen heere
>   Jhesus Xpristus...

* * *

Bruno Krusch, l'éditeur de la *Vita Amandi* dans les *Scriptores rerum merovingicarum,* indique en marge de son édition critique quelques réminiscences minimes – mais révélatrices – aux trois 'classiques' de l'hagiographie médiévale: la *Vie de saint Martin,* les *Gesta* (ou *Acta*) *Silvestri* et les *Dialogues* de Grégoire.[52] N'est-il pas significatif que l'auteur anonyme de la *Vita Amandi* mérovingienne et Gillis de Wevel, deux auteurs séparés par le temps et la langue, avaient finalement les mêmes 'prototypes' en tête en racontant des miracles, des apparitions diaboliques ou des discussions: saint Martin, Grégoire le Grand et le pape Silvestre.[53] Mis à part ces trois 'autorités' de l'hagiographie médiévale, Gillis a été inspiré par la légende de *Barlaam et Josaphat,* par la vie de Julien du

---

52. Pour saint Martin: *Vita Amandi,* p. 403, 434 n. 1, 448 n. 1 et pour Silvestre et Grégoire voir les annotations marginales p. 428, 429, 435, 437, 439, 445.

53. Leur présence – ainsi que celle de Barlaam et Josaphat, de Marguerite d'Antioche et de saint Julien –, dans l'hagiographie vernaculaire médiévale est bien connue, entre autres par le biais des traductions de la *Legenda aurea.* Pour la vaste littérature hagiographique en moyen néerlandais il nous manque malheureusement un inventaire. On essaye d'y remédier dans le cadre de différents projets, comme 'Narrative Sources', l'histoire de l'hagiographie médiévale sous la direction de G. Philippart et par une équipe de recherche autour de la *Légende dorée.*

Mans et par le combat héroique de sainte Marguerite d'Antioche.[54] Le poète flamand étale sa culture littéraire, non seulement par des paraphrases, mais en empruntant des passages entiers, des tournures, des rimes et leur combinaison. Ces différentes formes d'intertextualité se manifestent avant tout dans les miracles et les passages en style direct, comme les sermons, les prières, les dialogues et les débats. Le poème de Gillis met ainsi en évidence l'aspect artisanal de la littérature médiévale.

La relation de Gillis avec ses modèles varie pour des raisons peu transparentes.[55]

Son poème témoigne du succès de Maerlant, et particulièrement de son histoire universelle. Pendant des générations, il a inspiré les auteurs flamands, brabançons et hollandais. Gillis de Wevel montre jusqu'à quel point on a exploité son héritage littéraire.

La sélection intelligente des modèles dans le *Spiegel Historiael*, un ouvrage de plus de cent mille vers, contenant une part importante de légendes hagiographiques, fait ressortir l'expérience de Gillis en matière hagiographique. Il distingue clairement les 'classiques', ce qui souligne sa compétence à combiner avec habileté les prototypes de l'hagiographie médiévale et les exigences d'une littérature vernaculaire contemporaine dont il connaît les techniques – par exemple l'entrelacement – et les thèmes – comme 'le jeu du roi qui ne ment' –.

---

54. Il faut y ajouter les extraits concernant:
– un miracle de saint Bavon (*Amand*, II, 1393-98 – *Sp. Hist.*, III⁰ Partie, Livre VIII, ch. II, v. 1-13),
– les rois mages (*Amand*, I, 367-410 – *Sp. Hist.*, I⁰ Partie, Livre VI, ch. XLV, v. 1-62; voir W. Verbeke, 'Ave vinculum caritatis'),
– la sainte Vierge (*Amand*, I, 824-838 – *Sp. Hist.*, I⁰ Partie, Livre VI, ch. XLI, v. 1-18, voir W. Verbeke, 'O soete cruce'),
– la sainte Croix (*Amand*, I, 3618-3628 – *Sp. Hist.*, II⁰ Partie, Livre I, ch. XIV, v. 49-57 cf. Verbeke, 'O soete cruce...'.)
– et les dieux paiens (*Amand*, I, 1667-1677 – *Sp. Hist.*, II⁰ Partie, Livre I, ch. X, v. 10-21).

Il convient de signaler en plus quelques expressions passées en proverbe dont trois sont à attribuer à Sénèque, un à Statius.

Amand, I, 1708-1711 – *Sp. Hist.*, I⁰ Partie, Livre VIII, ch. LXXVIII, v. 37-40 (= Statius);
Amand, I, 1904-1908 – *Sp. Hist.*, I⁰ Partie, Livre VIII, ch. LX, v. 39-42;
Amand, II, 717-726 – *Sp. Hist.*, I⁰ Partie, Livre VI, ch. LV, v. 1-6;
Amand, II, 5405-5409 – *Sp. Hist.*, I⁰ Partie, Livre VIII, ch. LXIII, v. 45-49.

55. Sur la complexité de la 'réécriture hagiographique' voir par exemple: M. van Uytfanghe, *'Le remploi dans l'hagiographie: une "loi du genre" qui étouffe l'originalité?'*, dans *Ideologie e pratiche del reimpiego nell'alto medievo*, Settimane ..., 46 (Spoleto, 1999), I, p. 359-411; M. Goullet et M. Heinzelmann, *La réécriture hagiographique dans l'Occident médiéval: Transformations formelles et idéologiques*, Beihefte der Francia, 58 (Stuttgart, 2003).

On situe difficilement Gillis de Wevel dans l'histoire littéraire de Bruges où il a terminé son poème. S'il écrivait effectivement en fonction de la fête de saint Amand célébrée le 6 février 1367 dans la chapelle brugeoise qui porte le nom du saint, on songe inévitablement à l'auteur anonyme du *Roman de Baudouin de Sebourc*.[56] Ce contemporain de Gillis révèle qu'il a trouvé la source latine de son long poème dans la – supposée – bibliothèque de la même chapelle:

> Ceste canchon, signour, doit bien estre prisie,
> car translatee fu en divine clergie
> du latin en romans, nel tenez a folie,
> a Saint Amant a Brugez. En la liberarie
> en sont li fait escript (et) proprement la vie
> du bon roy Baudouïn de Sebourc le jolie.[57]

Bien qu'il s'agisse d'un topos, la mention d'une chapelle qui a laissé si peu de traces dans les archives de Bruges, intrigue. C'est une raison suffisante pour s'interroger sur sa place dans l'histoire de la littérature à la fois néerlandaise et française du Moyen Âge.

---

56. L. Boca, *Li Romans de Bauduin de Sebourc, IIIe Roy de Jhérusalem, poème du XIVe siècle* (Valenciennes, 1841; reprint Genève, 1972); nouvelle édition par L.S. Crist et R. F. Cook pour la Société des Anciens Textes Français (Abbeville, 2002). Les fragments d'une traduction en moyen néerlandais ont été publiés par G.H.M. Claassens, *De Middelnederlandse kruisvaartromans*, Thesaurus, 4 (Amsterdam, 1993), p. 160-229. Littérature: *Dictionnaire des lettres françaises: Le Moyen Age* (Paris, 1992), p. 132; J. F. Van der Meulen,'Bruges, Brendan et Baudouin de Sebourc', *Queeste*, 3 (1996), 1-17.

J'ai bien entendu recherché des parallèles entre *Bauduin de Sebourc* et Gillis de Wevel, mais le résultat est insuffisant pour arriver à des conclusions convaincantes.

57. Éd. Boca, Chant V, 1-18 = v. 4027- 4038 dans la nouvelle édition de L.S. Crist et R.F. Cook.

Pieter-Jan DE GRIECK

L'IMAGE DE LA VILLE ET L'IDENTITÉ MONASTIQUE DANS L'ŒUVRE DE GILLES LI MUISIS (1272-1353)[1]

Au bas Moyen Age, beaucoup de monastères se trouvaient dans les parages d'une ville ou dans la ville même. Plus particulièrement, les ordres mendiants, qui considéraient l'activité pastorale dans la ville comme leur mission principale, étaient bien présents dans la vie urbaine. Mais les ordres traditionnels possédaient également des abbayes dans les villes. Le monastère et la ville tiraient tous les deux profit de cette situation. Pour l'abbaye, le cadre urbain signifiait la sécurité, un accès facile aux marchés urbains et un grand potentiel de généreux donateurs. Dans la ville, le monastère constituait un pôle d'attraction religieux et économique; en outre, les moines s'occupaient souvent du salut de l'âme de ses habitants. Cette 'fonctionnalité réciproque' impliquait une gamme importante de contacts – et de conflits – entre les moines et les citadins.

La présence des monastères bénédictins dans les villes n'était pas du tout évidente. L'idéal bénédictin original, tel qu'il avait été formulé dans la Règle de Saint Benoît, prescrivait une vie entièrement vouée à Dieu, et isolée du monde. Une abbaye devait être autarcique dans la mesure du possible, ce qui éviterait aux moines les contacts avec le monde extérieur.[2] Le contraste entre les idéaux monastiques originels et le monde séculier se manifestait sans doute le plus distinctement dans la relation avec la ville. Dès lors, une question centrale s'impose: quelle était l'attitude des moines à l'égard de l'environnement urbain? Comment les bénédictins se positionnaient-ils avec leurs idéaux vis-à-vis de la société urbaine? Dans les sources monastiques la ville était-elle

---

1. Nous tenons à remercier MM. les Professeurs Werner Verbeke, Jean Goossens, Jacques Pycke et Theo Venckeleer pour leurs remarques critiques.
2. Benedictus, *Règle de Saint Benoît. Texte latin, traduction et concordance*, ed. P. Schmitz (Turnhout, 1987), p. 152-153: *'Monasterium autem, si possit fieri, ita debet constitui ut omnia necessaria, id est aqua, molendinum, hortum vel artes diversas intra monasterium exerceantur, ut non sit necessitas monachis vagandi foris, quia omnino non expedit animabus eorum'* (ch. LXVI, 6-7).

effectivement considérée comme 'l'antonyme du monachisme', comme on le prétend souvent?[3]

Dans ce contexte, l'ample œuvre de Gilles Li Muisis (1272-1353), abbé de Saint-Martin à Tournai, constitue une collection de sources intéressante. L'abbaye Saint-Martin fut fondée en 1092 à un endroit en bordure de la ville de Tournai et définitivement intégrée dans le tissu urbain par la construction de nouvelles murailles au dernier quart du XIIIe siècle. Tournai était une des villes les plus importantes et les plus florissantes des Pays-Bas méridionaux.[4] Au bas Moyen Age, la relation entre la ville et l'abbaye bénédictine sise à l'intérieur de ses murailles, était très solide. Ainsi, l'abbaye offrait du logement aux personnalités qui visitaient la ville. Comme l'a décrit Albert d'Haenens:

> '... les rois et leur cour bruyante, les princesses et leur suite, les légats pontificaux et royaux, les prélats friands d'agapes plantureuses, les comtes accompagnés de leurs hommes d'affaire ou de leur soldatesque, les évêques fêtant leur joyeuse entrée, le magistrat qui avait fait de l'abbaye un point de ralliement pour la défense de la ville, tout ce monde gâchait l'atmosphère de recueillement voulu par la règle de Saint Benoît. Le remue-ménage de ces visiteurs empêchait souvent les moines de prier sans être distraits, d'étudier avec concentration, d'éviter le contact avec les mondanités, bref de vivre dans un climat propice à une vie contemplative. (...) Nos pauvres moines durent souvent en oublier leur office. L'image d'une belle dame de la suite de la reine Jeanne, les bruits de festins et de grosses ripailles, ont pu éveiller plus d'une fois, dans leur conscience austère, la nostalgie des plaisirs du monde.'[5]

---

3. Cf. L.J.R. Milis, *Angelic Monks and Earthly Men. Monasticism and its Meaning in Medieval Society* (Woodbridge, 1992), p. 50-51. Déjà en 1987, A. Haverkamp formula des critiques sur la vision qui attribue aux auteurs bénédictins médiévaux une hostilité générale envers la ville: A. Haverkamp, '"Heilige Städte" im hohen Mittelalter', dans: F. Graus réd., *Mentalitäten im Mittelalter. Methodische und inhaltliche Probleme*, Vorträge und Forschungen herausgegeben vom Konstanzer Arbeitskreis für mittelalterliche Geschichte, 35 (Sigmaringen, 1987), p. 119-156. Cf. aussi H.-J. Schmidt, 'Societas christiana in civitate. Städtekritik und Städtelob im 12. und 13. Jahrhundert', *Historische Zeitschrift*, 257 (1993), p. 297-311.
4. P. Rolland, *Histoire de Tournai* (Tournai – Paris, 1956); F. Vercauteren, 'Doornik', dans: *Belgische steden in reliëf. Plannen opgenomen door Franse militaire ingenieurs – XVIIe-XIXe eeuw*, Pro Civitate. Historische uitgaven. Reeks in -4°, nr. 1 (Bruxelles, 1965), p. 163-206; J. Pycke, *Le chapitre cathédral Notre-Dame de Tournai de la fin du XIe à la fin du XIIIe siècle: son organisation, sa vie, ses membres*, Université Catholique de Louvain. Recueil de travaux d'histoire et de philologie. Série 6, 30 (Louvain-la-Neuve, 1986), p. 23-52; C. Dury, 'L'évolution démographique de Tournai au Moyen Age', dans: *Autour de la ville en Hainaut*, Études et documents du cercle royal historique et archéologique d'Ath, 7 (1986), p. 203; P. Stabel, *Dwarfs among Giants. The Flemish Urban Network in the Late Middle Ages* (Leuven – Apeldoorn, 1997), p. 69, 223-224.
5. A. d'Haenens, *L'abbaye Saint-Martin de Tournai de 1290 à 1350. Origines, évolution et dénouement d'une crise*, Université de Louvain. Recueil de travaux d'histoire et de philologie, IVe série, 23 (Louvain, 1961), p. 134-136.

Les relations étroites de l'abbaye avec la ville étaient-elles effectivement considérées par les auteurs monastiques comme une menace pour la vie claustrale? Dans cette contribution, nous allons à la recherche de l'image de la ville et des relations avec la ville dans les sources narratives rédigées par l'abbé Gilles Li Muisis. Nous comparons l'œuvre historiographique de Li Muisis (*Tractatus tertius* et *Tractatus quartus*) avec les *consuetudines* de l'abbaye qu'il avait notées (*Tractatus secundus*) et avec sa poésie moralisatrice. Ainsi, il est possible de confronter la vision de 'l'abbé-historien' à celle de 'l'abbé-moraliste' (encore que cette distinction soit dans une certaine mesure artificielle, surtout pour le *Tractatus quartus*). La présentation des écrits de Li Muisis et de leur contexte de rédaction (I) sera suivie de l'examen – à partir de l'œuvre historiographique – de l'attitude de Li Muisis face au pouvoir communal (II) et de sa perception de la société tournaisienne (III). Ensuite, nous étudierons comment, dans son œuvre moralisatrice, l'abbé se positionnait vis-à-vis de la ville (IV). Dans la conclusion (V), nous résumerons les observations.

GILLES LI MUISIS ET SON ŒUVRE[6]

La vie de Li Muisis a déjà été décrite de façon exhaustive dans les études de Philipp Wagner, Alfred Coville, Albert d'Haenens et Bernard Guenée.[7] Nous rappelons brièvement que ce descendant d'une famille tournaisienne aisée entra dans l'abbaye de Saint-Martin à l'âge de dix-huit ans, après avoir fait des études dans sa ville natale et à Paris. En 1300, il fit un pèlerinage à Rome à l'occasion de la première Année Sainte.[8] En 1331, il fut élu abbé. Suite à la mauvaise gestion de ses prédécesseurs, l'abbaye s'était détériorée au cours des premières décennies du XIVe siècle; Gilles avait des difficultés énormes pour empêcher sa faillite. En

---

6. Une bibliographie exhaustive sur Gilles Li Muisis se trouve dans le répertoire *Narrative Sources from the Medieval Low Countries*, à consulter sur l'Internet *(www.narrative-sources.be)*. Ce répertoire est un projet commun de l'Universiteit Gent, de la Katholieke Universiteit Leuven et de la Rijksuniversiteit Groningen. Les articles relatifs à Li Muisis sont A034-A043 et A139-A147.

7. P. Wagner, 'Gillon le Muisi, Abt von St. Martin in Tournai, sein Leben und seine Werke', *Studien und Mittheilungen aus dem Benediktiner- und Cistercienser-Orden*, 17 (1896), p. 547-577; A. Coville, 'Gilles li Muisis, abbé de Saint-Martin de Tournai, chroniqueur et moraliste', dans: *Histoire littéraire de la France, Tome XXXVII* (Paris, 1938), p. 250-280; A. d'Haenens, 'Muisis (Gilles Li)', dans: *Biographie nationale*, 32 (Bruxelles, 1964), col. 528-540; B. Guenée, 'Gilles Le Muisit (1272-1353)', dans: Id., *Entre l'Église et l'État. Quatre vies de prélats français à la fin du Moyen Age (XIIIe-XVe siècle)*, (Paris, 1987), p. 87-124.

8. Il a laissé un itinéraire du retour: cf. *Narrative Sources* A035.

tant que nouvel abbé, il remboursa les dettes contractées par ses prédécesseurs, il racheta des biens aliénés et il rétablit la discipline. Par son esprit pratique de comptable, Li Muisis se montra un excellent gestionnaire. Après vingt ans, l'abbaye de Saint-Martin était à flot grâce à lui, malgré les crises successives causées par la guerre, la famine et la peste.[9] En 1346, à l'âge de soixante-quatorze ans, l'abbé commençait à souffrir de cataracte. Il ne savait plus lire, ni faire l'administration de l'abbaye, et c'est pourquoi il décida de se mettre à dicter ses mémoires. En 1351 pourtant, deux ans avant sa mort, un bonheur inattendu lui échut. Un médecin allemand qui passait par Tournai – probablement à l'occasion de la Grande Procession – réussit à guérir sa cécité par une opération à l'oeil. Gilles nous a laissé des témoignages de ce fait remarquable tant dans sa poésie que dans sa prose.[10]

Toute la production de Gilles Li Muisis a été rédigée entre 1347 et 1353, la période de sa cécité et de sa guérison. C'est donc l'œuvre d'un abbé agé.

Tout ce qu'il a fait noter a été conservé dans des manuscrits de l'époque. Le manuscrit 135 de la Bibliothèque municipale de Courtrai, dont le texte fut constitué entre 1347 et 1349, contient les trois premiers ouvrages historiques (*Tractatus primus, secundus* et *tertius*), tous écrits en latin. Le *Tractatus primus* traite de la décadence de l'abbaye Saint-Martin sous les prédécesseurs de Gilles, et des efforts de celui-ci pour renverser la situation.[11] Le *Tractatus secundus* énumère les coutumes qui étaient en vigueur à l'époque où Gilles y était novice.[12] Le *Tractatus tertius*, qui occupe la plus grande partie du manuscrit, est une

---

9. A. d'Haenens, *L'abbaye Saint-Martin*, p. 169-198.
10. V. Deneffe, *Une opération de cataracte pratiquée à Tournai en 1351*, Extrait des Annales de la Société de médecine de Gand (Gand, 1892); A. d'Haenens, 'Gilles Li Muisis, abt van de Sint-Maartensabdij te Doornik, en zijn oogheelkundige operatie in 1351', *Verslagen en mededelingen van de Leiegouw*, 2 (1960), p. 199-220; N. Chareyron, 'Chirurgien et patient au Moyen Âge: l'opération de la cataracte de Gilles le Muisit en 1351', *Revue belge de philologie et d'histoire*, 74 (1996), p. 295-308.
11. Narrative Sources A036. Édition fragmentaire dans J.J. De Smet, *Corpus Chronicorum Flandriae*, Commission royale d'Histoire, tome II (Bruxelles, 1841), p. 115-130. Cf. P.-J. De Grieck, 'Gilles Li Muisis en de "Abbatum Memoria" van de Doornikse Sint-Maartensabdij', dans R. Bauer e.a. réd., *In de voetsporen van Jacob van Maerlant. Liber amicorum Raf De Keyser. Verzameling opstellen over middeleeuwse geschiedenis en geschiedenisdidactiek*, Symbolae Facultatis Litterarum et Philosophiae Lovaniensis, Series A/Vol. 30 (Leuven, 2002), p. 225-226.
12. Narrative Sources A037. Edition: A. d'Haenens, 'Le Tractatus de consuetudinibus de Gilles Li Muisis', *Bulletin de la Commission royale d'Histoire*, 124 (1959), p. 157-195.

chronique de Tournai et des Flandres de la fin du XIIIe siècle jusqu'en 1348.[13] Bien que cela ne soit pas indiqué dans les éditions, la division du troisième traité en huit parties ne date que du XVIIIe siècle. La structure de la chronique ne reflète pas de concept réfléchi. Après une brève chronique universelle (*pars prima* selon la division du XVIIIe siècle) et quelques anecdotes, elle contient une courte partie sur le châtelain et l'avoué du Tournaisis (*pars secunda*). La *pars tertia* traite de l'Eglise de Tournai et des évêques. Dans la *pars quarta*, il s'agit des 'nombreux événements qui eurent lieu dans la ville de Tournai' dans la période de 1267 à 1314. Après une généalogie des comtes de Flandre (*pars quinta*), vient la partie principale de la chronique, qui se compose de la *pars sexta* et de la *pars septima*. Ces parties traitent respectivement de la guerre franco-flamande et de la guerre franco-anglaise. Finalement, l'auteur s'étend brièvement sur le comte flamand Louis de Nevers (*pars octava*).

Le manuscrit Bruxelles B.R. 13076-7 fut constitué entre la fin de 1349 et les débuts de 1353. Gilles y reprend le fil de sa chronique *Tractatus tertius*; c'est pourquoi on désigne cet ouvrage comme *Tractatus quartus*. Il traite des événements historiques des années 1349-1352 et contient également des vers sur les papes et sur d'autres sujets. C'est sans doute l'œuvre la plus connue de Gilles Li Muisis: les passages sur la peste, le mouvement des flagellants et la persécution des juifs de l'an catastrophique 1349 constituent des témoignages souvent cités de la crise du XIVe siècle.[14] Le manuscrit bruxellois contient également une série de poèmes élogieux sur les abbés de Saint-Martin sous le titre d'*Abbatum memoria*.[15]

Finalement, nous mentionnons le manuscrit Bruxelles B.R. IV 119, contenant les poésies de Li Muisis. L'abbé commença ses poésies au printemps de 1350; il les écrivit complètement en français. La majorité des poèmes traitent de l'état moral des différentes couches de la société – le clergé régulier et séculier, les princes, les nobles, les marchands, les bourgeois etc.[16] Le manuscrit contient aussi le traité *Ch'est de l'estat*, un texte en prose sur la gestion des prédécesseurs de Gilles.[17]

---

13. *Narrative Sources* A038. Edition: H. Lemaître, *Chroniques et annales de Gilles Le Muisit, abbé de Saint-Martin de Tournai (1272-1352)*, (Paris, 1906), p. 1-219. Cette édition est lacunaire; pour les passages manquants nous nous basons sur l'édition plus complète mais négligente par J.J. De Smet, *Corpus*, p. 136-293.

14. *Narrative Sources* A039. Edition: H. Lemaître, *Chroniques*, p. 221-311; lacunaire, elle doit être complétée par l'édition par J.J. De Smet, *Corpus*, p. 305-448.

15. Voir P.-J. De Grieck, 'Gilles Li Muisis', p. 227-230.

16. *Narrative Sources* A042 et A139-147. Edition: J.M.B.C. Kervyn de Lettenhove, *Poésies de Gilles li Muisis*, 2 vols. (Louvain, 1882).

17. *Narrative Sources* A040. Edition: J.M.B.C. Kervyn de Lettenhove, *Poésies*, vol. 1, p. 124-141. Voir P.-J. De Grieck, 'Gilles Li Muisis', p. 226-227.

Au cours de sa vie, avant qu'il ne devienne aveugle, Li Muisis avait régulièrement pris des notes, qu'il devait utiliser pour la rédaction de ses ouvrages historiques. Plusieurs de ces notes ont été conservées, cependant la plupart ne sont pas autographes.

Un manuscrit qui se trouve dans les Archives de l'État à Tournai (cart. 91), et qui est en fait un amalgame hybride de parties provenant d'autres documents, contient entre autres des notes sur les difficultés que l'abbaye eut au début du XIVᵉ siècle. Gilles a probablement rédigé ces notes dans les années 1330;[18] dans son *Tractatus primus* il en a repris plusieurs littéralement. Le même manuscrit cart. 91 contient aussi une note sur la visite du cardinal Gaucelin à la ville de Tournai[19] et l'itinéraire mentionné ci-dessus.

Un manuscrit du même genre, le cart. 89bis des Archives de l'État à Mons, a été détruit en 1940. Il contenait des notes sur l'histoire de Tournai et des Flandres jusqu'en 1339. On a longtemps cru que ces notes étaient de la main de Jacques Muevin, le prieur et plus tard le successeur de Li Muisis; cependant Albert d'Haenens a démontré que Li Muisis les avait rédigées lui-même au fil des années. Une comparaison des notes dans le cart. 89bis (que nous appellerons *Chronicon*, suivant l'édition de De Smet) avec le contenu du *Tractatus tertius* nous montre que Li Muisis a littéralement repris certaines notes dans son troisième traité, qu'il en a repris d'autres de façon abrégée ou plus détaillée, et qu'il en a simplement omis certaines, selon la pertinence qu'il leur attribua pour son public de lecteurs.[20]

La méthode de travail concrète de Li Muisis peut être reconstruite de façon précise.[21] Comme le vieil abbé était aveugle, il n'a pas écrit ses traités de sa propre main. Dans le *Tractatus tertius* il se dit '*hujus operis*

---

18. A. d'Haenens, *Comptes et documents de l'abbaye de Saint-Martin de Tournai sous l'administration des gardiens royaux (1312-1355)*, Commission royale d'histoire, publications in -8° (Bruxelles, 1962), p. 33.
19. *Narrative Sources* A041.
20. *Narrative Sources* A034. Edition: J.J. De Smet, *Corpus*, p. 455-471. Cf. A. d'Haenens, 'Une œuvre à restituer à Gilles Li Muisis: la chronique dite de Jacques Muevin', *Bulletin de la Commission royale d'Histoire*, 127 (1961), p. 1-30; Id., 'Un exemple d'utilisation du papier à Tournai peu avant 1350', *Scriptorium*, 16 (1962), p. 89-92. L'interprétation du *Chronicon* qu'offre S. Vanderputten (S. Vanderputten, *Sociale perceptie en maatschappelijke positionering in de middeleeuwse monastieke historiografie (8ste-15de eeuw)*, Algemeen Rijksarchief en Rijksarchief in de Provinciën, Studia 87, Brussel, 2001, p. 245-246) ne tient pas suffisamment compte du dessein annalistique et 'provisoire' de ce texte.
21. A. d'Haenens, 'Gilles Li Muisis historien', *Revue bénédictine*, 69 (1959), p. 260-262.

et tractatus conditor et ordinator'.²² Il définit son activité utilisant des termes comme *compilare, scribere facere, in scriptis redigi facere*.²³ Faisant appel à sa mémoire, à ce que lui disaient les 'gens dignes de foi' ou à ses anciennes notes qu'il se faisait lire, il dicta son texte à son secrétaire. Ce secrétaire était probablement son prieur et futur successeur Jacques Muevin. Une miniature en tête du *Tractatus primus* représente cette méthode de travail: l'abbé aveugle dicte son texte à un moine assis à côté de lui. Cette façon de travailler et le fait que Gilles ne pouvait rien relire, expliquent sans doute l'incohérence dans la structure de ses textes.

A partir des 'brouillons' du secrétaire de Gilles, une équipe de copistes et de miniaturistes firent la version définitive. Les manuscrits conservés sont de telles versions au net; ils ont tous été achevés endéans trois ou, au maximum, cinq ans après que Gilles les avait dictés. Le manuscrit de Courtrai et le manuscrit Bruxelles IV 119 ont été copiés par au moins deux copistes; dans le manuscrit B.R. 13076-7 on distingue quatre mains différentes. Les miniatures proviennent elles aussi d'au moins deux enlumineurs. Pour copier et enluminer les manuscrits, l'abbaye Saint-Martin faisait appel à des professionnels venant de l'extérieur du cloître. Ainsi le nom de Pierart dou Tielt, miniaturiste laïc tournaisien, paraît dans les comptes de l'abbaye. A partir de certaines caractéristiques stylistiques on a été à même de conclure qu'il avait réalisé un grand nombre de miniatures dans les trois manuscrits de Li Muisis.²⁴

Les sources utilisées par Li Muisis montrent également qu'il existait des contacts entre les moines et la ville. L'abbé avait accès aux archives de la commune. Certaines pièces étaient à sa disposition pour les faire copier.²⁵ Dans un passage du *Tractatus tertius*, il mentionne comme sources les registres des gouverneurs de la ville et une œuvre en français d'un certain Jean Wallegrape, bourgeois (*civis*) de Tournai.²⁶

---

22. *Tractatus tertius*, éd. H. Lemaître, p. 212.
23. *Tractatus tertius*, éd. J.J. De Smet, p. 137; éd. H. Lemaître, p. 1, 34, 219; *Tractatus quartus*, éd. H. Lemaître, p. 221, 245 etc.
24. A. d'Haenens, 'Pierart dou Tielt, enlumineur des œuvres de Gilles Li Muisis. Note sur son activité à Tournai vers 1350', *Scriptorium*, 23 (1969), p. 88-93; D. Vanwijnsberghe, *"De fin or et d'azur". Les commanditaires de livres et le métier de l'enluminure à Tournai à la fin du Moyen Âge (XIVᵉ-XVᵉ siècles)*, Corpus of illuminated manuscripts, 10 (Leuven, 2001), p. 12, 94, 111 et 314.
25. A. d'Haenens, 'Gilles Li Muisis historien', p. 271.
26. *Tractatus tertius*, éd. H. Lemaître, p. 125: '*Et de ipsorum ordinatione omitto scribere causa brevitatis, quia gubernatores ville talia habent in suis registris registrata; et vidi penes quendam civem Tornacensem, dictum Johannem Wallegrape, omnia talia accidentia que omnia de gallico breviter transtuli in latinum.*' Jusqu'à présent, on n'a pas pu identifier l'œuvre de Wallegrape.

Quelle est en fait l'image de la ville que nous montre l'œuvre historiographique de Gilles Li Muisis?

L'IMAGE DU POUVOIR COMMUNAL

Dans la première moitié du XIIe siècle, la domination de l'évêque et du chapitre cathédral sur la ville de Tournai fut contestée par la classe croissante des marchands. Ceux-ci voulaient assurer leurs intérêts matériaux; c'est pourquoi marchands et riches bourgeois s'organisèrent en 1147 sous la forme d'une commune (*communia*), une association jurée. La ville était dès lors gérée par un collège de jurés présidé par deux prévôts. En 1188, Philippe Auguste confirma les institutions communales. Désormais, la ville était directement reliée à la couronne française et possédait une autonomie presque absolue. Bastion français sur la frontière avec l'Empire germanique, Tournai était 'une sorte de république bourgeoise'; c'était la commune la plus indépendante de France.[27] L'importance politique de Tournai, en raison de sa situation géographique, garantissait la persistance de la commune aux XIIIe et XIVe siècles.

Dans quelle mesure Gilles Li Muisis s'est-il intéressé – soit dans le sens positif, soit dans le sens négatif – à la politique communale?

Surtout la *pars quarta* du *Tractatus tertius* traite explicitement de l'histoire de la ville (toujours nommée *civitas*). Cette partie couvre la période de 1267 à 1314; elle ne nous apporte donc aucune information sur la constitution de la commune au XIIe siècle. Pour Li Muisis, la genèse de la commune faisait partie d'un passé reculé et inconnu; dans sa perception, la commune avait toujours existé.[28] Dans cette quatrième partie, Gilles donne surtout des informations sur les différentes actions militaires et juridiques que le gouvernement municipal entreprit au cours de la période mentionnée pour sauvegarder les intérêts de la commune. Ainsi, en l'an 1288, la commune étendit sensiblement son territoire par l'acquisition de la seigneurie du Bruille. Suite à l'annexion de ce domaine, la commune acquit aussi tous droits et justices au Bruille.[29] Gilles considérait cet événement comme une bonne affaire: 'Par la grâce de Dieu et par

---

27. C. Petit-Dutaillis, *Les communes françaises. Caractère et évolution des origines au XVIIIe siècle* (Paris, 1947), p. 53-55, 191; P. Rolland, *Histoire de Tournai*, p. 119-120; Id., *Les origines de la commune de Tournai. Histoire interne de la seigneurie épiscopale tournaisienne* (Bruxelles, 1931).

28. Cf. *Chronicon*, p. 461: '...civitas, quae a tanto longo tempore quod de contrario memoria non existebat consueta gubernari per cives suos libere, ...'.

29. Cf. P. Rolland, *Histoire de Tournai*, p. 96.

le zèle des bourgeois et des gouverneurs, ces endroits ont été unis et joints à la ville'. En outre, toute la ville fut renforcée par des fossés, des murs et des tours; ces fortifications pouvaient, 'avec l'aide de Dieu et de la Sainte Vierge, chaque fois qu'il serait nécessaire, résister à tous ceux qui veulent porter préjudice à la ville'.[30]

L'attitude positive de Gilles Li Muisis à l'égard de la commune apparaît aussi dans la *pars sexta* et la *pars septima* du *Tractatus tertius*. Ces parties traitent de l'histoire des conflits franco-flamand et franco-anglais, mais elles marquent aussi l'importance du rôle qu'a joué la ville de Tournai dans ces épisodes. La comparaison du texte du *Tractatus tertius* avec les notes préparatoires du *Chronicon* (cart. 89bis) montre que dans son troisième traité le but de Li Muisis était de mettre en lumière l'importance politique et militaire de la ville. Les notes préparatoires rendent surtout compte des actions militaires et administratives des rois et des comtes. Dans son *Tractatus tertius*, Li Muisis ajoute systématiquement des informations provenant d'autres sources sur le rôle que la ville de Tournai a joué lors de ces événements.

Le *Chronicon* signale, par exemple, qu'en 1328, le comte Louis de Nevers sollicita l'aide de Philippe de Valois pour combattre les rebelles flamands. Le roi de France vint à Cassel avec une grande armée et y livra bataille contre les Flamands, avec l'aide de six cents soldats tournaisiens.[31] Dans le *Tractatus tertius*, Li Muisis spécifie la composition du contingent tournaisien. Il comprenait deux cents arbalétriers et quatre cents[32] soldats munis d'épées et de lances; ils étaient tous habillés en tuniques rouges, ornés de l'emblème de la ville en argent. A leur arrivée à Cassel, le roi les accueillit avec reconnaissance. Mais la nuit, raconte Li Muisis, les rebelles flamands pénétrèrent dans le camp français, protégés par l'obscurité. Les Tournaisiens étaient les premiers à les remarquer. Tout de suite, ils commencèrent à les combattre. Finalement, les Français triomphaient de façon éclatante, et les Tournaisiens avaient eu une part décisive dans la victoire. Ils s'étaient comportés de façon si loyale et brave que le roi leur accorda, par gratitude, le privilège de

---

30. *Tractatus tertius*, éd. H. Lemaître, p. 38: '*Nunc autem, per Dei gratiam et per civium industriam atque gubernatorum, omnia sunt unita et civitati applicata. Et etiam de fossatis, de muris et turribus nobiliter totum in circuitu sunt fortificata ad repellendos omnes inimicos, et quod, auxiliante Deo et beata Virgine, quotiescumque fuerit necessarium et opportunum, possint resistere omnibus nocere volentibus civitati.*'

31. *Chronicon*, p. 460.

32. Le scribe écrivait erronément 'quadringentos'.

garder sa tente. Les capitaines tournaisiens pouvaient, selon Li Muisis, parler au roi chaque fois qu'ils le voulaient.[33]

Aussi la suite du *Tractatus tertius* montre-t-elle la fierté qu'inspiraient à Li Muisis les faits d'armes des troupes tournaisiennes dans le camp du roi de France.[34] Pour le siège de Calais en 1347, le Magistrat de la commune envoya à la demande du roi, un millier de soldats et d'ouvriers. Li Muisis décrit méticuleusement ces hommes et leur équipement. Il y avait quatre capitaines, quarante-cinq cavaliers et mille fantassins, dont deux cents arbalétriers, cent quarante archers, et aussi des lanciers et des soldats portant d'autres armes; en outre, il y avait des charpentiers et des ouvriers divers. Il est possible que l'abbé les ait vus de ses propres yeux, car avant leur départ, les troupes s'étaient assemblées dans l'abbaye Saint-Martin, sans doute pour implorer l'assistance de la puissance divine. Avec fierté, Li Muisis mentionne comment le roi de France louait l'équipement des Tournaisiens à Calais et comment les troupes dressaient leurs tentes le plus près de l'armée anglaise.[35]

La suppression de la commune en 1332 constituait un événement pénible pour Li Muisis. Suite à de fréquents abus des privilèges communaux par les Tournaisiens, le Parlement de Paris promulgua dans cette année un arrêt par lequel les citadins perdaient leur droit de commune. Même si la commune fut déjà réinstallée en 1340 par une charte de Philippe VI, la sentence avait laissé une forte impression dans la ville. Gilles Li Muisis, qui n'avait jamais connu d'autre gouvernement, se montre lui aussi impressionné par la condamnation. Dans les notes qui se trouvent dans le *Chronicon*, il transcrivit intégralement l'arrêt de 1332 qui accusait la commune d'avoir violé le droit royal, les libertés des marchands et les immunités du clergé.[36] Dans le *Tractatus tertius* pourtant, l'abbé ne mentionna cet événement que très brièvement. Il estimait qu'il n'était pas utile de s'étendre sur cet épisode regrettable de l'histoire tournaisienne.[37] Cependant, il a mentionné la cause de l'arrêt, à savoir le procès que le chapitre Notre-Dame avait intenté aux gouverneurs de la commune devant le Parlement de Paris. Les chanoines y avaient été soutenus par un nombre de vignerons et d'autres 'qui voulaient porter préjudice aux autorités

---

33. *Tractatus tertius*, éd. H. Lemaître, p. 99-101.
34. Ibid., p. 53, 119-120, 123-125, 185.
35. Ibid., p. 182-184.
36. *Chronicon*, p. 461-463; cf. C. Petit-Dutaillis, *Les communes françaises*, p. 192 et P. Rolland, *Histoire de Tournai*, p. 107-108.
37. *Tractatus tertius*, éd. H. Lemaître, p. 105: '*Articulos et formam arresti, et modum gubernationis et gubernatorum qui rexerunt usque ad tempus gratie facte a domino rege, omisi scribere propter multas causas, quia michi non videbatur expediens*'.

urbaines et qui les accusaient de beaucoup de choses'.[38] Chose remarquable, Li Muisis n'imputait pas la suppression à l'orgueil des bourgeois tournaisiens qui s'appropriaient trop de droits, mais à ceux qui s'y opposaient.

A la fin du *Tractatus quartus*, Li Muisis s'étend en détail sur la lutte acharnée qui opposa en 1350 la majorité des chanoines à une minorité soutenue par le Magistrat. Il s'agissait initialement d'une lutte pour le pouvoir entre les tribunaux ecclésiastique et échevinal, mais finalement ce conflit causa une grande discorde dans le chapitre même. Le roi Jean le Bon dut intervenir personnellement, mais sa sentence, reproduite *in extenso* par Gilles, ne fit pas disparaître la rancune entre les deux parties. En fin de compte, les chanoines réussirent à trouver un accord, grâce aux instances de l'abbé Li Muisis lui-même, qui était présent dans le chapitre pour présider aux négociations.[39]

L'IMAGE DE LA SOCIÉTÉ TOURNAISIENNE

La commune de Tournai était en fait une oligarchie. Une mince couche sociale fournissait les jurés et les échevins, et dominait la vie politique, économique et sociale de la ville. Cette élite était composée des grands lignages tournaisiens, qui devaient leur richesse surtout à leurs propriétés immobilières, et de quelques familles qui s'étaient enrichies par leurs activités commerciales.[40]

La famille Li Muisis faisait partie de ce deuxième groupe. A l'origine, ils étaient marchands, commerçants, propriétaires de l'*Hostellerie de la Couronne* sur le Grand Marché. Dès le début du XIIIe siècle, la famille jouissait d'un grand prestige dans la ville. Plusieurs parents de Gilles étaient échevin ou juré – c'était sans doute par leur truchement que l'abbé eut accès aux archives communales. Un cousin de Gilles, Pierre Li Mui-

---

38. Ibid., p. 104-105: '... *altercatio fuit et controversia grandis in parlamento Parisius inter gubernatores civitatis Tornacensis et decanum et capitulum ecclesie Beate Marie Tornacensis, pro venditione carbonum et quorumdam aliorum; junxeruntque se dictis canonicis quidam vinitores et alii quamplures, volentes nocere gubernatoribus ipsosque in multis accusantes*'.
39. Ibid., p. 283-293, 297-298, 307. Si le chapitre cathédral est mentionné dans le *Tractatus tertius* ou *quartus*, c'est presque toujours dans le contexte d'un conflit – un conflit interne ou un conflit entre le chapitre d'une part et la commune ou l'abbaye Saint-Martin d'autre part: *Tractatus tertius*, éd. H. Lemaître, p. 20-21, 24-25, 45-46, 104-105; *Tractatus quartus*, éd. H. Lemaître, p. 255.
40. J. Pycke, *Le chapitre cathédral*, p. 44-45.

sis, fut échevin, juré et prévôt et un des quatre capitaines des troupes tournaisiennes envoyées à Calais en 1347. Avec son frère Jean, Pierre participa en 1331 à la célèbre *Fête des 31 rois* à Tournai.[41] Cette fête était une variante des *tables rondes* tournaisiennes au cours desquelles les participants prenaient le nom ou les armes des héros arthuriens.[42] Il est possible que Gilles Li Muisis ait lui-même participé à une de ces tables rondes en 1290. En effet, dans un de ses poèmes il écrit qu'il était *'cancelier dou prince de le gale'*.[43] En 1290, Gilles, jeune moine, quitta l'abbaye pour régler une affaire d'héritage. Pendant 29 semaines il porta l'habit séculier; c'était peut-être dans cette période qu'il participa à la table ronde comme 'chancelier du prince des *galois*'.[44]

Dans ses œuvres historiques, Gilles Li Muisis consacre beaucoup d'attention aux fêtes urbaines, ces manifestations typiques de la culture bourgeoise qui étaient des moyens symboliques de resserrer la cohésion entre les grandes familles dirigeantes. Dans son *Tractatus tertius*, l'abbé mentionne les tables rondes de 1282 et de 1290.[45] Il cite également la fête des 31 rois en 1331 dans le *Chronicon*,[46] mais ne la reprend pas dans le troisième traité. Dans le *Tractatus quartus*, Li Muisis relate amplement une grande compétition d'arbalétriers, tenue à Tournai en août 1350.[47]

Il est clair que, tout moine qu'il était, Gilles Li Muisis continua à s'intéresser au mode de vie de son milieu d'origine, la riche bourgeoisie tournaisienne. Il aimait voir 'les richesses, les joyaux, les chevaux, les édifices, les villes, les pays'....[48] Même dans sa propre façon de vivre, Li Muisis ne renia jamais son origine bourgeoise. Il faisait ses délices des

---

41. N. Du Chastel de La Howarderie, *Notes pour servir à l'histoire de la famille li Muisis ou le Muisi* (Tournai, 1891).
42. E. Gachet, 'Les XXXI rois de Tournay', *Bulletin de la Commission royale d'histoire*, 1e série, III (1840), p. 117-124; E. Van den Neste, *Tournois, joutes, pas d'armes dans les villes de Flandre à la fin du Moyen Age (1300-1486)*, (Paris, 1996), p. 52, 133, 189.
43. *Ch'est li complainte des compagnons*, éd. J.M.B.C. Kervyn de Lettenhove, vol. 2, p. 261 et 266.
44. *Le gale* veut dire 'le plaisir', 'la joyeuse vie'; cf. les *compains de galle* de Villon et les *galois* (les 'gais lurons') d'Eustache Deschamps: J. Cerquiglini-Toulet, *La Couleur de la mélancolie. La fréquentation des livres au XIVe siècle 1300-1415* (Paris, 1993), p. 145-146; P. Wagner, 'Gillon le Muisi', p. 573. L'interprétation d'A. Coville, 'Gilles li Muisis', p. 263-264, que 'prince de le Gale' signifie 'le roi Galehot', nous semble plutôt recherchée.
45. *Tractatus tertius*, éd. H. Lemaître, p. 35, 38.
46. *Chronicon*, p. 461.
47. *Tractatus quartus*, éd. H. Lemaître, p. 272-273.
48. *Che sont les méditations*, éd. J.M.B.C. Kervyn de Lettenhove, vol. 1, p. 95: *'Volentiers rikèces veoie/ Chevaus, joyaus que jou amoie/ Edifices, villes, pays.'*

bons repas et des bons vins. Comme l'on peut lire dans son joli poème *Li complainte des compagnons*, Gilles aimait entonner une chanson et boire un verre de vin en bonne compagnie.[49] Il était passionné par la poésie vernaculaire. Avec les beaux dits on sert, selon lui, les seigneurs et on organise les bonnes fêtes, excellents dîners et soupers.[50] Il connaissait l'œuvre d'entre autres Jean de le Mote, Philippe de Vitri et Guillaume de Machaut, dont le premier était son contemporain, alors que les deux derniers étaient beaucoup plus jeunes que lui. L'abbé restait apparemment au courant des évolutions contemporaines dans la culture littéraire du Nord de la France.[51]

Evidemment, son origine familiale influençait également sa perception des groupes sociaux dans la ville. L'examen de la terminologie adoptée par Li Muisis dans ses ouvrages historiographiques, s'avérera révélateur.

Selon Li Muisis, la population de la ville se composait en premier lieu de *cives*: ceux qui bénéficiaient de tous les privilèges de la commune (*communia*). Dans un nombre limité de familles bourgeoises se recrutaient les gouverneurs (*gubernatores* ou *rectores*) – les magistrats de la ville – parmi lesquels les prévôts (*praepositi*) et les jurés (*jurati*) étaient les plus importants.[52] Outre le groupe des *cives*, il y avait dans la ville la grande masse de pauvres (*pauperes*) et d'artisans (*texentes, fullones* etc.), qui étaient d'office exclus de la gestion communale. Li Muisis parle de ce groupe en utilisant le nom collectif de 'commun' (*communitas*) ou des *habitatores*, qu'il distingue des *cives*.[53] Finalement il y avait encore la

---

49. *Ch'est li complainte des compagnons*, p. 259: '*Ch'estoit chius* [= Gilles] *qui prumiers devant trèstous cantoit,/ Des boins les compagnies amoit et les antoit/ Dou boin vin le milleur moult liement tantoit/ Tout disoit en appiert, de riens ne se vantoit.*' Aussi p. 263: '*Dou fort vin sans temprer à men plaisir buvoie;/ D'aus, d'ougnons et d'airun, de riens ne me wardoye*'; p. 265: '*Avoec les compagnons volentiers buveray./ Temprer me convient vin, que moult envis feray.*'
50. *Che sont les méditations*, p. 85: '*De biaus dis siert-on les signeurs/ Par tous les païs les grigneurs/ Et les gens de toutes manières/ Par quoy se facent boines chières/ En tous les lieus où sont ensamble. [...] Pour chou fait-il boin biaus dis dire/ Pour oster tous courous et yre/ As diners faire liement/ Et à soupers tout ensement.*'
51. B. Guenée, 'Gilles Le Muisit', p. 91-92; A. Coville, 'Gilles li Muisis', p. 281-283; P. Wagner, 'Gillon le Muisi', *Studien und Mittheilungen*, 18 (1897), p. 50-56. Cf. aussi J. Cerquiglini-Toulet, *La Couleur de la mélancolie*, p. 9-10, pour une belle description de l' 'amour des livres' de Li Muisis.
52. *Tractatus tertius*, éd. H. Lemaître, p. 34, 35, 41-45, 76, 177-178 etc.; *Tractatus quartus*, éd. H. Lemaître, p. 284-285 etc. Cf. P. Rolland, *Les origines*, p. 194-223.
53. *Tractatus tertius*, éd. H. Lemaître, p. 36, 40-43, 74, 105, 127, 132, 176, 187; *Tractatus quartus*, éd. H. Lemaître, p. 234-235, cf. aussi p. 225 et 226.

classe du clergé, dont faisaient partie entre autres les prélats (*prelati*: l'évêque et les abbés), les chanoines (*canonici* ou *decanus et capitulum*), les curés (*curati, presbiteri*), les chapelains (*capellani*), les frères mendiants (*religiosi mendicantes*) et les moines (*monachi*).[54]

La position que l'on occupait dans la société dépendait en premier lieu des biens et des ressources dont on disposait. Dans le groupe considérable des laïcs (*cives* et *habitatores*), Li Muisis établit une distinction entre les riches (*divites*) et les pauvres (*pauperes*), et entre ces deux groupes, il existait une classe moyenne (*mediocres*).[55]

Chaque groupe avait sa fonction et sa place bien définies dans la société. Les riches étaient ceux qui détenaient le pouvoir. C'est pourquoi le terme *divites* est interchangeable avec le terme *potentes* ou *magnes*, et le terme *pauperes* avec *parves*.[56] Les *gubernatores* se recrutaient, sans exception, dans la classe des riches. Ils étaient, dans la terminologie de Li Muisis, *personae authenticae*, des hommes sages qui prenaient des décisions justes pour le bien de la commune. Le peuple – la *communitas* ou les *pauperes* – devait leur obéir. Le peuple n'était-il pas ignorant, alors que les puissants étaient savants, sages et sains d'esprit?[57] Pour notre abbé, le peuple était une masse anonyme et indifférenciée. Dans ses chroniques le peuple ne sert que de spectateur – souvent grognant – des événements urbains, ou de victime de famines et d'épidémies.

Li Muisis était heureux quand l'ordre social était respecté, comme au moment du siège de Tournai en 1340, quand il y avait une grande union *inter gubernatores, cives et majores civitatis et communitatem*.[58] Lors de l'épidémie de peste en 1349, tout le monde continua également à remplir sa fonction. Pour limiter l'inquiétude du peuple, les autorités (*viri sapientes, villae gubernatores*) lancèrent quelques mesures 'pour le bien de la ville' (*pro civitatis bono*). Lorsque la *communitas* se mettait à se plaindre d'une des mesures (et Li Muisis adopte le discours direct pour rendre ces plaintes), les autorités décidèrent, 'prenant la bonne voie' (*capientes bonum iter*), d'abroger la mesure. Ainsi, les plaintes

---

54. *Tractatus tertius*, éd. H. Lemaître, p. 20-33, 90, 175-176 et passim; *Tractatus quartus*, éd. H. Lemaître, p. 230, 232-234, 240, 249, 258, 304 et passim.
55. *Tractatus tertius*, éd. H. Lemaître, p. 89, 131; *Tractatus quartus*, éd. H. Lemaître, p. 222, 258, 268, 304; cf. aussi *Des estas de tous gens seculers*, éd. J.M.B.C. Kervyn de Lettenhove, vol. 2, p. 2-8.
56. *Tractatus tertius*, éd. H. Lemaître, p. 43.
57. B. Guenée, 'Gilles Le Muisit', p. 97-100.
58. *Tractatus tertius*, éd. H. Lemaître, p. 131.

s'éteignirent.[59] Dans la vision de Li Muisis, le commun devait obéir aux puissants, mais les puissants devaient tenir compte des plaintes du peuple.[60]

Cependant, le fait qu'un grand groupe de citadins était exclu du pouvoir causa inéluctablement des tensions. À partir de 1280, ces tensions sociales s'accroissaient, comme dans de nombreuses villes flamandes. Cette année-là, les riches et les puissants de Tournai se regroupèrent dans la *Confrérie des Damoiseaux*, une association élitaire. En même temps, les magistrats publièrent un ban interdisant toute association de gens de métier. Ce ban était la cause d'un certain nombre de révoltes d'artisans, surtout de la part des tisserands et des foulons, qui étaient à chaque occasion gravement pénalisés par les magistrats.[61]

Gilles Li Muisis ne manifestait que très peu d'indulgence pour ces conspirateurs qui ne voulaient pas rester à leur place sociale naturelle. Dans ses chroniques, il ne mentionne leurs révoltes que très sommairement. Il s'intéresse plutôt à la punition des perturbateurs qu'aux motifs de leurs actions.[62] Pourtant, en avril 1307, il y eut une émeute dont Li Muisis s'indigna tellement qu'il y prêta plus d'attention dans sa chronique.[63] Le commun, 'nommément les tisserands, les foulons, les pauvres et les autres', refusait d'accepter une taille que le Magistrat avait imposée. Tous ces hommes complotaient contre les gouverneurs,[64] ils molestèrent les collecteurs des tailles et démolirent – acte symbolique – les

---

59. *Tractatus quartus*, éd. J.J. De Smet, p. 371-378; éd. H. Lemaître, p. 255-258. Cf. B. Guenée, 'Gilles Le Muisit', p. 113-114.

60. Cf. B. Guenée, 'Gilles Le Muisit', p. 109-111.

61. L. Verriest, *Les luttes sociales et le contrat d'apprentissage à Tournai jusqu'en 1424*, Académie royale de Belgique. Classe des Lettres et des Sciences morales et politiques et Classe des Beaux-Arts. Mémoires. Collection in -8°, 2ᵉ série, tome IX (Bruxelles, 1912), p. 8-9; P. Rolland, *Histoire de Tournai*, p. 123-126.

62. *Tractatus tertius*, éd. H. Lemaître, p. 35: '*Anno m° ducentesimo octogesimo primo, magna pars hominum texentium conspiraverunt contra rectores civitatis; et fuerint aliqui capti, ex quibus unus, Roussiaus li Kos nominatus, fuit per equos tractus et suspensus*'; p. 44: '*Anno predicto [1307], tercia die septembris, fullones fecerunt routam et voluerunt occidere prepositum. Et statim unus eorum qui se faciebat capitaneum, fuit per equos tractus et suspensus; et in crastina fuit Petrus de Moussein tractus et suspensus pro eodem facto. Et in crastino fuit Alardus de Bourgella, qui fuerat de consilio et auxilio fullonum et texentium in dicto facto, in foro, ante domum de Porco, capite detruncatus; et fuerunt plures proclamati et banniti.*'

63. Ibid., p. 40-43. Cf. L. Verriest, *Les luttes sociales*, p. 11-12 et P. Rolland, *Histoire de Tournai*, p. 126-127.

64. *Tractatus tertius*, éd. H. Lemaître, p. 40: '*Communitas autem, scilicet texentes, pauperes, fullones et alii, conspiraverunt contra dictos gubernatores…*'.

portes de la ville. Ils se stimulaient réciproquement à faire du mal. Le comportement de ces 'incontrôlés' causait chez l'élite de la ville une perplexité 'justifiée'.[65] Et la situation allait de mal en pis. Le jour après, les rebelles réclamèrent les *signa* de la ville, se rendirent aux maisons des *gubernatores* et les firent prisonniers. Ils menaçaient les proches des gouverneurs, les riches et les puissants: 'Venez, armez-vous et rejoignez-nous, sinon nous vous privons de votre liberté!'. C'était le monde à l'envers. Les riches 'obéissaient comme des moutons à ces personnes misérables et ils faisaient ce qu'ils leur commandaient'.[66] Finalement, la Vengeance de Dieu empêcha que cette perturbation insolente de l'ordre social s'aggravât encore. Une violente tempête éclata et dispersa les insurgés. Le jour après, sur les conseils d'un certain Mathieu de Haudion, '*homo sapiens et fidelis*', *armiger* qui résidait à l'abbaye Saint-Martin, les anciens magistrats furent déposés et d'autres furent nommés. Grâce à cette sage intervention d'une 'personne authentique', les esprits se calmèrent et l'ordre normal se réinstalla.

Entre la mince couche supérieure des riches et des puissants et la grande masse du commun, Li Muisis discernait un troisième groupe: le groupe des *mediocres*.[67] Ce terme *mediocres* (*li moyen* en français) qu'on retrouve aussi bien dans les ouvrages historiographiques que dans la poésie moralisatrice de l'abbé semble référer aux bourgeois qui ne faisaient pas partie de l'élite dirigeante. Ils profitaient des privilèges de la commune, mais contrairement à la classe des puissants, ils devaient travailler pour assurer leur propre subsistance. C'étaient probablement les marchands et les commerçants.[68]

---

65. Ibid., p. 41: '*Et incontinenti tota alia communitas et ribalditas, mutuo se ad malum faciendum provocantes, tota illa die mirabiliter gesserunt se. Ex quo gubernatores, potentes et divites merito fuerunt stupefacti...*'.
66. Ibid.: '*Et dicebant divitibus, et potentibus, et propinquis gubernatorum: "Ite, armate vos et venite nobiscum; alias, de vobis vindictam capiemus." Qui, sicut oves, obedientes talibus miserabilibus personis, faciebant quod imperabant, et pro certo, si aliquis collegisset copiam armatorum secum, sicut bestias eos occidissent.*'
67. Cf. note 55.
68. Cf. E. Maschke, 'Mittelschichten in deutschen Städten des Mittelalters', dans: E. Maschke et J. Sydow réd., *Städtische Mittelschichten: Protokoll der 8. Arbeitstagung des Arbeitskreises für Südwestdeutsche Stadtgeschichtsforschung, Biberach 14.-16. Nov. 1969*, Veröffentlichungen der Kommission für geschichtliche Landeskunde in Baden-Württemberg, Reihe B: Forschungen, Band 69 (Stuttgart, 1972), p. 1-31; réimprimé dans Id., *Städte und Menschen. Beiträge zur Geschichte der Stadt, der Wirtschaft und Gesellschaft 1959-1977*, Vierteljahrschrift für Sozial- und Wirtschaftsgeschichte, Beihefte, Nr. 68 (Wiesbaden, 1980), p. 275-305.

L'attitude favorable de Li Muisis envers le commerce et les commerçants saute aux yeux. Dans ses chroniques, l'abbé se montre préoccupé du trafic commercial en temps de guerre. Lors du siège de Tournai par les Flamands en 1303, on était capable de tenir une porte ouverte, de sorte que 'toutes les marchandises et toutes les denrées nécessaires puissent être importées', et que 'les marchands et leur marchandise puissent venir et sortir en toute sécurité; et tout le temps toute la commune y trouvait son avantage'.[69] La conséquence positive des armistices était que les marchands pouvaient voyager en toute sécurité.[70]

Ce qui est fort remarquable, ce sont les longs passages dans le *Tractatus quartus* concernant les dépréciations de la monnaie dans la période de 1349 à 1351, qui causèrent une augmentation du coût de la vie et des difficultés pour les marchands. Li Muisis parle des mutations monétaires comme quelqu'un qui s'y connaît. Il donne des informations précises sur le prix des denrées.[71]

Le positionnement comme religieux

Dans son œuvre historiographique, Li Muisis manifeste une attitude positive à l'égard de la commune tournaisienne. La ville et ses habitants sont présentés de façon concrète dans les *Tractatus tertius* et *quartus*. Par contre, le discours normatif de sa poésie moralisatrice et du *Tractatus secundus* offre une image différente de la ville. Celle-ci n'y est pas un espace concret et 'réel' – Tournai –, mais plutôt un lieu 'abstrait', un gouffre de péchés, qui, selon l'idéologie monastique traditionnelle, doit être évité par le moine.

Dans le *Tractatus secundus*, Li Muisis enregistre les coutumes telles qu'elles étaient en vigueur dans l'abbaye Saint-Martin dans le 'bon vieux temps'; il espère que ses propres moines en suivront l'exemple. A cette époque heureuse, la discipline fut très stricte: dans les autres monastères on considérait l'abbaye de Saint-Martin et celle d'Affligem comme des prisons.[72] Ainsi, les moines, lorsqu'ils voulaient aller en ville, étaient

---

69. *Tractatus tertius*, éd. H. Lemaître, p. 75: '*Portabanturque omnia venalia et necessaria civitati de Hannonia et de aliis patriis, ibantque et redibant secure mercatores et mercature; et tota communia toto illo tempore bene lucrabatur.*'
70. Ibid., p. 189, 211; *Tractatus quartus*, éd. H. Lemaître, p. 222.
71. *Tractatus quartus*, éd. H. Lemaître, p. 222, 268-269, 299, 302-303, 308-309. Cf. A. Coville, 'Gilles li Muisis', p. 307-308.
72. *Tractatus secundus*, p. 184: '*...monasterium Affliginense et monasterium nostrum pro carcere ab alijs monasterijs reputabantur*'.

obligés de passer par l'abbé ou le prieur, qui accordaient rarement la permission.[73] Seuls les officiers dans l'exercice de leurs fonctions sortaient librement.[74] Le sixième chapitre du *Tractatus secundus*, où il est question des *Consuetudines eundi in villam et alie quamplures*, mentionne que personne ne pouvait parler à une femme sans permission; même l'abbé devait toujours être accompagné de son chapelain lorsqu'il recevait une femme.[75]

Dans le poème moralisateur *Li Maintiens des monnes* Li Muisis fait également l'éloge du mode de vie des moines au temps jadis.[76] Ils passaient leur temps à prier et à étudier et ils vivaient en pauvreté. Maintenant, l'humilité s'est transformée en orgueil: les moines veulent imiter le style de vie des bourgeois et des nobles.[77] *'Or quert-on des fors vins, des mais délicieus;/ Et que plus sont coustant, plentiveus, prétieus,/ Tant plaist mieus as abbés, as couvens, as prieus'*.[78] Ne se contentant plus du simple habit noir, ils veulent de l'argent pour acheter eux-mêmes des vêtements. *'Li corps est au moustier, li coers est ou markiet'*.[79] Ils veulent toujours aller en congé en dehors du monastère; quand on le leur refuse, ils sont indignés. Gilles prévient que c'est le Satan qui les persuade de rompre le vœu monastique d'obéissance. *'Il te fera, s'il puet, par les villes router,/ Ès besoignes mondaines ten cuer dou tout bouter.'*[80]

Selon Gilles, c'est trop souvent la faute des abbés. En effet, ce sont eux qui donnent le mauvais exemple: ils mènent eux-mêmes une vie luxueuse et ils sont régulièrement absents pour se détendre. Li Muisis compare cette situation à un tournoi où les uns le font bien et où les autres le font

---

73. *Tractatus secundus*, p. 177-178: *'De licentiis eundi in villa difficile tradebantur tam sacerdotibus quam aliis et causam exprimere oportebat. Dyaconi et subdiaconi non nisi cum uno de senioribus ire poterant in spaciis. Poterant ire monachi per licentiam petitam per signa ad operatorium, pro suis necessitatibus'*.

74. *Tractatus secundus*, p. 185: *'Prepositus, cellarius, prior Sancti Amandi, de iure officiorum, et magister de Chantelus, quando sunt in monasterio, possunt ire in villa sine licentia ... Nullus alius debet exire extra septa monasterij absque licentia abbatis seu prioris vel eorum locum tenentis ... Alij officia habentes possunt ire ad sua officia exercenda'*. Cf. aussi *Ch'est de l'estat*, p. 134: *'... et des congiés d'aler en la ville faisoit li abbés grant difficultet, s'on ne monstroit cause ou grant nécessitet, exceptet chiaus del ordène et les officyers'*. Cf. A. d'Haenens, *L'abbaye Saint-Martin*, p. 51-53.

75. *Tractatus secundus*, p. 178; *Ch'est de l'estat*, p. 131.

76. *Li maintiens des monnes*, éd. J.M.B.C. Kervyn de Lettenhove, vol. 1, p. 142-208. Cf. C.V. Langlois, *La vie en France au Moyen Age de la fin du XIIe au milieu du XIVe siècle d'après des moralistes du temps*, Tome II (Paris, 1926-1928; réimpression Genève, 1970), p. 337-341.

77. *Li maintiens des monnes*, p. 159, 205.

78. Ibid., p. 151.

79. Ibid., p. 146.

80. Ibid., p. 149.

mal, mais où le juge (l'abbé), qui doit distribuer les prix, est absent. Le comportement des abbés contraste fortement avec celui de l'abbé 'idéal', saint Benoît lui-même. *'Sains Benois avoit-il dras des plus précieus,/ Palefrois sur lesquels gent fusses envieus?/ Avoit-il cescun jour des mais délicieus?/ Nenil, mais de ses monnes estoit moult curieus./ [...] Il ne chevauçoit mie, mais toudis demoroit/ En ce cielle, toudis Dieu prioit et oroit.'*[81] Saint Benoît se tenait toujours éloigné de la ville: *'Il ne se monstroit mie par villes, par cités,/ Anchois estoit li mundes en sen cuer despités'*.[82] Un bon abbé doit veiller au salut de l'âme de ses moines et il doit faire en sorte qu'ils ne quittent pas le cloître. En effet: *'Sicut piscis sine aqua, sicut monachus sine claustro'*.[83]

Li Muisis perçoit le monde de son époque comme un monde caractérisé par le péché. Il veut rappeler à son public l'exemple du 'bon vieux temps'. Profondément attaché à son devoir de sermonnaire, il dénonce amplement les progrès des trois vices fondamentaux par lesquels l'ordre social est perturbé – la cupidité, l'envie et l'orgueil.[84] Dans ses poésies il critique les différents états du monde. Ce faisant, il s'inspire largement des clichés de la littérature moralisatrice. Li Muisis commente successivement les moines, les nonnes, les béguines, les frères mendiants, les souverains et les nobles, les papes, les prélats, les chanoines, les prêtres et chapelains, les laïcs en général, les marchands et le clergé en général.

Les groupes urbains spécifiques, tels qu'ils figurent dans les chroniques, sont à peine détaillés ici. Dans les poèmes, la couche inférieure est totalement passée sous silence. Par contre, comme dans ses chroniques, Li Muisis porte un jugement assez favorable sur les classes moyennes: il loue les marchands, parce que ce sont eux qui prennent des risques pour assurer la prospérité des autres classes.[85] Ce sont *li moyen* qui paient pour les riches et pour les pauvres.[86]

---

81. Ibid., p. 157.
82. Ibid., p. 174.
83. Ibid., p. 147 (d'après saint Jerôme?).
84. Les conceptions morales de Gilles Li Muisis sont traitées en détail par C.V. Langlois, *La vie en France*, p. 321-373; B. Guenée, 'Gilles Le Muisit', p. 87-124; J. Devaux, 'Gilles li Muisis et la Complainte des Dames', *Les lettres romanes*, XLVI (1992), p. 3-17; C. Thiry, 'Les catégories sociales revues (et corrigées) dans quelques sources littéraires françaises des XIVe et XVe siècles', dans: J.P. Sosson réd., *Les niveaux de vie au Moyen Age. Mesures, perceptions et représentations. Actes du Colloque international de Spa 21-25 octobre 1998* (Louvain-la-Neuve, 1999), p. 344-353.
85. C. Thiry, 'Les catégories sociales', p. 352; C.V. Langlois, *La vie en France*, p. 359.
86. *Des estas de tous gens seculers*, p. 2: 'Moyens convient et grans et petis soustenir. [...] Pour rikes et pour povres li moyen souvent paient'.

Dans ses *complaintes* Li Muisis s'adresse explicitement à la couche urbaine supérieure. Ces poèmes ont été composés sous forme de dialogues entre l'auteur et, successivement, les femmes de Tournai, les hommes, et ses amis personnels.[87] Le poète critique leur façon de vivre; les bourgeois peuvent se défendre, mais après, il reprend l'offensive avec de nouveaux reproches. La critique toujours répétée est que personne ne parvient à rester à sa 'place naturelle'. Tout le monde veut 'de bas en haut venir', ce qui bouleverse l'ordre social. La confusion des états, contre laquelle Li Muisis fulmine si fortement, s'exprime pour lui en premier lieu dans la transgression des règles vestimentaires et des règles de conduite propres à chaque état.[88] Diverses miniatures dans le manuscrit de la poésie représentent l'abbé discutant avec un groupe d'hommes ou de femmes richement habillés.[89]

Li Muisis a-t-il réellement atteint son public ciblé? A-t-il effectivement réussi à accomplir une mission religieuse (ou éducative) dans la ville? Les hommes et les femmes de Tournai ont-ils lu ou entendu les poèmes qui leur étaient adressés? En tout cas, beaucoup moins que Li Muisis ne l'avait espéré. Il est fort probable que ce n'est que pendant sa vie que des non-religieux ont pu avoir connaissance de ses ouvrages – à savoir ses propres amis et ses proches. Après la mort de Gilles, les manuscrits sont restés dans la bibliothèque de l'abbaye pendant des siècles. Pour autant que nous sachions, l'œuvre de Li Muisis n'a connu aucune diffusion à l'extérieur de l'abbaye.[90]

Bien entendu, dans ses écrits moralisateurs Li Muisis exprimait également des critiques sur le clergé séculier (urbain). Une plainte qui revient plusieurs fois dans les poèmes sur les états du monde – et dans de nombreux autres textes du bas Moyen Age – c'est que le clergé s'enrichit et s'occupe trop d'affaires séculières. On la retrouve également dans le *Tractatus quartus*. Dans le passage traitant de la peste à Tournai, Li Muisis se plaint que les chanoines, tout comme le clergé paroissial, ne s'efforcent pas à diminuer la peur présente chez le peuple. C'était précisément grâce à cette peur qu'ils faisaient de bonnes affaires.[91]

---

87. *Ch'est li complainte de dames*, éd. J.M.B.C. Kervyn de Lettenhove, vol. 2, p. 170-211; *Ch'est des maintiens des hommes et chou qu'il doivent faire*, ibid., p. 212-229; *Ch'est li complainte des compagnons*, ibid., p. 259-279. Cf. J. Devaux, 'Gilles li Muisis et la Complainte des Dames'.
88. C. Thiry, 'Les catégories sociales', p. 349-350.
89. Ms. Bruxelles, Bibliothèque Royale, IV 119, f. 150v, 151r, 156v, 168v, 213r.
90. A. d'Haenens, 'Gilles Li Muisis historien', p. 262.
91. *Tractatus quartus*, éd. H. Lemaître, p. 255-257: '*Gubernatores civitatis, videntes quod decanus, et capitulum, et clerus totus, de remedio apponendo non curabant, quia sua*

La vraie mission du clergé devrait être l'instruction des laïcs. Les ecclésiastiques devraient donner le bon exemple. Gilles compare le clergé au soleil: la lumière de leur manière de vivre vertueuse rayonne (ou devrait rayonner) sur les laïcs, qui sont comme la lune.[92] Pour savoir bien instruire, les gens d'Église eux-mêmes doivent disposer de connaissances et d'une érudition suffisantes. Surtout les frères mendiants excellent en érudition. Par conséquent, ils sont bien placés pour instruire le peuple. L'attitude positive de Li Muisis à l'égard des ordres mendiants se lit également dans les chroniques. En 1349, quand les flagellants étaient entrés à Tournai, le franciscain Gerardus de Muro fit un sermon devant la masse attroupée dans la cour de l'abbaye; un sermon qui selon Li Muisis était *egregie* ('excellent') et *sagacissime* ('très sage').[93] Pareillement, Li Muisis écrit avec fierté sur les louanges que le célèbre dominicain Vincent de Beauvais avait exprimés lors de sa visite à la bibliothèque de Saint-Martin.[94] Cependant, tout comme les autres membres du clergé, les frères mendiants ne résistent pas eux-mêmes à l'attraction de la richesse temporelle.

Pourtant, dans sa poésie, Li Muisis s'intéresse à la situation pénible des prêtres non rentés qui devaient mendier pour survivre. Gilles leur fait prononcer une complainte au discours direct. Selon C. Thiry, le phénomène d'un prolétariat ecclésiastique était nouveau, et dès lors choquant pour l'abbé.[95]

Il ne faut pas s'étonner que l'image de la ville et de ses habitants soit moins 'concrète' dans les ouvrages moraux de Gilles que dans ses chroniques. Dans la poésie, l'abbé tournaisien observait les limites et les clichés du genre; il s'inspirait des modèles comme le Reclus de Molliens, Jaquemon Bochet et le *Roman de la Rose*.[96]

intererat et in facto lucrabantur, habito consilio, fecerunt ordinationes in modum qui sequitur [...] Predicta et alia multa pro utilitate civitatis fecerunt gubernatores in illis diebus proclamare, sub certis penis, ad voluntatem juratorum et consilii.'

92. *C'est des estas de tous prélas*, éd. J.M.B.C. Kervyn de Lettenhove, vol. 2, p. 350-354: 'Un pau voel le clergiet au soleil comparer/ [...] Sainte vie mener che fait le clergiet luire/ [...] Laye gent à le lune volentiers comparroie,/ Se le comparison faire bien je savoie./ [...] Laye gent, si con lune, se cangent et se muent/ Et les boines doctrines pluseur souvent respuent.'
93. *Tractatus quartus*, éd. H. Lemaître, p. 232; cf. aussi p. 230.
94. *Tractatus tertius*, éd. H. Lemaître, p. 1-3.
95. *C'est des curés et des capelains*, éd. J.M.B.C. Kervyn de Lettenhove, vol. 1, p. 378-379. C. Thiry, 'Les catégories sociales', p. 353; C.V. Langlois, *La vie en France*, p. 351-352.
96. C. Thiry, 'Les catégories sociales', p. 348. Cf. *Che sont les méditations*, p. 86-91. Jaquemon Bochet était un franciscain tournaisien qui, selon Li Muisis, rédigea un ouvrage intitulé *Tiaudelet* (probablement un remaniement de *Theodolus*): A. Coville, 'Gilles li Muisis', p. 282.

Conclusion

La situation de l'abbaye de Saint-Martin au bas Moyen Age est sans doute un exemple extrême d'interdépendance entre un monastère et une ville. L'abbaye se situait dans l'enceinte de Tournai et participait à la vie sociale, économique et religieuse de la ville. Gilles Li Muisis témoigne comment des princes et leur entourage séjournaient régulièrement dans l'abbaye, comment des fêtes plantureuses y étaient organisées, comment les habitants de Tournai se rassemblaient dans la cour de l'abbaye pour écouter les serments des franciscains et des dominicains.

Toutefois, ce qui était plus important que la proximité 'physique', c'était la proximité 'mentale' de la ville – l'influence de la culture urbaine sur la culture monastique. On peut en effet reconnaître chez Gilles Li Muisis des éléments trahissant une 'mentalité bourgeoise'. Sa prise d'habit à l'âge de dix-huit ans n'avait pas causé une rupture totale avec son milieu d'origine. Il restait en contact avec ses parents et ses amis et donc aussi avec leur façon de vivre et de penser. Il aimait bien les plaisirs de la table et la bonne compagnie.

Par ses chroniques, il voulait clairement atteindre la population urbaine: alors que dans son *Tractatus primus* et *secundus* – décrivant l'histoire récente de l'abbaye de Saint-Martin – il ne s'adressait qu'à ses propres moines,[97] l'abbé s'adressait dans le *Tractatus quartus* 'tant aux hommes qu'aux femmes qui liront mes ouvrages entièrement ou partiellement.'[98] Dans ses poésies aussi, Gilles visait un public qui ne se composait pas uniquement de moines. Il les a écrites en français pour qu'elles puissent être lues par des laïcs. Dans ses *complaintes*, il s'adressait explicitement à la riche bourgeoisie tournaisienne.

Dans ses chroniques, Li Muisis s'intéressait toujours à l'élite urbaine de bourgeois puissants et riches. Il faisait l'éloge de leurs accomplissements politiques et militaires en tant que dirigeants de la commune, de leur gouvernement juste, des fêtes splendides par le biais desquelles ils procuraient une grande renommée à la ville. Li Muisis s'intéressait à l'économie urbaine et il reconnaissait le rôle central de l'argent. Il considérait comme un état spécifique la classe moyenne des marchands et des commerçants, qui s'occupaient de l'approvisionnement de la ville. Il

---

97. [Praefatio], éd. J.J. De Smet, p. 111: *'Vos omnes, qui in monasterio beati Martini Tornacensis habitum regularem assumpsistis, et qui ibidem stabilitatem et conversionem morum et obedientiam professi estis et novistis, tam moderni quam futuri...'*.
98. Tractatus quartus, éd. H. Lemaître, p. 307: *'...supplicans tam viris quam mulieribus qui legerint omnia per me ordinata vel partem eorumdem...'*.

n'ignorait pas la couche urbaine inférieure, mais la jugeait de façon froide, brève et de temps en temps ouvertement méprisante.

L'attitude négative face à la ville dans une poème comme *Li maintiens des monnes* ne semble pas être beaucoup plus qu'un *topos*. La critique se concentre surtout sur ce que représente la ville dans le discours moralisateur, à savoir le déclin moral, la cupidité, la mobilité sociale. Le rejet du monde, ce noyau central de l'idéologie monastique originel, n'occupe qu'une place marginale chez Li Muisis.

On constate un décalage entre l'idéal de la vie de moine et la réalité d'un style de vie plutôt bourgeois. Gilles aime la vie luxueuse, il aime voir les hommes et les villes et les richesses. Pourtant, en tant qu'abbé, c'est son devoir de critiquer ce style de vie et de prôner plus d'ascèse et plus de sobriété. Est-il exagéré de parler d'un conflit entre une identité monastique et une identité 'urbaine'? L'opposition entre ces deux identités est moins profonde qu'il n'y paraît. Gilles ne considérait comme étant 'problématique' que son style de vie. Pour lui, sa loyauté vis-à-vis de la commune et de l'élite urbaine n'était pas en contradiction avec celle par rapport à l'abbaye et à la Règle de saint Benoît. La conception de la société idéale était la même pour le supérieur du monastère que pour le membre de l'élite urbaine: le *conventus* doit obéir à l'abbé, le peuple doit obéir aux magistrats, tandis que l'abbé et les magistrats ont la tâche de gouverner justement. C'est un péché grave de s'opposer à cet ordre voulu par Dieu, ordre qui au fond est identique au monastère et dans la ville.

L'attitude positive de Li Muisis à l'égard de la ville semble atypique pour un auteur monastique et surtout pour un auteur bénédictin.[99] Il faut cependant mettre l'accent sur le fait que chez les auteurs bénédictins il n'existait pas d'hostilité générale face à la ville, et certainement pas au bas Moyen Age.[100] Une vision concrète de la vie urbaine, non déterminée par des images religieuses, n'était pas seulement une caractéristique de l'historiographie franciscaine ou dominicaine, comme on fait souvent croire.[101]

---

99. L'œuvre historiographique de Li Muisis semble en tout cas occuper une position particulière dans l'historiographie monastique des Pays-Bas méridionaux. Dans son étude quantitative à grande échelle de cette historiographie, Steven Vanderputten n'a pas pris en considération l'œuvre de Li Muisis (sauf le *Chronicon*), précisément parce qu'il l'a estimée trop atypique: S. Vanderputten, *Sociale perceptie en maatschappelijke positionering*.
100. Cf. A. Haverkamp, 'Heilige Städte', p. 154.
101. Cf. H.-J. Schmidt, 'Societas christiana', p. 327-351.

Néanmoins, l'œuvre historiographique de Li Muisis fait preuve d'un intérêt singulier pour l'environnement urbain. Indubitablement, l'emplacement de l'abbaye Saint-Martin dans une ville comme Tournai et la personnalité particulière de Gilles Li Muisis ont-ils joué un rôle décisif.

Janick APPELMANS

THE ABBEY OF AFFLIGEM AND THE EMERGENCE OF A HISTORIOGRAPHIC TRADITION IN BRABANT (1268-1322)

The field of the historiography in Brabant has received in recent years a lot of attention.[1] Some separate texts have been studied with convincing results, but a global approach has often been missing.[2] Despite the efforts of literary scholars and historians, especially the Latin genealogies and chronicles have not been granted the study they deserved. These historical texts were written in the second half of the thirteenth century and the first decades of the fourteenth century and are the earliest extant narratives that clearly focus on the reigning ducal dynasty.

This contribution proposes to study where and by whom these first historiographical texts about the dukes of Brabant were written and to find out the relationship between the different genealogies and chronicles, both in Latin and the vernacular.

---

1. P. Avonds and J.D. Janssens, *Politiek en literatuur. Brabant en de slag bij Woeringen. 1288* (Brussels, 1989); A.-J.A. Bijsterveld, J.A.F.M. Van Oudheusden and R. Stein, eds., *Cultuur in het laatmiddeleeuwse Noord-Brabant. Literatuur – Boekproductie – Historiografie* (Bois-le-Duc, 1998); M. Ceunen and J. Goossens, *Jan I, hertog van Brabant. De dichtende en bedichte vorst. Catalogus. Tentoonstelling naar aanleiding van de 700ste verjaardag van de dood van hertog Jan I van Brabant, ingericht in het historisch stadhuis van Zoutleeuw van 21 mei tot 31 augustus 1994* (Louvain, 1994); R. Stein, *Politiek en historiografie. Het ontstaansmilieu van de Brabantse kronieken in de eerste helft van de vijftiende eeuw*, Miscellanea Neerlandica, 10 (Louvain, 1994).
2. J. Goossens, 'Herzog Jan I. von Brabant und der limburgische Erbfolgekrieg in der mittelalterlichen niederländischen und deutschen Literatur', in: H. Tervooren and H. Beckers, eds., *Literatur und Sprache im rheinisch-maasländischen Raum zwischen 1150 und 1450, Zeitschrift für deutsche Philologie*, 108 Sonderheft (Berlin, 1989), 178-192; A.L.H. Hage, ' "De beste man die nie in hondert iaren was" : Keizer Hendrik VII in Velthems voortzetting van de Spiegel Historiael', in: R.E.V. Stuip en C. Vellekoop, eds., *Koningen in kronieken*, Utrechtse bijdragen tot de mediëvistiek, 16 (Hilversum, 1998), 143-161; A.L.H. Hage, 'Lodewijk van Velthem: pastoor tussen kerk en wereld', *De nieuwe taalgids. Tijdschrift voor neerlandici*, 87 (Groningen, 1994), 210-216; R. Stein, 'Jan van Boendales Brabantsche Yeesten: antithese of synthese?', *Bijdragen en mededelingen betreffende de geschiedenis der Nederlanden*, 106 (The Hague, 1991), 185-197; W. Van Anrooij, 'De literaire ambities van Hennen van Merchtenen', *Tijdschrift voor Nederlandse taal- en letterkunde*, 109 (Leyde, 1993), 291-314.

The dukedom of Brabant emerged during the high Middle Ages. From the eleventh till the thirteenth century the successive counts of Louvain and dukes of Brabant (from 1106) subdued a more or less homogeneous territory in Lower Lotharingia. By the end of the thirteenth century Brabant was firmly established and figured among the mightiest lordships.

From 1200 onwards the name *Brabant* was well-known throughout the Low Countries. Many *vitae* that related the lives of contemporary saints, had seen the dukedom as their heroes's natural habitat. Thomas of Cantimpré (†1270/1272) located some of the exempla from the *Bonum universale de apibus* in his native Brabant.[3] The Cistercian monks of Villers promoted throughout their writings the name of Villers-en-Brabant. The grey monks had geopolitical motives for this propaganda. Amongst the early benefactors the noble family of Marbais is pre-eminent. Their contribution to the foundation is well documented in the abbey archives, but the chronicle omits the name of this powerful family.[4] The reason for this deliberate omission was, as G. Despy pointed out, merely political. During the first hundred years of its existence the abbey came under the influence of the dukes of Brabant, whilst the Marbais were in support of the counts of Namur. Even the rulers themselves were pressed by the success of the name and added in the charters their tautological honour of dukes of Brabant to their official titles of dukes of Lower Lotharingia and margrave of the Holy Roman Empire.

In the first half of the thirteenth century the name Brabant frequently appeared in historiographic writings, but there was as yet no sign of a historiography in Brabant, describing the ancient and noble ancestry and the memorable acts of the dukes. The first extant texts can only be spotted at the end of that thirteenth century. Compared to the other territories in the Southern Low Countries the Brabantine historiography emerged fairly late. In the middle of the tenth century the Flemish priest Witger composed a genealogy of count Arnulf I.[5] Influential monastic authors such

---

3. Thomas Cantimpratanus, *Bonum universale de apibus*, G. Colvenerius, ed. (Douai, 1627³), second book, c. 32, §5, p. 369; c. 36, §4, p. 386 and c. 40, §4, p. 402-403.

4. The first author limits the contribution of the Marbais family by narrating that Saint Bernard was 'exortatus a quibusdam personis' in order to found a new convent: 'Cronica Villariensis monasterii', G.W. Waitz, ed., in: *Monumenta Germaniae Historica, Scriptores*, 25 (Hannover, 1880), c. 1, l. 26, p. 195; E. Brouette, 'Abbaye de Villers, à Tilly', in: *Monasticon belge*, 4 (Liège, 1968), 341-405 (363); G. Despy, 'La fondation de l'abbaye de Villers', *Archives, Bibliothèques et Musées de Belgique*, 28 (Brussels, 1957), 3-17.

5. *Narrative Sources. De verhalende bronnen uit de middeleeuwse Nederlanden – The Narrative Sources from the Medieval Low Countries*, [www.narrative-sources.be], W037.

as Heriger of Lobbes (†1007), Anselm of Liège (†after 1056) and Gilles of Orval (†c. 1251) described the reigns of the successive bishops of Liège in the *Gesta episcoporum Leodiensium*.[6] Even the house of Boulogne, that reigned in the later half of the eleventh century over Lower Lotharingia, had its parentage brought together in the *Genealogia comitum Buloniensium*.

In the decade starting with the premature death of duke Henry III (†1261) Brabant was at the edge of an internal war. Mighty barons from within the dukedom and powerful ecclesiastical and secular princes from the Low Countries, all kinsmen of the young heir, duke Henry IV (†1272), wanted to share the government with Alice (†1273), Henry III's widow.

Only after several military campaigns and the abdication in 1267 of the physically and mentally disabled heir Henry IV in favour of his younger brother John I (†1294) Brabant overcame the dynastic crisis.

During this period of political instability the earliest narrative sources focussing on the house of Louvain were written from 1268 onwards. They include four Latin genealogies and a chronicle on the origins of the dukes of Brabant.

Table 1: The ducal genealogies

Narrative sources	**Title**	**redaction**
G022	*Genealogia ducum Brabantiae, heredum Franciae-1*	1268-1270
G022	*Genealogia ducum Brabantiae, heredum Franciae-2*	1268-1270
G021	*Genealogia ducum Brabantiae ampliata*	1270-1271
G023	*Genealogia ducum Brabantiae metrica*	1272-1285/1288

These *Genealogiae ducum Brabantiae* retrace the ancient origins of the ducal house from Priamus, the mythological founder of the Carolingian dynasty, over Charlemagne (†814), to the reigning duke John I. They aimed at legitimatising the ducal government and stressing its political pretentions by revealing the family ties between the house of Louvain and their powerful or royal ancestors, the Carolingian dynasty, the Merovingian saints and Geoffrey of Bouillon (†1100), the leader of the first crusade and liberator of the Holy Land.

---

6. *Narrative Sources*, A028, A098 and H025.

Many nineteenth and twentieth century historians have promoted Affligem as the literary center where the different genealogical texts have been written. J. Heller, the editor of the four *Genealogiae ducum Brabantiae*, argues that both versions of the oldest genealogy as well as the text of the *Genealogia ampliata* were written by a single monk from Affligem.[7] Opposite to this largely spread theory the Dutch medievalist R. Stein held some years ago the view that these narrative sources had been drawn up in Nivelles.[8] In the seventeenth century J.J. Chifflet had already argued that Nivelles was the cradle of the dynastic historiography in Brabant. He considered the *Genealogia ampliata* as a *Chronicon genealogicum Nivellense*.[9] The earliest history of Nivelles was closely linked with the emergence of the Carolingian dynasty. Pippin of Landen (†640) owned a large estate there and his widow, Ida, founded a famous abbey about 646. Soon a flourishing industrial and mercantile community grew around the abbey. By the thirteenth century however the town's growth and prosperity halted.

The name of Nivelles appears in different chapters in the genealogies and it refers to an epoch, when the dynasty of the Pippinids was indissolubly linked with this religious center. The authors strongly stress the ties of Saint Gertrude (†659), the founder's daughter and the second abbess, with the Louvain dynasty. Opposite to the Trojan and Roman ori-

---

7. P. De Ridder, 'Dynastiek en nationaal gevoel in Brabant onder de regering van hertog Jan I. 1267-1294', *Handelingen van de Koninklijke Zuidnederlandse Maatschappij voor Taal- en Letterkunde en Geschiedenis*, 33 (Brussels, 1979), 73-100 (77); R. Folz, *Le souvenir et la légende de Charlemagne dans l'empire germanique médiéval*, Publications de l'Université de Dijon, 7 (Paris, 1950), 377; 'Genealogia ducum Brabantiae ampliata', J. Heller, ed., in: *Monumenta Germaniae Historica, Scriptores*, 25 (Hannover, 1880), 391-399 (391); 'Genealogia ducum Brabantiae heredum', J. Heller, ed., in: *Monumenta Germaniae Historica, Scriptores*, 25 (Hannover, 1880), 385-391 (385); C. Lemaire, 'Een kroniek vol "quade truffen"', in: E. Cockx-Indestege and F. Hendrickx, eds., *Opstellen voor Dr. Jan Deschamps*, 2 (Louvain, 1987), 279-295 (287); *Narrative Sources*, G021-G023; Stein, *Politiek en historiografie*, 6; *Van den derden Eduwaert. Uitgegeven met een inleiding over de Brabantse historiografie tussen ca. 1270 en ca. 1350*, J.G. Heymans, ed., Tekst en Tijd, 10 (Nijmegen, 1983), 10; W. Verleyen, 'Een overzicht van de geschiedenis van de abdij Affligem', *Eigen Schoon en de Brabander*, 66 (Brussels, 1983), 123-138 (138).

8. R. Stein, 'Brabant en de Karolingische dynastie. Over het ontstaan van een historiografische traditie', *Bijdragen en mededelingen betreffende de geschiedenis der Nederlanden*, 110 (The Hague, 1995), 329-351; R. Stein, 'De kroniek van Peter van Os en de Brabantse historiografie', in: A.-J.A. Bijsterveld, J.A.F.M. Van Oudheusden and R. Stein, eds., *Cultuur in het laatmiddeleeuwse Noord-Brabant. Literatuur – Boekproductie – Historiografie* (Bois-le-Duc, 1998), 122-138 (130); W. van Anrooij, *Helden van weleer. De Negen Besten in de Nederlanden, 1300-1700* (Amsterdam, 1997), 81.

9. *Narrative Sources*, G021.

gin the ancestry of Pippin of Landen was experienced as a unique and characteristic feature of the Brabantine lords. The tenth chapter mentions that seven rulers of Brabant were buried in Nivelles, but in contrast with Affligem only Gerberga's and count Henry III's funerals were exploited to refer to the monastery.[10] At the moment that the genealogical tales were written, Affligem had taken over for more than hundred years the functions of dynastic necropolis.

A strong argument in favour of Nivelles is the use of the *Vita sanctae Gertrudis tripartita* as a source. This life of Saint Gertude is the first work to mention the family ties down to the grandchildren of Charlemagne.[11] Spread beyond Nivelles, the *vita* was however not the exclusive source of the genealogies. Other narrative texts, such as Sigebert of Gembloux's (†1112) chronicle and the genealogy of the counts of Boulogne, were far more important.[12] As R. Stein correctly pointed out, it seems that the Carolingian dynastic features were drawn at Saint Gudula's tomb in Moorsel and at Saint Gertrude's relics in Nivelles, but only at the start of John I's reign the link with the rulers of Brabant has been definitively made by the genealogies. This concept of the ancient, royal and saintly extraction of the dukes of Brabant proved successful during more than five centuries.[13]

The saints stressed by R. Stein refer indeed to an epoch during which Nivelles was pre-eminent amongst the monasteries within Pippin's realm. But the saintly Carolingian relatives of the Brabantine dynasty were not specifically linked with Nivelles. They enjoyed a flourishing veneration in other ancient religious institutions, such as Sainte-Waudru in Mons, Maubeuge, Maroilles, Saint-Ghislain, Saint-Vincent at Soignies and Lobbes.[14]

The genealogies supply beyond the information about Nivelles and the saints from Hainaut much more data. For the recent periods they contain many references to the monastery of Affligem and to the narrative texts circulating there. This Benedictine abbey was founded in 1063 by the

---

10. 'Genealogia ampliata', Heller, ed., c. 2, p. 392-393, l. 43, 2 and 3 and c. 10, p. 396, l. 5-8; 'Genealogia heredum', Heller, ed., c. 3, p. 388, l. 56 and c. 4, p. 389, l. 8; Stein, 'Brabant en de Karolingische dynastie', 342 and 344.
11. Stein, 'Brabant en de Karolingische dynastie', 340-343.
12. *Narrative Sources*, G020 and S042.
13. Stein, 'Brabant en de Karolingische dynastie', 351.
14. A.-M. Helvétius, *Abbayes, évêques et laïques. Une politique du pouvoir en Hainaut au moyen âge. VIIe-XIe siècle*, Credit Communal, Collection Histoire in-8°, 112 (Brussels, 1994), 314-345.

family of margrave Henry II of Verdun (†1085) between Alost and Brussels. Almost from the very first years of its foundation the rulers of Brabant favoured the extension of its domain. The Benedictine convent with its ascetic lifestyle functioned as the dynastic necropolis for the lords of Brabant, in the way that Nivelles had functioned in a distant past. In the period from 1139 to 1254 several members of the dynasty were buried in the abbey church.[15] The genealogies did not omit to mention the separate counts and dukes who got their final resting place in the sanctuary of Affligem. The ruler to whom the genealogies paid most attention, Geoffrey I with the Beard (†1139), was buried there. The metrical genealogy praises him from a mere monastic point of view as 'utilior monachis'. This text, that is generally characterized by its vagueness and brevity, mentions one peculiar detail about the tomb of the first duke: his bones were buried in the crypt of the abbey church. On the eve of the thirteenth century the monastery church still functioned as the burrial ground for the Brabantine dynasty. Marie of France, the second wife of Henry I (†1235), was granted there in 1223 or 1224 her last resting place.[16] The Benedictine convent was not only a sepulchre for the dead members of the ducal house, but also a dynastic and religious centre where living family members could vow their bodies and souls to God. Henry, a son of duke Geoffrey I, prayed and dwelt there under the rule of Saint Benedict.[17] The monastery did not solely serve as a ducal necropolis, but functioned also in other ways for the dynasty. Until the fifteenth century the abbey took care of the Brabantine standard. The Cistercian chronicle writer Gilles of Orval mentions that the Brabantine coat of arms was already stored at the abbey of Affligem in the first half of the thirteenth century.[18] The lords of Asse, a few miles east of Affligem, fulfilled the task of hereditary ensign from 1234 onwards.[19]

---

15. Verleyen, 'Overzicht', 130.

16. Marie of France (†August, 15 1223/1224) was the daughter of the French king Philip II August (1180-1223) and the widow of count Philip of Namur (1195-1212).

17. 'Genealogia ampliata', Heller, ed., c. 11, p. 396, l. 15-16, c. 12, p. 396, l. 30 and c. 14, p. 398, l. 2; 'Genealogia heredum', Heller, ed., c. 5, p. 385 and p. 389, l. 37-43 and c. 7, p. 390, l. 22; 'Genealogia ducum Brabantiae metrica', J. Heller, ed., in: *Monumenta Germaniae Historica. Scriptores*, 25 (Hannover, 1880), 399-404 (403, l. 9, 12 and 43); *Van den derden Eduwaert*, Heymans, ed., 8-9.

18. Gilles of Orval was mentioned as prior in 1241 and died around 1251: *Narrative Sources*, A028.

19. Verleyen, 'Overzicht', 132; Jan van Heelu, *Chronique en vers ou relation de la bataille de Woeringen – Rymkronyk betreffende den slag van Woeringen, van het jaer 1288*, J.-F. Willems, ed., Collection de chroniques belges inédites (Brussels, 1836), LIV.

Not only because of its bonds with Brabant's dukes the abbey deserved the chroniclers's attention. The first genealogist praises the convent as a jewel within the Benedictine order, a 'decus in ordine nigro'.[20] A manuscript of the *Genealogia ducum Brabantiae ampliata*, in which the *Nomina sanctorum* are added, contains an explicit reference to Affligem. The author mentions his membership of the monastic community. The Benedictine monk testifies to the generosity of the house of Boulogne with the following words: 'Hii et mater eorum, sancta Ida, soror nostra, dederunt monasterio nostro Haffligem decimas Genapie et Hugolini curiam'.[21] An other indication for the longest genealogy's creation in the Dutch abbey of Affligem rather than in Nivelles, that is situated in the *Roman pays du Brabant*, may be the importance accorded to the ducal ancestor Charlemagne in the spread of the Dutch language. The genealogist confirms three times that the emperor prescribed the use of the vernacular for the teaching of elementary grammar, for the names of the months and for the twelve wind directions. These affirmations were made upon the authority of Sigebert of Gembloux, whose *Chronografia* was often used at Affligem.[22] The monk Gislebert (†after 1176), later an abbot at Ename in Flanders, continued the universal chronicle in the abbey until 1164.[23]

The genealogies refer always to places in Walloon Brabant where the Benedictines of Affligem had major domanial exploitations or important revenues. Ida of Boulogne granted the monks the tithes of Genappe. In 1147 the chapter of Nivelles gave sixty-six hectares in Genappe to the abbey of Affligem in rent. Abbot Godeschalk (†1195) supported duke Geoffrey III (†1190) in 1160 at the erection of new franchises at Frasnes and Baisy.[24] According to the first genealogist Geoffrey of Bouillon and his brothers Baldwin of Jeruzalem and Eustach of Boulogne grew up in Baisy.[25] The black monks of Affligem had additional points of support in Walloon Brabant such as the priories of Frasnes and Basse-Wavre. Other Brabantine place names can often be related to Affligem as well. Although Louvain was the original ducal residence, Brussels and its area are far more stressed throughout the genealogies.[26]

20. 'Genealogia heredum', Heller, ed., c. 5, p. 389, l. 38.
21. 'Genealogia ampliata', Heller, ed., p. 391 and 398, l. 13-14: the fifteenth century manuscript Paris, Bibliothèque Nationale, ms. lat., 14194, f. 223r-224r (*nomina sanctorum*).
22. 'Genealogia ampliata', Heller, ed., c. 4, p. 393, l. 41-43.
23. *Narrative Sources*, G089.
24. A. Despy-Meyer and C. Gérard, 'Abbaye d'Afflighem, à Hekelgem', in: *Monasticon belge*, 4 (Liège, 1964), 17-80 (28 and 29).
25. 'Genealogia heredum', Heller, ed., c. 5, p. 389, l. 26.
26. 'Genealogia heredum', Heller, ed., c. 3, p. 388, l. 21-31 and c. 4, p. 389, l. 1-22; 'Genealogia metrica', Heller, ed., p. 404, l. 32-33 and 35.

The Merovingian saints do not only refer to Hainaut or to Nivelles. With the exception of Gertrude only a single saint with a veneration in Brabant enjoys the specific attention of the genealogists. Gudula, whose cult was celebrated in the collegiate church of Brussels, was a native of Moorsel, a village at three miles distance from Affligem. The *Genealogia ampliata* pays a lot of attention to the transfer of Gudula's (†c. 710) relics from Moorsel to Brussels under the supervision of duke Charles of Lower Lotharingia (†before 995).[27] Even the poet of the *Genealogia metrica*, who is very sparse with digressions, relates the transfer.[28] The first genealogy focuses on the second transfer of the saint in 1047 from the church Saint Géry to the church dedicated to the archangel Michael in the upper town.[29] Places such as Hamme[30] or Moorsel, that are linked with Gudula's life, refer to the area between Asse and Alost. The first genealogist links her name explicitly with Moorsel, in which neighbourhood she was born. Her relics were transferred around 800 from Hamme to a monastery situated over there. The author does not pay any attention to Gudula's education in the abbey of Nivelles.[31]

In contrast with the genealogies a *consensus opinionum* exists concerning the origin of the *Chronica de origine ducum Brabantiae*. A member of the abbey community of Affligem terminated the chronicle during the reign of John II (1294-1312), presumably before 1298.[32] The unfortunate death of John I, who had in his own time already achieved eternal

27. 'Genealogia ampliata', Heller, ed., c. 7, p. 394.
28. 'Genealogia metrica', Heller, ed., p. 402, l. 4.
29. 'Genealogia heredum', Heller, ed., c. 4, p. 389, l. 21.
30. An alternative identification, Ham near Alost, lies also in the vicinity of the abbey of Affligem: *Vita Gudulae*: J. Verbesselt, *Het parochiewezen in Brabant tot het einde van de 13de eeuw*, 4 (Pittem, 1965), 201-208.
31. 'Genealogia heredum', Heller, ed., c. 4, p. 389, l. 21.
32. 'Comes de Nassowe Adolphus, postea electus in regem Alemanie' and 'Iohannes primus genuit Iohannem secundum, nunc ducem Lotharingie, Brabancie et Lemburgensem. Amen': 'Chronica de origine ducum Brabantiae', J. Heller, ed., in: *Monumenta Germaniae Historica. Scriptores*, 25 (Hannover, 1880), 405-413 (c. 53, p. 412, l. 31-32 and 413, l. 54-55); The editor J. Heller incorrectly wrote in his introduction that the chronicle was written between 1298 and 1304: 'Chronica de origine', Heller, ed., p. 405, l. 15-20 and especially l. 16; A number of historians copied the wrong date: A. Bayot and A. Cauchie, 'Chroniques de Brabant', *Bulletin de la Commission royale d'histoire*, 5e série 10 (Brussels, 1900), XXXVII-C (LVI); *Van den derden Eduwaert*, Heymans, ed., 31; Two historians give a correct datation for the final version between 1294 and 1298: P. Avonds, 'Brabant en de slag bij Woeringen. Mythe en werkelijkheid', in: P. Avonds and J.D. Janssens, eds., *Politiek en literatuur. Brabant en de slag bij Woeringen, 1288* (Brussels, 1989), 15-99 (57); Stein, 'Brabant en de Karolingische dynastie', 347; Stein, 'Kroniek van Peter van Os', 130.

glory because of his chevalresque behaviour, could have been the immediate cause for the definitive version of the chronicle.[33] The author seems to have begun the chronicle one or two decades earlier. This presumption is based on an indication that he started the chronicle before the end of the war of succession in Limbourg. At the discussion of the titles of the dukes of Lower Lotharingia, he stresses that the rulers of Limbourg did reserve in his time the ducal dignity for themselves.[34] This affirmation can only be fully true until the start of the wars in Limbourg. In 1279 or 1280 Walram IV (1247-1279/1280), the last male heir of Limbourg, died. Three years later his heiress Irmgard followed him into the grave without children. In 1288 her widower, count Rainout of Gelre, gave up all hope to become duke. The treaty of May 19, 1289 ratified the definitive annexation of Limbourg by Brabant. At each of these dates the use of the title of dukes of Lower Lotharingia by the house of Limbourg *usque ad hodiernum diem* became more and more an element of a past perfect. In this view the dynastic chronicle has to be situated before 1280, because after this date there are no more male dukes of Limbourg. These remarks almost close the chronological gap between the writing of the Latin genealogies and the beginning of the dynastic chronicle. In the successive versions of the *Genealogia ducum Brabantiae heredum Francie*, the *Genealogia ducum Brabantiae ampliata* and the *Chronica de origine ducum Brabantiae* one may easily perceive an increasing use of one single source, Sigebert of Gembloux's *Chronografia*.

Although the contrary has many times been pretended, the genealogies have seldom been used as a source for the *Chronica de origine ducum Brabantiae*.[35] The *Chronica* is much more dependent upon Sigebert's chronicle and its continuations at Gembloux and Affligem.[36] Some chapters draw completely upon the *Chronografia* and provide the chronicle with a geographically large Lotharingian scope. The compiler integrated different passages with few or no connection with the history of Brabant and its rulers in his narrative. The rebellion of the Lotharingian duke Geoffrey II († 1069) from the house of Ardennes is completely copied from Sigebert. The destruction of the imperial palace in Nijmegen by

---

33. 'Chronica de origine', Heller, ed., p. 405, l. 1-5.
34. 'Extunc tamen usque ad hodiernum diem Lemburgenses non comites, sed duces se nominant': 'Chronica de origine', Heller, ed., c. 46, p. 408, l. 45.
35. The *Genealogia ampliata* seems to be a more likely source than the earliest genealogy.
36. The use of the two continuations can be spotted in 'Chronica de origine', Heller, ed., c. 49, p. 409, l. 14-32.

duke Geoffrey II and the burning of Saint Mary's church in Verdun were events that took place far beyond the borders of the dukedom of Brabant.[37]

At different occasions the chronicle aims more clearly than the genealogies towards the abbey of Affligem and its neighbourhood. The genealogists had divided their attention between the chapters of Brussels and Louvain, both founded in the eleventh century. The author of the *Chronica de origine* pays exclusively attention to the church of Brussels. He deals with the transfer of Saint Gudula from Saint Géry's to Saint Michael's church. This sanctuary, where a college of twelve canons administered the offices, received the local tithes.[38] At the exception of Brussels, Affligem is the most mentioned place in Western Brabant. The twenty-fourth chapter focuses on the foundation of the Benedictine abbey. The chronicler found this information in the *Exordium Affligemense*, where he learned that twenty-three years after the settlement in 1063 bishop Gerard of Cambrai confirmed the foundation by solemnly consecrating the church.[39] Finally he tells about duke Geoffrey with the Beard as a most marvellous man in his time. He could not refrain from mentioning twice his sepulchre in the abbey church.[40] Throughout his chronicle the author shows a clear vision in political affairs and in chronology. He disposed of a well-defined perception of time, including a view on the past, the present and the relativity of time.

The direct influence of the genealogies and the chronicle can be spotted at the ducal court. In a charter dated December 1289 John I considered Geoffrey of Bouillon as his 'old ancestor'.[41]

During the first decades of the fourteenth century a genealogy as well as the chronicle were translated into Dutch poetry. These translations and adaptations clearly show the ties between the monastic genealogies and the historiography of the fourteenth century Antwerp school. The *Chronica de origine ducum Brabantiae* was integrated by Jan van Boendale

---

37. 'Chronica de origine', Heller, ed., c. 39-40, p. 405, c. 42, p. 407, l. 40-52 and c. 43, p. 407-408.
38. 'Chronica de origine', Heller, ed., c. 41, p. 407, l. 35-39.
39. 'Chronica de origine', Heller, ed., p. 408, l. 7-22; *Narrative Sources*, C014.
40. 'Succedit frater eius Godefridus cum Barba, postea dux Lotharingie, qui in Haffligenio sepultus est' and 'Godefridus dux Lotharingie, magnum patrie sue decus, vir suo tempore et tempori et honori sciens se decenter conformare, moritur et Haffligemensis templi sepultura honoratur': 'Chronica de origine', Heller, ed., c. 45, p. 408, l. 27-28 and c. 48, p. 409, l. 2-3.
41. J.F.D. Blöte, *Das Aufkommen der Sage von Brabon Silvius, dem brabantischen Schwanritter*, Verhandelingen der Koninklijke Akademie van Wetenschappen te Amsterdam. Afdeeling Letterkunde, nieuwe reeks V 4 (Amsterdam, 1904), 22.

(†1351) in his *Brabantsche yeesten*.[42] He linked the Benedictine chronicle and the information on Brabant's past in the *Spieghel Historiael* of Jacob van Maerlant (†c. 1300). Both sources based their information about the dukedom's earliest history on Sigebert's *Chronografia*.

The translation of a Latin genealogy has not yet been recognised. Mostly a linear evolution between the Latin genealogies, the Latin chronicle, the Middle Dutch chronicle and the Middle Dutch short chronicle has been proposed or silently adopted. This scheme can not be held any longer.

A short vernacular history of the ducal ancestry, known as the *Rijmkroniek van Brabant-B*, is conserved in four manuscripts and as many versions.[43] All these texts go back, two by two, as W. van Anrooij pointed out, to a single text that may be written in Antwerp shortly after 1322. It is traditionally ascribed to the alderman's clerck Jan van Boendale. When he had finished the first version of his *Brabantsche yeesten*, he would have made a summary. Firstly there is no relation between the five books in his large historic overview of the Brabantine rulers and the short vernacular chronicle. Secondly the original text of the *Rijmkroniek van Brabant-B* does not seem to be an abstract of the *Brabantsche yeesten*, but rather a fairly correct translation of a genealogy, most probably the *Genealogia ducum Brabantiae ampliata*.

Since there are also formal differences between a chronicle and the *Korte Rijmkroniek van Brabant-B*, like the brevity of the Brabantine text and the poor elaboration of the non-genealogical themes, the *Rijmkroniek* must be perceived as a genealogy. A change in its denomination is therefore inevitable: the *Rijmgenealogie van Brabant*-B (or Metric Genealogy of Brabant-B) would be a more fitting name for the *Korte Rijmkroniek van Brabant-B* (or Short Metric Chronicle of Brabant-B). The primary aim of the text was to create a vernacular overview of the illustrious extraction of the ducal family from Priamus over Charlemagne to the contemporary rulers.

Still one question remains, whether Jan van Boendale can or can not be identified as the poet of this *Rijmgenealogie* (or Metric genealogy)? Boendale's connection with Affligem, as the translator of the *Chronica de origine ducum Brabantiae* in his historiographic masterpiece, the *Brabantsche yeesten*, points to an identification. But why should a writer start off with a brand new text when he has already dealt with the

---

42. *Narrative Sources*, J038.
43. *Narrative Sources*, K003-K005 and K008.

subject matter in much more depth and with more valuable sources?[44] Further investigation into Boendale's redaction methods may answer this question.

With this vernacular text there came in 1322 a temporary end to the boom of a historiographic tradition, including genealogies and chronicles, both in Latin and in the vernacular. The *Brabantsche yeesten*, with their sixteen thousand verses, became a standard history of Brabant. It was continued by Boendale himself up to 1350 and by an anonymous author in the fifteenth century. Other fifteenth century authors used his texts for new histories of Brabant. The Dutch genealogy was copied and emendated in different manuscripts, beyond the borders of Brabant. It is clear that this evolution started with the genealogies and the *Chronica de origine ducum Brabantiae*.

During the thirteenth and fourteenth century new mythical tales on Brabant's origin came into being. Hennen van Merchtenen incorporated these materials in the Brabantine historiography in 1415. Due to a lack of space he may have been more creative in integrating different matters and sources into his narrative than his great predecessor Jan van Boendale.

The historiographic tradition, started at Affligem, continued beyond the reign of the Louvain dynasty, during the Burgundian and Habsburg era. In the fifteenth century an anonymous Dutch poet continued Boendale's deeds of the dukes till 1441.[45] Under the reign of Philip the Good (†1467) the ducal officers Emond de Dynter (†1449) and Peter a Thymo (†1474) compiled Latin stories of Brabant's history.[46] By the end of the fifteenth century the Antwerp publisher Roland van den Dorpe edited *Die alder excellenste Cronyke van Brabant*.[47]

Complementary to the science where the first dynastic chronicles were written this contribution aims at elaborating the profile and questioning the identity of the first ducal historians. A fifth historiographical writing from the same monastic environment at Affligem is the continuation of

---

44. Boendale started his *Brabantsche yeesten* about 1316, while the genealogy was translated into Dutch in 1322, 'Dertien hondert ende xxij mede' or 'XIIIc ende XXII mede': *Narrative Sources*, K004 and K008.
45. *Narrative Sources*, B021.
46. *Narrative Sources*, E001 and P008.
47. *Narrative Sources*, W008.

De viris illustribus, that has been written between 1270 and 1273.[48] The work unites biographical and bibliographical information on Christian writers and is for that reason also known as *De scriptoribus ecclesiasticis*. The Church father Jerome (†419/420) was at the survey's origin. In the later half of the fifth century the priest Gennadius of Marseille (†492/505) added some ninety authors. In the seventh century the Spanish bishop Isidore of Seville (†636) and his younger contemporary, the archbishop Ildefons of Toledo (†667), continued the inventory. During the High Middle Ages their work was continued by famous authors such as Honorius of Autun (twelfth century) and Sigebert of Gembloux, who included references to one hundred seventy-two writers in his list.[49] The thirteenth century compiler of *De viris illustribus* clearly wished to place himself in this glorious tradition. He wanted the work 'ad hoc nostrum tempus ultra extendere'.[50]

During many centuries the continuation has been mistakenly attributed to the theologian Henry of Ghent (†1293).[51] This incorrect attribution to the philosopher and secular canon appears in a manuscript and in the successive editions of the biographical and bibliographical survey.[52] On the eve of the twentieth century F. Pelster linked the name of Henry of Brussels, a monk of Affligem and an expert in chronology, with the catalogue.[53] He listed sixty authors from the period from 1050 till 1270

---

48. Henry of Brussels wrote the survey probably before 1273, because in that year Peter of Tarantaise was appointed archbishop of Lyons and Bonaventure was created a cardinal. The compiler finished his inventory certainly before 1276, because he omits the papal election of Peter of Tarantaise (Innocent V, 1276): *De illustribus Ecclesiae scriptoribus*, S. Petri, ed. (Cologne, 1580) c. 41, 417; G.I. Lieftinck, 'Middelnederlandse handschriften uit beide Limburgen', *Tijdschrift voor Nederlandse taal- en letterkunde*, 72 (Leyde, 1954), 184-200 (197).

49. 'Der Literaturkatalog von Affligem', N. Häring, ed., *Revue bénédictine*, 80 (Maredsous, 1970), 64-96 (64-65); G. Hendrix, 'Der Literaturkatalog von Affligem. Some notes on a Catalogus virorum illustrium', in: A. Raman and E. Manning, eds., *Miscellanea Martin Wittek: Album de codicologie et de paléographie offert à Martin Wittek* (Louvain-Paris, 1993), 181-188 (181); O. Weijers, *Dictionnaires et répertoires au moyen âge. Une étude du vocabulaire*, Etudes sur le vocabulaire intellectuel du Moyen Age, 4 (Turnhout, 1991), 148.

50. *De illustribus Ecclesiae scriptoribus*, Petri, ed., prologus, 397.

51. The philisopher Henry of Ghent (†1293) was from 1267 a member of the cathedral chapter at Tournai and was archdeacon of Bruges (1276) and thereafter of Tournai (1278).

52. *De illustribus Ecclesiae scriptoribus*, Petri, ed., prologus, 396 with the title: 'Prologus in librum sequentem, de viris illustribus authore Henrico de Gandauo'.

53. G. Hendrix, 'Cistercian Sympathies in the 14th-century Catalogus virorum illustrium', *Cîteaux*, 27 (1976), 267-278 (275) correctly wrote 'I conjecture [...]'; 'Two catalogues of Medieval Authors', N. Häring, ed., *Franciscan Studies*, 26 (Saint Bonaventure, 1966), 195-211 (195-197); P. Lehmann, 'Philippe d'Harvengt', *Historisches Jahrbuch*, 45

and dealt with their profane and sacred writings. In the second but last chapter he commented his own scientifical work. The catalogue especially enumerates Henry's merits as an expert in chronology: 'Henricus, Bruxellae ordiundus, monachus Affligeniensis, calculatoriae artis pertitus, discordiam naturalis computi lunae et cycli decemnovenalis diligenter absolvens calendarium, ita distinxit, ut positis secundum cyclum decemnovenalem suo loco primilunis, ipse e regione non solum qua die vel qua hora singularum lunationum singulis mensibus accensio contingeret, annotaret'.[54] Philippe of Bergamo, who edited the *Supplementum supplementi chronicon* (Venice, 1503), stressed also his scientific activities while characterising the monk Henry.[55]

Although the catalogue has been transmitted anonymously in most manuscripts, there are several arguments to situate the list at Affligem and to point to Henry of Brussels as its compiler. The writer pays a lot of attention to the Southern Low Countries and Northern France.

Table 2: The notices on the authors from the Low Countries
in the *Catalogus de viris illustribus* by Henry of Brussels
according to the edition by S. Petri (Cologne, 1580)

CHAPTER	PAGE	AUTHOR	DEATH
4	398-399	Odo of Cambrai	1113
19	406	Walter of Châtillon	after 1176
20	406	Walter of Châtillon	after 1176
21	406-407	Alain of Lille, O.Cist.	1202
24	408	Simon of Tournai	1202
25	408-409	Hugues of Saint-Victor, O.S.A.	1141
37	414-415	James of Vitry	1240
38	415	John of Abbeville	1239
39	416	Franco of Affligem, O.S.B.	1134

(München, 1925), 556-557 (556); *Narrative Sources*, C007; F. Pelster, 'Der Heinrich von Gent zugeschriebene Catalogus virorum illustrium und sein wirklicher Verfasser', *Historisches Jahrbuch*, 39 (München, 1918-1919), 253-268 (254-255); E. Van Arenbergh, 'Henri, surnommé de Bruxelles', in: *Biographie Nationale*, 9 (Brussels, 1886-1887), col. 187-188 (187); J. van Mierlo, *De letterkunde van de Middeleeuwen tot omstreeks 1300. Geschiedenis van de letterkunde der Nederlanden*, 1 (Brussels-Bois-le-Duc, 1939), 194, 262 and 265-266; Weijers, *Dictionnaires et répertoires*, 148-149.

54. *De illustribus Ecclesiae scriptoribus*, Petri, ed., c. 58, 425.
55. 'Henricus de Brusellis monachus per hoc tempus floruit. Qui cum in diversis scripturis studiosus et continuo exercitatione philosophus, magnus computista habetur et ipse monumentis mandavit nonnnulla commendanda, quibus suo tempore longe innotuit et inter cetera librum unum *De ratione computi* et alium *De incencionibus* et quaedam alia': Pelster, 'Catalogus', 261.

51	421	Thomas of Cantimpré, O.S.A./O.P.	1270/1272
52	422	Guerric of Saint-Quentin, O.P.	c. 1245
53	422-423	Gerard of Louvain, O.P.	c. 1250
54	423	Guibert of Tournai, O.F.M.	1288
56	423-424	Simon of Affligem, O.S.B.	Possibly after 1214
57	424	William of Affligem, O.S.B.	1297
58	425	Henry of Brussels, O.S.B.	after 1270
60	425	Eberhard of Béthune	Shortly before 1212

The abbey of Affligem was not only situated at the heart of the author's thematic and geographical interests, the separate notices contained different references to the Benedictine community as well. The fourth biographical article shows the first affinities between the catalogue and the monastery. Odo of Cambrai (°1050) informed a monk of Affligem about a dispute he had with a Jew concerning the mystery of our Lord's incarnation. The founder of the abbey of Saint Martin at Tournai (1092) and bishop of Cambrai (1105-1113) 'scripsit', according to the *Catalogus de viris illustribus*, 'etiam ad Vulbodonem, monachum Affligemiensem, disputationem quam habuerat cum quodam Iudaeo de mysterio incarnationis Dominicae'.[56] The fifteenth chapter, dealing with the writings of Peter the Chanter (†1197), mentions a copy of a grammar conserved at Affligem.[57] The thirty-ninth notice pays attention to the literary heritage of prelate Franco (†1134). The second abbot of Affligem wrote at the instance of his predecessor a treatise on the divine grace, that he finished after the death of Fulgence (†1122). Therefore he ended his treatise with a eulogy of the first abbot of Affligem. He also sent a consolatory letter to the nuns of Grand-Bigard and Forest and composed some hymns in honour of the virgin Mary.[58]

---

56. *De illustribus Ecclesiae scriptoribus*, Petri, ed., c. 4, 399.
57. Hendrix, 'Cistercian Sympathies', 274.
58. 'Literaturkatalog', Häring, ed., c. 39, 89: 'Dominus Franco abbas Haffligeniensis. Rogatus a domino Fulgentio predecessore suo antequam ipse dominus Franco abbas esset scripsit opusculum quod appelauit *De gratia Dei*. Et antequam consummaret idem opusculum decente abbate Fulgentio ipse successit et iam abbas factus predictum opusculum consummauit in eiusdem opusculi fine laudes sui predecessoris declamans, metrice etiam statum future glorie eleganter describens'; Despy-Meyer and Gérard, 'Abbaye d'Afflighem', 27; E. Vaerenbergh, 'Francon', in: *Biographie Nationale*, 7 (Brussels, 1880-1883), col. 269-270.

An important indication for the authorship of a monk of Affligem are the three contemporary notices on the literary fellow monks at the very end of the list. These notices reveal the profound interest of the Brabantine Benedictines. They cherished the history as well as the exegesis and the chronology. The prior William of Affligem (†1297) translated the *Vita Lutgardis* of Thomas of Cantimpré in the vernacular and wrote about the many marvellous events in the nun's life. The monk Simon of Affligem (after 1214) compiled an abstract of the *Moralia in Job* of pope Gregory the Great (590-604) and wrote a commentary on that didactic writing of the Church father. He also composed some commentaries on the Song of Songs and compiled a collection of sermons.[59] Finally there is the notice on Henry of Brussels himself, who is the last author in a row of three writers from Affligem.[60] The two ecclesiastical writers from around 1200 who close the narrative, have to be considered as 'Nachträge aus früher Zeit', just as F. Pelster did.[61]

The familiarity with the authorship of Thomas of Cantimpré indicates also in the direction of an abbey in Brabant that had multiple connections with other regular clergymen. The catalogue mentions that the dominican friar wrote the *vitae* of Christina of Brustem (†1224) and of Lutgart of Tongres (†1246).[62] This accurate information was available in Affligem, where around the same time a Middle Dutch poetic translation of the *Vita piae Lutgardis* has been composed. The poet points several times to 'die iacobite, Bruder Damaes van Bellengem', the dominican friar Thomas of Bellingen, as the author of the Latin story.[63] A century later this

---

59. 'Literaturkatalog', Häring, ed., c. 56, 95: 'Symon, monachus Haffligeniensis, breuiauit libros Moralium expositionis beati Gregorii in Iob moralem expositionem per totum opus beati Gregorii excerpens et littere libri beati Iob apte apponens totum librum beati Iob moraliter exposuit. Scripsit etiam idem Symon quosdam sermones de Canticis canticorum. Scripsit et quandam uisionem cuiusdam conuersi ordinis Premonstratensis de quodam monasterio quod dicitur Postele. Collegit etiam excerpta quedam de sermonibus beati Gregorii pape in Ezechielem de collationibus Patrum et de opusculo Richardi de Xii patriarchis'; U. Berlière, 'Simon, moine d'Affligem', in: *Biographie Nationale* 22 (Brussels, 1914-1920), col. 537; *De illustribus Ecclesiae scriptoribus*, Petri, ed., c. 56, 423-424.

60. Pelster, 'Catalogus', 263.

61. Pelster, 'Catalogus', 267.

62. 'Literaturkatalog', Häring, ed., c. 51, 93: 'Frater Thomas ordinis Predicatorum Louanii habitans. Scripsit uitam cuiusdam sancte mulieris in Hesbania que uocabatur Cristina. Scripsit etiam uitam cuiusdam monialis de aquiria, domine scilicet Lutgardis'.

63. Bellingen, near Léau-Saint-Pierre, was the birthplace of Thomas of Cantimpré. Therefore he is sometimes refered to as Thomas of Bellingen; 'Sente Lutgart', M. Gysseling, ed., in: M. Gysseling, *Corpus van Middelnederlandse teksten (tot en met het jaar 1300)*, II, *Literaire handschriften*, 5 (Leyde, 1985), 5-500 (c. 35, v. 11764-11765, p. 289, l. 34-35).

knowledge was not any more at hand. The grey friar Gerard was not acquainted with the author of these works when he translated them. A correct survey of the bibliography of Thomas of Cantimpré, as given in *De viris illustribus*, was by no means an easy task. During a long time one of the two most extensive works of the friar, the *Liber de natura rerum*, has been attributed to the Dominican philosopher Albertus Magnus (†1280). Even the Bollandist Daniël van Papenbroeck (1628-1714) identified an unknown Nicolas of Cantimpré by mistake as the writer of the third book of Marie d'Oignies's life.[64]

An other reason to see Henry of Brussels as the compiler of the Affligem catalogue of ecclesiastical writers is his acquaintance with the work of Sigebert of Gembloux. The similarities between these two Benedictines are striking. Henry did not only live in a monastery where a century earlier the universal chronicle of the monk of Gembloux had been continued, he also shared his interest for the astronomy, the techniques and the chronology. The titles of his scientific treatises are the *Calendarium pro accensionibus lunae ad punctum investigandis*, the *Liber de ratione computandi ecclesiastici* and the technical writings *De compositione astrolabii* and *De esu et utilitate astrolabii*.[65] Like his examples and predecessors, Jerome and Sigebert, Henry concluded his overview with listing his own writings. In this context it does not seem illogical at all to credit Henry of Brussels with the continuation of Sigebert's *De viris illustribus*.[66]

The comparison of Henry of Brussels with the author's profile of the different Latin genealogies is worthwhile. The anonymous compiler of the *Genealogia ducum Brabantiae heredum Francie* and the *Genealogia ducum Brabantiae ampliata* elaborated the parentage of the houses of Boulogne and Louvain largely thanks to the information supplied by Sigebert's chronicle. The striking resemblances between Henry of Brussels and the historian of Gembloux may give way for further speculation upon the authorship of the *Chronica de origine ducum Brabantiae*. This chronicle draws almost exclusively on Sigebert's narrative and his continua-

---

64. 'Supplementum auctore coaevo fratri Nicolao, canonico regulari coenobii Cantimpratani', D. Papebrochius, ed., in: *Acta Sanctorum Junii* 5 (Paris-Rome, 1867³), 572-581.

65. *De illustribus Ecclesiae scriptoribus*, Petri, ed., c. 58, 425; U. Engelmann, 'Heinrich von Brüssel', in: *Lexikon für Theologie und Kirche*, 5 (Freiburg, 1960), col. 177; G. Michiels, 'Henri de Bruxelles', in: *Dictionnaire d'histoire et de géographie ecclésiastiques*, 23 (Paris, 1990), col. 1106-1107 (1106).

66. *Narrative Sources*, S065: Sigebert ended his career with this work in Gembloux in 1111-1112.

tors in its attempt to reconstruct the dynastic history of the counts of Louvain and the dukes of Brabant. A single reference to this often used source is of major importance. The chronicler strengthens his description of the different houses that claimed the dignity of dukes of Lotharingia for themselves with the words 'sicut et manifeste patet ex cronicis illustris viri Sigeberti quondam Gemblacensis monachi'.[67] Maybe this sentence contains more than a mere reference to Sigebert's universal chronicle. The praising depiction of Sigebert as a *vir illustris* can be seen as an allusion to the catalogue *De viris illustribus*. In this terminology a supplementary argument for Henry of Brussels's authorship of the *Chronica de origine ducum Brabantiae* can be perceived.

In a thirty years time, from 1268 to 1298, the core of the Brabantine historiography was composed at a single Benedictine abbey in the dukedom, Affligem. During the first decades of the fourteenth century the two major works of this Latin historiography, the *Genealogia ampliata* and the *Chronicon de origine* were translated into Dutch in Antwerp. In the fifty years from 1268 to 1322 the foundations of a new historiographic tradition, both in Latin and the vernacular, were laid. Could this whole processus of creating a history for the Brabantine dukes be the achievement of two authors, a Benedictine monk and a lay poet? In any case, we must reconsider the contribution of the abbey of Affligem and its prolific author Henry of Brussels to the earliest historiography of Brabant and its rulers.

---

67. 'Chronica de origine', Heller, ed., c. 52, p. 410, l. 42.

Thomas KOCK

SELBSTVERGEWISSERUNG UND MEMORIA IN DER DEVOTIO MODERNA: DIE TRADITIONSCODICES DER BRABANTISCHEN AUGUSTINER-CHORHERRENSTIFTE

Die aus religiosen Gemeinschaften überlieferten Traditionscodices können folgende Funktionen erfüllen:
- sie überliefern die Geschichte des Konvents, d.h. sie bieten im klassischen Sinn Historiographie;
- eingefügt werden wichtige Urkunden: Bestimmungen bei der Fundation, Auszeichnungen durch Ablaß, Übertragungen von Besitz. Die Codices erfüllen die Funktion eines Kopiars;
- in tabellarischer Form oder auch mit kurzen Lebensbeschreibungen wird der verstorbenen Angehörigen des Klosters oder Stiftes gedacht. Die Handschriften dienen als Nekrolog;
- angeführt werden die Wohltäter des Konvents; erwähnt werden können dabei die Schenkungen im einzelnen sowie insbesondere die dadurch entstandenen Verpflichtungen wie das Lesen von Messen oder das Spenden von Almosen.

Elisabeth van Houts spricht davon, daß monastische Gemeinschaften nach etwa drei Generationen die Notwendigkeit sähen, 'to support their collective memory'.[1] Statt von 'kollektiver Erinnerung' könnte man auch die von Jan Assmann eingeführten Begriffe des 'kommunikativen' oder 'kulturellen Gedächtnisses' verwenden; für Assmann bilden 40 Jahre die Schwelle, sich literarisch auf eine rezente Vergangenheit zu beziehen.[2] Solche Traditionscodices wurden also nicht mit der Fundation oder auch kurze Zeit danach erstellt. Als Grund für die Anlage der Handschrift wird in den Prologen häufig angeführt, der ursprüngliche *fervor*, das Feuer und die religiöse Leidenschaft der Gründergeneration, der *patres primitivi*, sei

---

1. S.E.M.C. van Houts, *Local and regional chronicles*, Typologie des sources du moyen âge occidental, 74 (Turnhout, 1995), S. 28, vgl. auch S. 19. S. auch St. Molitor, 'Das Traditionsbuch. Zur Forschungsgeschichte einer Quellengattung und zu einem Beispiel aus Südwestdeutschland', *Archiv für Diplomatik*, 36 (1990), S. 61-92.
2. S.J. Assmann, *Das kulturelle Gedächtnis. Schrift, Erinnerung und politische Identität in frühen Hochkulturen* (München, 1992), S. 48ff.

verlorengegangen. Die Codices sollen als Korrektiv und Exemplum dienen. Oft sind es Krisensituationen, die den Anstoß zur Aufzeichnung geben, seien es spirituelle Krisen, aber auch äußere Katastrophen wie Krieg, Verwüstung oder Seuchen. Die Codices dienen der Selbstvergewisserung und der Memoria, sie werden in der Regel von einem Mitglied der Gemeinschaft angelegt, dann aber über Generationen fortgeführt, ergänzt und korrigiert, sodaß hier idealiter der ganze Konvent als Autor fungiert.

Fragt man nach dem Aufbau, der Funktion und der Rezeption solcher Handschriften im Bereich der Devotio moderna, so gilt es auch die Übernahme, die Vermittlung in andere Textzusammenhänge oder an andere Gemeinschaften, also den Transfer von Texten und die Veränderungen, die sich dadurch für die Interpretation ergeben, in den Blick zu nehmen. Der brabantische Raum soll dabei im Mittelpunkt stehen, da von dort eine Vielzahl solcher Handschriften überliefert ist, und die Auswahl es zusätzlich, en passant, ermöglicht, auf die These von John Van Engen einzugehen, wie sie im Titel seines Aufsatzes in der Gedenkschrift für Willem Lourdaux zum Ausdruck kommt: 'A Brabantine perspective on the origins of the modern devotion'.[3]

1402 wird das Groenendaaler Kapitel gegründet, ein Zusammenschluß von Augustiner-Chorherrenstiften, die sich bewußt in die Tradition der Mystik eines Jan van Ruusbroec stellen. Es handelt sich um die Konvente Groenendaal, Rooklooster, Zevenborren sowie die *Domus beatae Mariae in Bethlehem* in Herent.[4] Beginnen möchte ich mit einem Codex aus dem von Zevenborren aus gegründeten Augustiner-Chorherrenstift in Ophain (Bois-Seigneur-Isaac). Die Handschrift hat in der Forschung bisher wenig Beachtung gefunden, was auch darin begründet liegt, daß sie nach wie vor in dem Priorat in Ophain, das heute Prämonstratenser bewohnen, aufbewahrt wird und daher schwer zugänglich ist.[5] Während

---

3. J. Van Engen, 'A Brabantine Perspective on the Origins of the Modern Devotion: the First Book of Petrus Impens's *Compendium decursus temporum monasterii Christifere Bethleemitice puerpere*', in: W. Verbeke u.a. (Hgg.), *Serta devota in memoriam Guillelmi Lourdaux*, Bd. 1: *Devotio Windeshemensis*, Mediaevalia Lovaniensia, Series 1, Studia 20 (Löwen, 1992), S. 3-78.

4. Vgl. L. Janssens – E. Persoons, *Klooster in het Zoniënwoud (Hertoginnedal, Groenendaal, Rooklooster, Zevenborren en Ter Kluizen)*. Ausstellungskatalog (Algemeen Rijksarchief en Rijksarchief in de Provinciën, 83), (Brüssel, 1989), (mit Literaturangaben).

5. Die Handschrift wird aufbewahrt in Ophain, Archief Abdij Bois-Seigneur-Isaac, Nr. 34 (künftig zitiert als: Ophain; die neuzeitliche Seitenzählung in der Handschrift ist nicht konsequent, später eingefügte Blätter werden z.T. nicht mitgezählt; die folgenden Angaben folgen dieser trotzdem). Vor einigen Jahren hatten Mitarbeiter des von Nikolaus Staubach in Münster geleiteten Forschungsprojekts zur Devotio moderna die Möglichkeit,

die anderen Konvente des Groenendaaler Kreises früh den Weg in die Klausur, die *inclusio*, wählen, ist Ophain eine Kapelle zum Hl. Blut angeschlossen, die sich zum Wallfahrtsziel von Pilgern entwickelt.[6] Anzunehmen ist, daß ein solcher Ort großen Wert auf die Propagierung der Wunderberichte und der zu gewinnenen Ablässe legt, ein Interesse an der Verbreitung der eigenen Geschichte besteht. Bereits auf dem Vorsatzblatt des Ophainer Codex wird eine erste Aussage zur Funktion der Handschrift getroffen: *Hoc registrum est valde necessarium pro arcario.* Der Inhalt wird als *registrum* bezeichnet, das sehr nützlich für den *arcarius* sei, den Prokurator, und damit denjenigen, der für das Archiv und damit auch für die Finanzen des Konvents zuständig ist. Ein anderer Titel als der des Registers wird im Prolog verwendet: *Prologus in descriptionem originis monasterii beate Marie in Busco Domini Isaac.* Zu Beginn des Prologs hebt der Autor die *ars litteratoria* hervor. Die Generationen kommen und gehen, vom menschlichen Handeln bleibe nur das im Gedächtnis, was auch schriftlich aufgezeichnet werde.[7] Hervorgehoben wird die

---

das Buch vor Ort einzusehen und zu fotographieren. In dem Archiv sind darüber hinaus auch einige Urkunden überliefert; die wichtigste Darstellung stammt von D. van den Auweele – A. Verrycken, 'Imago fundatoris: Jean de Huldenberghe († 1458) et le prieuré de Notre-Dame à Bois-Seigneur-Isaac', in: Verbeke (wie Anm. 3), S. 79-114; vgl. zur Geschichte des Konvents F. Baix, 'Bois-Seigneur-Isaac', in: *Dictionnaire d'histoire et de géographie ecclésiastiques*, Bd. 9 (Paris, 1937), Sp. 547-572; Pl. Lefèvre, 'A propos du corporal miraculeux de Bois-Seigneur-Isaac', *Analecta Praemonstratensia*, 39 (1963), S. 347-351; J. Vanderborght, in *Monasticon Belge*, Bd. 4: *Province de Brabant* (Liège, 1970), S. 1025-1066; D. van den Auweele, in *Monasticon Windeshemense*, Bd. 1: *Belgien*, hg. von W. Kohl – E. Persoons – A.G. Weiler, Archief- en Bibliotheekwezen in België, Extranummer, 16 (Brüssel, 1976), S. 31-44; R. de Keyser – D. van den Auweele, 'Le prieuré de Notre Dame à Bois-Seigneur-Isaac face aux deux pouvoirs', in: *Recht en instellingen in de Oude Nederlanden tijdens de Middeleeuwen en de Nieuwe Tijd. Liber amicorum Jan Buntinx*, Symbolae A 10 (Löwen, 1981), S. 227-255; A. Verrycken, 'Volksvroomheid in de late middeleeuwen', *Volkskunde*, 83 (1992), S. 28-36.

6. Zur Klausur s. F. Prims, *De kloosterslot-beweging in Brabant in de XVde eeuw* (Antwerpen – Utrecht, 1944), sowie R. De Keyser – P. Trio, 'De *inclusio* van Melle uit 1447: Bijdrage tot de insluiting van Windesheimse kloosters', in: Verbeke (wie Anm. 3), S. 189-202. Vgl. auch die Auflistung bei Johannes Busch, *Chronicon Windeshemense und Liber de reformatione monasteriorum*, hg. von K. Grube, Geschichtsquellen der Provinz Sachsen und angrenzender Gebiete, 19 (Halle, 1886), S. 370-372.

7. Ophain, S. 1: *Inter omnia divine pietatis humano generi collata remedia, quibus mortalis sustentatur infirmitas, ars litteratoria non infimum locum tenet, dum per hanc immortalitatis naturaliter avidi homines quodammodo etiam post mortem vivunt et temporalium actionum memoria quadam perpetuitate ad posteros propagatur. Siquidem iuxta dictum sapientis 'generatio preterit et generatio advenit' (Eccl. 1,4), et per singulas generationes multa geruntur in tempore, quorum noticia post futuris generationibus non modo delectabilis sed perutilis ac necessaria admodum invenitur, sola autem scriptura est, que temporalium actionum memoriam scientie immortalitate perpetuat et apud posteros nullam permittit obrepere vetustatem.*

besondere Auszeichnung des Ortes. Der Autor habe gesammelt, was ihm von den älteren Mitbrüdern erzählt wurde, und was er aus schriftlichen Quellen erfahren konnte.[8] Bereits im Prolog werden die Freunde und Wohltäter des Konvents angeführt, denen gegenüber die Gemeinschaft eine besondere Verpflichtung eingegangen ist.[9] Die fünf Teile des Ophainer Codex werden im Prolog genannt:

1. Die Errichtung einer Kapelle, die Erscheinung des heiligen Blutes, Wunderberichte sowie die Gründung des Klosters,
2. kurze Lebensbeschreibungen der Prioren und der von ihnen eingekleideten Brüder sowie die wichtigsten Ereignisse,
3. ein Verzeichnis der verstorbenen Brüder, wie auch der *clerici*, der Konversen und der Laien, die auf dem Klosterfriedhof beerdigt sind,
4. ein Verzeichnis der Wohltäter, für die der Konvent Messverpflichtungen und Anniversarien übernommen hat,
5. ein Verzeichnis derjenigen Wohltäter, denen gegenüber keine rechtlichen Verpflichtungen bestehen, die gleichwohl aber in die Gebetsleistungen aufgenommen werden.[10]

---

8. Ophain, S. 1f.: *Hinc quoque nosipsi, ut de communibus ad propria descendamus, ob singularem divini respectus evidentiam et quam plurima manifeste electionis indicia, quibus hunc locum ad sui nominis gloriam devotionemque fidelium propensius incitandam a multis retro annis invisere dignata est divina clementia ac inter omnes huius occidui orbis ecclesias insigniter illustrare sue beatissime passionis insignia in eadem mirifice renovando, dum in eo instar loci calvarie agnus sine macula vero rubet sanguine, qui mundavit secula ab antiquo crimine, propterque alia multa, que circa initium ac progressum huius monasterii contigisse cognovimus, que non sine gravi dispendio animarumque periculo in oblivionis absorta voraginem successorum nostrorum evadent noticiam, nisi litterarum vinculis alligata permanserint, ea que de premissis nota nobis vel seniorum nostrorum relatu tradita aut ab eisdem litteris mandata nobis certa fide comperta sunt, in hoc scripto quamquam agresti sermone colligere atque hinc abeuntes ad patres nostros, ut cognoscat generatio altera, posteris nostris relinquere dignum duximus et necessarium arbitrati sumus.*
9. Ophain, S. 2: *... qui deinde amici ac benefactores in construendis edificiis aliisque divino cultui necessariis comparandis, terris, pratis, nemoribus atque redditibus acquirendis, suas manus porrexerint adiutrices, postremo que, quales et pro quibus capellanie missarum perpetue seu que vel qualia anniversaria defunctorum aut alia officia ecclesiastica et onera quelibet spiritualia per dictos benefactores hic instituta sint et fundata et per conventum domus huius, matura deliberatione prehabita, perpetuis futuris temporibus fideliter observanda suscepta sint ac firmiter stabilita.*
10. Ophain, S. 4: *Dividitur autem hoc originale in quinque partes, quarum in prima tanguntur aliqua de prima capella et de eventu sacri sanguinis miraculosi aliisque miraculis inde secutis et de fundatione monasterii. In secunda agitur de prioribus, qui huic loco prefuerunt, et de fratribus, qui sub eis professi sunt, et de quibusdam eventibus, qui eorum temporibus contigerunt. In tercia notantur secundum ordinem temporis fratres defuncti, clerici et conversi, deinde alii layci, postremo quidam extranei hic sepulti. In quarta ponuntur nomina specialium benefactorum cum insinuatione beneficiorum et onerum in missis et anniversariis seu quibuslibet aliis ab eisdem susceptorum. In quinta asscribuntur*

Im ersten Kapitel wird über den Bau einer Kapelle berichtet. Maria selber fordert in einer Erscheinung den Ritter Isaac, der von einem Kreuzzug nach Hause kommt, auf, sie sucht den Ort aus; ein Motiv, das sich in der Historiographie des öfteren nachweisen läßt. Erzählt wird dann ausführlich von dem Blutwunder, das sich während des Lesens der Messe im Jahre 1405 ereignet. Wichtig ist, daß während dieser Messe der Gründer des Klosters Johannes de Busco oder Johannes le Familleur anwesend ist, der die besondere Bedeutung des Wunders für den Ort erkennt und ihm Publizität verschafft. So werden Boten in die umliegenden Provinzen entsandt, um über das Blutwunder zu berichten und den Aufbau eines Klosters zu ermöglichen.[11]

Erzählungen über Blutwunder nehmen im späten Mittelalter stark zu, sie können neben der Marienverehrung als ein Kennzeichen der Frömmigkeit dieser Zeit bewertet werden. Zu unterscheiden ist zwischen einer Verehrung des reliquiaren Blutes Christi, also des Blutes, das Christus am Kreuz vergossen hat, so in Brügge seit dem 12. Jahrhundert, sowie des eucharistischen Blutes Christi, also von wundertätigen, blutenden Hostien.[12] Solche Hostienwunder finden im späten Mittelalter besonders in zwei Formen Verbreitung: der Aufdeckung von Hostienfreveln sowie einer Versinnbildlichung der Transsubstantiation, des Wandlungsgeheimnisses während der Messe, wie in Ophain.[13] Wir haben es hier mit einer sehr dinglichen, sehr materiellen Frömmigkeit zu tun. Gerade von

---

nomina aliorum specialium amicorum ac benefactorum, pro quibus ad aliqua specialia onera obligati non sumus, sed ad communes tantum orationes. Zum fünften Abschnitt vgl. ebd., S. 197: *Incipit quinta pars, in qua recitantur nomina et beneficia quorundam specialium amicorum, quibus ad aliqua specialia onera obligati non sumus, sed ad communes et inde terminatos orationes, et quedam alia necessaria annotantur.* Zum Aufbau der Handschrift vgl. *Monasticon Belge* (wie Anm. 5), S. 1024f. Es folgen noch weitere Zusätze, insbesondere eine zweite Redaktion des 4. und 5. Teils, s. ebd., S. 1025f.

11. Ophain, S. 4ff.

12. Maßgeblich ist die Darstellung von P. Browe, *Die eucharistischen Wunder des Mittelalters*, Breslauer Studien zur historischen Theologie, Neue Folge 4 (Breslau, 1938); vgl. auch W. Brückner, Art.: 'Blutwunder (Blut, Heiliges; Bluthostien)', in: *Lexikon des Mittelalters*, Bd. 2, Sp. 292f.; Ch. Zika, 'Hosts, Processions and Pilgrimages: Controlling the Sacred in Fifteenth-Century Germany', *Past and Present*, 118 (1988), S. 25-64; Ch.M. Caspers, *De eucharistische vroomheid in het feest van sacramentsdag in de Nederlanden tijdens de late middeleeuwen*, Miscellanea Neerlandica, 5 (Löwen, 1992); R. Sprandel, *Chronisten als Zeitzeugen. Forschungen zur spätmittelalterlichen Geschichtsschreibung in Deutschland*, Kollektive Einstellungen und sozialer Wandel im Mittelalter, Neue Folge 3 (Köln-Weimar-Wien, 1994), S. 277-285; A. Angenendt, *Geschichte der Religiosität im Mittelalter* (Darmstadt, 1997), S. 506-508.

13. Ein dritter Bereich sind die Speisungswunder, wie sie im besonderen von Liedwina van Schiedam oder Nikolaus von der Flüe überliefert sind, s. Sprandel (wie Anm. 12), S. 278.

den sich stark ähnelnden Geschichten um einen Hostienfrevel gingen sehr häufig Pogrome gegen Juden aus.[14] Kritische Stimmen gegen die Ausbreitung solcher Kultstätten sind nicht selten, das bekannteste Beispiel ist eine entsprechende Bulle des Nikolaus von Kues, der während seiner Legationsreise 1451/52 versucht, hier einschränkend zu wirken.[15] In den südlichen Niederlanden ist die Verehrung des eucharistischen Blutes Christi weit verbreitet, so in Brüssel – der Hostienfrevel von 1370 ist in 18 Festerbildern in St. Gudula dargestellt –, Gent und auch in Löwen.[16] Für die Devotio moderna gibt es zu Ophain allerdings nur zwei Parallelen: Die Gründung des Chorherrenstifts in Blomberg in der Diözese Paderborn ging auf den Diebstahl konsekrierter Hostien im Jahre 1460 zurück, die eine Frau in einen Brunnen geworfen haben soll. Über dem Brunnen wird eine Kapelle errichtet, aus der das Stift hervorgeht.[17] Ebenfalls an der Stelle eines Hostienwunders ist das Chorherrenstift Herrenleichnam in Köln entstanden.[18]

Die blutende Hostie in Ophain wird Pierre d'Ailly, dem Bischof von Cambrai zwei Jahre zur Begutachtung übergeben, dessen 'Bulla confir-

---

14. Erinnert sei hier an das Wilsnacker Wunderblut oder die Sternberger Hostienschändung, s. den Artikel 'Wilsnacker Wunderblut' von V. Honemann, in: *Verfasserlexikon*, Bd. 10, Sp. 1171-1178 (mit umfangreichen Literaturangaben) sowie ders. 'Die Sternberger Hostienschändung und ihre Quellen', in: H. Boockmann (Hg.), *Kirche und Gesellschaft im Heiligen Römischen Reich des 15. und 16. Jahrhunderts* (Göttingen, 1996), S. 75-102. Vgl. auch F. Lotter, 'Hostienfrevelvorwurf und Blutwunderfälschung bei Judenverfolgungen von 1298 (Rintfleisch) und 1336-1338 (Armleder)', in: *Fälschungen im Mittelalter*, Bd. 5, MGH Schriften 33,5 (Hannover, 1988), S. 533-583 sowie F. Graus, *Pest – Geissler – Judenmorde. Das 14. Jahrhundert als Krisenzeit,* Veröffentlichungen des Max-Planck-Instituts für Geschichte, 86 (Göttingen, 1987).
15. E. Meuthen – H. Hallauer (Hgg.), *Acta Cusana. Quellen zur Lebensgeschichte des Nikolaus von Kues,* Bd. 1, Lieferung 3a (Hamburg, 1996), Nr. 1454, sowie Browe (wie Anm. 12), S. 159ff. S. dazu jetzt N. Staubach, 'Cusani laudes. Nikolaus von Kues und die Devotio moderna im Reformdiskurs des Spätmittelalters', *Frühmittelalterliche Studien,* 34 (2000), S. 259-337.
16. Zu Brüssel s. Pl. Lefèvre, 'Le miracle eucharistique de Bruxelles en 1370', *Analecta Bollandiana,* 51 (1933), S. 325-336, Browe (wie Anm. 12), S. 137 u.ö., zu Gent und Löwen, ebd., S. 143f., s. auch die von Johannes Gielemans überlieferte '*Historia de miraculosa revelatione venerabilis Sacramenti in civitate Bruxelensi*', in: *Anecdota* (wie Anm. 54), S. 329-340.
17. Zu Blomberg s. den Artikel von H.-P. Wehlt, in: K. Hengst (Hg.), *Westfälisches Klosterbuch. Lexikon der vor 1815 errichteten Stifte und Klöster von ihrer Gründung bis zur Aufhebung,* Teil 1, Münster 1992, S. 84-88 (mit Literaturangaben). Kritisch zur Blomberger Wallfahrt äußert sich 1471/72 der Kartäuser Johannes Hagen, von J. Klapper, *Der Erfurter Kartäuser Johannes Hagen, ein Reformtheologe des 15. Jahrhunderts,* Bd. 2, Erfurter Theologische Studien, 10 (Leipzig, 1961), S. 92-112; Staubach (wie Anm. 15).
18. S. dazu von den Brinken, in: *Monasticon Windeshemnse* (wie Anm. 5), Bd. 2: *Deutsches Sprachgebiet* (Brüssel, 1977), S. 261-267.

mationis' in die Chronik eingefügt wird.[19] Er zeichnet die Kapelle auch durch Ablässe aus. Pierre d'Ailly, dessen Karriere manche Parallele zu der des Nikolaus von Kues aufweist, gehört zu den wichtigsten Förderern der Devotio moderna in Brabant.[20] Die Devoten haben es ihm durch eine umfangreiche Überlieferung seiner Schriften, insbesondere seiner Predigten, gedankt. Die Kapelle wird 1413 den Besitzungen von Zevenborren inkorporiert, über erste Wallfahrten wird berichtet. Der prominenteste Pilger ist 1416 Wilhelm von Flandern, der Graf von Namur.[21]

Für die Fundation des Chorherrenstiftes ist allerdings in erster Linie der Augustiner Aegidius Breedeyck verantwortlich, der 1416 mit zwei oder drei Brüdern aus Zevenborren nach Ophain geht. Über seine Zeit in Zevenborren berichtet seine Vita, Aegidius sei dorthin gemeinsam mit sieben Priestern gekommen. Mit der Unterstützung der Herzogin Johanna von Brabant versuchten sie in Zevenborren, nachdem sie zunächst in Brüssel gelebt hatten, ihre Vorstellungen eines gemeinsamen Lebens in der Einsamkeit umzusetzen. Betont wird sein Bemühen, Kleriker und Laien zu integrieren; die Zahl seiner Anhänger nimmt rasch zu, was als Beleg für die Attraktivität der neuen Lebensform gewertet wird.[22]

19. Ophain, S. 12ff. Die Bulle ist in Ophain, Archief Abdij Bois-Seigneur-Isaac, erhalten.
20. An Literatur zu Pierre d'Ailly, die allerdings auf sein Verhältnis zur Devotio moderna kaum eingeht, s. F. Oakley, *The Political Thought of Pierre d'Ailly. The Voluntarist Tradition* (New Haven – London, 1964); A.E. Bernstein, *Pierre d'Ailly and the Blanchard Affair. University and Chancellor of Paris and the Beginning of the Great Schism*, Studies in Medieval and Reformation Thought, 24 (Leiden, 1978); M. Chappuis, *Le Traité de Pierre d'Ailly sur la Consolation de Boèce, Qu. 1*, Bochumer Studien zur Philosophie, 20 (Amsterdam, Philadelphia, 1993). Pierre d'Ailly gehört auch zu den wichtigsten Verteidigern der Brüder vom gemeinsamen Leben, s. dazu Theo Klausmann, *Consuetudo consuetudine vincitur. Die Hausordnungen der Brüder vom gemeinsamen Leben im Bildungs- und Sozialisationsprogramm der Devotio moderna* (Frankfurt/M., 2003), S. 110ff.
21. Ophain, S. 35.
22. Ophain, S. 69-71: *Primus itaque prior huius domus, ut dictum est, fuit frater Egidius de Breedeyke, sanctus videlicet ac reverendus pater, amator iusticie et omnis virtutis ac religionis zelator sanctorum Ieronimi et Iohannis Crisostomi amator precipuus, et corporalis austeritatis cultor, in sacris litteris non mediocriter exercitatus, potens in opere et sermone, sicut ex quibusdam scriptis eius, necnon ex epistolis magni illius ac famosissimi viri magistri Gerardi Magni eidem directis satis intelligi datur, et sicut fama ad nos usque deferente ac multorum relatu cognovimus... Deinde inspiratus a Domino cum aliis septem presbiteris sociis suis pauco tempore in opido Bruxellensi iuxta capellam Sancti Laurentii martiris habitavit ibique pariter in communi viventes expectabant, donec viderent, quis eos sic affectos, ut ipsi erant ad ambulandum in via Dei, ad bene vivendum locus haberet utilius. Denique communi consilio anno ab incarnatione Domini millesimo trecentesimo octogesimo accesserunt ad locum Septem Fontium in nemore Zonie solitarium tunc et solis pene feris silvestribus habitabilem, ubi per dominam Iohannam, illustrem Brabantie ducissam, dato eis habitandi spacio pariter confidentes multisque*

Aegidius würde man heute als einen unbequemen, einen schwierigen Menschen bezeichnen, worüber das 'Originale' allerdings keine Auskünfte gibt.[23] Er war in Zevenborren wegen seiner Strenge als Prior abgesetzt worden; dem Anschluß des Konvents an die Windesheimer Kongregation der Devotio moderna, dieser erfolgt erst 1443, stand er kritisch gegenüber, und für Ophain versuct er zunächst einen unabhängigen Weg zu gehen. Er beschreibt seine eigenständigen Auffassungen mit Hilfe von normativen Traktaten und vermag so das neue Stift, dem er bis 1424 vorsteht, zu prägen.[24] Vielleicht läßt sich die Gründung des Chorherrenstiftes in Melle und die Übersiedlung mehrerer Kanoniker aus Ophain dorthin auch als Protest gegen die Statuten von Aegidius Breedeyck interpretieren.[25] Im 'Originale' wird seine Ankunft in Ophain stilisiert.

temporibus in magna paupertate degentes de labore manuum suarum pauperem ac sobrium victum transigebant. Anno autem Domini millesimo trecentesimo LXXXVIII° ordinem canonicorum regularium assumpserunt atque ex tunc in magno rigore penitencie et austeritate viventes, cum cotidianis fatigarentur laboribus, omnem tamen pene cibum et potum in pondere et mensura sumebant. Cupiens vero devotissimus pater hanc suam vivendi formam ad multorum salutem latius propagare, plurimos ex diversis locis clericos et laycos congregare studuit atque ita in brevi factus est in gentem magnam, adeo ut preter laycos fratres, quorum non parvus numerus erat, aliquando XXVIII fratres chorales haberet. Evolutis autem post receptionem ordinis vigintiquinque vel amplius annis destitutus, ut supra dictum est, ab officio prioratus, non diu post, anno scilicet Domini M°CCCC° sextodecimo, missus est a successore suo, secundo Septem Fontium priore, ad istum locum de Busco, divina interius agente providentia, et Iohanne de Busco exterius procurante. Ubi infra octo annorum spacium quibus eidem loco prefuit, in spiritualibus eum et temporalibus promovendo non parvum fructum fecit. Nam inter alia eius temporibus nova ecclesia nostra fundata et supra terram muri eius evecti fuerunt.

23. Zu Aegidius Breedeyck vgl. A. Van der Taelen, 'Gillis van Breedeyck, stichter van de priorij van Zevenborren', *Eigen Schoon en de Brabander*, 43 (1960), S. 439-450.

24. Ophain, S. 69: *Scripsit namque idem venerabilis pater luculento sermone quasdam epistolas eruditione et exhortationibus plenas, et ex sermocinationibus eius plurima reportata habentur, ex quibus bonus zelus eius et devotio perpendi possunt. Quendam preterea tractatum ex dictis Iohannis Crisostomi compilavit, quem in quinque capitula distinctum ac totidem rubricis pretitulatum 'De quinque punctis' inscribi voluit. Scripsit etiam pro canonicis regularibus librum statutorum quatuordecim capitulis intercisum pro domo Septemfontium, que primo per episcopum Cameracensem ac deinde per summum pontificem confirmata etiam nos in domo ista servavimus, quoadusque Windesimensi capitulo generali submissi et colligati fuimus.* Vgl. Anm. 78. Zu seinen Schriften s. W. Lourdaux – E. Persoons, *Petri Trudonensis Catalogus scriptorum Windeshemensium*, Universiteit Leuven. Publicaties op het gebied van de geschiedenis en de filologie, 5e Reeks, Deel 3 (Löwen 1968), S. 2f. Von seinen Schriften ist einer großer Teil nicht überliefert, so u.a. seine Briefe an Geert Grote und eine '*Apologia de se ad fratres suos*'. Vgl. zu seinen Schriften auch Th. Kock, *Die Buchkultur der Devotio moderna. Handschriftenproduktion, Literaturversorgung und Bibliotheksaufbau im Zeitalter des Medienwechsels. Traditon – Reform – Innovation*, Studien zur Modernität des Mittelalters, 2 (Frankfurt/M. u.a. ²2002), S. 178f.

25. So de Keyser – Trio (wie Anm. 6) S. 190-192.

Vorbild ist die Chronik aus Groenendaal, insbesondere die Vita des Jan van Ruusbroec.[26]

Etwa die Hälfte des ersten Teiles im 'Originale' umfasst Wunderberichte. Es handelt sich um Heilungs-, Straf- und Bekehrungswunder. Viele der Pilger stammen aus weit entfernten Regionen, oft sind sie zu anderen Wallfahrtsstätten unterwegs, etwa nach Rom, und erfahren die Erfüllung ihrer Wünsche bereits in der Hl.-Blut-Kapelle.[27] Die Erzählungen sind oft sehr drastisch, so wenn ein Pastor, dem die Gläubigen wegen des Wunders in Ophain ausbleiben, den Mirakelbericht anzweifelt, und er zur Strafe in der Messe nach der Wandlung mit dem heiligen Blut Christi im Mund auf einen Stein aufschlägt und kurz darauf verstirbt, ohne das Bewußtsein zurückzuerlangen.[28] Verarbeitet ist hier der Konflikt mit der für die Kapelle zuständigen Pfarrkirche von Haut-Ittre. In einem anderen Bericht wird Johannes de Busco von einem Wilhelmiten aus Nivelles herausgefordert, einen Gottesbeweis über die Wahrheit des Blutwunders herbeizuführen. Es spricht sicherlich für die sehr dingliche Frömmigkeit, die mit den Blutwundererzählungen verbunden ist, daß Johannes auf diesen Vorschlag eingeht. Der Wilhelmit bricht einen Ast von einem Baum, der Beweis besteht darin, daß demjenigen Recht gegeben werden soll, dessen Holz innerhalb von zwei Wochen zu grünen beginnt. Zur Überraschung des Lesers schlägt der Stab des Wilhelmiten grün aus und der des Johannes verdorrt. Die Antwort des Johannes entbehrt dann allerdings nicht einer subtilen Logik: Siehst du, sagt er sinngemäß, daß dein Ast ausschlägt, ist ein Werk des Teufels und zeigt, daß du von Dämonen besessen bist. So einfach gibt sich der Mönch nicht geschlagen, er verhöhnt Johannes, indem er zur Messe ein Tuch mitnimmt, ein Nasenbluten verursacht und das Blut in das Tuch tropfen läßt: 'Hier, Johannes, ist das Blut eures Herrn, das ich dir versprochen habe.' Johannes handelt

---

26. S. '*De origine monasterii Viridisvallis et de gestis patrum et fratrum in primordiali fervore ibidem degentium*', *Analecta Bollandiana*, 4 (1885), S. 263-334; zu Henricus Pomerius s. den Artikel von A. Ampe, in: *Dictionnaire de Spiritualité*, Bd. 12 (Paris, 1986), Sp. 1908-1913 (mit Literatur).

27. Ophain, S. 47: *De romipeta qui lumen amissum recuperavit. Alter quidam vir de opido Valenchenarum in itinere constitutus, qui Romam pergere cupiebat, una dierum qua nescio occasione oculorum lumen amisit, et per biduum densis tenebris involutus in cecitate permansit. Implorata deinde omnipotentis Domini misericordia per suum sacrum sanguinem miraculosum de Busco emissoque voto, quo eundem preciosum sanguinem, si repatriare contingeret, visitaret, confestim omni detorsa caligine ceci pridem oculi claro rursus lumine vestiuntur tandemque reversus in patriam illuminatoris sui limina petiit et vota persolvens ea, que sibi contigerant, recitavit.*

28. Ophain, S. 25-27: *De presbitero obtrectatore sacri sanguinis miraculosi, qui ad terram cadens exspiravit.* Vgl. dazu De Keyser – van den Auweele (wie Anm. 5), S. 232.

sofort und resolut: er stopft dem Mönch das Tuch in den Mund: *Quod tuum est comedas!* Der Teufel kann sich nicht halten und muß aus dem Mönch ausfahren. Der Wilhelmit erfährt seine endgültige Heilung, wie könnte es anders sein, in der Kapelle von Bois-Seigneur-Isaac.[29] Sicher kommt in dieser Geschichte auch die Konkurrenz zu den benachbarten Klöstern in Nivelles zum Ausdruck.

Auf die Mirakelberichte folgt ein Epilog sowie Eintragungen von anderen Schreibern, die bis 1700 reichen. Verwiesen wird auf eine alte Handschrift, die sich im Augustinerkloster in Oignies befinde, und die vorher im Besitz von Ophain gewesen sein müsse. Dort seien Wunder des hl. Blutes aufgezeichnet, die in der eigenen Handschrift, sie wird hier als *registrum nostrum* bezeichnet, fehlen und noch hinzugefügt werden müßten.[30] In Oignies war 1499 der Kanoniker und Historiograph Gaspar Ofhuys Prior geworden, möglicherweise hat er Aufzeichnungen aus Ophain dorthin mitgenommen, von ihm stammt u.a. das 'Originale Cenobii Rubee Vallis in Zonia', also eine Chronik Rookloosters.[31]

Deutlich ist das Bemühen, den Traditionscodex jeweils zu aktualisieren. Die fünf Teile der Ophainer Chronik wurden zunächst von einer Hand angelegt, der Schreiber läßt dann Seiten für die Fortsetzungen frei, im Laufe der Zeit werden weitere Zettel eingefügt.[32] Er verwendet eine Hybrida formata, also die für die Devotio moderna typische Buchschrift.[33] Diese anlegende Hand wollte man dem sechsten Prior des Konvents, Johannes Bellens, Prior von 1450-1458, zuweisen. Dafür gibt es ein gewichtiges Argument: Johannes geht 1458 als Rektor und Beichtvater in das Augustinerinnenkloster St. Agnes nach Gent und bleibt dort mit einer Unterbrechung bis 1474, gestorben ist er 1483. Aus St. Agnes ist

---

29. S. die Erzählung '*De monacho blasphemo, qui obsessus a dyabolo per sanguinem miraculosum liberatus fuit*', Ophain, S. 28-30.

30. Ophain, S. 54: *In monasterio canonicorum regularium Oignacensi est liber manuscriptus olim, ut apparet proveniens ex nostris patribus, et ex contextu historie ex scriptura amplissime cognoscitur, in quo omnia ad sanctissimum sanguinem miraculosum tam que precesserint mirabilia quam que subsecuta sunt continentur, prout fert registrum nostrum hoc addito, quod in illo libello Oignacensis continentur...* Der Eintrag bezieht sich im folgenden auf Erscheinungen des Klostergründers, die in volkssprachliche Bearbeitungen der Mirakelberichte Eingang gefunden habe, s. dazu u. bei Anm. 45.

31. Brüssel, KB, II 480, s.u. bei Anm. 64. Vgl. zu seinen Schriften *Monasticon Belge* (wie Anm. 5), S. 1034 sowie den Artikel von G. Hendrix, in: *Nationaal Biografisch Woordenboek*, Bd. 13 (Brüssel, 1990), Sp. 599-604, *Petrus Trudonensis* (wie Anm. 24), S. 42f.

32. Ophain, S. 4: *Post quarum etiam singularum partium finem spacium relinquitur, ut ea, que processu temporis scribenda occurrerint, suis in locis continentur.*

33. Zu den Schriftarten s. J.P. Gumbert, *Manuscrits datés conservés dans les Pays Bas*, Bd. 2 (Leiden, 1988), S. 23ff.

ebenfalls ein Traditionscodex überliefert.[34] Die ersten 30 Blätter der Handschrift stammen nach einer Zuweisung der Schwester Josina Des Plancques von Johannes Bellens: *Ter eeren Gods ende tot stichticheit van ons allen heeft de goede eerweerdeghe vader broeder Jan Bellens, wijsen rectoer van desen huuse, de voerscreven cronijcke dus verre ghecopuleert ende bescreven, bewijsende hoe dit godshuus van sente Agneeten sijn eerste begin ghenomen heeft.* Dieser an Johannes Bellens zugewiesene Teil erinnert in der Tat an die Handschrift aus Ophain bis hin zu wörtlichen Anklängen im Prolog. Berichtet wird über die ersten Schwestern, eine Pestkatastrophe, die Umwandlung der Gemeinschaft in ein Augustinerinnenkloster, es folgen Lebensbeschreibungen der Priorinnen sowie der Schwestern und als vierter Teil eine Übersicht der Wohltäter des Konvents. Die Viten der Schwestern stammen dann allerdings nicht von Johannes Bellens, sie werden 1533 von der genannten Josina Des Plancques dessen Bericht hinzugefügt, wobei auch sie auf ältere Vorlagen zurückgreift; ihr Schwesternbuch und die Chronik werden zusammengebunden.[35] Der Johannes Bellens zugewiesene Teil ist nicht als Autograph überliefert. Typische Fehler lassen darauf schließen, daß es sich um eine Abschrift handelt, sodaß für den Ophainer Codex aufgrund eines Vergleichs der Hände keine Rückschlüsse gezogen werden können. Ein Argument spricht allerdings gegen Johannes Bellens als Schreiber der Ophainer Handschrift. Unter den Lebensbeschreibungen der Prioren im zweiten Teil des 'Originale' findet sich auch eine kurze Vita des Johannes Bellens, und zwar von der anlegenden Hand, ebenso wie die seines Nachfolgers. Zwar fehlen hier die sonst üblichen auszeichnenden Epitheta, verwiesen wird hier ausschließlich auf die Baugeschichte.[36]

---

34. Ich danke Anne Bollmann (Groningen), die eine Edition des Textes vorbereitet, daß sie mir Kopien der Handschrift zur Verfügung stellte. Die Literatur zu St. Agnes ist zusammengestellt bei C. Lingier, 'Boekengebruik in vrouwenkloosters onder de invloed van de Moderne Devotie', in Th. Mertens (Hg.), *Boeken voor de eeuwigheid. Middelnederlands geestelijk proza* (Amsterdam, 1993), S. 280-294, 454-466.

35. Zu den Autorinnen s. C. Morlion, 'De onuitgegeven kloosterkroniek van het St. Agneeteconvent als bron voor de deugdenspiegel en spiritualiteitsbeleving bij de vrouwelijke moderne devoten (Gent, 1434-1535)', *Ons Geestelijk Erf*, 56 (1982), S. 342-362. Die Ähnlichkeit und Übereinstimmung zwischen dem Traditionscodex aus Ophain und dem ersten Teil des Codex aus St. Agnes geht allerdings nicht so weit, daß sie unzweifelhaft von einem Autor stammen müssen, wie dies van den Auweele – Verrycken (wie Anm. 5), S. 93 behaupten: 'Une comparaison entre les prologues de ces deux chroniques prouve qu'ils sont, indubitablement, l'œuvre d'un seul et même auteur, à savoir Jean Bellens.'

36. Ophain, S. 78: *Huic sexto loco successit frater Iohannes Bellens huius domus conventualis. Cuius temporibus deposita domo antiqua, que in medio cymiterii constituta prima huius loci habitatio fuit una cum ambitu ligneo partis australis, in eodem latere iuxta ecclesiam inceptus ambitus novus et quedam alia inchoata fuere. Huius tempore professi*

Trotzdem erscheint es sehr unwahrscheinlich, daß Johannes Bellens hier seinen eigenen Eintrag verfaßt. Der Wechsel der Hände erfolgt mit dem Priorat von Nicolaus de Cruce (1469-1485), der von Johannes Bellens eingekleidet worden war.[37] Im dritten Teil stammt der letzte Eintrag der anlegenden Hand zum Jahre 1465, der Wechsel der Hände folgt mit dem Seitenumbruch innerhalb eines Eintrags zum Jahre 1466.[38] Wahrscheinlicher erscheint es daher, entweder Nicolaus de Cruce selber als Schreiber anzunehmen oder einen Bruder, der zu dieser Zeit im Konvent lebte.

Der dritte Teil des Traditionscodex aus Ophain ist überschrieben: *Incipit tertia pars, in qua continentur nomina fratrum defunctorum et quorundam aliorum hic sepultorum*.[39] Bezeichnet wird dieser Abschnitt auch als 'Cathalogus defunctorum'. Der 'Cathalogus'-Titel findet sich in solchen Traditionscodices der Devotio moderna häufig, u.a. in Rookloooster bei dem schon genannten Gaspar Ofhuys. Der vierte und fünfte Teil behandelt die Wohltäter. Die Funktion der Viten besteht darin, die besonderen Leistungen für den Konvent hervorzuheben, etwa der Bereich der Baugeschichte, einschließlich von Geldgaben für einen Neu- oder Umbau, überhaupt werden die herausragenden Legate oder Schenkungen angeführt, die Übertragung von Besitz oder das Ausstellen von Privilegien. Dazu gehört auch das Schreiben oder Schreibenlassen von Büchern oder bei den Wohltätern der Bereich der Buchschenkungen. Die Nachrichten zum Scriptorium und zur Bibliothek sind in Ophain allerdings sehr viel seltener als in anderen Memorialquellen aus dem Groenendaaler Kreis.[40] Auffallend ist in Ophain die enge Verbindung zum brabantischen Herzogshaus, dem Adel kommt im Wohltäterverzeichnis eine herausragende Rolle zu. Der vierte Teil beginnt mit einer Vita des Gründers Johannes de Busco, der selbst dem Adel angehört. Das zweite Kapitel ist überschrieben *De domino comite et domina comitissa Namurensis*, es schließt sich an *Johannes dux Brabantie comesque Hannonie, Rex Francorum*

---

sunt: frater Iudocus Rogerii, frater Stephanus Predare, frater Vincentius Stoop, frater Nycholaus de Cruce, frater Iohannes Amoury presbiter et frater Iohannes Rooms conversus. In fine autem octavi anni absolutus est tempore visitationis. Der Eintrag zu Johannes Bellens im 3. Teil lautet, Ophain, S. 119: *Frater Johannes Bellens, sextus prior huius monasterii prior* (sic) *obiit rector monialium de Zichenis* (Ten Elze), *ibique sepultus est anno domini MCCCC LXXXIII° nona die mensis maii.* Vgl. zu ihm *Monasticon Belge* (wie Anm. 5), S. 1051f.

37. Ophain, S. 80.
38. Ebd., S. 118f.
39. Ebd. S. 115.
40. S. die Angaben bei van den Auweele, in: *Monasticon Windeshemense* (wie Anm. 5), S. 37. Vgl. dazu Kock (wie Anm. 24), S. 34ff.

Ludovicus sowie *Dominus Philippus dux Burgundie*, vom denen jeweils reiche Schenkungen verzeichnet sind.[41] Die Beziehungen einzelner Prioren zum Herzogshaus finden des öfteren Erwähnung.

Der Traditionscodex enthält unterschiedlichste Nachrichten und erfüllt Funktionen, die sich mit der Doppelformel Selbstvergewisserung – das Vorbild und Exemplum der Patres, wie auch der Sicherung des Besitzes und der gewählten Lebensform – sowie Memoria – Gedenken an die verstorbenen Brüder und Wohltäter – beschreiben läßt. Verschriftlicht findet sich hier der Kern des eigenen Selbstverständnisses. Bestimmt war eine solche Handschrift zum häufigen Vorlesen in der Gemeinschaft, dafür spricht auch die verwendete Buchschrift. Der Codex dürfte der regelmäßigen gemeinsamen Lektüre im Refektorium gedient haben. Verwendung finden konnte er darüber hinaus auch bei den Gesprächen der Brüder untereinander, bei der täglichen Kollation.[42]

Natürlich sind zur schriftlichen Sicherung der eigenen Traditon noch andere Handschriften notwendig, so wurden die Urkunden des Konvents nicht nur in einem solchen Traditionscodex abgeschrieben. Anzunehmen ist daneben noch die Anlage eines Kopiars.[43] Einem solchen Kopiar ging dann wiederum häufig eine kurze Chronik voran, oft nur wenige Seiten, in der über die Gründung der Gemeinschaft berichtet wird. Gleichzeitig wurden weitere Nekrologien benötigt. In der Handschrift aus Bois-Seigneur-Isaac wird davon gesprochen, daß Namen auch in das Martyrologium eingetragen werden.[44] Eine solche Handschrift wurde in der Kirche verwahrt und stellte sicher, daß der Konvent seinen Mess- und Gebetsverpflichtungen nachkommen konnte. Informationen aus unterschiedlichen Handschriften werden also kompiliert, abgeschrieben und zusammengetragen. Der Wechsel der Schreiberhand innerhalb eines Eintrags im Nekrolog spricht dafür, daß wir es auch in Ophain mit einer Abschrift aus verschiedenen Quellen zu tun haben könnten, sozusagen mit einer kleinen Bibliothek in einem Band. Die Rezeption eines solchen Traditionscodex

---

41. Ophain, S. 149-157.
42. Die Konzeption der Handschrift verkennen van den Auweele – Verrycken (wie Anm. 5), S. 91: 'La Chronique latine du prieuré de Notre-Dame à Bois-Seigneur-Isaac est une œuvre hétérogène, déséquilibrée et de valeur inégale. Elle mérite autant la qualification de source juridique et administrative que celle de source narrative.'
43. Überliefert ist ein Kartular: Brüssel, ARArch., KerkArch. 15443 (zu den Jahren 1335-1474). Ein zweites Kartular wird im Kloster in Ophain aufbewahrt.
44. Aus Ophain ist weder das Martyrolog noch ein eigenständiges Nekrologium überliefert, wohl allerdings aus dem Chorherrenstift Ten Hole in Melle, dessen sechs erste Kanoniker aus Bois-Seigneur-Isaac stammen: Gent, Rijksarchief, Fonds de Melle 1. Zu den Beziehungen der beiden Konvente vgl. Ophain, S. 71-75.

beschränkte sich auf das eigene Kloster, das eigene Stift, es handelt sich in der Regel um Unikate. Dies gilt natürlich nicht für die einzelnen Textblöcke, die in andere Zusammenhänge gestellt, eine Verbreitung über den eigenen Konvent hinaus erfahren konnten.

Aus Ophain ist eine volkssprachliche, niederländische Bearbeitung des ersten Teils erhalten, allerdings keine reine Übersetzung.[45] Die Gründung der Kapelle wird ausführlicher erzählt als in dem Traditionscodex, der Bearbeiter könnte hier auf eine ältere Überlieferung zurückgegriffen haben. Vor die Kapitel zum Blutwunder setzt er einen Prolog, er begründet die Bedeutung der Wunder für seine Zeit: die alten Mirakel würden auch jetzt noch erneuert, um die Menschen zum christlichen Glauben zu bewegen.[46] Das Blutwunder wird ausführlicher dargestellt, als in der lateinischen Fassung: *Vanden welken ende van vele anderen mirakelen, die daer na ghevolcht sijn, wij ghebeden sijn, een ghescrifte te makene in dietscher talen ter ghesterkinghen vanden heileghen kersten gheloeve ende om de devocie van meneghen mensche daer mede te verwecken. Ende hebben daer omme de gheschiedenisse ende oppenbaringhe vanden heileghen bloede ende van anderen dinghen, die daer aen cleven, met corten woerden bescreven in deser manieren.*[47] Zur Beglaubigung der Wunder beruft sich der Bearbeiter auf mündliche Berichte der Pilger,[48] auch hier handelt es sich nicht um reine Übersetzungen, sondern um Bearbeitungen und Kürzungen mit der Tendenz, daß die Drastik noch zunimmt. Der Bearbeiter fügt weitere Berichte hinzu, so eine Vision des Klostergründers. Die Bedeutung des Wallfahrtsortes wird den Hörern insbesondere bei der Erzählung über die Schwester Marie van Mostroel, die als Inklusin in der Pfarrkirche von Nivelles lebte, verdeutlicht. Marie möchte zum heiligen Grab nach Jerusalem pilgern, sie erhält durch ihre Obersten die Erlaubnis. Sie geht nach Rom, dort hört sie in einer von Donner und Wetterleuchten begleiteten Vision eine Stimme, das neue Jerusalem finde sie in Ophain. Sie kehrt zurück, bleibt für den Rest ihres Lebens dort und stirbt als heilige Frau. Gerade auf diese Erzählung wird in der Handschrift durch einen am Rand gezeichneten Engel, der als Nota-Zeichen dient, besonders

---

45. Brüssel, KB, 13524 (3658), s. auch *Monasticon Belge* (wie Anm. 5), S. 1028f.
46. Brüssel, KB, 13524, fol. 1r-9v.
47. Brüssel, KB, 13524, fol. 11r.
48. Ebd., fol. 16r: *Want vele andere mirakelen, die doe int beghinsel ghevielen ende daer na dicwijls ghevallen sijn ende noch dicwile tot opten tijt van nu, alsoe ons die pelgherijns vertrecken, die hier altemet comen om theilghe bloet te visiterenne, dier es soe vele, dat sij te lanc te srivene waren.*

aufmerksam gemacht.[49] Dem Bericht dürfte zumindest ein wahrer Kern zugrunde liegen, im dritten Teil des Traditionscodex wird auch einer Reklusin Maria gedacht, der Eintrag dürfte sich auf Marie van Mostroel beziehen: *Soror Maria reclusa, qui a principio fundationis monasterii multis annis inclusa permansit, usque ad obitum suam in parva cellula primo iuxta antiquam et post modum infra novam ecclesiam hic iacet.*[50] Ausgelassen hat der Bearbeiter in der volkssprachlichen Fassung die Kapitel über die Gründung des Klosters. Die Handschrift war nicht zur Lektüre im Konvent, also für die Laienbrüder, bestimmt. Wahrscheinlicher ist, daß der Codex zum Vortrag in der Kapelle gedacht war, er zur Predigt vor den Laien diente.

Der Text ist datiert. Nach der Übersetzung des Epilogs folgt: *Hier endet die hystorie ende mirakelen vanden heilighen bloede van Boschysaac. Int iaert ons heeren MCCCC ende LXVIII.*[51] Angehängt sind noch weitere Wunderberichte, die sich nur teilweise auch im lateinischen Text finden. So gibt der vorletzte Bericht einen Hinweis auf den Schreiber. Er handelt über einen Bruder aus Ophain, und der Bearbeiter spricht über *mijn heere, de prioer.*[52] Die Handschrift wurde also von einem Bruder aus Bois-Seigneur-Isaac angelegt, und es handelt sich nicht um den Prior. Die Anlage des lateinischen Traditionscodex etwa um 1465 wird durch diesen Befund bestätigt, will man nicht von der unwahrscheinlichen Annahme ausgehen, daß der volkssprachliche Text vor dem lateinischen entstanden sei. Bereits kurz nach der Anlage der Handschrift bemühte sich der Konvent demnach, die Wunderberichte auch in der Volkssprache zu propagieren. Eine zweite volkssprachliche, französische Darstellung ist erst aus dem Jahre 1560 überliefert, nach der Stiftung eines neuen

---

49. Ebd., fol. 39r/v: *Van eender clusenerssen gheheeten suster Marie van Mostroel. Dit is van eender cluseneersen gheheeten suster Marie van Mostroel, de welke woende inde stat van Nivele inde parochiekerke vanden heileghen grave, die gheloeft hadde eenen wech te doene te Iherusalem int heilich lant omme dat heileghe graf te visenteren ende te besuekene, orlof ghecreeghen hebbende van haren oversten, es ghetrocken met huerer voer sustere tot Rome. Te Rome wesende so hief daer een grodt tempeest van dondre ende van weerlichte, dat sy daer afblent wert, doen quam haer groten druc int herte want sy niet voerder gaen en mochten. Corts daer naer so quam een stemme inder nacht ende seide tot haer: "Suster Marie van Mostroel, keert weder omme den wech, die ghy comen sijt ende gaet tot eender plaetsen gheheeten te Bossche Ysaac by Nivele in Brabant, daer seldi vinden een capelle ghesticht van onser liever Vrouwen, daer Iherusalem vernieut es." Ende sy ghinc daer ende bleef daer al haer leven lanc ende sy staerf daer als een heilich wijv.* Der Engel als Nota-Zeichen findet auch ansonsten in der Handschrift Verwendung.
50. Ophain, S. 141.
51. Brüssel, KB, 13524, fol. 36v.
52. Ebd. fol. 40r.

Reliquiars, von dem auch als Übersetzer hervorgetretenen Hubert Lescot (1527-1575); sie geht auf die Bearbeitung von 1468 zurück.[53] Um eine Verbreitung der Mirakelberichte durch den Druck scheint sich der Konvent nicht bemüht zu haben. Überliefert sind allerdings drei aus dem 16. Jahrhundert stammende Einblattdrucke – Maria mit dem Jesuskind, sowie zwei Engel vor dem Reliquiar, dieses Motiv ist in zwei Fassungen erhalten –, die in die Ophainer Handschrift eingeklebt worden sind.

Teile des Ophainer Traditionscodex sind auch über den eigenen Konvent, den eigenen inner-circle, hinaus verbreitet worden. Ein erstes Beispiel bilden die Sammlungen des Johannes Gielemans aus Rooklooster († 1487). Gielemans schreibt und kompiliert umfangreiche Handschriften mit historiographischen und hagiologischen Texten, deren ausschnitthafte Veröffentlichung durch die Bollandisten einer Erforschung seiner Werke eher im Wege gestanden hat als daß es ihr nützte.[54] Der bereits erwähnte Gaspar Ofhuys berichtet über Gielemans, er sei ein sehr sorgfältiger Schreiber gewesen, die Bibliothek verdanke ihm mehr als zwanzig Handschriften (*volumina*), *omnium fere sanctorum sanctarumque Brabantie vitam inquisivit et scripsit*.[55] Angelegt hat er vier Sammlungen, zwei sollen hier behandelt werden: das 'Novale Sanctorum' und das 'Hagiologium Brabantinorum'.[56] Das 'Novale Sanctorum' ist zwischen 1483 und 1485 entstanden, es umfaßt zwei Bände im Folioformat auf Pergament mit zusammen 648 Blättern. Beiden Teilen stellt Gielemans einen Prolog voran. Demnach würde auf die Exempla Heiliger der eigenen Zeit aufmerksamer gehört, und sie würden leidenschaftlicher und bereitwilliger als Vorbild gewählt. Daher habe er Berichte über solche

---

53. Ophain, Archief Abdij Bois-Seigneur-Isaac, Nr. 35: Histoire du Saint-Sang et du Convent de Bois-Seigneur-Isaac. S. *Monasticon Belge* (wie Anm. 5), S. 1026-1028, 1056f. S.J. Van den Gheyn, 'Hubert Lescot, prieur de Bois-Seigneur-Isaac. Notice bibliographique', *Annales de l'Académie royale d'archéologie de Belgique*, 53 (1901), S. 417-440.

54. S. *Anecdota ex codicibus hagiographicis Iohannis Gielemans Canonici Regularis in Rubea Valle prope Bruxellas*, ediderunt Hagiographi Bollandiani (Brüssel, 1895). Einen Überblick zu den Werken vermittelt G. Hendrix, in: *Nationaal Biografisch Woordenboek*, Bd. 13 (Brüssel, 1990), Sp. 317-332 (mit Literatur).

55. Zitiert nach Hendrix (wie Anm. 54), Sp. 318.

56. Alle vier Werke werden in der Österreichischen Nationalbibliothek in Wien aufbewahrt: das *Novale Sanctorum* (Cod. ser.n. 12708-9, 2 Bde.), das *Hagiologium Brabantinorum* (Cod. ser.n. 12706-7, 2 Bde.), das *Sanctilogium* (Cod. ser.n. 12811-4, 4 Bde.) sowie das *Historiologium Brabantinorum* (Cod. ser.n. 12710). Zu den Handschriften s. D. Thoss, *Flämische Buchmalerei. Handschriftenschätze aus dem Burgunderreich. Ausstellungskatalog* (Graz, 1987), Nr. 52f.; 'De codicibus hagiographicis Iohannis Gielemans Canonici Regularis in Rubea Vallis prope Bruxellas', *Analecta Bollandiana*, 14 (1895), S. 5-88.

Heilige gesammelt, die nach 1300, nach Cölestin V., der hier nicht zufällig gewählt ist, gelebt haben.[57] Gielemans betont, er sei bei der Anlage des Bandes natürlich darauf angewiesen gewesen, was er in seiner Einsamkeit (*in vasta solitudine*), also in der Bibliothek Rookloosters, zur Verfügung habe.[58] Der erste Band folgt in seiner Ordnung der Chronologie. Er beginnt, auch das wohlbedacht, mit einem Text von Pierre d'Ailly. Es überwiegen Heilige und Wunderberichte aus dem brabantischen Raum, eingefügt werden auch Viten aus dem burgundischen Herrscherhaus. In diesen Zusammenhang eines 'Novale Sanctorum' werden die historiographischen Texte der Devotio moderna eingeordnet. Johannes Gielemans inseriert in sein Werk die Lebensbeschreibungen Geert Grotes sowie von Florens Radewijns und dessen Schülern, also die Bücher 2-4 aus dem 'Dialogus noviciorum' des Thomas von Kempen, die er noch um ein Reimgedicht über Grote erweitert.[59] Eingefügt ist der 'Liber de origine monasterii Viridis Vallis', also der Gründungsbericht Groenendaals von Henricus Pomerius sowie der erste Teil des Traditionscodex aus Ophain, die 'Historia sanguinis miraculosi de Busco Domini Isaac'.[60] Gielemans setzt dem Text einen neuen Prolog voran: die Werke des Herrn an diesem ausgezeichneten Ort seien noch nicht genügend bekannt. Gielemans beruft sich hier auf zwei Quellen, auf das, was er selber gesehen hat sowie auf Zeugnisse, die in Heften oder Kladden (*in aliis schedulis*) der Alten (*seniorum nostrorum*) aufgezeichnet seien.[61]

---

57. *Novale Sanctorum*, Bd. 1, Wien, Österreichische Nationalbibliothek, Cod. ser.n. 12708, fol. 1v: *Inter quos hiis in quos fines seculorum devenerunt, qui sumus utique nos, summos divina clementia utriusque sexus delegavit sanctos, qui circa nostra tempora in virtutibus et miraculis venustissime floruerunt, Celestinum videlicet papam sanctissimum, institutorum ordinis Celestinorum, atque alios diversos post ipsum, qui quanto nobis tempore viciniores, tanto eorum gesta nos reddant ad audiendum attentiores et ad sequendum ferventiores ac promptiores...*

58. Ebd.: *... assumpsi colligendi gesta huiusmodi sanctorum, qui citra tempora beatissimi Celestini pape prefati, videlicet ab anno domini M° CCC° ac deinceps floruerunt queque ad meam notitiam pervenire potuerunt... Sed nec omnium, qui citra prefata tempora claruerunt, a me virtutes digeste sunt, neque enim de hiis, que non legi, nosse potui, et quod aliis forsitan est notum, mihi in vasta solitudine degenti est incognitum, sed ea, que quoquo modo reperiri valui, in hoc volumine inserere curavi.* Der zweite Band enthält neben Nachträgen, Entscheidungen des Basler Konzils, insbesondere in der marianischen Frage, verschiedene Papstbullen, so den Ablaß zum Jubeljahr 1450 oder die verschiedenen Aufrufe zum Kreuzzug.

59. Der *'Dialogus noviciorum'* ist ediert durch M.I. Pohl, *Thomas von Kempen, Opera omnia*, Bd. 7 (Freiburg, 1922), S. 1-329; zu dem Reimgedicht s. T. Brandsma, 'Twee berijmde levens van Geert Groote', *Ons Geestelijk Erf*, 16 (1942), S. 32-51.

60. S. die Teiledition in *Anecdota* (wie Anm. 54), S. 379-389.

61. Ebd., S. 380: *Quamobrem iuxta iniunctum nobis spiritualis patris imperium, immo iuxta quod Dominus dederit, de apparitione sacrosancti sanguinis miraculosi, qui in ista*

Zur Beglaubigung der Mirakelerzählungen aus Ophain fügt er im Anschluß die Urkunde des Pierre d'Ailly hinzu. Den Text aus Ophain kürzt er um zwei Kapitel, die Inkorporation der Kapelle durch Zevenborren sowie den Bericht über die Pilgerfahrt des Grafen Wilhelm von Namur und über dessen unehelichen Sohn, einem Klausner in Ophain.

Zwei Texte zur Devotio moderna verfaßt Gielemans selbst, ein 'Tractatulus de origine monasterii Septem Fontium', also einen Gründungsbericht über das Chorherrenstift Zevenborren.[62] Hier lag ihm möglicherweise keine entsprechende Quelle vor, ein solcher Traditionscodex ist in Zevenborren erst später angelegt worden. Der zweite Text handelt über seinen eigenen Konvent: das 'Primordiale monasterii Rubee Vallis'.[63] Es ist wie der 'Dialogus noviciorum' des Thomas von Kempen in Dialogform aufgebaut. Ein Senior erzählt einem Junior, also einem Novizen, die Gründungsgeschichte des Klosters. Gielemans führt auch Lebensbeschreibungen an, wobei er exemplarisch aus jeder Gruppe der Klosterangehörigen eine Vita auswählt. Der Aspekt der Memoria findet Berücksichtigung durch Namenslisten, mit denen Gielemans sein Werk abschließt. Das 'Primordiale' ist kurz nach 1460 entstanden, fortgesetzt wird es bis 1521.

Das 'Novale Sanctorum' erweist sich damit als eine sehr bewußt angelegte Textsammlung, es erfüllt die Kriterien, die ich anfangs für einen Traditionscodex genannt habe. Was den Rezipienten des Gielemannschen Oeuvres offensichtlich fehlte, ein ausführlicheres Eingehen auf die Memoria, wurde durch den bereits erwähnten Chorherren Gaspar Ofhuys ergänzt. Ofhuys stellte, bevor er nach Bois-Seigneur-Isaac ging, für Rooklooster einen weiteren Traditionscodex zusammen, der aus vier Teilen bestand, einem 'Originale cenobii Rubee Vallis in Zonia', einem 'Catalogus fratrum choralium', also von Lebensbeschreibungen aller Professbrüder des Klosters, drittens 'De benefactoribus' und viertens 'De onere

---

ecclesia de Busco Domini Isaac honorifice conservatur, eiusque approbatione et confirmatione sollemni deque multis aliis signis ac prodigis inde secutis aliquanta dicemus, sicut ea partim oculata fide conspeximus, partim vero in aliis schedulis exarata seniorumque nostrorum veridico testimonio nobis intimata recepimus; praetermittentes causa brevitatis ea quae de initio et progressu monasterii alio in loco descripta sunt, sed de veteri capella beatae Dei genetricis Mariae, prout exigit ordo narrationis, aliqua praemittentes ad laudem Domini et Salvatoris nostri Iesu Christi.

62. *Anecdota* (wie Anm. 54), S. 396-417.
63. Ebd., S. 109-197.

missarum'.⁶⁴ Wie in Ophain wurde dieser Codex nach dem Weggang von Gaspar Ofhuys weitergeführt.

Das spirituelle Konzept von Gielemans geht allerdings über Codices wie den in Ophain oder in Rooklooster durch Gaspar Ofhuys angelegten hinaus. Die Selbstvergewisserung der Brüder wird bei Gielemans wie in Ophain durch die Geschichte, insbesondere die Gründungsgeschichte des eigenen Konvents sowie über beispielhafte und vorbildliche Lebensbeschreibungen verstorbener Mitbrüder vermittelt. Das eigene Kloster wird hier allerdings, und das ist das neue, und nur aus dem Aufbau der gesamten Handschrift erschließbare Moment, anders als in Ophain in einen heilsgeschichtlichen Zusammenhang eingeordnet. Da ist zunächst die Fokussierung auf den Raum, auf Brabant, als gewichtigen Schwerpunkt eines 'Novale Sanctorum'. Zweitens wird hier die eigene Bewegung, die Devotio moderna, von Ruusbroec über Grote bis hin zu den Angehörigen des eigenen Konvents, in dieses 'Novale Sanctorum' integriert. Die 'neuen' Heiligen, die Mitglieder des eigenen Reformkreises, werden den 'alten' Heiligen gleichgesetzt.

Eine zweite Sammlung von Johannes Gielemans beschäftigt sich explizit mit den Heiligen Brabants, das zwischen 1476 und 1484 angelegte 'Hagiologium Brabantinorum'. Es umfaßt ebenfalls zwei Bände im Folioformat mit zusammen 685 Blättern. Die Unterteilung der zwei Bände erläutert er in einem Prolog: *ut in primo ponantur illi, qui de genere Karoli Magni sunt nati; in secundo vero illi, qui aliunde sunt propagati ratione praedicta.*⁶⁵ Der erste Band umfaßt also Heilige aus dem Brabanter Raum, die von Karl dem Großen abstammen. Gielemans macht sich damit die vom brabantischen Herzogshaus seit dem 13. Jahrhundert propagierte Ansippung an die Karolinger zu eigen. Über Karl verfaßt er eine eigene Biographie, Karls Titel lautet bei Gielemans anachronistisch: *imperator Romanorum, rex Francorum et dux Brabantinorum*. Für Parallelen zum 'Hagiologium' und zur Einordnung in die brabantische dynastische Historiographie kann hier auf die Untersuchung von Robert Stein über 'Politiek en Historiografie' verwiesen werden.⁶⁶ Für Johannes Gielemans ist allerdings das Lob der Herzogsfamilie kein Selbstzweck, sondern auf die eigene Gemeinschaft rückbezogen. Zur Selbstvergewisserung

---

64. Brüssel, II 480 (3369). Der dritte und der vierte Teil sind nicht erhalten. Ein Ausschnitt aus dem 'Originale' ist veröffentlicht in den *Anecdota* (wie Anm. 54), S. 303-329, zum 'Catalogus' s. ebd., S. 201-303.
65. Zitiert nach: *De codicibus hagiographicis* (wie Anm. 56) S. 11.
66. R. Stein, *Politiek en Historiografie. Het onstaansmilieu van Brabantse kronieken in de eerste helft van de vijtiende eeuw*, Miscellanea Neerlandica, 10 (Löwen, 1994).

der Kanoniker gehört die immer wieder aufgezeigte Verbindung zum Herzogshaus. Es ist Johanna von Brabant, die den Konventen des Groenendaaler Kreises ermöglicht, im Zonienwald um Brüssel die neue Lebensform zu realisieren.[67] Die enge Beziehung zum Adel wurde bereits anhand des Wohltäterverzeichnisses aus Ophain deutlich. Brabant als *terra sancta* zeigt sich bei Johannes Gielemans in der großen Zahl von Heiligen, in den heiligen Patronen des Herrscherhauses, in der heiligmäßen Lebensform der eigenen Gemeinschaft. Es ist diese Trias, die das Selbstverständnis des Groenendaaler Kreises ausmacht. Eine eigenständige brabantische Perspektive der Devotio moderna, wie sie John Van Engen formuliert hat,[68] läßt sich somit an drei Punkten nachweisen. Neben den Bezug auf Jan van Ruusbroec statt Geert Grote als *fons et origo* der eigenen Bewegung in Abwehr des Geschichtsbildes von Johannes Busch, neben den Weg in die Klausur, tritt als dritter Punkt die Verbindung zum Herzogshaus und damit ein auf den Adel bezogenes Selbstverständnis.

Die Beziehung zum brabantischen Adel findet ihren Ausdruck auch in einer ganzseitigen Miniatur zu Beginn des 'Hagiologium'. Dargestellt ist Karl der Große als Schutzmantelheiliger. Eine weitere Miniatur zu Beginn des zweiten Bandes zeigt brabantische Heilige in Form der Wurzel-Jesse-Ikonographie. Für die Wertschätzung der Codices spricht, daß diese Miniaturen nicht im Scriptorium von Rooklooster ausgeführt wurden. Sie stammen nach den Untersuchungen von Maurits Smeyers aus dem Atelier des Brügger Illuminators Loyset Liédet.[69] Neben den Miniaturen zeigt auch das verwendete Folioformat, das ansonsten fast ausschließlich Liturgica und Werkausgaben der Kirchenväter vorbehalten war, den Repräsentationcharakter dieser Handschriften. Der auch sonst in Rooklooster oft verwendete Eintrag *pro libraria* zu Beginn des 'Hagiologium' beweist, daß der Codex für die eigene Bibliothek bestimmt war. Er dürfte, wie auch die anderen Sammlungen von Gielemans, regelmäßig im Konvent vorgelesen worden sein.

Eine andere Linie innerhalb dieser Vernetzung zwischen den einzelnen brabantischen Chorherrenstiften führt nach Zevenborren, in die *Domus*

---

67. Vgl. z.B. den Bericht im 'Primordiale monasterii Rubee Vallis', in: *Anecdota* (wie Anm. 54) S. 123.
68. Wie Anm. 3.
69. S.M. Smeyers, *Flämische Buchmalerei. Vom 8. bis zur Mitte des 16. Jahrhunderts* (Stuttgart, 1999), S. 270 (mit einer Abbildung der zweiten Miniatur). Die Miniatur zum 1. Band ist abgebildet in: W. Braunfels – P.E. Schramm (Hgg.), *Karl der Große. Lebenswerk und Nachleben*, Bd. 4 (Düsseldorf, 1967), S. 484. Vgl. E. Quadflieg, 'Eine Brüsseler Karls-Miniatur um 1480', *Aachener Kunstblätter*, 27 (1963), S. 188-194.

beatae Mariae ad Septem Fontes. In Zevenborren hatten sich bereits im 14. Jahrhundert Eremiten niedergelassen, hierhin kam Aegidius Breedeyck, der erste Prior von Ophain, um 1380 mit einigen Gefährten.[70] 1388 schenkt Johanna von Brabant den Einsiedlern die Klause und erteilt ihnen die Erlaubnis, hier ein Augustinerkloster zu errichten, das dann zum Mutterhaus für die Brüder in Ophain werden sollte. Von daher steht zu erwarten, daß in Handschriften aus Zevenborren auch der Entwicklung in Ophain gedacht wird. Ein solcher Traditionscodex ist allerdings erst im 17. Jahrhundert zusammengebunden worden, wobei hier ältere Texte zu einer Handschrift vereinigt werden.[71] Von Aegidius van der Hecken († 1538) stammt ein 'Cathalogus' mit kurzen Lebensbeschreibungen. Auf eine reine Namensliste folgt der 'Decursus priorum', ein 'Cathalogus fratrum' sowie ein 'Memoriale benefactorum'. Eingebunden in den 'Cathalogus' sind kurze historiographische Texte, ein Reimgedicht über das Kloster sowie ein Bericht über einen Brand 1518, der einen verheerenden Schaden verursacht hat. Bei diesem Brand könnte auch eine ältere Chronik des Klosters von Wilhelmus Catthem zerstört worden sein. Die Beziehung dieses Textes zu dem Gründungsbericht, den Johannes Gielemans in sein 'Novale Sanctorum' einfügt, läßt sich also nicht mehr rekonstruieren. Ersetzt wird diese Chronik erst im 17. Jahrhundert, in dem die brabantische Historiographie der Devotio moderna eine Renaissance erlebt, durch den Kanoniker Ambrosius Pontanus († 1643) mit seinem 'Gazophylacium Zoniacum sive Historia sacra Nemoris Zonie'. Die Chronik geht zunächst allgemein auf die Geschichte der Augustinerchorherren ein. Es folgt ein Gründungsbericht sowie ein ausführliches Kapitel über den ersten Prior Aegidius van Breedeyck. An kurze Viten der Prioren, ein Kapitel 'De viris illustribus monasterii Septem Fontis' schließt ein Verzeichnis der Wohltäter an. Neben das 'Gazophylacium' stellt Pontanus ein 'Compendium historiale' aus Bois-Seigneur-Isaac. Für die drei Kapitel 'De eiusdem loci antiquitate et situ', 'De prima fundatione' sowie 'De continuata successione priorum', einer Aufreihung der Prioren bis zur Mitte des 17. Jahrhunderts, benutzt Pontanus den Traditionscodex aus Ophain, ohne allerdings diesen zu kopieren. Der 'Cathalogus' sowie die Chronik werden dann gemeinsam mit einigen weiteren Texten, so Generalkapitelspredigten des Ordens, die hauptsächlich von Prioren aus Bois-Seigneur-Isaac stammen, zu einer Handschrift vereinigt.[72]

---

70. S.o. Anm. 22.
71. Brüssel, KB, 11974-11985 (3672).
72. Die Chronik ist 1688 in Druck erschienen: *Historia Septifontana celeberrimi monasterii canonicorum regularium S.P. Augustini in Sylva Soniaca. Instituti, propagati,*

Die bisher behandelten Handschriften zeigen, daß es in den brabantischen Chorherrenstiften zu einem Austausch der Codices, zu einem Handschriftentransfer gekommen ist. Johannes Gielemans etwa betont bei einem der Gründungsberichte, er habe die Nachrichten aus glaubwürdigen Manuskripten zusammengestellt. Er muß also neben dem umfangreichen Bestand der eigenen Bibliothek, für Rooklooster lassen sich ungefähr 400 Handschriften nachweisen, auch über einen Leihverkehr die Möglichkeit gehabt haben, Bücher anderer Konvente einzusehen und abzuschreiben.[73]

Einzelne Texte, die Gielemans bearbeitet oder kopiert, werden aus Rooklooster dann wiederum weiter verbreitet. So ist seine Fassung aus dem Ophainer Traditionscodex in zwei weiteren Handschriften erhalten. Den Prolog überliefert eine nicht lokalisierte Sammlung aus dem 17. Jahrhundert, die Texte über Kreuzwunder (*De sancta cruce*) vereinigt.[74] Noch aus dem 18. Jahrhundert stammt eine Abschrift in einem Heft von nur 22 Blättern des vollständigen Textes.[75] Das 'Primordiale' aus Rooklooster ist in drei weiteren Textzeugen überliefert, so in einer Brügger Handschrift, die u.a. verschiedene Klosterchroniken aus Gielemans zu einem Buch vereinigt.[76] Aus der Devotio moderna stammen einige Sammelhandschriften, in der die Historiographie einzelner Häuser, zusammengefügt sind, Texte von Henricus Pomerius, Johannes Busch, Thomas von Kempen oder auch weniger bekannter Autoren. Sie gehören ebenfalls in den Bereich der Traditionscodices, indem sie über die Geschichte des eigenen Hauses hinausgehen, diese ergänzen und hinführen zu einer Chronik der gesamten Bewegung. Diesen letzten Schritt der Darstellung

---

perfecti, & trino hinc saeculo, in descriptione Insignium Virorum suorum jubilantis. Accedit Historia Monasterii eiusdem Ordinis dictis a Sylva Domini Isaac. Authore R.D. Joanne Baptista Wiaert canonico regulari Septifontano (Brüssel, 1688), zu Bois-Seigneur-Isaac S. 110-156. Hierbei handelt es sich bis auf wenige Nachträge ausschließlich um den Text des Ambrosius Pontanus. Vgl. auch R.P. Marcus Mastelinus, *Necrologium Monasterii Viridis Vallis* (Brüssel, um 1630), S. 51ff.

73. Kock (wie Anm. 24) S. 225ff. Das Thema des Handschriftentransfers innerhalb der Devotio moderna behandelt am Beispiel des Böddeker Reformkreises Th. Kock, 'Zur Produktion und Verbreitung von Handschriften im 15. Jahrhundert. Das Rechnungsbuch aus dem Augustiner-Chorherrenstift Kirschgarten', in: R.A. Müller (Hg.), *Kloster und Bibliothek. Zur Geschichte des Bibliothekswesens der Augustiner-Chorherren in der Frühen Neuzeit* (Paring, 2000), S. 23-58.

74. Brüssel, KB, 8146-9 (3588).

75. Brüssel, KB, 8181 (4554).

76. Brügge, Stadtbibliothek, 425 s. A. de Poorter, *Catalogue des manuscrits de la Bibliothèque Publique de la ville de Bruges*, Catalogue général des manuscrits des bibliothèques de Belgique, 2 (Gembloux- Paris, 1934), S. 478-481. S. auch die Handschrift Brüssel, KB, 13525-26 (3663).

der Devotio moderna als religioser Bewegung, geht neben Johannes Busch, dessen Werk die Forschung maßgeblich bestimmt, der Herenter Chorherr Petrus Impens († 1523), nur daß er, im Gegensatz zu Johannes Busch, die Konvente in Brabant, und nicht die Tätigkeit eines Geert Grote, Groenendaal statt Deventer, als Ausgangspunkt seiner Chronik wählt.[77] Petrus Impens verwendet den Traditionscodex aus Ophain, er faßt die Gründung kurz zusammen und geht ausführlicher auf das Werk des Aegidius Breedeyck ein.[78]

Bei dem Versuch, einige Traditionscodices aus den Brabanter Chorherrenstiften vorzustellen, geht es darum, den Blick stärker weg vom einzelnen Text, hin zur gesamten Handschrift zu lenken, und deren Funktion für das Leben der einzelnen Gemeinschaft zu interpretieren. Eine Untersuchung des Abschreibens, Bearbeitens, Umstellens oder auch des Übersetzens einzelner Teile dieser Codices zeigt deutlich den Prozeßcharakter dieser Texte.[79] Einordnen läßt sich dieser Vorgang auch in das

77. Zu den Werken von Petrus Impens und Johannes Busch s. in Kürze die Dissertationen von Aloysia Jostes und Bertram Lesser.
78. Wien, ÖNB, Ser. n. 12816, fol. 105r: *Fundatio monasterii Busci Domini Ysaac iuxta Nivellam anno XIIII^{c}XVI°. Eodem pene sub tempore contigit Deo permittente circa venerabile corpus Christi in sacramento altaris per cuiusdam sacerdotis notabilem incuriam ac negligentiam insigne periculum in capella quadam sub patronatu nobilis et potentis viri domicelli Iohannis Familieur alias de Busco constituta, quem capelle locum vulgares Buscum Dominum Ysaac nuncupabant idipsumque nomen presens tempus conservat. Commendata est exinde eadem capella accedente consensu Cameracensis antistitis domini Petri de Aliaco sollicitudine et devotione predicti nobilis viri ac patroni eiusdem in relevamen paupercule fundationis monasterii beate Marie Septemfontium ordinis canonicorum regularium. Missi sunt ergo illic a priore primo eiusdem monasterii duo fratres professi sacerdotes regimen et curam ipsius capelle cum cunctis dependentiis suis tam emolumenti quam oneris perpetui amministrarunt. Post biennium absoluto interea ab officio primo priore Septemfontium instantia nobilis comitis et comitisse Namurcensis intercedente, frater Alardus de Ghelier prior et conventus Septemfontium resignarunt capellam prefatam cum omnibus suis pertinentiis fratri Egidio Breedeycke acceptanti cum plenaria potestate construendi eodem in loco novum monasterium canonicorum regularium. Cuius rei gratia tres fratres chorales illi adiuncti sunt, qui auxiliante Deo in eam qualitatem, quam nunc cernere licet, monasterium extruxerunt. Fuit autem primus huius monasterii prior frater Egidius Breedeycke venerandus pater, amator iusticie, cultor virtutis et religionis, sanctorum Iheronimi et Crisostimi zelator precipuus ac corporalis austeritatis observator exactus. Scripsit epistulas quasdam luculento sermone eruditione plenas. Edidit et tractatum ex dictis Crisostimi in quinque capitulis distinctum, quem 'De quinque punctis' pretitulavit. Scripsit et fratribus suis canonicis regularibus librum statutorum XIIII capitulis distinctum per Cameracensem episcopum primum, deinde per dominum apostolicum confirmatum. Ex hoc monasterio nova plantatio domus beate Marie in Mello iuxta Gandavum tamquam filia illius processit et ortum habuit.*
79. N. Staubach, 'Text als Prozeß. Zur Pragmatik des Schreibens und Lesens in der Devotio moderna', in: Ch. Meier u.a. (Hgg.), *Pragmatische Dimensionen mittelalterlicher Schriftkultur* (München, 2002), S. 251-276; vgl. auch DERS., 'Von der persönlichen

besonders in der französischen Forschung und auf hagiographische Texte bezogene Konzept 'Re-écriture'.[80] Gerade die für die Selbstvergewisserung und die Memoria der Konvente maßgeblichen Aufzeichnungen waren einer ständigen Veränderung und Anpassung unterworfen. Eine genauere Untersuchung der Beziehungen der Handschriften untereinander wird allerdings erst möglich sein, wenn sich die Editionslage verbessert haben wird.

Erfahrung zur Gemeinschaftsliteratur. Entstehungs- und Rezeptionsbedingungen geistlicher Reformtexte im Spätmittelalter', *Ons geestelijk Erf,* 68 (1994), S. 200-228, bes. S. 226f.

80. S. dazu G. Philippart, 'Hagiographes et hagiographie, hagiologes et hagiologie: des mots et des concepts', in: *Hagiographica. Rivista di agiografia e biografia della Società internazionale per lo studio Medio Evo latino,* 1 (1994), S. 1-16 sowie Ders., 'Introduction', in: Ders. (Hg.), *Hagiographies. Histoire internationale de la littérature hagiographique latine et vernaculaire en Occident des origines à 1550,* Bd. 1 (Turnhout, 1994), S. 9-24. Vgl. jetzt auch den Sammelband: D.R. Bauer – K. Herbers (Hgg.), *Hagiographie im Kontext. Wirkungsweisen und Möglichkeiten historischer Auswertung,* Beiträge zur Hagiographie, 1 (Stuttgart, 2000).

Rudi KÜNZEL

ORAL AND WRITTEN TRADITIONS IN THE *VERSUS DE UNIBOVE*[1]

There are four reasons why we medievalists should devote attention to the interplay of oral and written tradition in medieval texts.

1. When we investigate the Middle Ages, we are concerned with a society that long consisted primarily of illiterates, a society where the necessary transmission of knowledge and information was largely conducted through oral communication. This is a powerful reason for us to seriously address the oral tradition of transmitting culture and information. If we want to do justice to the oral tradition in medieval society, we should not regard it as a preliminary stage in the rise of written culture, but as a phenomenon *sui generis*. However, we can only approach the oral tradition via a different, written derivation that does not do sufficient justice to the original phenomenon. Historical philological research into oral tradition should be aimed at identifying as many of its traces as possible in written texts.

2. By conducting this research we can also learn a great deal about the force of oral and written tradition and the proportion of these forces that changes in time and varies in space. If for example in a given text, the written tradition originating from clerical culture appears to be permeable to elements of an oral tradition, this reveals something about the proportion of forces of the two traditions at the time.

3. The writings of clerics about other social groups contain *their* images, their representations of these groups, not the self-representations

---

[1]. Earlier versions were presented at the Colloquium *Geheugen en cultuuroverdracht in de Middeleeuwen* (Memory and the Transmission of Culture in the Middle Ages), Flemish Medieval Studies Work Group, University of Ghent, 28 October 1994, and at a meeting of historians from the Westphalia Wilhelm University of Münster and the (Dutch) Medieval Studies Research School, Wassenaar, 3 November 1998. I was given valuable bibliographical information and advice by Prof. A. Welkenhuysen, E. Doelman, M.A., Dr. J. Koopmans, Dr. E. Mantingh, Dr. T. Meder and L.C. Meijer, M.A., which I would like to express my gratitude for. I would also like to thank Anne-Ruth Wertheim for her stimulating comments on an earlier version of this article, Henk Bonke and Els Schuringa for their help with the first English version and Sheila Gogol for her translation of the final English version.

of the groups' members. The clerical images of other groups are images from *outside*. Traces of oral tradition can put us on the track of representations of social groups from *within*, representations that can differ substantially from the clerical ones.

4. A great deal of interesting research has been conducted on the differences and similarities between oral and written tradition and on how the two influence each other. Contributions have been made by experts from any number of disciplines, including anthropologists, historians, historians of literature and psychologists. The field of medieval studies can make its own contribution to the research on the interaction between oral and written tradition: Western Europe is a case that, as a result of the relatively early advent of written tradition, can be followed over a longer period of time than in many other parts of the world.

The eleventh-century poem *Versus de Unibove* (Poem on One-ox) is known as a work deeply rooted in written literary as well as oral tradition, and viewed from the research perspectives referred to above, it is consequently a 'case' that is relevant. Thanks to the excellent way A. Welkenhuysen edited and translated the *Versus de Unibove*,[2] it is possible to conduct research into the ramifications and interaction of the two traditions in this poem.

---

2. A. Welkenhuysen (ed. and transl.), *Het lied van boer Eenos (Versus de Unibove). Kluchtig versverhaal uit de elfde eeuw. Inleiding, facsimile-weergave, teksteditie, metrische vertaling, bijlage ter verantwoording en duiding*, Syrinx tekstuitgaven, 1 (Leuven, 1975). Th.A.-P. Klein, '*Versus de Unibove*. Neuedition mit kritischem Kommentar', in: *Studi medievali*, Serie terza, 32 (1991), pp. 843-886. W. Evenepoel et al. (eds), *A. Welkenhuysen, Latijn van toen tot nu. Opstellen, vertalingen en teksten*, Symbolae Facultatis Litterarum Lovaniensis, Series A, 18 (Leuven, 1995), pp. 281-305, 'Het lied van boer Eenos (Versus de Unibove)'. Improved text edition and translation. The 1975 edition remains indispensable because of the introduction and the appendix with the acknowledgements and explanations, including a bibliography, a memorandum accompanying the manuscript, text critical notes and explanatory comments. They are quoted here as Welkenhuysen, 'Inleiding' (Introduction) and Welkenhuysen, 'Bijlage' (Appendix). As regards the text, I follow the 1995 edition. To be complete, I would also like to mention M. Wolterbeek, 'Unibos: the earliest full-length fabliau (text and translation)', in: *Comitatus*, 16 (1985), pp. 46-76. M.W. Wolterbeek, *Ridicula nugae satyrae. Comic narratives of the tenth, eleventh and early twelfth centuries* (Berkeley, 1984), pp. 73-86, 98-100 and 322-365, introduction, notes, text and translation. M. Wolterbeek, *Comic tales of the Middle Ages. An anthology and commentary* (New York etc. [1991]), pp. 28-34, 41 and 150-171, introduction, notes, text and translation.

The *Versus de Unibove*: the contents of the poem

This poem tells a story composed of four episodes.[3]

First episode. A peasant only has one ox. Every time he buys another one, one of them dies. That is why his neighbours gave him the nickname One-ox. One day he loses his last ox. He goes to the market in a nearby town and sells its hide for a low price. On his way back he passes through a forest to defecate and finds three jars filled with coins. At home he borrows a measuring cup from the provost (*praepositus*, probably a local manager of ecclesiastical property). The provost accuses One-ox of theft, but he says he got the money for the hide of his ox. Now the provost, the bailiff and the priest kill their oxen and go to the market with the hides. The exorbitant prices they are asking get them into a conflict with some shoemakers, their prospective customers. They are fined and the hides are confiscated. They want to take revenge against One-ox.

Second episode. One-ox smears his wife with the blood of a pig. She pretends to be dead. The three revengeful village magistrates enter. One-ox takes out a horn, blows it as he walks around her three times. She pretends she has suddenly come alive again and the three magistrates think she rose from the dead more beautiful than ever. They want their wives to be rejuvenated the same way, so they buy the horn from One-ox and murder their wives. At their funerals they swear to take revenge.

Third episode. One-ox puts coins into his mare's behind. His three enemies believe she shits money; they are willing to abandon their revenge if One-ox sells them the animal. It is not difficult to guess the outcome.

Fourth and last episode. One-ox is to be put to death by the three village potentates. He can decide how he wants to be executed, and chooses death by drowning. Tied up and locked in a barrel, he is carried out to sea. He has put some money in his pocket and tempts the three to have a drink at an inn. Meanwhile a swineherd passes by with his herd and hears shouts from the barrel: 'I don't want to be a provost.' The herdsman is interested in this job and changes places with One-ox. He drowns. Three days later the trio meets One-ox again, with the swine of the drowned herdsman. He pretends to have found the swine at the bottom of the sea. The provost, the bailiff and the priest throw themselves into the sea and One-ox is liberated from his foes.

3. The structure of the poem is as follows: the first episode is described in strophes 9 to 66, the second in strophes 70 to 114, the third in strophes 120 to 158 and the fourth in strophes 160 to 215.

The Author, His Audience, the Genre

The poem *Versus de Unibove* consists of 216 strophes, each with four verses. The poem was written in the eleventh century.[4] It was passed down in just one manuscript, a codex probably part of the library of St. Peter's Monastery in Gembloux at the beginning of the twelfth century.[5] The poem is part of a codex that contains treatises on the theory of music, astronomy, mathematics, and philology.[6] So the poem is in a compilation of texts that served a function within the intellectual culture of monks. This provides some information about the potential reading audience the author of the *Versus* was addressing.

The author probably came from the north of the Romance language region, and might have been from Wallonia. Welkenhuysen has quite a convincing linguistic argument to support this idea.[7] The stress in the *Versus* is often on the last syllable of a word that had the stress on the first syllable in Classical Latin, for example: *bovés emít paupér homó* (strophe 5.1). This is typical of the Latin of an author from the Romance language region. Since the codex the poem was in probably belonged to the library of St Peter's Monastery in Gembloux, quite a few researchers feel the author is apt to be from northern France or Wallonia.[8]

Although the author remained anonymous, it is possible to say something about his cultural background. He must have been a person with considerable erudition, which he can only have acquired in learned clerical circles. The eloquent Latin points in that direction, as do the numerous quotations from the Bible[9] and some very rare Aramaic words.[10] The

---

4. Welkenhuysen, 'Inleiding', pp. VI-VII.
5. Welkenhuysen, 'Bijlage', pp. 5-7.
6. Welkenhuysen, 'Bijlage', p. 6. Klein, '*Versus de Unibove*. Neuedition mit kritischem Kommentar', pp. 845-846.
7. Welkenhuysen, 'Inleiding', p. VIII.
8. K.C. Peeters, 'De oudste West-Europese sprookjestekst. Unibos-problemen', in: *Volkskunde*, 71 (1970), pp. 8-23, pp. 19-21 summarizes the hypotheses of previous research. As regards this I follow Welkenhuysen, 'Inleiding', p. VIII. L. Genicot did express certain doubts as to whether the poem originated in Gembloux in his review of Welkenhuysen's edition (*Revue d'histoire ecclésiastique*, 71, 1976, p. 231). According to him the term *praepositus* occurs more frequently in Hainault and northern France than in the vicinity of Gembloux.
9. G. La Placa, 'I *Versus de Unibove*, un poema dell' XI secolo tra letteratura e folklore', in: *Sandalion*, 8-9 (1985-1986), pp. 285-305. See also the edition by Klein.
10. D.A. Wells, 'Die biblischen Wörter im "Unibos": Ein Beitrag zur Bedeutungsforschung und zum Verständnis des Antiklerikalismus im Frühmittelalter', in: K. Grubmüller et al. (eds), *Kleinere Erzählformen im Mittelalter*, Schriften der Universität-Gesamthochschule Paderborn, Reihe Sprach- und Literaturwissenschaft, 10 (Paderborn, 1988), pp. 83-88.

poem is a learned text, written in Latin. It exhibits a markedly ironic humour. One-ox's meeting up with his adversaries three days after his presumed death might in fact be an allusion to the resurrection of Christ. This combination of clerical erudition and ironic distantiation from clerical conventions might have given Welkenhuysen the idea the author was a young monk or a wandering scholar.

Strophes 2 and 3 could contain some information about the social framework the poem functioned in:

> Ad mensam magni principis
> est rumor Unius Bovis,
> praesentatur ut fabula
> per verba iocularia.
>
> Fiunt cibis convivia,
> sed verbis exercitia;
> in personarum drammate
> Uno cantemus de Bove.

[At the table of a great lord / the story of One-ox goes around; / it is presented as fiction / in playful words./ With delicacies a feast is created / but style exercises are created with words / so let us sing of One-ox/ in the form of a dialogue.]

Are these only *topoi* or do the verses actually contain real information? If they do, they might indeed describe a declamation given at a festive meal. The fact that the story (*rumor*) about One-ox is depicted (*praesentatur*) might be indicative of a declamation. Was it perhaps a mimetic performance in song (*cantemus, in personarum drammate*)?[11] The terms *rumor* and *fabula* are indicative of what a medieval audience perceived as fiction. *Verba iocularia* is indicative of a comical presentation. Was the *magnus princeps* a prestigious cleric? If so, he could well have been an abbot, which could mean the Poem on One-ox was for an audience of monks. Or was he a secular nobleman? In that case, we should consider the possibility that the poem went through a secular aristocratic, orally transmitted preliminary stage.

Whatever the case may be, in its written form the poem was very probably meant for a monastic audience. From the moment the text was recorded in writing, there was no longer any possibility of an oral *creation* – as is characteristic of oral tradition – and at most of an oral *performance*. Well-educated monks would probably have been able to follow

---

11. F. Bertini, 'Il contadino medievale, ovvero il profilo del diavolo (una nuova interpretazione dei *Versus de Unibove*)', in: *Maia,* 47 (1995), pp. 325-341 (p. 331).

this kind of performance in Latin. The Romance mode of the Latin used in the *Versus* reinforces the impression that the poem was recited.[12]

The Poem on One-ox is related to the fabliaux, and is known as the first specimen of this genre.[13] Fabliaux are short stories in verse,[14] comical works, often with a rather drastic kind of humour; the scene is usually set in the countryside. So the similarities to the *Versus* are obvious.[15] Fabliaux lend themselves to a theatrical transposition. The Poem on One-ox contains any number of themes appropriate to a theatrical reproduction, for example the scene where One-ox walks around his purportedly dead wife's bed three times blowing his horn, and she, smeared with blood, seems to awake from the dead.[16] The events in the fabliaux are events that occur in everyday life. The same applies to the *Versus*.

The French fabliaux flourished from about 1200 into the fourteenth century.[17] Most of the fabliaux were composed in the north of France; Picardy made an important contribution.[18] The Latin Poem about One-ox was, as is noted above, most probably written down in Wallonia or in the north of France. In a geographical respect, as Welkenhuysen has remarked, this links up rather well with the area where the fabliaux originated.[19] Enough said about the written literary, genre-related similarities between the *Versus* and the fabliaux. Are there also similarities as regards the influences of oral tradition?

---

12. Cf. A.P. Orbán, 'Was verraten die Horaz-Zitate in der *Ecbasis Captiui* über die Herkunft des Autors und die Darstellungsweise des Gedichtes?', in: *Mediaevistik*, 4 (1991), pp. 265-295 (pp. 284-290).

13. This was already the opinion of Gaston Paris at the end of the nineteenth century, quoted by P. Nykrog, *Les fabliaux*, Publications romanes et françaises, 123 (Genève, 1973), p. 264; see also Welkenhuysen, 'Inleiding', pp. V-VI.

14. Nykrog, *Les fabliaux*, pp. 245-248; H.H. Christmann, 'Fabliau', in: K. Ranke et al. (eds), *Enzyklopädie des Märchens. Handwörterbuch zur historischen und vergleichenden Erzählforschung*, 4 (Berlin and New York, 1984), col. 773-780 (col. 773).

15. In addition, the fabliaux have the following features in common with the *Versus*. The most prevalent category of characters are the priests; the peasants are the second most prevalent (O. Jodogne, *Le fabliau*, Typologie des sources du Moyen Âge occidental, 13, Turnhout, 1975, pp. 26-27), and in the Poem on One-ox a peasant is the main character and a priest is one of his three adversaries. Many fabliaux contain a moral (Jodogne, *ibid.*, pp. 15-16, 23); the moral of the *Versus* is in the last strophe (216): this story demonstrates once and for all that people should never take the clever advice of their enemies.

16. Jelle Koopmans drew my attention to this point. This makes it all the more probable that a reference is made in strophes 2 – 3 to a theatrical depiction.

17. C. Muscatine, *The Old French fabliaux* (New Haven and London, 1986), p. 4.

18. Christmann, 'Fabliau', col. 774. Jodogne, *Le fabliau*, pp. 24-25.

19. Welkenhuysen, 'Inleiding', p. VIII.

A certain extent of research has been conducted on the influence of oral tradition in the fabliaux: not enough to draw any generalising conclusions, but enough for a tentative judgment.[20] It has been noted that the narrative material in a number of fabliaux is related to narrative motifs that also occur in the oral tradition. It looks as if the genre was suitable for this, as it were: what a successful fabliau needed was juicy humorous narrative material that could be colourfully depicted. It is easy to imagine that if authors were familiar with narrative material of this kind from the oral tradition, they would be happy to use it.

The themes and atmosphere of the *Versus* are related to those of the fabliaux. The similarity of the *Versus* to the later fabliaux is not necessarily linked though to written literature. This similarity can be derived in part from the fact that like the authors of the fabliaux, the author of the *Versus* took his narrative material from the oral tradition and selected according to the same criteria. This is why it is conceivable that future systematic research into derivations from the oral tradition in the fabliaux will help gain greater insight into the Poem on One-ox.

The succesion of narrative motifs and the updating of the narrative material are often cited as properties of oral tradition. I would like to see whether the Poem on One-ox exhibits these properties and whether any conclusions can be drawn from this as regards the possible oral origin of the narrative material in the *Versus*.

THE SUCCESSION OF NARRATIVE MOTIFS

If an orally transmitted story consists of a succession of motifs,[21] it is usually not one whole with a comprehensive main motif and secondary side motifs, as we know for example from the nineteenth-century novel. It is far more apt to be a collection of separate motifs side by side.[22] According to Walter Ong, oral style is additive rather than subordinative

---

20. No inventory has been made of the narrative motifs in the fabliaux. Christmann, 'Fabliau', col. 777-778, gives a number of examples of the narrative material incorporated in the fabliaux. An interesting book is P.-Y. Badel, *Le sauvage et le sot. Le fabliau de Trubert et la tradition orale*, Essais sur le Moyen Âge, [5] (Paris, 1979), in which links are drawn between the oral tradition and the contents of one fabliau.

21. I use the terms type and motif in the meanings customarily adhered to in folklore research, the term *type* to refer to a story-as-a-whole and the term *motif* to refer to a building stone of a story. I use the term *episode* to refer to the parts of the *Versus de Unibove* cited in footnote 2.

22. W.J. Ong, *Orality and literacy. The technologizing of the word* (London and New York, 1990⁹), pp. 37-39.

and aggregative rather than analytic. But he does add that these features would continue to play a role in written literature for a long time to come.[23] They are consequently not *exclusively* characteristic of orally transmitted literature.

There is also evidence of successions of narrative motifs in written medieval literature.[24] This is not necessarily indicative of oral creation. It can also be quite adequately explained by noting that the authors were familiar with the procedures of oral tradition because it was the most widespread form of cultural transference. In much the same way, train compartments were built at the start of the railroad era that looked like stagecoaches. More generally, even if the succession of narrative motifs is a characteristic of much of the oral tradition, we still can not use this feature as a criterion for identifying oral tradition.

The Poem on One-ox consists of a succession of narrative motifs; this does not necessarily mean the poem derives from an earlier version that was orally created and transmitted. However, if orally transmitted versions of this story were already in circulation before the *Versus de Unibove* came into existence, then like so much oral tradition, they could have consisted of successions of narrative motifs. In that case, the author did not necessarily invent the succession of motifs in the *Versus*. I will elaborate upon this point later.

UPDATING NARRATIVE MATERIAL

It has been argued that updating is a feature of much of the oral tradition because narrators have a tendency to alter stories that have been in circulation for some time to suit the situation they and their audience are now in.[25] Concreteness is another property of oral tradition. In general, the narrated material is close to the human lifeworld.[26] It is also the case however with written literature incorporating narrative material that is already circulating that an author can adjust the narrative material to his own lifeworld and 'fill up' the story with concrete details he knows from his own experience. So these are not all-weather criteria. Bearing this in mind, let us consider the contents of the *Versus de Unibove*.

---

23. Ong, *Orality and literacy*, pp. 141-147.
24. I would like to thank Erwin Mantingh for the information about this.
25. Ong, *Orality and literacy*, pp. 46-49 and the literature cited there.
26. Ong, *Orality and literacy*, pp. 42-43.

The poem refers again and again to socio-economic reality, the world of farming, cattle-breeding, and commerce.[27] One-ox is a farmer. His plough is drawn by oxen. The more notable inhabitants of his village also work with oxen. In the first episode, One-ox has an animal he rides to the market, and it is probably the very same animal as the mare that emerges in the third episode as a miraculous producer of money. He also has a pig (one pig at least). We see cattle-breeding in the last episode: the swineherd with his herd. The swineherd has a bundle of arrows on his back. From time to time he might also be active as a hunter.

From the poem we learn about the domanial relations in the countryside. There is a village aristocracy: a provost, probably the local manager of the property of a religious institution (*praepositus*), a village bailiff (*maior villae*), and a village priest. Whether they themselves work the land is not clear from the text. The priest has some servants.

It is not possible to determine the exact status of One-ox. It is true that the villagers disparagingly nickname him One-ox, but this only goes to show that had he not been out of luck, he would have had two oxen. Obviously oxen are the animals used to draw ploughs in his region, and not yet horses. The three village magistrates also use them.[28] According to an estimate by L. Genicot, less than ten per cent of the agrarian population had a plough and animals to pull the plough.[29] One-ox and his three adversaries are thus members of the well-to-do rural population. Moreover One-ox has a horse to ride. All this doesn't make an

---

27. See the penetrating analysis of the market scene by B. Schmeidler, 'Kleine Forschungen in literarischen Quellen des 11. Jahrhunderts', in: *Historische Vierteljahrschrift*, 20 (1920-1921), pp. 129-149, (pp. 129-138 about the *Versus de Unibove*, pp. 131-133). Afterwards L. Genicot pointed out the importance of this text for socio-economic historical research in his review of Welkenhuysen's edition.

28. In the eleventh century, in these parts of Europe oxen were still the animals ordinarily used to pull a plough, and not yet horses. See L. Genicot, *L'Économie rurale Namuroise au Bas Moyen Âge*, III, *Les hommes – Le commun*, Université de Louvain, Recueil de travaux d'histoire et de philologie, 6ᵉ série, fasc. 25 (Louvain-la-Neuve and Brussels, 1982), pp. 255-257; R. Fossier, *La terre et les hommes en Picardie jusqu'à la fin du XIIIᵉ siècle*, 2 vols. (Paris and Louvain, 1968), I, pp. 254, 377-378. Strophe 144 contains an inconsistency: when the mare assumed to be able to defecate money awakes, it expects to be put to the plough. But this slip of the pen on the part of the author might well indicate that horses were sometimes used to pull a plough.

29. L. Genicot, 'Entre l'empire et la France (de 925 à 1429)', in: Idem (ed.), *Histoire de la Wallonie* (Toulouse, 1973), pp. 123-185 (p. 145). The smokey hut of One-ox in strophe 24 is not necessarily indicative of poverty. Many peasants had houses with stokeholes instead of chimneys. This can be an (ironically intended?) observation from another lifeworld, such as that of the castle or monastery.

impression of poverty.[30] If there are any differences between One-ox and the village magistrates, they are not material ones.

There is a market every day in a nearby city. Goods, in this case oxhides, are conveyed the short distance to the market. Shoemakers buy hides directly from the peasants and pay for them in cash. In this economy, money is important.

So we find a variety of economic activities in the countryside described in the poem: breeding swine and hunting, agriculture in a domanial context, an agrarian economy at least partly oriented to marketing.

Some elements originating from the socio-economic reality of those days serve an indispensable function in the plot. The fact that for a long time One-ox only has one ox, while two of them are needed, has an obvious effect in the tale: in relation to the three village magistrates it makes him a loser. Money is an essential element in the progress of the action: a sale takes place in three of the four episodes; the prospect of pecuniary advantage is the motor in the third episode (about the mare), and the fourth episode: first the swineherd is seduced by it, then the three village magistrates are.

In its more imaginary aspects, the text also bears traces of socio-economic reality. Transformed into a fairy-tale motif, there is money in the form of a treasure One-ox finds. His mare seems to be capable of miraculously generating vast wealth. There are also animals as a fairy-tale source of prosperity: the swine at the bottom of the sea.

Now, what are the consequences of all this for the position of the *Versus* with respect to written and oral tradition? There are definitely traces of eleventh-century reality in the *Versus*. But this is no reason to assume the story has either an oral or a written origin. There is no way to know whether narrative material that was already in existence was updated here, because we have no earlier version of the same or a related story to compare it with. Even if we did, it would still be true that though updating narrative material is a characteristic of much oral tradition, it can also play a role in written works.

There is one detail that could have been taken from older, orally transmitted versions. If I am not mistaken, it is not a matter of updating

---

30. L. Genicot doubted whether One-ox was a poor peasant in his review of Welkenhuysen's edition. A. Borst (*Lebensformen im Mittelalter*, Frankfurt on Main and Berlin, 1973; 1986, pp. 97-101) erroneously argued that One-ox was the poorest man of the village. He did however rightly emphasize the antagonism between One-ox and his adversaries.

however, but quite the opposite, a pure case of adopting an existing motif where adaptation would have been quite feasible: the sea One-ox is to be thrown into and that his adversaries drown in. Not a single other passage in the poem shows that the story takes place anywhere near a coast. Other researchers who studied the *Versus* all situate the story inland. A river or a lake would be a more logical location. Indeed this is the case in some of the stories related to the story in the *Versus* that were orally transmitted before they were recorded in writing.[31] Is the motif of the sea a petrified remainder of older versions? Perhaps. But it is also possible that the poet deliberately preserved – or invented – this motif because a sea, so much vaster and deeper than a river, produces a better dramatic effect. What is more, though the poem is filled with true-to-life details, there is nothing to keep the author from giving his imagination free rein. The sea is very much in keeping with the other imaginary elements in his work.

LITERARY IMAGES OF PEASANTS

The images of the main character of the poem, the peasant One-ox, partly originate from literary tradition, and partly from oral tradition. Let us first look at some of the medieval traditions in written literature on peasants and examine the role they play in the images of One-ox.

One comment should be made beforehand. The author of the *Versus de Unibove* clearly keeps an ironic distance from written tradition and Christian doctrine. For example the moral in the final strophe – do not take the advice of cunning enemies – closes with the solemn statement that the story illustrates this moral 'for all eternity' (*per saeculorum saecula*), which is undoubtedly meant to be ironic.[32] Bertini holds that the punishment designed for One-ox, being tied up in a barrel and tossed into the sea, refers to a passage in Revelation (20:1-3) about how Satan is bound and cast into the abyss; based in part on this, he assumes the poet intended to portray One-ox as satanic.[33] I tend to agree with the first point,

---

31. There are various examples in: J. Bolte and G. Polívka, *Anmerkungen zu den Kinder- u. Hausmärchen der Brüder Grimm*, 5 vols. (Leipzig, 1913-1932), II, pp. 1-18, 'Das Bürle'.

32. J. Beyer (*Schwank und Moral. Untersuchungen zum altfranzösischen Fabliau und verwandten Formen*, Studia Romanica, 16 Heidelberg, 1969, pp. 78-79) sees the same ironic intention.

33. Bertini, 'Il contadino medievale, ovvero il profilo del diavolo (una nuova interpretazione dei *Versus de Unibove*)', p. 340. La Placa however sees the irony here ('I *Versus de Unibove*, un poema dell' XI secolo tra letteratura e folklore', p. 302).

but not the second. How certain is it that this reference to Revelation was meant seriously? Let us compare it with the meeting between One-ox and his adversaries three days after his assumed death by drowning in strophe 197. This is undoubtedly an allusion to the resurrection of Christ, but definitely with a very ironic slant. We should consequently never lose sight of the fact that irony can play a role, as can also be the case in the literary images of peasants in the *Versus* that I shall now address.

1. The attitude of the clerical and secular elite to the peasants – the majority of the population – was ambivalent. The members of these elite groups realized they depended on the peasants' productivity for their very livelihood, but they often felt far superior to them.[34] The impression is given that as long as the peasants were resigned to being the lower strata in society, they were described relatively charitably. This mechanism is perhaps also recognisable in the images of One-ox in the poem. He is certainly not described more negatively than the three village magistrates. Perhaps the people the Poem on One-ox was meant for felt so superior to the quarreling villagers that they could be amused by the greedy magistrates made to look like fools by the tricks of a sly peasant.[35]

2. Texts written by clerics in the early Middle Ages often contain images of peasants as thoroughly earthy beings, coarse and ridiculous.[36] They are images formed from above and outside in circles of clerical *litterati*. The same stereotypes occur in courtly literature, where people who share in the courtly culture are contrasted with *villains*, uncivilised peasants.[37] This image is found in the beginning of the *Versus*: One-ox is an underdog and hardly a human being. In strophe 4 he is depicted as a ridiculous yokel:

> Natis natus ridiculis
> est rusticus de rusticis;
> natura fecit hominem,
> sed fortuna mirabilem.

---

34. P. Freedman, *Images of the medieval peasant* (Stanford California, 1999), pp. 15-39, 'Peasant labor and the limits of mutuality', pp. 143-150, 'The domesticated peasantry'.

35. As regards the depiction of the village priest, many commentators have been struck by the fact that of the village magistrates, he is portrayed in by far the most negative way. A link is drawn in this connection to the aversion of the monastic clergy to the lay clergy.

36. J. Le Goff, 'Les paysans et le monde rural dans la littérature du haut Moyen Âge (V^e-VIe siècle)', in: Idem, *Pour un autre Moyen Âge. Temps, travail et culture en Occident: 18 essais* ([Paris], 1977), pp. 131-144.

37. E. Faral, *La vie quotidienne au temps de saint Louis* ([Paris], 1938), pp. 115-127. J. Bumke, *Höfische Kultur. Literatur und Gesellschaft im hohen Mittelalter*, 2 vols. (Munich, 1994^7, in one volume), I, pp. 79-80.

[Born from a ridiculous offspring / here is a peasant born from peasants; / nature made him a human being, / but fortune an exceptional one.]

This scornful characteristic may be a *topos*, a vehicle for a *litteratus* to express his disdain of peasants or meet the expectations of his audience. But this is not quite certain. The poet might have written these lines purely for the dramatic effect, to emphasize the contrast with the cleverness and fighting spirit One-ox later exhibits. After this, One-ox is only called foolish (*stultus*; strophe 22) on one occasion. Once he has found the treasure, he sends his son to the provost to borrow a measuring cup and seems to be acting against his own interests. Further on in the text he calls himself a *pauper*, but only does so to fool his enemies (strophe 29).[38]

Scatological stories and images are an important component of the negative stereotyping of peasants. The manure of the animals they work with day after day serves as the material basis; in the literary representation, this can be enlarged to become grotesque. Freedman has collected a huge file on these images, and adds astute comments.[39] Scatological elements play a prominent role in the Poem on One-ox: returning to the town, One-ox defecates in the woods; his mare produces manure instead of the promised riches. Here again, the scatological element contributes to the negative representation, but the links drawn between manure and wealth are intriguing. In the first episode One-ox finds the treasure immediately after he has defecated, and in the third episode there is the suggestion that the animal's belly contains money. It is possible that side by side with the negative connotations, positive scatological ones that are rooted in orally transmitted folk tradition also play a role here.[40]

---

38. The word *rusticus* (peasant) has numerous negative connotations that might have added to the impression given here: uncultivated, ignorant, ridiculous. The word *pauper*, which is used in strophes 5, 29, 37 and 120, can have any number of meanings. In the *Versus* it is used in the purely economic meaning of 'poor'. *Agricola* in strophe 5, where One-ox wants to plough *sub exemplis agricolae*, has the neutral meaning of 'person who farms the land'.

39. Freedman, *Images of the medieval peasant*, pp. 150-156, 'Stupidity and excrement'.

40. Bertini, 'Il contadino medievale, ovvero il profilo del diavolo (una nuova interpretazione dei *Versus de Unibove*)', pp. 331 and 337 sees links with the folk culture and refers to Bakhtin's observations about the importance of the symbolism of the lower body there, alluding to M. Bakhtine, *L'oeuvre de François Rabelais et la culture populaire au Moyen Âge et sous la Renaissance* (Paris, 1970; original Russian edition 1965), pp. 366-432, 'Le "bas" matériel et corporel chez Rabelais'. Comparable ideas can be found in Freedman, *Images of the medieval peasant*, p. 153.

3. In addition, medieval texts contain an image of peasants with a different tint. Although the secular and clerical elites often looked down upon peasants as uncivilised outsiders, they realized that the peasants had effective means to escape their economic obligations and distress, for example sabotage and evasion. In the literary imagination, this is presented as unreliability.[41] The inventive One-ox, able to survive any danger by being so smart, seems compatible with this stereotyped expectation. One-ox often exhibits conduct that is strikingly calculating.[42] He carefully stages his ruses: the woman who seems to be dead, the mare that seems to defecate money. Before he disappears in the barrel, he makes sure he has got enough money to get his executioners drunk. With carefully chosen words, he repeatedly plays his opponents for fools and entices the swineherd to take his place.

4. There is yet another aspect of the elitist image of the peasant, an aspect narrowly interwoven with the previous one: the peasant who lives outside the culture and lives so close to nature that he is nearly an animal, and who is therefore unpredictable and dangerous.[43] One-ox has some of these traits. He is portrayed as a man who abruptly exchanges his role of a passive victim for that of a very efficient manipulator. This happens when he tempts the provost, the bailiff and the priest to kill their oxen. From then on, he is the one who takes the initiative.

The nearest parallel of the *Versus* in this respect is the *Fabliau de Trubert* about a man who lives outside the culture and uses tricks to get the better of his mighty adversary. It is even more fantastic and cruel than the story about One-ox. One-ox and Trubert have some traits in common; they are both unpredictable and sadistic. Their first act is performed on

---

41. On tensions in agrarian societies E.R. Wolf, *Peasants*, Foundations of modern anthropology series (Englewood Cliffs, N.J., 1966), pp. 77-95 and J.C. Scott, *Weapons of the weak. Everyday forms of peasant resistance* (New Haven and London, 1985). On images influenced by these tensions: P. Freedman, 'Peasant anger in the late Middle Ages', in: B.H. Rosenwein (ed.), *Angers past. The social uses of an emotion in the Middle Ages* (Ithaca and London, 1998) pp. 171-188; Idem, *Images of the medieval peasant*, and R. Künzel, *Beelden en zelfbeelden van middeleeuwse mensen. Historisch-antropologische studies over groepsculturen in de Nederlanden, 7de – 13de eeuw* (Nijmegen, 1997) p. 66.

42. This aspect is also emphasized by F. Bertini, who however views it as an indication of a more positive evaluation of peasants ('Il "nuovo" nella letteratura in latino', in: *L'Europa dei secoli XI e XII fra novità e tradizione: sviluppi di una cultura*, Miscellanea del Centro di studi medioevali, 12, Milan, 1989, pp. 216-238, esp. pp. 222-224 and 228).

43. Le Goff, 'Les paysans et le monde rural dans la littérature du haut Moyen Âge', pp. 139-140; Badel, *Le sauvage et le sot. Le fabliau de Trubert et la tradition orale*, pp. 27-30.

their own initiative, and is an act of totally unreasonable aggression, enigmatic and therefore sinister.[44]

Oral tradition

The question has been posed above as to whether influences of oral tradition can be found in the *Versus de Unibove*. The fact that like the later fabliaux, the poem contains humourous, everyday narrative material, the succession of motifs, the wealth of factual details, the scatological elements – all these traces have failed to produce conclusive answers. But there is more.

The relationship between the sexes is described in the *Versus* in ways that are not in keeping with the clerical tradition. As far as we can look back, in Western Europe the married couple and the nuclear family around it was the basic unit. This is also the case in the *Versus*. Not only are the two worldly magistrates married, so is the priest. One-ox and his wife cooperate closely in the ruse with the resuscitating horn. Cooperation between a husband and wife will often have been everyday practice. There is not much evidence of it though in clerical writings because it does not fit in with the misogynous picture the medieval clergy had of women. Solidarity between man and wife belongs in the lay world. This is why stories about it in texts from clerical circles are probably of oral origin.[45]

The nature of the main character would also seem to be indicative of oral tradition. The ridiculed underdog from the beginning of the poem soon changes into a resourceful man who settles account with his adversaries in a series of tricks. He is cunning and calculating and constantly promotes his own interests; he is aggressive and cruel and keen on harming his enemies.

Although there is a great deal in the poem that has the flavour of reality, the success of One-ox is supernatural. It seems to belong to the world of the fairy tale. Does the material of the *Versus* originate indeed from

---

44. Cf. Badel, *Le sauvage et le sot*, especially pp. 24-25. Jelle Koopmans pointed out this parallel to me.
45. It is also interesting that the three would have liked their wives to be objects of lust, but that is no longer the case since they are old now. So in this poem, beauty is also something that matters to the villagers. This is not something one would expect to find in a work meant for the higher classes, whether clerical or secular. These images of the relation between the sexes are not included in the widely varied assortment in Freedman, *Images of the medieval peasant*, pp. 157-173, 'Peasant bodies, male and female'.

this genre of oral literature? In *The types of the folktale*, their catalogue of folk tales from all over the world, Aarne and Thompson classify the narrative material in the *Versus* as Type 1535, 'The poor and the rich peasant'.[46] Before and after Aarne and Thompson it has often been argued that the poem contains elements from oral tradition and more specifically from the fairy tale.[47]

The story of the *Versus* belongs to a large family of stories. There are similarities between the members of this family: in all the versions there is the constantly underlying theme of a seemingly weak person who, by way of his own cunning, gets the better of one or more seemingly strong persons. This thematic core is elaborated upon in the *Versus de Unibove* in a succession of episodes that have one thing in common, i.e. that the main character fools his adversaries into thinking certain magical objects (a horn, a mare) or certain acts (selling oxhides, being in a barrel or at the bottom of the sea) can be very profitable in an economic, erotic or social way.

There is a similarity between the various versions classified by Aarne and Thompson as Type 1535, but there are also differences due to processes of addition and wear. Some versions contain fewer motifs than the *Versus* or contain motifs the poem does not. One example is the version from Westphalia recorded in 1829.[48] A peasant is so poor he has to slaughter his last cow, and he takes the hide to town. When it starts raining, he covers himself with the hide, turning its bloody inner side to the outside. A raven comes flying to the blood, and the peasant catches it. Then the peasant manages to convince an innkeeper that the raven can predict the future. The peasant returns to his village with the money he has received for the raven. He leads his fellow villagers to believe he earned the money with the cowhide. We are already familiar with the outcome: the villagers slaughter their cows, only to have their hopes smashed when they get to the market. In this version, there is then the motif of the barrel and the cattle at the bottom of a river.

If these narrative motifs are put side by side with the ones in the *Versus*, it is clear that the virtually identic first motif occurs in both of

---

46. A. Aarne and S. Thompson, *The types of the folktale. A classification and bibliography*, FF Communications, 184 (Helsinki, 1964[2]), no. 1535. The whole family of Type 1535 belongs to a still larger complex, the stories about a trickster. Stories of this kind have been found all over the world.

47. Welkenhuysen, 'Inleiding', p. IX.

48. Bolte and Polívka, *Anmerkungen zu den Kinder- u. Hausmärchen der Brüder Grimm*, II, pp. 4-6.

them, but the Westphalia variant also includes the motif of the bird predicting the future; the motif in the second episode of the *Versus* (the resuscitating horn), and in the third (the money-producing animal) do not appear in the Westphalia variant, but the narrative material of the fourth episode does. This combination of similarities and differences is incompatible with the properties of written tradition and fits in very well with what is known about the properties of oral tradition.[49]

An important factor in this connection is that the version in the *Versus de Unibove* and the related stories consist of successions of narrative motifs. By nature, orally transmitted stories that consist of successions of narrative motifs are unstable.[50] Successions of this kind have something arbitrary about them; they can easily be made shorter or longer. If a story consists of this kind of succession of motifs, the various versions can consequently differ sharply from each other. This also holds true of the stories classified as Type 1535.[51] There are also variations in the separate narrative motifs. The resuscitating horn for example can sometimes be replaced by a flute.[52] But this is variation within certain borderlines: the object changes, but the function in the plot remains the same.

---

49. R. Künzel, 'Mondelinge overlevering in verhalende bronnen uit de Middeleeuwen. Enige historische en antropologische benaderingen', in: M. Mostert (ed.), *Communicatie in de Middeleeuwen. Studies over de verschriftelijking van de middeleeuse cultuur*, Amsterdamse historische reeks, Grote serie, 23 (Hilversum, 1995), pp. 21-38 (p. 32).

50. S. Thompson, *The folktale* (New York, 1946), pp. 165-168.

51. Aarne and Thompson have taken into consideration all the versions of a story that were known to them and they have given a sum total as it were of all the motifs that occur in the variants known to them. The motifs they list under I, II and III do not occur in the *Versus*. The parts IVa and b and Va and b correspond with three episodes of the *Versus* (1, 2 and 4). The third episode of the *Versus* (the mare that produces the money) is not registered as part of Type 1535.

The following motifs have been identified: S. Thompson, *Motif-index of folk-literature. A classification of narrative elements in folktales, ballads, myths, fables, mediaeval romances, exempla, fabliaux, jest-books and local legends* (Bloomington Ind., 1932-1936), Motif N 478. *Secret wealth betrayed by money left to borrowed money-scales*; K 941.1. *Cows killed for their hides when high price is reported by trickster*; K 113. *Pseudo-magic resuscitating object sold. Dupe kills his wife (mother) and is unable to resuscitate her*; B 103.1.1. *Gold producing ass* (cf. Type 563, *The table, the ass, and the stick*; in both of them the animal really produces wealth); K 842. *Dupe persuaded to take prisoner's place in a sack: killed. The bag is to be thrown into the sea. The trickster keeps shouting that he does not want to go to heaven (or marry the princess); the dupe gladly substitutes for him*; K 1051. *Diving for sheep. Dupe persuaded that sheep have been lost in river*.

52. See the survey of the motifs in M. De Meyer, *Vlaamsche sprookjesthema's in het licht der Romaansche en Germaansche kultuurstroomingen*, Koninklijke Vlaamsche Academie voor Taal- en Letterkunde, Reeks VI, no. 63 (Leuven, 1942), pp. 133-163, 'Het Unibos-thema', pp. 142-145; cf. p. 153 there.

The name of the main character provides another piece of information indicative of oral tradition. The name One-ox only occurs in the *Versus*, not in other stories related to the *Versus*. There is a Flemish version though with the name Eentand (One-tooth) and a German one with the name Einhirn.[53] As De Meyer notes, they are probably corruptions of the name One-ox. The notion of 'one and only one' was still preserved, though the second element of the name was changed. This is in keeping with what we know of oral tradition.[54]

The Poem on One-ox contains the oldest known written recording of four narrative motifs also evident in nineteenth and twentieth-century recordings of oral tradition. There these narrative motifs – isolated or in combination with each other and, in so far as they are clustered, in varying combinations – appear to have a vast distribution. They occur all across Europe and far beyond its borders.[55] As has been noted above, the Poem on One-ox has been passed down in only one manuscript, which was probably meant for the monks of St Peter's Monastery in Gembloux. It is extremely improbable that from that one manuscript meant for internal use at one monastery, the narrative motifs were disseminated all across the entire region where they were observed in the nineteenth and twentieth centuries.[56] This vast a dissemination region can only have been

---

53. De Meyer, *Vlaamsche sprookjesthema's in het licht der Romaansche en Germaansche kultuurstroomingen*, p. 141. Bolte and Polívka, *Anmerkungen zu den Kinder- u. Hausmärchen der Brüder Grimm*, II, pp. 8-10. In addition, numerous other names for the main character occur in other versions, but they are not relevant here.

54. A suggestion made by Theo Meder. In addition, as regards the German version with Einhirn, it should be noted that it dates back to 1559 (V. Schumann, *Nachtbüchlein*, I, no. 6, ed. J. Bolte, Publikationen des Literarischen Vereins in Stuttgart, Stuttgart, 1893) and thus can not have been influenced by the first edition of the *Versus* dated 1838 (J. Grimm and A. Schmeller (eds), *Lateinische Gedichte des X. und XI. Jh.*, Göttingen, 1838; reprint Amsterdam, 1967, pp. 354-383). This is why the name One-ox was probably once part of other, unregistered versions that the version with the corrupted name Einhirn goes back to. Since these unregistered versions, as I argue below, are not derived from the *Versus*, the name One-ox was probably part of the orally transmitted story that the poem goes back to.

55. W. Liungman, *Die schwedischen Volksmärchen. Herkunft und Geschichte*, Veröffentlichungen des Instituts für Deutsche Volkskunde, 20 (Berlin, 1961), pp. 304-305, 'No. 1535. Der grosse und der kleine Klaus'. T. Dekker, J. van der Kooi and T. Meder, *Van Aladdin tot Zwaan kleef aan. Lexicon van sprookjes: ontstaan, ontwikkeling, variatie* (Nijmegen, 1997), pp. 154-155, 'Grote Klaas en Kleine Klaas (Unibos)', and the literature cited there.

56. Even if the manuscript did serve a function as a performance procedure, the range of its influence must have been extremely limited, not nearly enough to explain the later distribution of the narrative material. This is also the case if we assume that various elements were lost in the written transmission. Say the Poem on One-ox goes back to a written example that has since been lost, as Klein posits in '*Versus de Unibove*. Neuedition

the result of an extremely strong oral component in the transmission process.

Since dissemination from the earliest written version could not possibly have led to this vast a distribution, the relation between the narrative motifs in the *Versus* and the ones in the versions recorded later can only be explained by assuming there was an oral tradition which the author of the *Versus* as well as the later narrators who operated orally were consulting.[57] We should not envisage this common oral tradition as one given spoken text that was conceived at a certain moment in time. Instead we should see it as a complex of related, orally transmitted narrative motifs from which, at various places and moments in time, unique oral versions could be separately derived.

On the grounds of all these arguments, the version in the *Versus de Unibove* does not have the status of an original that all the later versions are derived from. The poem makes the impression of being a written rendition based on one or more orally transmitted versions amidst other orally transmitted versions that have been lost, and would seem to be based upon a selection from the narrative material available at the time.

Is there anything to be said about this narrative material? The vast majority of the orally transmitted stories collected by folklore scholars date back to the nineteenth and twentieth centuries. A great deal of medieval narrative material has been discovered by erudite researchers such as Bolte, Polívka, Wesselski and Hilka. Unfortunately this knowledge was never systematically made accessible by means of a motif index for the medieval oral tradition. Monographs have been written about some of the Types, in which all the versions from the earliest known ones to the contemporary ones have been collected and analysed as regards their interdependence. Up until now, no monograph has been devoted to the complex of stories referred to in this article, i.e. Type 1535. But a study was written in 1942 on part of the material, the book *Vlaamsche sprookjesthema's in het licht der Romaansche en Germaansche kultuurstroomingen* (Flemish Fairy Tale Themes in the Light of Romance and Germanic Cultural Trends) by Maurits de Meyer, which has a comprehensive scope and is still well worth reading. This work is based upon

---

mit kritischem Kommentar', p. 847. Then this hypothetically written *Vorlage* to the *Versus* would similarly lack the capacity to have caused the present distribution of the narrative motifs.

57. Only in the early modern period are there, in addition, several authors who operate in writing; cf. De Meyer, *Vlaamsche sprookjesthema's in het licht der Romaansche en Germaansche kultuurstroomingen*, pp. 149-150.

material from France, the Netherlands, Belgium, Luxembourg and Germany. Up to now, in my opinion the chapter on the narrative material in the *Versus* and the related folk tales is the most important analysis any folklore scholar has ever written on this material.[58] De Meyer bases his conclusions on a total of 97 versions, 26 of which are from France, three from Wallonia, 17 from Flanders, six from the Netherlands, one from Luxembourg and 44 from Germany.

Is it feasible to place the narrative material of the *Versus* within the larger entirety researched by De Meyer on the grounds of this work? This is only the case to a limited degree. It was De Meyer's aim, as is clear from the title of his book, to investigate the Flemish narrative material on One-ox against the background of the narrative material in a large part of Western Europe, whereas this kind of investigation into the Walloon narrative material would be more relevant to the question I am posing. What is more, his study only includes three Walloon variants. That is not nearly enough to base any conclusions on that are specifically related to Wallonia. One outcome of De Meyer's research is the placement of the narrative material from Flanders with respect to two large groups of stories, a French and a German one. In this spirit I shall suffice with a placement of the narrative material in the *Versus* with regard to these two groups of stories.

If we compare the results of De Meyer's research with the narrative material in the *Versus*, the following pattern emerges. There is evidence of the narrative motif in the first episode of the poem, the adventure with the ox, throughout the region De Meyer studied, i.e. in France, Germany, Belgium, Luxembourg and the Netherlands. The same holds true for the last episode, the one about the escape from the barrel and the defeat of the adversaries. (The fact that One-ox is to be killed in a barrel rather than a sack alludes more to the German than the French narrative material. Barrels are quite common in the German variants whereas sacks are more frequently referred to in the French ones.) The narrative motif in the second episode about the sale of the pseudo-magic musical intrument is similarly found throughout the region, but with a striking difference in

---

58. De Meyer, *Vlaamsche sprookjesthema's in het licht der Romaansche en Germaansche kultuurstroomingen*, pp. 133-163: 'Het Unibos-thema'. In this study the conclusions drawn by J. Müller, *Das Märchen vom Unibos*, Deutsche Arbeiten der Universität Köln, 7 (Jena, [1934]) are summarized and numerous improvements have been made. The article by Peeters, 'De oudste West-Europese sprookjestekst. Unibos-problemen', was published afterwards. It is useful as synthesis, but there is not sufficient evidence to convincingly support specifying Flanders as the region where the *Versus* first emerged.

frequency between France, Belgium and the Netherlands on the one hand and Germany on the other: it is common in the French variants (in De Meyer's documentation, 19 times of a total of 26 researched variants), and in the Belgian and Dutch ones, and uncommon in the German ones (4 times in a total of 44 variants). However, the motif in the third episode, the sale of the animal that is supposed to produce money, solely occurs in France, be it quite infrequently (4 times in a total of 26 variants), and only in the northern half of the country. So there is only one region where all four motifs occur in the nineteenth and twentieth centuries, namely the north of France.

If we now examine the provenance of the poem, in the first instance the region where it probably originated seems to bear a surprising resemblance to this outcome. After all, the author was very probably from the north of the Romance language region, possibly from Wallonia and perhaps Gembloux. The region where the poem probably originated and the region where a succession of narrative motifs were found in the nineteenth and twentieth centuries that are identical to the succession in the *Versus* thus largely coincide.

It is tempting to conclude that the poet could have heard the very same succession of motifs being told in the eleventh century as were told there eight centuries later, and that we are perhaps observing the continuity in a spatial sense[59] of a cluster of narrative motifs over a distance of eight centuries. But caution is called for. Monks did not live in total isolation; sometimes they had contact with the outside world, and could thus have taken narrative material from outside their immediate lifeworld. If perchance the poem did indeed originate in Gembloux, we have to take into account the fact that this monastery was in contact with other monasteries in more southern French regions,[60] so that narrative material could have been conveyed from there to Gembloux. What is more, wandering scholars, the other category mentioned before in connection with the authorship of the *Versus*, frequently lived in the outside world and were often extremely mobile, which could definitely have led to 'cross-pollination'.

A more cautiously formulated conclusion might be feasible. It we bear in mind that the 'niche' the author lived in can have been wider than his

---

59. In a *spatial* sense: other forms of continuity are distinguished; cf. H. Bausinger, 'Zur Algebra der Kontinuität', in: H. Bausinger and W. Brückner (eds), *Kontinuität? Geschichtlichkeit und Dauer als volkskundliches Problem* (Berlin, 1969), pp. 9-30.

60. Welkenhuysen, 'Inleiding', p. VIII, based upon J. Toussaint, *L'abbaye de Gembloux. Les origines et l'âge d'or (940-1136)*, (Gembloux, [1972]), pp. 44-55.

immediate geographical surroundings, perhaps we ought to situate this 'niche' in the region where the succession of motifs characteristic of the *Versus* occurred in the nineteenth and twentieth century, i.e. the north of the Romance language region.

Lastly, the fact remains that since the *Versus de Unibove* did originate in that region, the other way around a global localisation is thus possible of the region where the motifs that occur in the poem were being orally transmitted in the eleventh century. For comparative historical research into the One-ox motifs, this remains an interesting point.

CONCLUSION

In the beginning of this article I argue that in view of the predominantly oral nature of medieval Western European culture, it is worth while to try and identify the original oral cores in written medieval texts, that written texts sometimes reflect the balance between oral and written literary tradition, that orally transmitted stories can contain the self-images of groups that do not write, and that as a result of the relatively early spread of literacy and the tendency to record in writing, the differences and similarities between oral and written tradition and how they influence each other in Western Europe can be examined over a long period of time. Viewed from these research perspectives, what have we learned from the study described here of the *Versus de Unibove*?

The poem has been passed down in a codex produced in and meant for extremely literate monastic circles. It is written in eloquent Latin and in a purely literate verse form. These features are indicative of the world of written literary tradition.

The Poem on One-ox is closely related to the fabliaux recorded in the north of France starting around the year 1200; it is a comic narrative in verse, it has theatrical aspects, and takes place in the countryside. The similarity in the theme and atmosphere can reflect the fact that like the authors of the fabliaux, the author of the *Versus* got his narrative material from the oral tradition at the time.

The Poem on One-ox consists of four successive episodes. Concatenation is a feature of many orally transmitted stories as well as early written literature, and consequently is not necessarily an indication of the influence of oral tradition on written literature. But since the same clustering of motifs observed in the *Versus de Unibove* also occurs in a number of folk stories recorded later, perhaps there is a new way to assess the compositional input of the author. Honemann puts a strong emphasis on his compositional capacity. Suchomski however notes that the middle two episodes could very well have been left out without harming the logic of the story. Beyer – the only author cited here who takes the possibility into account that the oral tradition at the time could have influenced the poem – sees the *Versus* as a series of episodes that could also have been shorter or longer; he feels this series consists of hitherto separate stories joined together by the author.[61] In view of the similarity between the succession of motifs in the *Versus* and a number of folk stories recorded later – a similarity, which as I have stated, is not generated by dispersion from the *Versus* to these later versions – it does not seem probable that the author of the *Versus* is their designer.

Are there any traces of updating in the *Versus de Unibove*, a property of much of the oral tradition? The poem takes place in the everyday world at the time, but for lack of comparative material there is no way to tell whether this is the result of adaptations in orally transmitted stories that had circulated earlier, or of the author's updating already existing narrative material in the *Versus*.

The description of the main character coincides in part with stereotypes the secular and clerical elites had about peasants, who they felt were earthy, coarse, ridiculous, unreliable, unpredictable and dangerous. However, the image of One-ox as a formidable character feared for his slyness, a trickster, probably stems from the oral tradition.

The cluster of narrative motifs is unmistakably indicative of oral tradition. This cluster is related to numerous folk stories with an immense distribution that were recorded later. Dispersion from the first recorded version, the *Versus*, can not have caused this expansion. It is indicative instead of a complex of shared oral sources for both of them. This is a convincing pirce of evidence that unambiguously indicates that the narrative material in the *Versus* is from the oral tradition: the similarity to other stories that were solely orally transmitted at the moment of recording in the early modern period.[62] Within this large complex, perhaps one specific

---

61. V. Honemann, 'Unibos und Amis', in: Grubmüller et al. (eds), *Kleinere Erzählformen im Mittelalter*, pp. 67-82, especially p. 74. J. Suchomski, *'Delectatio' und 'Utilitas'. Ein Beitrag zum Verständnis mittelalterlicher komischer Literatur*, Bibliotheca Germanica, 18 (Bern and Munich, 1975), pp. 106-110: 'Unibos', p. 108. Beyer, *Schwank und Moral. Untersuchungen zum altfranzösischen Fabliau und verwandten Formen*, p. 74. Suchomski could have explained the fact he observed if he had referred to the structural instability of *orally* transferred stories that consist of successions of narrative motifs.

62. In addition, the positive relation between the sexes, the element 'one' in the name of the main character in some versions of the story, and the slight variations within structurally identical motifs in the various versions are valid arguments.

succession of motifs was orally transmitted for centuries on end in a certain region, namely in the north of the Romance language region from the time of the recording of the *Versus de Unibove* – and if this is true, then probably from an earlier date – up until today.

Some features of the *Versus* – the everyday aspect of he narrative material and in part the description of the main character – can go back to either oral or written literary tradition. During the writing of the Poem on One-ox, a vast mutual penetration of oral and written tradition must have been taking place. After all, the written version came into being in a culture still predominantly an oral one, but it is simultaneously the product of a cultivated, literate brain. The effect of oral and written tradition alike on a text like this does not mean the influence of the one was at the expense of the other. The manifest presence of orally transmitted narrative material coincides with an equally manifest presence of purely written literary style features.

Here the phenomenon can have occurred that is called over-determination in psychoanalysis. This term is used if one and the same element in a dream, one specific slip of the tongue or one neurotic symptom is the expression of very different psychological drives.[63] This can also be a way of viewing the simultaneous influencing exerted by oral and written tradition on a literary text such as the *Versus*. With a result similar to the psychological mixed symptoms, a compromise that exhibits the signs of heterogeneous tendencies: this poem belongs to written literature, but is no less 'oral' for this reason.

Whether the cultural heterogeneity in the poem that was later discerned was experienced as such by the audience at the time and, if so, how it was perceived – as stimulating, amusing or shocking, or all of these at the same time – is a question that will have to remain open. Or maybe there is yet another way to look at it, because in the eleventh century, orally transmitted and written literature might have sometimes been very close. We might tend to see written authorship and oral transmission as two quite different traditions, but apparently the author of the *Versus de Unibove* had no trouble taking material from either of them.

The various traditions that played a role in the creation of the *Versus de Unibove* can also be approached from the aspect of *time*. Side by side, various types of durability (*durées*) can be discerned, each with its own

---

63. Several examples in the section on condensation in S. Freud, *Die Traumdeutung, Gesammelte Werke*, 2-3 (Frankfurt am Main, 1968[4]), pp. 284-310, 'Die Verdichtungsarbeit'.

duration and very different origins.[64] The literary form features in the *Versus de Unibove* are medieval continuations and transformations of Classical Latin literary traditions. The Christian elements in the poem are part of a long religious tradition, but the frequently ironic use the author makes of them is very much linked to the time and situation. The narrative motifs that occur in the *Versus* belong to a comprehensive tradition that has gone on for ages. The fact that the author of the *Versus* exhibits a certain openness vis a vis the oral tradition of his day can be viewed as part of a tendency that was to become stronger in the course of the twelfth century;[65] the Poem on One-ox is a harbinger of it. In this poem, there is also the formulation in words of the stereotype images the upper classes of pre-industrial Western Europe had of the peasant, i.e. as an inferior and ridiculous creature, and the peasant who may have been weak in some ways, but who had something unmanageable and dangerous about him. These are images that were to prevail for quite some time. The setting of the story in the *Versus* is typical of the era when the poem was written: the battle for material possessions in the social elite of a village in the larger context of a market-oriented agrarian economy, and many other elements taken from everyday life at the time. The prevailing image of the peasant One-ox is certainly not a purely positive one, but he definitely is a man who stands up for himself. This too would seem to be a product of the time. It reflects a growing awareness on the part of the clerical and secular elite that some of the peasants are not taking part in the social process in a purely passive way.

On a micro-scale – if one examines the text in itself – the Poem on One-ox presents an intriguing mixture of extremely heterogeneous components. Viewed on a macro-scale – in the light of more comprehensive contexts in time and space – there is once again a perception of heterogeneity, ambiguity and multiplicity.

---

64. The following observations have been inspired by a discussion between M. Soriano and J. Le Goff, E. Le Roy Ladurie and A. Burguière, 'Les Contes de Perrault', in: *Annales. Économies, Sociétés, Civilisations*, 25 (1970), pp. 633-653, included in the reprint of Soriano's book *Les Contes de Perrault. Culture savante et traditions populaires* ([Paris], 1977²), pp. II-XXX, especially pp. X-XIII, and a comment by Le Goff: 'L'étude de la culture populaire ou de phénomènes ou d'oeuvres imprégnées de culture populaire met l'historien en contact avec un "temps historique" qui le déconcerte. Rythmes lents, flashbacks, pertes et résurgences s'accordent mal avec le temps unilinéaire dans lequel il est à tout le plus accoutumé à discerner çà et là des "accélérations"ou des "retards". Raison de plus pour se féliciter que l'élargissement du champ de l'histoire au folklore remette en cause ce temps insuffisant'. ('Mélusine maternelle et défricheuse', in: Idem, *Pour un autre Moyen Âge*, pp. 307-331, footnote 12, pp. 314-315).

65. Le Goff, 'Mélusine maternelle et défricheuse'.

Geert H.M. CLAASSENS

THE 'SCALE OF BOENDALE': ON DEALING WITH FACT AND FICTION IN VERNACULAR MEDIAEVAL LITERATURE*

I

In preparing this contribution I have toyed with quite a few titles. Provocative ones, such as 'Leopold von Ranke did not belong to the thirteenth century', or more ominous ones such as 'On the spiritual hazards of writing history in the Middle Ages' – and many similar ones have all come up. The various possibilities all elucidated one or the other aspect of my thinking about the hardly visible borderline between literature and historiography in the vernacular *Schrifttum* of the Middle Ages. Yet in a collection of articles devoted to mediaeval 'narrative sources', featuring many contributions by prominent historians, and undoubtedly counting a large number of historians among its readers, I, as a literary historian specializing in Middle Dutch literature, ultimately feel called upon to stand up for vernacular texts as historical sources. I will not do so, however, by making a plea for the reliability of those Middle Dutch texts. Instead I am envisaging a *reductio ad absurdum*. I want to show something of the struggle with 'truth' that many writers and poets of the Middle Dutch language area experienced, hoping to convince you of two ideas: firstly that the modern distinction we make between fiction and non-fiction is irrelevant for mediaeval literature, and secondly that vernacular texts should not in principle be judged differently in their relationship to historical truth than Latin ones. I would hereby like to emphasize that I am not so much concerned with the question of whether vernacular texts

---

* An earlier, less expanded version of this article was published as 'De dichter liegt, maar hij spreekt toch de waarheid. Over feit en fictie in middeleeuwse literatuur', in: Ria Jansen-Sieben, Jozef Janssens and Frank Willaert (eds), *Medioneerlandistiek. Een inleiding tot de Middelnederlandse letterkunde* (Hilversum, 2000), 179-191. I would like to stress that this paper should be considered 'work in progress' and that I would welcome any comments, such as I have already received from Paul Arblaster, Katty De Bundel, Ortwin De Graef, An Faems and Paul Wackers (for which I am very grateful). I am indebted to Paul Arblaster and Roger Janssens for the English translation of this contribution.

offer a reliable reproduction of historical factuality as with the stance – implicitly or explicitly – taken by the authors of the texts concerned *vis à vis* the description of past events.

If I now start my 'story', I do so in the hope that at the end of it the reader will be able to classify it as true or untrue.

II

At the beginning of the fourteenth century Melis Stoke, clerk to the counts of Holland, wrote his part of what is now known as the *Rijmkroniek van Holland* [*Rhyme Chronicle of Holland*].[1] In it he describes the succession in 1299 of count John II to John I in these words:

> Doe hij vernam, wert hi droeve;
> Doch pensede hi om sine behoeve
> Ende quam int lant, als hi eerst mochte.
> Als hire quam, hi bedochte
> Sijn orbaer, ende deden ter eerden,
> Sijn neven Jan, met groter weerden,
> Te Reynsborch, in des vader graf.
> De anders dan wel seghet hieraf,
> Hi mesdoet herde zere:
> Dat weet God, de overste here,
> Dat de stucken dus toe quamen.
> Des moghen si hem sere scamen,
> De so gherne spreken quaet.
> Ombaren sijs, dat waer mijn raet,
> Ende wreken hem metter tonghe niet.
> Alst God woude, eest ghesciet.[2]

[When he [= John II] learnt of this [= the death of John I] he became sad. He considered what was necessary for him, and went to the country [= Holland] as quickly as possible. When he arrived there, he considered what was fitting, and interred his cousin John with great dignity, at Rijnsburg, in his father's grave. Whosoever speaks anything but good of this occasion commits a serious crime; God, the highest Lord, knows that it took place this way. Those who so much like to speak ill, should be very much ashamed. My counsel would be for them to leave it and not to take revenge with the tongue. As God wanted it, so did it take place.]

---

1. The *Rijmkroniek van Holland* is quoted after the edition by W.G. Brill, *Rijmkroniek van Melis Stoke*, 2 vols (Utrecht, 1885; [WHG, nieuwe serie 40, 42, rpt. Utrecht, 1983]). A short introduction in English is given in Wim van Anrooij, 'Stoke, Melis', in: John M. Jeep (ed.), *Medieval Germany. An Encyclopedia* (New York & London, 2001), 736-737.
2. *Rijmkroniek van Holland*, VI, ll. 1313-1328 (Brill, *Rijmkroniek*, II, 132-133).

Burgers, in his recent study of the *Rijmkroniek van Holland*, has shown that what Melis Stoke is doing here can be characterized in only one way: he is lying. At the same time a lack of factual knowledge cannot be called upon as an excuse for the lie, as it is precisely the charters that Stoke drew up as a clerk to the counts that tell us the true circumstances concerning the succession. John II did not dash off to Holland to bury his deceased cousin in great grief – he first had himself installed as successor at Middelburg and only afterwards travelled on to Zierikzee, Dordrecht and other Dutch towns. This means that some two weeks must have passed between the moment John II received the news of John I's demise and the latter's burial, which presents an entirely different picture of the successor.[3]

Elsewhere in his work Stoke presents himself as the epitome of reliability:

> Want ic en can in ghenen wegen
> Yement belieghen teniger stonde;
> Wat ics scrive dats bi orconde.[4]
> [For I cannot in any way ever lie to anyone; what I write is truly true.]

Among later historians, too, Stoke has a good reputation as historiographer. Yet in the passage quoted above Stoke twists the facts, paints a distorting picture, blurs the true circumstances – whatever we want to call it: he does not give a correct representation of the course of events here and he knows so. Melis Stoke is lying here, and will have had his motives to do so: after all, John II of Holland was his patron.[5]

Taking into account his position we will not blame Stoke too much for this 'white lie'. St. Augustine would have condemned him much harder. In *De mendacio* he rigorously refuses to accept any form of lying.[6]

---

3. Cf. J.W.J. Burgers, *De Rijmkroniek van Holland en zijn auteurs. Historiografie in Holland door de Anonymus (1280-1282) en de grafelijke klerk Melis Stoke (begin veertiende eeuw)*, (Hilversum, 1999), 303-305, which moreover gives another example of Stoke's 'tinkering with historical truth'.

4. *Rijmkroniek van Holland*, V, ll. 660/59-61 (lines 59-61 of an insertion of 127 lines, found in two manuscripts of the *Rijmkroniek van Holland*; Brill, *Rijmkroniek*, II, 35).

5. In this respect the words *als hi eerst mochte* (as quickly as possible) in Stoke's description (quoted above) of the succession are revealing. One could read this as Stoke's implicit acknowledgement that there was a delay, subtly suggesting that it was a necessary one, rebutting the suggestion of unnecessary or improper delay. In this way he seems to cover for his patron as well as for himself as 'reporter of the events'.

6. Such a categorical position was taken by many theologians, of whom Augustine was one of the most important and influential. Comp. S. Bok, *Lying: Moral Choice in Public and Private Life* (Hassocks, 1978), 33-46. In an appendix some relevant excerpts from Augustine's treatises are printed in English translation (250-255).

According to the moral code of Christianity, lying is a serious sin, a choice in favour of the Evil One, against Christ. Satan is the 'father of the lie' (John 8:44), the 'master of the forked tongue', while Christ is 'the way and the truth and the life' (John 14:6).[7]

From this perspective all speaking in general – and therefore writing as well – must be considered risky business. The fact that writers realized this is clearly borne out by a passage from the work of the Brabantine poet Jan van Boendale († ca.1351). In the fifteenth chapter of the third book of his *Der leken spiegel* [*The Laymen's Mirror*],[8] written between 1325 and 1330, we can read the following:

> Vintmen sine scrifture valsch dan,
> So en sal nemmermeer man
> Hem van rechte gheloven voort;
> Want hi heeft dichten verboort
> Ende verloren dichters name
> Ende sal hebben des ewelike blame.[9]
> [Should it be found out that his [= a poet's] writings are not true he will, quite justly, never again be believed; he has forfeited the right to write and lost the title of writer, and will consequently forever stand in ill repute.][10]

Should Boendale, who was familiar with Stoke's work,[11] have known that the latter had not strictly stuck to the facts, he would surely – I assume – have banned him from the Pantheon of 'true poets'. Boendale also takes up a strict, Biblically-founded stance *vis à vis* lying:

> Die heilighe scrifture seit albloot
> Dat loghenen die ziele slaen te doot,

---

7. The Biblical foundations of this stance against lying can easily be expanded. See, e.g., Ps. 5:7, I Tim. 1:9-10, Proverbs 6:17, Psalm 101:7, and – last but not least – in the eighth of the Ten Commandments (Exod. 20:19 and Deut. 5:20).

8. Edition in M. de Vries, *Der leken spieghel, leerdicht van den jare 1330, door Jan Boendale, gezegd Jan de Clerc, schepenklerk te Antwerpen*, 3 vols (Leiden, 1844-1847), vol. III, 158-172. Also see W.P. Gerritsen, 'De dichter en de leugenaars. De oudste poetica in het Nederlands', in: *De nieuwe taalgids*, 85 (1992), 3-27 and W.P. Gerritsen *et al.*, 'A fourteenth-century vernacular poetics: Jan van Boendale's "How Writers Should Write" (with a Modern English translation of the text by Erik Kooper)', in: Erik Kooper (ed.), *Medieval Dutch Literature in its European Context* (Cambridge, 1994), 245-260. A short introduction in English is given in Geert H.M. Claassens, 'Jan van Boendale (ca. 1280-1351)', in: John M. Jeep (ed.), *Medieval Germany. An Encyclopedia* (New York & London, 2001), 405-407.

9. Jan van Boendale, *Der leken spiegel*, III, 15, ll. 61-66 (De Vries, *Der leken spieghel*, III, 161).

10. The translation given above is by Erik Kooper, in Gerritsen et al. (1994), 253-258, quote on 254.

11. Cf. Burgers, *De Rijmkroniek van Holland*, 366-368.

Ende dat wi zullen antwoorden
Van allen ydelen woorden,
Daer die rechte rechtre sal
Doemen dese wereld al.[12]
[Holy Scripture states clearly that lies lead the soul to damnation and that we shall have to answer for all idle talk when the just Judge will pass judgement on this entire world].[13]

This utterance can obviously be understood in a general sense, but the first quote clearly shows that more is at stake. After all, Boendale passes this judgement in a poetical context. The relevant chapter from *Der leken spiegel* [*The Laymen's Mirror*] is entitled *Hoe dichters dichten sullen ende wat si hantieren sullen* [*How Writers Should Write and What They Should Pay Attention To*] and is wellknown as the oldest poetics in Dutch, even though it is more of a 'defence of poetry' than an extensive literary-technical treatise. If we look at the direct context of the quote, we will immediately be struck by the literary dimension of the opposition 'lie *versus* truth'. Boendale uses the reference to the Bible as an argument in his plea for veracity in historiography: one must not lie in a history. He here makes a connection between ethics and literature which then was, but nowadays no longer is self-evident: in the mediaeval world view literature is not an independent category, but a part of ethics. As far as Boendale's stance is concerned we may wonder whether the ban on lying only holds for historiography (to which sacred literature mostly belongs), or that it also extends to other kinds of texts. The fact that lying is morally reprehensible means that for Boendale (and his contemporaries) invented stories were probably at least problematical, but we would be going too far to claim that for him these stories – which we would now call fiction – were by definition unacceptable. Precisely because of the fact that in mediaeval literature the opposition 'lie *versus* truth', in its meaning of 'invented' *versus* 'historical', can never be separated from its religious and moral foundations; restrictions are imposed on the use of fiction, while at the same time the principle of its possible use is safeguarded. Some examples from Middle Dutch literature will presumably be able to clarify this point.

---

12. Jan van Boendale, *Der leken spiegel*, III, 15, ll. 113-118 (De Vries, *Der leken spieghel*, III, 163).
13. The translation given above is by Erik Kooper, in Gerritsen et al. (1994), 253-258, quote on 255.

III

At his birth Seghelijn of Jerusalem, the hero of the eponymous fourteenth-century chivalric romance, receives christening presents from three prophetesses.[14] Firstly he will always be victorious in combat, secondly he will never be refused a request provided he looks the person concerned in the eye, and thirdly he will end his life in holiness. Only the second present is linked to a condition: if Seghelijn lies, he will lose his gift for a limited period of time.[15] With this condition upon the second christening gift and its rôle in the story the poet proclaims his view that lying is a sin in the eyes of God: if and when the hero of *Seghelijn van Jherusalem* because of circumstances resorts to a lie he will be heavily punished for it by God.

At the same time, however, the question may be asked whether the poet himself always tells the truth. In his story he presents a fictional hero – child of an equally fictional pagan king of Jerusalem and his crypto-Christian wife –, a hero whom the poet after many adventures has end up as pope. In his lifetime Seghelijn fights pagan giants, begets seven sons by as many pagan princesses, is therefore condemned by God to spend fifteen years in a dungeon, is granted mercy after this penance and subsequently relieves Rome, which is being besieged by pagans. To reward him for his dedication the Roman emperor Constantine offers him the hand of his daughter Florette, and at the wedding his mother-in-law Helena persuades him to join her to the Holy Land to find the Holy Cross. After their return – with the Cross! – Seghelijn for a while bears the crown of Rome, but when he kills his parents 'by accident', he withdraws into a tree as a hermit. Fifteen years later he will be taken away from the tree as the ruling pope Celestin – just before his death – had nominated Seghelijn his successor. When he accepts that office and assumes the papal name Benedict I the prophecy of the third christening present is fulfilled: he ends his life as an exemplary saint.

---

14. The *Seghelijn van Jherusalem* is quoted after J. Verdam (ed.), *Seghelijn van Jherusalem naar het Berlijnsche handschrift en den ouden druk van wege de Maatschappij der Nederlandsche Letterkunde uitgegeven door...* (Leiden, 1878). The most recent reflection on this text is Geert H.M. Claassens, 'Dat en is sonder reden niet. Over de zeven vragen van Seghelijn van Jherusalem', in: *Spiegel der Letteren* 40 (1998), 25-54. A short introduction in English is given in: Geert H.M. Claassens, '*Seghelijn van Jherusalem*', in: John M. Jeep (ed.), *Medieval Germany. An Encyclopedia* (New York & London, 2001), 715.

15. Cf. *Seghelijn van Jherusalem*, ll. 224-251 (Verdam, *Seghelijn*, 4).

From a modern point of view we would not hesitate to consider *Seghelijn van Jherusalem* fiction. The poet creates a chronotope – a space-time-constellation – in which a number of referential elements (Jerusalem, Rome, Emperor Constantine) do admittedly play a rôle, but in which the fictional, non-referential elements prevail: the character Seghelijn and his parents, the fights with giants, and Seghelijn's marriage into the imperial family – and these are only a few of the narrative elements that have come up in the extremely abbreviated summary given above. Assessing the story 'with the eyes of the times' is a lot more difficult: we cannot find out for each narrative element whether it was considered referential or non-referential by the story's contemporary audience. That mediaeval literature portrays much which at the time was considered referential, but which we now consider non-referential, may be deduced from the prominent place of hagiography in the literary spectrum of the Middle Ages. The miracles of the numerous saints' lives were assumed to be true: skepsis on that part would not only disqualify the story, but would also take the ground from under the cherished concept of 'sanctity'.[16] An historical criticism of mediaeval narrative sources will therefore always have to take into account this distinction, at the risk of a completely distorted assessment of authorial possibilities and intentions, and of the contemporary interpretations of mediaeval sources.

Does this mean that we cannot draw sensible conclusions on the degree to which the mediaeval audience experienced *Seghelijn van Jherusalem* as referential or non-referential? No reception evidence for this chivalric romance has come down to us to be interrogated, but the text itself offers the possibility of sensible speculation.

At the wedding of Seghelijn and Florette his new mother-in-law Helena speaks to him:

> 'Soete vrient Seghelijn,
> Wiltu mi ghehulpich sijn,
> Wi souden soeken gaen dat cruys,
> Daer aen hinc die soete Jhesus,
> Ende bringhent hier in dese stede.
> So hadden wi al daer God mede
> Was ghepassijt dore us.'
> Seghelijn sprac: 'Vrouwe, dat cruys
> So willic u helpen halen.'

---

16. The *Wahrheitsanspruch* of hagiographies is discussed in Aviad M. Kleinberg, *Prophets in their own Country. Saints and the Making of Sainthood in the Later Middle Ages* (Chicago, 1992), particularly 40-70.

Die vrouwe dancte hem der talen.
Si ghinghen reeden hare vaert,
Te varen te Jherusalem waert.[17]

['Dear friend Seghelijn, if you are willing to assist me then we might be able to find the cross on which sweet Jesus hung, and bring it to this town. Then we would have brought everything together with which God for our sake underwent the passion.' Seghelijn spoke: 'Lady, I want to help you fetch the cross.' The lady thanked him for these words. They went and prepared their journey to Jerusalem.]

If you really want to find the Holy Cross, then you have to travel to Jerusalem. Indeed, Golgotha lies just outside that town, and it is at that spot that the important passion relic lies hidden. But this is the only passage in *Seghelijn van Jherusalem* in which the Holy Cross is directly linked with Jerusalem. The further development of the story shows that Helena, Seghelijn and their retinue are looking for and find the cross near the town of Ysona, and not in Jerusalem. Ysona is admittedly attributed the same *grandeur* as Jerusalem, but the explicit statement that these two towns are 'seven miles' from each other makes it impossible factually to identify the two.[18]

It seems unlikely to me that the contemporary audience would not have noticed this historical 'untruth'. The story of Christ' passion as it is recounted in the gospels may be assumed to have been well-known to everyone concerned. Moreover it is not only in relation to the gospels that the *Seghelijn*-Poet 'is lying': by moving the finding of the cross to Ysona he deviates from the *Inventio crucis*-legend as it was spread by *inter alia* the *Legenda aurea* of Jacobus de Voragine (†1298).[19] Our poet took several elements from this legend for his own version of the finding of the cross, but all in all gave the story his own twist. What is remarkable, however, is the fact that he did not in any way disguise a relationship with the *Inventio crucis*-legend. On the contrary, in the prologue to *Seghelijn van Jherusalem* he very explicitly drew the attention to the fact with the words:

Want men in die kerke mach lesen,
Hoe dat soete cruys wart vonden,
Daer God aen sterf doer onse sonden.

---

17. *Seghelijn van Jherusalem*, ll. 8715-8726 (Verdam, *Seghelijn*, 118).
18. *Seghelijn van Jherusalem*, ll. 9983-10.010 (*descriptio* of Ysona) and 10.021 (the distance between Jerusalem and Ysona) (Verdam, *Seghelijn*, 135-136).
19. The *Legenda aurea* of Jacobus de Voragine is quoted after Giovanni Paolo Maggioni (ed.), *Iacopo da Varazze, Legenda aurea*, 2 vols (Firenze, 1998 [2nd, revised edition]). The *Inventio crucis*-legend in vol. I, 459-470.

Men seyt dat Helena vant: (...).²⁰
[For in church one can hear how the sweet cross was found on which God died for our sins. It is said that Helena found it.]

From the way in which *Seghelijn van Jherusalem* has been handed down to us – one nearly complete manuscript has been preserved, plus one incunable and another five sixteenth-century printings, in addition to which at least one excerpt testifies to the story's popularity²¹ – we cannot but infer that the audience did not hold his failure to adhere strictly to historical truth against the poet. At the same time, and from a mediaeval perspective, the finding of the cross cannot be considered a negligible footnote in history.

Why the poet took some liberties with history can be explained quite easily. After all the prophecy had said that Seghelijn, following the Judas and Julian legends on which this part of the text is based,²² would kill his parents, and in a repetition of this prophecy by a divine messenger he was told not to return to Jerusalem:

'Hoerdijt, Seghelijn, joncheer?
Ter stat waert niet en keer:
Dat ontbiet u ons Here God.
Doedijt oec, du biste sot:
U soude ghescien veel rouwen.
Ghi en moeght nemmermere scouwen
Vader noch moeder op ghenen dach,
Ghi en sout hem gheven den dootslach.
Scouwe tlant ende die stede.'²³
['Did you hear that, master Seghelijn? Do not return to the town, this is what God our Lord bids you do. If you do so, you are foolish: much sadness would come over you. You must never again look at your father and mother, at no time, for otherwise you would kill them. Avoid the country and the town.']

The poet was therefore unable to have Seghelijn and Helena find the cross in Jerusalem, as in that case Seghelijn's parents would die a premature death. Yet however simple and plausible this narrative explanation is for

---

20. *Seghelijn van Jherusalem*, ll. 42-45 (Verdam, *Seghelijn*, 1).
21. The manuscript and printed versions of the *Seghelijn van Jherusalem* are discussed in I. Van de Wijer, 'Segheliin van Jherusalem. Tekstoverlevering van een Middelnederlands ridderdicht', in: *Quaerendo*, 14 (1984), 273-304.
22. On the use of sources in the *Seghelijn van Jherusalem*, cf. J.D. Janssens, *Dichter en publiek in creatief samenspel. Over interpretatie van Middelnederlandse ridderromans* (Leuven, 1988), 106-142 and Claassens, 'Dat en is sonder reden niet', 45-48.
23. *Seghelijn van Jherusalem*, ll. 2717-2725 (Verdam, *Seghelijn*, 37).

the historical twist under consideration, it does not in any way explain why the contemporary audience accepted it.

My interpretation is that the *Seghelijn*-Poet prepared his audience for such an acceptance through his prologue. He opens the prologue with an invocation of Mary – may she ask her Son to assist the poet in his venture – which turns into a *captatio benevolentiae* through which the poet wants to bring his audience to the desired receptive attitude. He seems to anticipate 'mixed' reactions:

> Dese hystorie ende schone dinghen,
> Die ic hier te dichten ghere
> Soe dat ic blive in mijn ere,
> Sonder scande ende lachter
> Van hem diet sullen lesen hier achter
> Ende hoeren sullen, sijnt leec of clerc.[24]
> [This history and the pretty stories that I want to versify here, so that my honour remain intact and I do not suffer shame and slander from those who shall read or hear it afterwards, be they laymen or clerics.]

Apparently he does not exclude the possibility that someone or other, learned or not, would not agree with his view and story. Why not? The following lines raise a corner of the veil, when the poet says:

> Want het wort een sonderlike werc
> Ende ene aventure waer,
> Die gheviel dertich jaer
> Na dat God die doot ontfinc
> Ende doer ons aent cruce hinc.[25]
> [For it will become an exceptional story and a veritable adventure, which took place thirty years after God received Death and hung from the cross for our sake.]

The combination of 'exceptional story' and 'veritable adventure', followed by the very specific historical positioning of the story thirty years after Christ's death on the cross, has to prepare the audience for a story that is all but common, but that at the same time cannot be seen as separate from the history of salvation. Yet the preparation of the audience has not come to an end yet. Using a rhetorical trick the poet tries to establish a relationship between himself, his story, and the audience:

> Wonder heeft mi, dat si vergaten,
> Die hem wilen dichtens vermaten

---

24. *Seghelijn van Jherusalem*, ll. 14-19 (Verdam, *Seghelijn*, 1).
25. *Seghelijn van Jherusalem*, ll. 20-24 (Verdam, *Seghelijn*, 1).

Van boerden ende menighen jeesten,
Ende si lieten metter keesten
Dese edel hystorie achter.[26]

[I am surprised that they should have forgotten this, those who formerly took it upon themselves to versify many a fabliau and geste, and that with the cores they should also have left behind this noble history.]

In other words, he asks his audience to go along with his amazement at the fact that this 'noble history' has not been told before. Compared to all the *boerden* (fabliaux) – a term I want to interpret here as 'fabrication' – and *jeesten* (gestes) – to be understood as 'account of actions in the past' – which have been made public, the history of Seghelijn has strangely enough fallen by the wayside. Moreover by associating this story with the concept of *keest*, 'the pith, the core, the marrow, the best', the poet seems to call up an interpretative framework founded on the Bible. Mediaeval biblical exegesis is familiar with a comparison – based on Matthew 13:24-30 – in which the literal and the symbolic meanings of the Bible are compared with chaff and wheat, or with the hard shell and the sweet core of a nut.[27] Is the poet, in alluding to this biblical-exegetical comparison, asking his audience to accept a story that is yet untold, a story that should moreover not be taken literally? It definitely looks like it.

Of course this story has not been told before: the poet has composed it himself. The lines quoted above already suggest that the story positions itself somewhere between a fabrication (*boerde*/*fabliau*) and a realistic account (*jeeste*/*geste*), although the poet will later in the prologue make it clear in an almost paradoxical way that the audience should not expect a 'true' history. The lines quoted above, in which he links his own story with the *Inventio crucis*-legend and with Helena, are followed by this announcement:

Men seyt dat Helena vant:
Het was waer, mer een wigant
Wasser mede, een deghen fijn,
Van Jherusalem Seghelijn,
Daer ic u af segghen sal.[28]

---

26. *Seghelijn van Jherusalem*, ll. 25-29 (Verdam, *Seghelijn*, 1).
27. On the comparison between the chaff and the wheat in biblical exegesis see for example G.R. Evans, *The Language and Logic of the Bible. The Earlier Middle Ages* (Cambridge, 1984), 13-17. The comparison also occurs elsewhere in Middle Dutch literature, e.g. in the prologue to Jacob van Maerlant's *Scolastica* (c. 1271).
28. *Seghelijn van Jherusalem*, ll. 45-49 (Verdam, *Seghelijn*, 1-2).

[It is said that Helena found it [= the Holy Cross], which is true, but with her was some warrior, a good knight, Seghelijn of Jherusalem, of whom I will now tell you].

Everyone who was familiar with the story — and we may assume them to have been many — will surely have known that nowhere in the legend surrounding the finding of the Cross do we find any references to a brave knight Seghelijn of Jherusalem who assisted Helena in her search for the Holy Cross. Stronger yet: everyone who knew the version of the *Legenda aurea* might have known that the legend of the finding of the Cross contained an historical 'problem' — even without Seghelijn —, and that problem is, moreover, explicitly mentioned.[29] In the legend Helena is said to meet an eye-witness of Christ's death on the cross, while Jacobus de Voragine points out that more than 270 years must have passed between the crucifixion and Helena's quest, which makes her alleged meeting with an eye-witness rather less credible (unless people lived longer in those days).[30] It is this historical impossibility which is also expressed in the prologue to *Seghelijn van Jherusalem*: if the story ties in with Helena's quest then it is of course impossible for it to have taken place thirty years after Christ's death on the cross.[31]

In this way the prologue seems to contain a number of clear signals to the audience, warning it not to expect *Seghelijn van Jherusalem* to be pure historiography. At the same time the poet nowhere explicitly mentions that he is writing fiction. If the Bible prohibits the use of 'idle words' it is not, of course, self-evident for him to claim bluntly that he is writing fiction. What the poet does do, however, is to point out explicitly to the audience that his story contains a meaning:

Men machse lesen sonder lachter
Voer elken die aen Gode gheloeft,

---

29. In my opinion the *Seghelijn*-Poet was closely familiar with Jacobus's *Legenda aurea*. Elsewhere I have pointed out that he used a part of the legend of St Andrew from this collection. Cf. Claassens, 'Dat en is sonder reden niet', 45-48.

30. Cf. Jacobus de Voragine, *Legenda aurea*, lxiv (De inventione sancte crvcis): *Non uidetur autem multum probabile quod pater istius Iude tempore passionis Christi esse potuerit, cum a passione Christi usque ad Helenam, sub qua Iudas fuit, fluxerunt plus quam ducenti septuaginta anni, nisi forte diceretur quod tunc homines plus quam modo uiuebant* (Maggioni, *Iacopo da Varazze*, I, 466). [It does not seem very probable, however, that this Jew's father could have lived at the time of Christ's passion, because from that time to Helena's, when this Judas is supposed to have told his story, more than 270 years had elapsed – unless, perhaps, it could be said that men lived longer then than they do now. (translation by William Granger Ryan, *Jacobus de Voragine, The Golden Legend, Readings on the Saints*. Princeton 1993, I, p. 281)].

31. *Seghelijn van Jherusalem*, ll. 22-24 (Verdam, *Seghelijn*, 1).

Ende al waer een mensche verdoeft,
Van redene dom ende blent,
Hi warde saen bekent,
Indien dat hi reden verstoede.[32]
[The story may be read without shame to everyone who believes in God, and even if a human being were to be dazed, of weakened mind and blind, it would be immediately clear to him when he learns of its meaning.]

Here too he is manipulating his audience with rhetorical means: there are no elements in this story which would be shameful for a good christian, and it is unthinkable that a human being would be so foolish, stupid and blind as not to te able to understand this story.

Using these means the *Seghelijn*-Poet tries to enter into a pact with his audience: 'I know that you know that this story will contain some elements that are historically untrue, but let us agree not to make a fuss about them, for the meaning is much more important than the historical or factual truths which are here or there stretched somewhat.' In fact the poet is offering his audience a kind of contract: the story may contain certain untruths on the historical level, on the moral level it is a true story.[33] In other words, he is asking the audience not to judge the story purely by its referentiality, but to read it primarily as a linguistic vehicle for a message that is of great educational value within the entire framework of the history of salvation – to which the story is explicitly linked.

IV

In this way the religious *cum* moral foundation of the opposition between 'true' and 'untrue' precisely creates the possibility of using a (largely) invented story for ethical purposes. In fact this is acknowledged by Jan van Boendale in his poetics referred to earlier. When he brings up Aesop's and Avianus's fables and the stories about Reynard the Fox, he specifies their non-referential nature by pointing out the fact that in these stories animals can talk: talking animals do not exist, so these stories are by definition non-referential. Yet that does not mean that they are utter lies to Boendale: they are untrue, because impossible, at the level of their link with extra-literary reality, but on the ethical level they are true, for

---

32. *Seghelijn van Jherusalem*, ll. 30-35 (Verdam, *Seghelijn*, 1).
33. I found much inspiration for this approach in Monika Otter, *Inventiones. Fiction and referentiality in twelfth-century English historical writing* (Chapel Hill, 1996).

they contribute to our understanding of moral meanings. He puts the argument in the following words:

> Dat dese dinc vonden was,
> Was al om lere ende wijsheit,
> Als ic u voren hebbe gheseit;
> Want een sin, die is zwaer,
> Die maken exemple claer;
> Want in parabolen God selve sprac
> Sine sermoene die hi vertrac.[34]
>
> [These [= stories about Reynard] have been composed entirely for the purpose of instruction and wisdom, as I told you before, for a meaning that is difficult to grasp can be elucidated by instructive examples; after all, God himself couched the sermons that he preached in parables.][35]

For Boendale these invented stories are therefore acceptable only as didactic aids in clarifying a difficult message. The argument he adduces cannot really be refuted: Jesus too used stories – parables, allegories – to explain his teachings to his disciples. Everyone can read so in the gospels! Boendale incidentally does not say explicitly that Jesus's parables were invented, but by putting them in this context he is at least suggesting so. Slightly later Boendale warns the reader that this use of fiction should not be exclusively aimed at entertaining the audience, and that it had even better be omitted:

> Want wi van allen ydelen woorden
> Ten oordele sullen antwoorden.
> Dus en salmen lieghen niet
> In hystorien, wats ghesciet.[36]
>
> [Yet one had better refrain from this, for on the Day of Judgement we shall have to account for all idle talk. Therefore, when writing history one must on no account tell lies.][37]

In other words: although the use of fiction may in some cases be defensible, mixing non-referential matters into a text that strives for referentiality remains so hazardous as to endanger the writer's spiritual salvation and eternal life.

---

34. Jan van Boendale, *Der leken spiegel*, III, 15, ll. 192-198 (De Vries, *Der leken spieghel*, III, 166).
35. The translation given above is by Erik Kooper, in Gerritsen et al. 1994, 253-258, quote on 256.
36. Jan van Boendale, *Der leken spiegel*, III, 15, ll. 205-208 (De Vries, *Der leken spieghel*, III, 166-167).
37. The translation given above is by Erik Kooper, in Gerritsen et al. 1994, 253-258, quote op 256.

V

As far as mediaeval literature is concerned we could – following Boendale – see 'true' and 'untrue' as the two extremes of a sliding scale, which I shall at this occasion christen the 'Scale of Boendale'. On this scale the various texts take up their position as being to a larger or to a smaller degree referential. It is of course impossible to describe the 'non-referential' pole in absolute terms: through the very use of language as a medium every text retains some form of referentiality. Yet the further a story moves away from historical reality as it was then seen, the more that text will approach the 'non-referential' pole.

The mediaeval beast stories will undoubtedly have been situated close to the pole of 'non-referentiality' on the 'Scale of Boendale'; nevertheless they were very popular. Their highly non-referential nature was therefore no argument to reject them categorically as stories, or at least Boendale by no means does so. At the same time, though, he only accepts these non-referential animal stories because they are true in a moral sense, and because they can be appreciated as significant and meaningful metaphors. If that is not the case, the text concerned – or a part thereof – should be considered a lie.

At the other end of the scale should be situated the *artes*-texts and the encyclopaedic works such as *Der naturen bloeme* [*The Bloom of Nature*] (c.1270) by the famous Flemish poet Jacob van Maerlant († ca. 1290).[38] These kinds of texts are themselves closely followed by those historical texts that aimed for a high degree of referentiality. A good example of the latter to me seems to be another work by Jacob van Maerlant, namely *Ystory van Troyen* [*History of Troy*] (c.1264).[39] He too offers his audience a contract, but one with clearly different terms from that of *Seghelijn van Jherusalem*. Maerlant also ties in with an existing text – the Middle Dutch *Trojeroman* [*Romance of Troy*] by Segher Diengotgaf[40] – which

---

38. On Jacob van Maerlant and his oeuvre see Frits van Oostrom, *Maerlants wereld* (Amsterdam, 1996). A short introduction in English is given in Geert H.M. Claassens, 'Jacob van Maerlant (ca. 1230-ca. 1290)', in: John M. Jeep (ed.), *Medieval Germany. An Encyclopedia* (New York & London, 2001), 403-405.

39. Jacob van Maerlants *Istory van Troyen* is quoted after Nap. De Pauw and E. Gaillard (eds), *Die Istory van Troyen*, 4 vols (Gent, 1889-1892). An important study of this text is L. Jongen, *Van Achilles tellen langhe. Onderzoekingen over Maerlants bewerking van Statius' Achilleis in de Historie van Troyen* (Deventer, 1988).

40. The *Trojeroman* by Segher Diengotgaf has been edited in Jozef Janssens and Ludo Jongen, *Segher Diengotgaf, Trojeroman* (Amsterdam, 2001). A short introduction in English is given in Geert H.M. Claassens, 'Segher Diengotgaf (fl. 1200-ca. 1260)', in: John M. Jeep (ed.), *Medieval Germany. An Encyclopedia* (New York & London, 2001), 715-716.

he intends to complete. The history of the Trojan War should, according to him, definitely start with the story of Jason and his quest for the Golden Fleece.[41] Maerlant continues with a prayer for inspiration, in which he simultaneously defines his position *vis à vis* the audience:

> Nu bid ic Gade dat Hy my sende
> Synen geest, daer ic by vinde
> Vray, reyn ende scone woert,
> Ende by synre cracht ghestoert
> Die ghene syn, te alre tyt,
> Om myn ghedichte draghen nyt.[42]
> [Now I pray to God that He may let the spirit come over me, so that I may be able to find true, pure and beautiful words, and that through His power those who hold spite in their hearts because of my poem may always be ruined.]

Compared to the *Seghelijn*-Poet Maerlant takes up a much more robust position: he does not try to find a rhetorical 'we' uniting the poet and his audience, but posits a self-confident 'I', convinced of his own abilities against those who treat his work unfairly.

While the *Seghelijn*-Poet ties in with a legend passed down from the pulpit, Maerlant introduces an eyewitness of his history, Dares Phrygius. He does not mention the title of the latter's work, namely *De excidio Troiae historia*, but does underline Dares's impartiality in presenting the facts. He even reveals the detours along which this important book has come down to him.[43] Next Maerlant identifies his other sources, Homer, Ovid and Statius, and says that he will offer his audience a verifiable argument by indicating in his work where he has borrowed from these *auctoritates*.[44] The main source of his work is revealed last, namely the *Roman de Troie* (c.1160) by Benoît de Sainte Maure, of which he emphasizes that even though it is a rhyming French text, it is based on a Latin source, thus suggesting that it is a reliable text.[45] Lastly Maerlant

---

41. Jacob van Maerlant, *Ystory van Troyen*, ll. 4-20 (De Pauw & Gaillard, *Die Istory van Troyen*, I, 1).
42. Jacob van Maerlant, Ystory van Troyen, ll. 21-26 (De Pauw & Gaillard, Die Istory van Troyen, I, 1-2).
43. Jacob van Maerlant, *Ystory van Troyen*, ll. 27-42 (De Pauw & Gaillard, *Die Istory van Troyen*, I, 2). Comp. Jongen *Van Achilles tellen langhe*, 178-180.
44. Jacob van Maerlant, *Ystory van Troyen*, ll. 43-49 (De Pauw & Gaillard, *Die Istory van Troyen*, I, 2).
45. Jacob van Maerlant, *Ystory van Troyen*, ll. 50-52 (De Pauw & Gaillard, *Die Istory van Troyen*, I, 1-2). Comp. Jongen (*Van Achilles tellen langhe*, 179-180) who points out that Maerlant must have been aware that his use of Benoit's *Roman de Troie* enhanced the risk of historical incorrectness. Here, as elsewhere in his oeuvre, Maerlant does not hesi-

identifies himself as the author of the *Ystory van Troyen*: with his name and reputation, and referring to his earlier works he offers himself as a guarantor of the quality of the work at hand.[46]

The contract Maerlant offers his audience clearly leaves less room for doubt on the referential quality of his text. He joins the established historiographical tradition and does not try to strike a bargain with his audience,[47] but on the contrary takes up a highly self-confident position. When he writes at the end of the prologue:

> In den Duytsche dichtet Jacop
> Van Merlant: doer nyemans scop
> So en wilt hys niet begheven,
> Eer dit boeck is al volscreven.[48]
> [This was versified in Dutch by Jacob van Maerlant: and he will not cease for anyone's mockery before this book is completely finished.]

he almost seems to be formulating a challenge: try to prove that my history of the Trojan war is not all correct!

The fact that Maerlant's strict historiographical stance is no guarantee for perfect historical reliability is also made clear in his invocation of Dares Phrygius. The latter, whom Maerlant so explicitly advances as an eyewitness, did not take part in the Trojan War at all. The war in question in all probability took place at the beginning of the thirteenth century *before* Christ, while *De excidio Troiae historia* was written only in the fifth century *after* Christ.[49] At the same time, though, this is an anachronistic comment: just like his contemporaries Maerlant was fully convinced that Dares had actually lived through the Trojan war and put it on record as an eyewitness. We would be unjustly imposing our own norms on Maerlant if we were not to accept him as historiographer because of Dares.

---

tate to correct his sources. On Maerlant's use of sources in general see Petra Berendrecht, *Proeve van bekwaamheid. Jacob van Maerlant en de omgang met zijn Latijnse bronnen* (Amsterdam, 1996).

46. Jacob van Maerlant, *Ystory van Troyen*, ll. 53-60 (De Pauw & Gaillard, *Die Istory van Troyen*, I, 2).

47. The importance of being in line with the tradition as a warrant for historical truthfulness was very clearly acknowledged by Jan van Boendale in his poetical treatise. He lists a number of important writers, ranging form Moses to ... Jacob van Maerlant! Cf. Jan van Boendale, *Der leken spiegel*, III, 15, 235-296 (De Vries, *Der leken spieghel*, III, 168-170).

48. Jacob van Maerlant, *Ystory van Troyen*, ll. 53-56 (De Pauw & Gaillard, *Die Istory van Troyen*, I, 2).

49. On Dares Phrygius as authority on the Trojan war cf. Jongen, *Van Achilles tellen langhe*, 16-18.

If Maerlant's *Ystory van Troyen* approaches one end of the 'Scale of Boendale' and the mediaeval beast epic the other, the *Seghelijn van Jherusalem* will be relatively equidistant from either end. Yet precisely where a text should be positioned on the line between fiction and non-fiction cannot be laid down in absolute terms. Moreover this will not have been the same spot for each mediaeval man or woman.

As I have said before: the way the *Seghelijn van Jherusalem* has come down to us suggests that the audience accepted the contract offered by the poet. That that interpretation may not be valid for each member of the audience will be self-evident. Moreover it seems improbable to me that Jan van Boendale would have accepted this text, which presents itself as 'history', as such. After all, in his poetics he rejects the tale of *Karel ende Elegast* [*Charlemagne and Elegast*] – a short Middle Dutch romance about Charlemagne – as untrue. The latter text relates how Charlemagne went out stealing one night and thus discovered a conspiracy against his life.[50] The order to go stealing was allegedly passed on to him by an angel from God, yet Boendale does not seem to accept this, as may become clear from the following quote from his poetics:

> Men leest dat Kaerle voer stelen:
> Ic segt u, al zonder helen,
> Dat Kaerl noit en stal.[51]
> [The story goes that Charlemagne went out to steal; I tell you, quite frankly, that Charlemagne never stole.][52]

When we confront this firm rejection with the beginning of *Karel ende Elegast*, we can only conclude that Boendale did not accept the contract that this anonymous poet had offered his audience, despite the fact that it shows similarities with that of the *Seghelijn*-Poet. *Karel ende Elegast* also subtly warns against the singularity of the story, which is clearly woven around an historical figure, and goes on to trie to make a connection with the audience as a guarantee for the story:

> Hoort hier wonder ende waerhede!
> Wat den coninc daer ghevel,

---

50. *Karel ende Elegast* is quoted after Geert Claassens (ed.), *Karel ende Elegast* (Amsterdam, 2002), its relationship with history and historiography is surveyed on p. 10. A short introduction in English is given in Irene Spijker, 'Charlemagne Epics, Middle Dutch', in: John M. Jeep (ed.), *Medieval Germany. An Encyclopedia*. (New York & London, 2001), 102-103.

51. Jan van Boendale, *Der leken spiegel*, III, 15, ll. 133-135 (De Vries, *Der leken spieghel*, III, 163-164).

52. The translation given above is by Erik Kooper, in Gerritsen et al. (1994), 253-258, quote on p. 255.

Dat weten noch die menige wel, (...).⁵³
[Hark here, wonder and truth! What happened to the king there many will remember, (...).]

That *Karel ende Elegast* will not be far removed from the *Seghelijn van Jherusalem* on the line between referential and non-referential will hereby hopefully have become clear, as will the probability that the relative positions of diverse texts will not have been identical to every mediaeval man or woman.

VI

I am nearing the end of my argument. Even if it has been only minimally convincing, we may at least claim that fictionality is not a real problem in a mediaeval literary context. We can obviously question the extent to which a mediaeval text is referential or non-referential, but for the contemporary audience that will have been a question that went further than a look at the similarities between the story and historical reality: reliability is a moral rather than an historical category. A non-referential text may propagate a moral truth and thereby become acceptable, while a text intended to be referential may contain so many 'historical errors' as to be morally unacceptable. Moreover, specific medieval views of individual texts can only be traced in approximation. If there happen to be judgements on texts by third parties, such as Boendale's on *Karel ende Elegast*, they may of course be clues.⁵⁴ But as individual assessments and points of view play a rôle in the matter, we cannot always accept those judgements as decisive and as generally accepted.

There can be no doubt that a number of other elements played a rôle in mediaeval conceptions of (non-)referentiality and the moral value of texts:⁵⁵ is a text written in the vernacular or in Latin – with Latin, as the language of the Church and of scholarship obviously weighing in more

---

53. *Karel ende Elegast*, ll. 8-10 (Claassens, *Karel ende Elegast*, 20).

54. See, for example, Jacob van Maerlant's judgement on a number of Arthurian romances (cf. Geert H.M. Claassens and David F. Johnson, 'Arthurian Literature in the Medieval Low Countries: An Introduction', in: *King Arthur in the Medieval Low Countries,* Mediaevalia Lovaniensia, Series I, Studia XXVIII (Leuven, 2000), 1-34, esp. 1-4).

55. I deliberately refrain from giving extensive bibliographical references on these elements, precisely because there are so many available. And, moreover, I know of no contribution which convincingly argues for an absolute criterium by which to distinguish between referentiality and non-referentiality in mediaeval literature.

heavily? Is it written in prose or in verse – after all, bound language imposes restrictions on the writer? Are there any links with oral tradition? Have any sources been used and if so, which ones? And along the same lines: how does the writer position himself and his text *vis à vis* tradition, to what links does he commit himself?

The key to this seems to me to be the contract an author offers his audience, in which the elements summed up above clearly have their rôle, and which often after careful analysis reveals where on the 'Scale of Boendale' a text should be situated.

Maybe someone will – after reading this contribution – conclude that even though I have shown that the opposition between fiction and non-fiction does not constitute a real problem in mediaeval literature, I have not got round to my second thesis. Well, the fact that vernacular texts should not in principle be judged differently from Latin texts with regard to their relationship to historical reality follows quite logically from a very simple premise: lying is just as easy in Latin as in any vernacular you may care to think of.

Steven VANDERPUTTEN

UNE ICONOGRAPHIE DE L'HISTORIOGRAPHIE MONASTIQUE: RÉALITÉ OU FICTION?[1]

Au cours des dernières décennies, ceux qui étudient l'iconographie des manuscrits médiévaux ont largement abandonné une approche purement axée sur l'histoire de l'art. Celle-ci a été remplacée par un modèle interprétatif, qui place résolument au centre du débat la relation entre le texte et l'image et la fonction communicative de l'image elle-même. A l'issue de cette révolution paradigmatique, les traditions iconographiques sont aujourd'hui traitées comme des facteurs déterminants dans l'interprétation des textes, surtout si celle-ci doit permettre de comprendre les contextes dans lesquels ces derniers étaient lus.[2] Il faut, pourtant, admettre que cette 'nouvelle vague' dans l'étude des manuscrits s'est souvent faite sentir à travers les études de textes (ou de manuscrits) singuliers.[3] Plutôt que de répéter cet exercice, je voudrais m'inspirer d'une nouvelle tendance qui consiste à examiner la relation entre texte et image de façon structurelle, autrement dit de voir à quel point le discours d'un certain type de texte (hagiographie, historiographie, etc.) s'appuie sur des programmes iconographiques.[4] Malgré les désavantages évidents de cette

---

1. S. Vanderputten est *'Chargé de Recherches du Fonds de la Recherche Scientifique – Flandre (F.W.O.-Vlaanderen)'*.
Le texte de cet article est une version révisée d'une présentation que j'ai faite le 8 Octobre 2002 à la Bibliothèque Nationale Albert I à Bruxelles, à l'occasion du congrès 'Manuscripts in transition'. Je me borne ici à donner un aperçu général de la situation telle qu'elle résulte de l'étude des manuscrits. Pour une étude plus approfondie voir mon article '"Historical imagery"? The social meaning of the image in monastic historiography', *Scriptorium*, 57 (2003), p. 194-222.
2. S. Ringboom, 'Some pictorial conventions for the recounting of thoughts and experiences in late medieval art', dans *Medieval Iconography and Narrative. A Symposium* (Odense, 1980), p. 41.
3. Voir, par example, V.F. Fines, 'Reading Medieval Images: Two Miniatures in a Fifteenth-Century Missal', dans M.M. Manion et B.J. Muir, *Medieval Texts and Images. Studies of Manuscripts from the Middle Ages* (Chur, Reading, Paris, Philadelphia, Tokyo, Melbourne et Sydney, 1991), p. 127.
4. J.G. Alexander, 'Facsimiles, Copies, and Variations: The Relationship to the Model in Medieval and Renaissance European Illuminated Manuscripts', dans *Retaining the Original. Multiple Originals, Copies, and Reproductions (Center for Advanced Study in the Visual Arts Symposium Papers VII)*, (New England, 1989), p. 63.

approche, les résultats d'une étude pareille permettent de mieux évaluer la représentativité des manuscrits splendides qui ont fait l'objet de nombreuses études.

L'un des types de texte dont les mécanismes de transmission et de reproduction restent peu documentés est sans doute l'historiographie monastique. Dans le cadre de cet article, j'ai choisi de soumettre à un examen analytique l'imagerie utilisée dans les manuscrits de provenance monastique contenant des annales, gestes et chroniques écrites par des moines qui vivaient dans les Pays-Bas Méridionaux.[5] Vu que l'étude de l'histoire profane n'occupait qu'une place marginale dans l'ensemble de la vie intellectuelle des moines,[6] il est surprenant de voir l'intensité avec laquelle l'historiographie monastique s'est manifestée durant une grande partie de l'époque médiévale. Dans la région qui nous concerne ici, plus de cent soixante-dix textes ont été produits entre le neuvième et le quinzième siècle. De cette masse de textes, il nous reste environ deux cent soixante-cinq témoins manuscrits médiévaux, dont deux cent dix sont de provenance monastique.[7] Notre attention se concentrera ici sur les exemplaires illuminés dont on peut supposer qu'ils ont assisté les historiographes dans les efforts qu'ils accomplissaient en vue de fournir aux moines une identité collective, basée sur un sens d'historicité et de légitimité.

Au cours de mes recherches sur les manuscrits en question, il m'est vite apparu que les ressources financières et matérielles, investies dans la reproduction d'annales, de gestes et de chroniques restaient souvent assez limitées. Rien ne permet de reconnaître une tendance particulièrement développée à alléger (ou alourdir) l'expérience visuelle du texte historique à l'aide d'une multitude de rubrications, d'initiales et d'autres marques visuelles. Cette remarque doit immédiatement être suivie par une autre, qui concerne la décoration historiée et les miniatures. Dans la plupart des cas, les textes historiques sont préservés dans des contextes

---

5. Un aperçu détaillé des textes en question est à consulter dans les appendices de mon livre *Sociale perceptie en maatschappelijke positionering in de middeleeuwse monastieke historiografie (8ste-15de eeuw)*, 2 volumes (Bruxelles, 2001).

6. Voir mon article 'De plaats van de historiografie in het mentale blikveld van een middeleeuwse kloostergemeenschap: de getuigenis van de bibliotheekcatalogi', dans *Millennium*, 16 (2002), pp. 38-57.

7. Grâce à la base de données *Narrative Sources*, le répertoire qui couvre toute la production médiévale de textes narratifs dans la région, il est devenu facile de consulter cette information pour chaque texte individuel (http://www.narrative-sources.be/). Dans les pages suivantes, j'utiliserai les codes du répertoire pour renvoyer aux listes des manuscrits et aux bibliographies.

manuscrits (souvent miscellanés) où l'iconographie n'est généralement pas utilisée comme outil discursif supplémentaire. En d'autres mots, les manuscrits de notre sélection ne comportent que rarement des images: sur deux cent dix manuscrits, seuls vingt-six ont été reconnus comme illustrés. Parmi ces derniers, dix-huit (ou moins de dix pour cent du total) portent des illustrations dans la partie historique du manuscrit.

Répartition à travers les siècles des manuscrits illustrés à l'historiographie monastique

Siècle de production	Nombre total de manuscrits	Manuscrits illustrés dans des sections non historiques	Manuscrits illustrés dans des sections historiques	
			Origine monastique	Origine non monastique ou incertaine
9	2	1	0	0
10	5	0	0	0
11	17	1	0	0
12	74	2	2	2
13	37	1	1	1
14	37	1	4	0
15	93	2	11	5

Ces chiffres, augmentés par ceux du tableau, ne sont pourtant pas décevants. Bien au contraire: ils permettent de formuler une conclusion à deux implications. En premier lieu, il n'a jamais été question d'une tendance structurelle chez les moines à agrémenter le discours du texte historique d'images, sauf peut-être à l'extrême fin du Moyen Âge. En deuxième lieu, ce manque d'intérêt pour l'imagerie historique est la cause première du fait que l'iconographie monastique ne s'est jamais développée un arsenal d'images et de représentations qui touchaient à des aspects de l'histoire profane.[8] Dans les pages qui suivent, nous verrons par exemple que l'iconographie dans les manuscrits du Moyen Âge tardif est presque systématiquement tributaire de celle utilisée dans les volumes destinés à un public non monastique. Cette évolution se laisse expliquer par l'impact croissant des ateliers laïcs (qui suivaient les modes contemporaines) sur la production des manuscrits.

8. M. Gill, 'The role of images in monastic education: the evidence from wall painting in late medieval England', dans G. Ferzoco et C. Muessig (eds.), *Medieval monastic education* (Londres et New York, 2000), p. 118.

En dépit de ces observations, il reste nécessaire de se demander à quel point le texte et l'image historique interagissent dans ces dix-huit manuscrits, dont on sait qu'ils ont été illustrés spécifiquement pour un public monastique.[9] Les premiers exemples de décoration iconographique dans les manuscrits historiques de notre sélection datent des alentours de l'année 1200.[10] Il s'agit de deux exemplaires de la chronique universelle de Sigebert de Gembloux († 1114).[11] Le premier, de la fin du douzième siècle, provient du monastère de Hautmont,[12] tandis que l'autre, remontant aux premières années du siècle suivant, a été produit pour (et probablement par) les moines d'Aulne-sur-Sambre.[13] Sur une trentaine de copies contemporaines (12e-13e siècles) de ce texte extrêmement répondu,[14] les deux manuscrits en question sont les seuls de provenance monastique dans lesquels j'ai retrouvé des preuves de décoration iconographique. Dans le premier volume (celui de Hautmont), on retrouve deux miniatures de confection rustique.[15] La première image, située sur le folio 1r, représente Ninus, le légendaire premier roi assyrien. Il est facile de deviner pourquoi cette figure obscure s'est vue attribuer une place si importante dans ce manuscrit. Sigebert avait eu l'intention explicite d'arranger l'histoire profane comformément la théorie des grands empires, dont il utilisait le symbolisme pour s'exprimer avec force sur la situation politique contemporaine. Il est parfaitement compréhensible que les

---

9. J.J.G. Alexander, 'Iconography and Ideology: Uncovering Social Meaning in Western Medieval Christian Art', dans *Studies in Iconography*, 15 (1993), pp. 6-8.

10. Pour des raisons typologiques, je passerai sur le manuscrit de la cartulaire-chronique de l'abbaye bénédictine de Saint-Bertin, qui contient un grand nombre de reproductions de sceaux dont les originaux étaient attachés aux chartes transcrites (Boulogne-sur-Mer, Bibliothèque Municipale, 146 et 146A (voir les fiches NaSo F014, S091 et G055)). Les reproductions de sceaux dans les cartulaires sont assez rares (J.L. Chassal, 'Dessins et mentions de sceaux dans les cartulaires médiévaux', dans O. Guyotjeannin, L. Morelle et M. Parisse (eds.), *Les cartulaires. Actes de la Table ronde organisée par l'École nationale des chartes et le G.D.R. 121 du C.N.R.S. (Paris, 5-7 décembre 1991)*, (Paris, 1993), pp. 154 et 165-166; voir, pour d'autres exemples, S. Lewis, *The Art of Matthew Paris in the Chronica Majora* (Aldershot, 1987), pp. 76-77 et A. De Loisne, 'Les miniatures du cartulaire de Marchiennes', dans *Bulletin archéologique du comité des travaux historiques et scientifiques* (1903), pp. 476-489).

11. C. Ondracek, 'Die lateinischen Weltchronicken bis in das 12. Jahrhundert', dans U. Knefelkamp (ed.), *Weltbild und Realität: Einführung in die mittelalterliche Geschichtsschreibung* (Pfaffenweiler, 1992), p. 2.

12. Paris, Bibliothèque Nationale, Nouvelles Aquisitions Latines, 1543. Voir J. Leclercq, 'Les manuscrits de l'abbaye d'Hautmont', dans *Scriptorium*, VII (1953), p. 65.

13. Bruxelles, Bibliothèque Royale, II 1055bis.

14. Voir la fiche dans *Narrative Sources* (NaSo S042).

15. Une troisième image a été sauvagement excisée de la feuille 52r.

artistes de ce manuscrit aient tenu à se présenter au lecteur avec une image introductrice représentant Ninus comme le 'premier' d'une lignée de souverains universels, qui s'étendait jusqu'à leur propre époque.

La deuxième image, située sur la feuille 50r, est un portrait de Sigebert lui-même, plongé apparemment dans ses pensées. Une initiale historiée dans le manuscrit d'Aulne-sur-Sambre permet de déduire que cette image a été inspirée par un désir de démontrer la qualité presque surhumaine de la chronique. Les artistes de ce dernier se sont laissés inspirer par l'iconographie des évangéliaires, dans lesquels l'auteur de chaque texte est souvent représenté au travail derrière son pupitre, pendant que l'inspiration divine (représentée par un pigeon) l'assiste dans ses efforts. La même imagerie se retrouve dans la deuxième copie de notre chronique (f. 1r voir illustration p. 266), où on constate que le 'portrait' de Sigebert a été inspiré plutôt par une volonté de mettre en évidence l'inspiration divine dans la composition de ce travail immense que par une volonté d'honorer l'auteur comme individu. L'attention des décorateurs des manuscrits universels se portait donc plutôt sur le caractère téléologique et rationnellement scandé (en *aetates*) de l'historiographie universelle et sur l'inspiration divine appuyant la rédaction d'œuvres de ce type que sur les faits historiques proprement dits. Aussi difficile qu'il fût de visualiser la théorie de l'histoire, l'histoire elle-même se laissait encore moins représenter par les moines.

Il faudra attendre jusqu'au quinzième siècle avant de trouver quelques rares exemples d'une iconographie en rapport avec des faits historiques concrets. La seule exception à cette règle est à trouver dans les manuscrits de Gilles li Muisis, abbé de la communauté bénédictine de Saint-Martin à Tournai depuis 1331. Son élection avait marqué le début d'une politique de réformes vigoureuses qui avaient pour but de réorganiser la communauté, d'instaurer une version réformée de la Règle et de redresser les finances de l'abbaye après des décennies de déclin institutionnel et moral.[16] En 1348, l'abbé fut frappé d'une cataracte aiguë provoquant une cécité passagère. N'étant jamais enclin à se laisser décourager par un accident de parcours, il compensa l'arrêt des réformes par la rédaction d'une œuvre littéraire, historique, moralisante, normative et généralement

---

16. A. D'Haenens, *L'abbaye Saint-Martin de Tournai de 1290 à 1350. Origines, évolution et dénouement d'une crise* (Louvain, 1961), pp. 175-176; 'La crise des abbayes bénédictines au bas Moyen Age: Saint-Martin de Tournai de 1290 à 1350', dans *Le Moyen Age*, LXV (1959), pp. 75-95 et 'Une oeuvre à restituer à Gilles li Muisis: La Chronique dite de Jacques Muevin', dans *Bulletin de la Commission Royale d'Histoire – Handelingen van de Koninklijke Commissie voor Geschiedenis*, CXXVII (1961), p. 16.

didactique (aujourd'hui connue comme les quatre *Tractati*), dont le contenu se concentra surtout sur la légitimation de la réforme et l'exposé systématique de ses principes de conduite et de gouvernement monastique. Ces activités ont été suivies par la confection d'un nombre de manuscrits somptueusement décorés et illustrés par le Tournaisien Piérart dou Tielt, qui dirigea un atelier dans la ville.[17]

A en juger par la décoration iconographique des *Tractati*,[18] li Muisis et ses associés les plus proches ont accompli des efforts considérables pour promouvoir le charisme du premier et l'image qu'on avait de lui dans la communauté monastique. Une série impressionnante d'images montre li Muisis en sa qualité de réformateur, de législateur et de diplomate (avec une multitude de partenaires: rois, papes, évêques, abbés, abbesses et citadins).[19] Aucun effort n'a également été ménagé pour démontrer que li Muisis était bien au courant de la situation politique contemporaine.[20] Les images du manuscrit de Courtrai nous montrent comment les moines de

---

17. Courtrai, Bibliothèque de la Ville, Fonds Goethals-Vercruysse, 135, vers 1350 (NaSo A036-A038; voir J. Casier et P. Bergmans, *L'art ancien dans les Flandres (région de l'Escaut). Mémorial de l'exposition rétrospective organisée à Gand en 1913. Tome deuxième. Orfèvreries - Miniatures de manuscrits - Tapisseries* (Bruxelles et Paris, 1921), pp. 43-45); Bruxelles, Bibliothèque Royale, 13076-13077, vers 1353 (Naso A039) et Bruxelles, Bibliothèque Royale, IV 119 (olim Dyson-Perrins, 53), de la même époque (Naso A040). Voir les dossiers dans *Narrative Sources* pour les éditions des textes. En ce qui concerne le débat touchant à la manière dont les *Tractati* ont été composés, voir G. Caullet, 'Les manuscrits de Gilles Le Muisit et l'art de la miniature au XIVe siècle. Le relieur Tournaisien Janvier', dans *Bulletijn van den Geschied- en Oudheidkundigen Kring te Kortrijk – Bulletin du Cercle Historique et Archéologique de Courtrai*, 5 (1907-1908), p. 205 et A. D'Haenens, 'Le Tractatus de consuetudinibus de Gilles Li Muisis', dans *Bulletin de la Commission Royale d'Histoire – Handelingen van de Koninklijke Commissie voor Geschiedenis*, CXXIV (1959), pp. 143-195). Je renvoie à mon étude approfondie (voir la note 1) pour une bibliographie et de plus amples commentaires.

18. M. Smeyers, *Vlaamse miniaturen van de 8ste tot het midden van de 16de eeuw. De middeleeuwse wereld op perkament* (Louvain, 1998), p. 151. A l'heure actuelle, des chercheurs à la KULeuven ont mis en cours des recherches approfondies relatives à l'oeuvre et les manuscrits de li Muisis. Sans doute seront-ils capables de reconsidérer plusieurs aspects de ce dossier.

19. Images de li Muisis comme érudit (Bruxelles, Bibliothèque Royale, IV 119, f. 21v), dictant ses oeuvres (Courtrai, Bibliothèque de la Ville, Fonds Goethals-Vercruysse, 135, f. 9r; voir *Medieval Mastery. Book illumination from Charlemagne to Charles the Bold 800-1475*, Louvain, 2002, pp. 246-247), abbé administrateur, promulguant ses *consuetudines* revisées aux membres de sa communauté (f. 29r). Pour ses relations avec à peu près toutes les ordres reconnus de la société contemporaine, le manuscrit du *Ch'est de l'estat* (Bruxelles, Bibliothèque Royale, IV 119) offre une iconographie qui ne laisse que peu de doutes à l'égard de l'image qu'on voulait projeter de lui (voir G. Warner, *Descriptive catalogue of illuminated manuscripts in the library of C.W. Dyson Perrins D.C.L., F.S.A.* Vol. I. *Text* (Oxford, 1920), pp. 105-107).

20. Voir Courtrai, Bibliothèque de la Ville, Fonds Goethals-Vercruysse, 135, f. 73r, 95r, 131v, et Bruxelles, Bibliothèque Royale, 13076-13077, f. 12v, 16v et 24v.

Saint-Martin se voyaient confrontés (assez soudainement, on peut le supposer) à une imagerie dont il n'avaient pas l'habitude: scènes de bataille, images de la joyeuse entrée du comte de Flandre dans les grandes villes de son territoire, des ravages de la peste, des pogroms sur les juifs dans le duché de Brabant et plus à l'est, et, finalement, de l'horreur des flagellants. Il faut, pourtant, attirer l'attention sur le fait qu'aucune de ces images évoque le milieu monastique auquel ces images étaient destinées, et que la première série d'images se concentre sur la personne de l'abbé lui-même, et ceci dans un contexte strictement contemporain. On peut ajouter que les décorateurs du manuscrit ne se sont jamais laissé séduire à confectionner des images de la communauté ou des édifices de l'abbaye, bien que la plus grande partie de l'activité littéraire de l'abbé portât sur l'histoire récente de son abbaye. En effet, dans la liste des quelques textes appartenant aux manuscrits des *Tractati* dépourvus de toute illustration, son aperçu de l'histoire récente de l'abbaye figure de façon prominente.[21] Apparemment, le déclin de l'autorité abbatiale, les catastrophes financières et le piètre état des bâtiments de l'abbaye dans le dernier demi-siècle suscitèrent des sentiments suffisamment vifs (ou traumatiques) chez les moines pour que le besoin d'une évocation en images ne se fasse nullement sentir.

L'attitude ambiguë des moines à l'égard du passé le plus récent est documentée de façon encore plus claire dans le manuscrit du *Tractatus quartus*.[22] A partir de la feuille 56r, li Muisis présente à ses lecteurs un aperçu concis et objectif de l'histoire de l'abbaye et de ses abbés depuis la fondation par Odon, qui remonte à la fin du onzième siècle. Les responsables de la décoration du manuscrit ont décidé de faire précéder ce texte par une image qui occupe presque la moitié de la page et qui a pour thème la destruction de l'abbaye par les Normands en 882.[23] Pour li Muisis et ses contemporains, il était assez évident que cette phase mythique de l'histoire de la communauté de Saint-Martin avait été conçue par des auteurs du douzième siècle désirant de se défendre contre les chanoines de Tournai, qui s'étaient violemment opposés à la fondation d'une abbaye bénédictine.[24]

---

21. Bruxelles, Bibliothèque Royale, IV 119, f. 36v-43v.
22. Bruxelles, Bibliothèque Royale, 13076-13077. Voir illustration p. 267.
23. Voir G. Caullet, 'Les manuscrits', p. 215.
24. P. Rolland, 'Les *Monumenta Historiae Tornacensis* (Saec. XII). Etude critique', dans *Annales de l'Academie Royale d'Archéologie de Belgique*, LXXIII (1925), pp. 270-272 et C. Dereine, 'Odon de Tournai et la crise du cénobitisme au XIe siècle', dans *Revue du Moyen Age Latin* (1948), pp. 137-141.

Le résultat de cette intervention consiste en un mariage unique du travail d'un érudit réformateur qui se concentra plutôt sur l'histoire récente (dont on n'a jamais voulu présenter des images) et d'une décoration permettant de compléter l'histoire sémi-imaginaire d'une communauté. Dans les contextes historiographiques, les moines se montraient donc extrêmement réticents (ou désintéressés) à faire représenter leur propre histoire récente en images, alors que celle-ci se voyait en même temps élaborée de façon exemplaire dans l'oeuvre de li Muisis. Ce qui est plus intéressant encore, c'est que (en ce qui concerne leur propre identité et histoire) l'intérêt des moines se concentra sur leurs 'origines' lointaines et, inversement, sur le rôle de l'abbé dans la société contemporaine, ce qui explique la présence de l'image présentant la destruction de l'abbaye en 882 et des images franchement non historiques (didactiques et propagandistes) de li Muisis lui-même.[25]

Bien que le pourcentage des exemplaires illustrés s'accroisse quelque peu dès les premières années du quinzième siècle, les tendances présentes dans l'iconographie des manuscrits de li Muisis continuent à s'observer jusqu'à la fin du Moyen Âge. On peut distinguer deux groupes de manuscrits qui se distinguent entre eux par l'identité du destinataire. En effet, les analyses des bibliothèques monastiques démontrent que les collections des communautés monastiques et celles d'un grand nombre d'abbés évoluèrent dans des directions différentes, marquées soit par le contenu des textes, soit par la décoration. En ce qui concerne l'historiographie, on observe que les abbés de grandes institutions comme Saint-Pierre et Saint-Bavon à Gand, Saint-Bertin et Les Dunes s'érigèrent en mécènes de la production de livres dans la grande tradition bourguignonne. Les manuscrits intégrant les collections abbatiales se distinguaient par leur décoration raffinée, qui correspond parfaitement aux goûts et aux thèmes préférés de l'élite cléricale et laïque. Il devient alors difficile de retrouver, dans les miniatures, des touches supposées 'typiquement monastiques' ou même des thématiques qui touchent à l'essence de la vie des moines.[26]

---

25. Les mêmes remarques valent pour les images dans le manuscrit supposé autographe des *Annales Hannoniae* de Jacques de Guise (NaSo J015), à Valenciennes (Bibliothèque Municipale, 768-770 (olim 578)).

26. L'exemple le mieux documenté est celui des manuscrits du *Compendium historiae universalis* par Aegidius de Roya (vers 1460-1463), moine cistercien de l'abbaye des Dunes. J'ai pu tracer au moins cinq ou six exemplaires (dont trois illustrés) qui ont été offerts à des prominents de l'élite monastique et Bourguignonne entre les années 1464 et 1491 (voir mon article 'Wetenschap en cultureel kapitaal aan het einde van de vijftiende eeuw. Een onderzoek naar de handschriften van Aegidius de Roya's *Compendium historiae universalis*', dans *Handelingen van het Genootschap voor Geschiedenis*, CXL (2003), p. 42-65).

Un deuxième groupe de manuscrits se présente comme des volumes à caractère didactique, dont le contenu s'adressait aux besoins intellectuels de la communauté monastique bien plus qu'à ceux de l'abbé. Dans ces copies, qui contiennent dans la plupart des cas des textes à caractère universel, on retrouve les préoccupations essentielles des moines dont les manuscrits de li Muisis avaient déjà témoigné. D'une part, l'identité contemporaine des communautés monastiques s'abstraite, voire se transforme en des images qui renvoient aux idéaux de la vie spirituelle et conventuelle. D'autre part, l'identité historique d'une communauté est représentée dans des contextes très spécifiques et extrêmement significatifs, comme la fondation d'une institution monastique, ou la vie et les miracles du saint fondateur.

Les deux tendances se retrouvent dans les manuscrits de la chronique de Jean d'Ypres (NaSo J104), abbé de Saint-Bertin († vers 1383).[27] Neuf copies médiévales en sont préservées, dont au moins sept proviennent de la bibliothèque de Saint-Bertin. Ce nombre élevé et le programme iconographique dans deux exemplaires portent à croire que les abbés utilisèrent le texte et son contexte manuscrit pour donner un sens d'historicité à la communauté monastique, mais également pour leur communiquer l'essence de la vie monastique à Saint-Bertin. A part une copie présentant une vue sur l'abbaye et la ville de Saint-Omer,[28] deux exemplaires de 1405[29] et de 1437[30] portent une décoration élaborée et basée sur le même prototype (peut-être le manuscrit de 1405 lui-même). Dans les images, on retrouve d'abord les éléments essentiels des pratiques de vénération monastique: le f. 14v dans le manuscrit de 1405 nous montre Saint Pierre et Saint Jean Baptiste en adoration devant la Vierge et l'Enfant, tandis que le f. 15r complète l'image en montrant l'auteur et l'entière congrégation suivant l'exemple des saints.[31] Sur les ff. 15v et 16r, les principaux saints de l'abbaye sont représentés: Bertin, Omer, Folcuin, et Silvin.

---

27. L. Van der Essen, 'Jean d'Ypres ou de Saint-Bertin († 1383). Contribution à l'histoire de l'hagiographie médiévale en Belgique', dans *Revue Belge de Philologie et d'Histoire*, I (1922), pp. 484-485.

28. London, British Library, Additional Manuscripts, 30033, f. 1r (commissionné en 1456 pour l'abbé Pierre Courauld de Saint-Pierre à Gand). L'image panoramique elle-même semble être reprise d'une aquarelle dans un rouleau contemporain (Saint-Omer, Bibliothèque Municipale, 1489).

29. Saint-Omer, Bibliothèque Municipale, 739 (olim 630).

30. Saint-Omer, Bibliothèque Municipale, 740.

31. Voir aussi J. Naughton, 'A Minimally-intrusive Presence: Portraits in Illustrations for Prayers to the Virgin', dans M.M. Manion et B.J. Muir (eds.), *Medieval Texts*, pp. 117-118.

L'auteur qui a donné son histoire à sa communauté est célébré par un deuxième portrait au f. 16v.

En ce qui concerne le texte de la chronique, seul un passage repris du *Speculum Historiale* de Vincent de Beauvais a retenu l'attention des artistes. L'histoire illustrée traite du moine Jocio, qui se distinguait de ses collèges par son zèle particulier dans la récitation des prières et des psaumes en l'honneur de la Vierge. Après son décès, ceux qui étaient présents à son lit de mort virent des roses jaillir de ses yeux, de ses oreilles, et de sa bouche. Cette anecdote assez innocente, qui est traduite en images pour le bénéfice moral des moines, se présente comme un *exemplum* idéal de l'utopie du monachisme (f. 113v et 114r).[32] Dans ce contexte didactique plutôt qu'antiquaire on retrouve donc uniquement des éléments illustrés qui servent à l'exploration d'un idéal dépassant le cadre du temps humain, et dont l'expression ne présente que peu de rapports au déroulement de l'histoire, qu'elle soit profane ou liée aux institutions monastiques.

Les manuscrits de Saint-Bertin ne font pas exception à une situation générale, comme en témoigne un codex encyclopédique de l'abbaye d'Oudenburg, daté vers 1458.[33] Composé de textes à contenu biblique, universaliste, dynastique et généalogique, ce volume offre aux moines Bénédictins un aperçu global de l'histoire du monde et des principaux acteurs de l'histoire contemporaine. Bien que l'illustration des premières pages du manuscrit soit composée d'images cosmologiques,[34] comme un plan de Jérusalem et un plan du monde, l'iconographie de la partie cen-

---

32. Dans la copie de 1437, les miniatures se trouvent respectivement sur ff. 9v-11v et, sous forme condensée, sur le f. 90v.

33. Bruges, Grand Séminaire, 127/5. Pour une description détaillée, voir R. Vander Plaetse, dans *Sint-Arnoldus en de Sint-Pietersadbij te Oudenburg 1084-1984. Tentoonstellingscatalogus* (Oudenburg, 1984), pp. 273-277 et le catalogue dactylografié du professeur E.I. Strubbe.

34. Le style et le contenu de ces images permettent de supposer que les artistes ont utilisé des modèles du douzième siècle (M. Smeyers et B. Cardon, 'Vier eeuwen Vlaamse miniatuurkunst in handschriften uit het Grootseminarie te Brugge', dans A. Denaux et E. Vanden Berghe (eds.), *De Duinenadbij en het Grootseminarie te Brugge. Bewoners/Gebouwen/Kunstpatrimonium* (Tielt et Weesp, 1984), p. 166 et M. Smeyers, *Vlaamse miniaturen*, p. 273). Par contre, une image de Jérusalem par l'atelier de Loyset Liédet dans une copie du *Historiologum Brabantinorum* de Johannes Giellemans (NaSo J207) montre que les mêmes images se voyaient aussi adaptées pour entrer en accord avec les goûts contemporains (Vienne, Österreichische Nationalbibliothek, Series Nova 12710 (olim Familien-Fideicommiss-Bibliothek, 9365), f. 2v; vers 1486-87, or. Rouge-Cloître; voir O. Pächt et D. Thoss, *Flämische Schule II. Textband* (Vienne, 1990), pp. 116-118 et *Tafelband*, planche XV).

trale, le *Chronicon Aldenburgensis monasterii majus* (NaSo C015), reprend les thèmes dont j'ai déjà fait mention. Bien que cette chronique universelle ne contienne que peu de références au passé de l'abbaye d'Oudenburg, les passages qui nous rappellent cette histoire sont les seuls à avoir été sélectionnés pour la décoration. Comme à Saint-Bertin, les images démontrent que l'intérêt des moines se portait sur la vénération des saints, comme Godelieve de Ghistel, mais surtout sur le patron, en l'occurence Arnoul de Soissons (f. 28r, XXXVr et LXVr). Cette préférence nette, observable au niveau des faits et des thèmes qui sont sélectionnés pour la décoration, met en évidence le fait que l'iconographie de ce manuscrit réfère aux contextes que l'historiographie 'profane' avait en commun avec les traditions hagiographiques. En ce qui concerne l'histoire de la communauté monastique elle-même, on ne s'étonne point de trouver une représentation de la fondation de l'église d'Oudenburg au f. LXIIIr.

Il me semble difficile d'imaginer un point de vue monastique plus idiosyncrasique que celui dont on retrouve l'expression iconographique dans les manuscrits de Saint-Bertin et d'Oudenburg. La docilité dont témoignent les artistes de manuscrits confectionnés pour les abbés mécènes à l'égard du goût et des thèmes préférés de l'élite bourguignonne contraste fort avec l'expressivité de la décoration des textes historiques qui se concentre sur les intérêts et les objectifs de la communauté monastique en tant que groupement religieux. Un dernier exemple particulièrement intrigant du contraste entre ces deux programmes iconographiques est constitué par le seul manuscrit de la *Chronique [rimée] de Floreffe* (NaSo H022-S084), écrite entre 1462 et 1465 par le Norbertin Simon.[35] Selon le prologue, la chronique se veut un texte didactique présentant l'administration des abbés de Floreffe comme un exemple pour ceux qui dirigent les institutions ecclésiastiques et séculières.[36] C'est avant tout la personnalité de Lucas d'Eyck (1444-1465) qui mérite l'attention des lecteurs,

---

35. Bruxelles, Bibliothèque Royale, 18064-18069, f. 187v ff. Voir A Langfors, 'Simon, auteur de la *Chronique de Floreffe*', dans *Romania. Recueil trimestriel consacré à l'étude des langues et des littératures romanes*, XLV (1918-1919), pp. 268-270 et N. Backmund, *Die mittelalterlichen Geschichtsschreiber des Prämonstratenserordens* (Averbode, 1972), pp. 239-240.

36. Dans son prologue, l'auteur mentionne qu'il est '...chose tres prouffitable aux seigneurs et prelas avoir plusieurs livres vieulx et nouveaulx pour y avoir recours en temps et en lieu et pour recreacion selonc les divers cas qui de jour en jour aviennent...' (H. Peters, 'Über Sprache und Versbau der Chronik von Floreffe', dans *Zeitschrift für romanische Philologie*, XXI, 1897, p. 356).

et plus particulièrement ses efforts pour renouveler la vie intellectuelle dans son institution[37] et pour obtenir des exemptions et la permission d'utiliser les insignes pontificaux.[38] Pour compenser ce désir de mettre en lumière les réformes à Floreffe et faute d'histoire vraiment captivante pour un public non monastique, la dernière partie de la chronique se concentre presque entièrement sur l'histoire régionale et internationale.

Malgré cet objectif assez ambitieux, il semble que la chronique n'a jamais eu d'impact en dehors des murs de l'abbaye de Floreffe. Quoi qu'il en soit, la seule copie de ce texte fort intéressant montre comment les moines eux-mêmes récupérèrent le texte pour l'intégrer dans un univers imagé typiquement monastique. Les miniatures, dont le style rustique laisse deviner qu'ils ont été confectionées par un membre de la communauté, sont composées pour la plupart d'entre-elles d'images allégoriques, comme 'La damme representant l'église de Floreffe' qui protège ses moines sous son manteau (f. 198r), la 'liesse' ou la joie démodérée (f. 203v) et la mort (f. 204r).[39] L'artiste avait pourtant bien compris la divergence entre les ambitions littéraires de Simon et le milieu où cette copie devait être lue, comme en témoigne la miniature au f. 191v. (Voir illustration p. 269). L'image est dominée par une forêt dense, avec à l'extrême gauche un panorama schématique de l'abbaye de Floreffe, où l'on observe certains personnes essayant de regarder par-dessus les murs pour voir ce qui ce passe dans le monde extérieur. Au centre de l'image, un homme accoudé et habillé à la mode contemporaine se laisse identifier comme l'"home moult tristes et tres infortunez" du prologue.[40] L'utilisation de ce motif commun à la littéraire vernaculaire s'inscrit dans la stratégie de l'auteur qui consiste à se manifester comme un écrivain accompli qui connaît ses antécédents classiques et contemporains. Plus important encore est le fait que, en tant que chroniqueur, il se positionne quelque part entre son propre statut monastique et le rôle adopté

---

37. [F.] de Reiffenberg, (ed.), *Monuments pour servir à l'histoire des provinces de Namur, de Hainaut et de Luxembourg,* VIII (Bruxelles, 1848), pp. 155-157.

38. Voir U. Berlière, 'Abbaye de Floreffe', dans *Monasticon Belge. Tome I. Province de Namur et de Hainaut. Premier fascicule* (Liège, 1890), p. 120.

39. Des espaces vides (folios 193r, 195v, 196r, 199v, 201r et v, f. 206r et 210r), presque tous dans un contexte allégorisant, montrent que quelques aspects des 'decisions préliminaires importantes' de l'artiste (voir J.G. Alexander, 'Facsimiles', p. 63) n'ont jamais été implémentés.

40. 'Chi commenche l'aucteur de ce livre et traittie tout premier a parler en fourme d'ung home moult tristres et tres infortunez et poursieut avant par maniere de dyaloghue en tenant signe de soigne et de ficcion jusques ad ce qu'i vient a parler et touchier des cronicques et hystoires.' (H. Peters (ed.), 'Über Sprache', p. 357).

d'écrivain qui connaît son monde. L'iconographie du manuscrit de la *Chronique de Floreffe* nous montre donc comment les Norbertins se trouvaient coincés entre leur propre sens d'identité et le fait que le discours qui accompagnait ce sentiment n'avait presque aucune résonance dans le monde extérieur.

Pour conclure ce bref survol, j'estime qu'il m'est permis de dire que l'analyse des manuscrits de notre sélection de textes confirme l'hypothèse selon laquelle une iconographie historique 'typiquement' monastique n'existe pas. L'une des causes majeures réside dans le fait que les moines ne portaient que peu d'intérêt à la représentation picturale d'événements profanes qui ne référaient que marginalement à leurs idéaux spirituels, intellectuels et institutionnels. D'où le fait que l'iconographie la plus ancienne que j'ai pu retrouver met l'accent sur le caractère téléologique et inspiré de l'historiographie universelle. Cette réticence à l'égard de l'histoire factuelle ou profane persistera jusqu'à la fin du Moyen Âge, sauf dans les manuscrits réservés à l'usage exclusif de quelques abbés mécènes. Dans les manuscrits des communautés monastiques, la vénération des saints, le rôle déterminant du saint fondateur en les origines d'une abbaye sont mis en évidence comme étant les passages essentiels du récit, quel que soit le genre auquel celui-ci appartient. En ce qui concerne l'histoire récente, l'iconographie des manuscrits semble se concentrer sur une imagerie qui se veut normative, abstraite. Tout cela nous montre comment, en dépit des ambitions universalistes de quelques historiens monastiques comme Jean d'Ypres et Simon de Floreffe, le passé non hagiographique fut inséré dans la *lectio* des moines. Ceux-ci tentaient de compenser la futilité de l'histoire terrestre par une tendance à se concentrer sur le *soi*, sur le groupe de moines comme unité de vénération et sur le caractère organisé mais fondamentalement asocial de l'initiative monastique.[41]

Aperçu provisoire des manuscrits illustrés contenant de l'historiographie provenant des Pays-Bas Méridionaux

1. *Manuscrits provenant de milieux monastiques*
   – 12e siècle (2): Boulogne-sur-Mer, Bibliothèque Municipale, 146 et 146A (cartulaire-chronique de Saint-Bertin) et Paris, Bibliothèque Nationale, Nouvelles Acquisitions Latines, 1543 (*Chronique* de Sigebert de Gembloux; fin du 12e siècle, or. Hautmont).

---

41. Je tiens à remercier le professeur Ludo Milis, dr. Ann Kelders, Bart Defrancq, André Vanderputten et Melissa Provijn pour leur aide précieuse.

- 13e siècle (1): Bruxelles, Bibliothèque Royale, II 1055bis (*Chronique* de Sigebert de Gembloux; début du 13e siècle, or. Aulne-Sur-Sambre).
- 14e siècle (4): Bruxelles, Bibliothèque Royale, 13076-13077 et IV 119, et Courtrai, Bibliothèque de la Ville, Fonds Goethals-Vercruysse, 135 (oeuvres de Gilles li Muisis; tous vers 1350-1353, or. Saint-Martin à Tournai) et Valenciennes, Bibliothèque Municipale, 768-770 (olim 578) (*Annales Hannoniae* par Jacques de Guise; autographe ou copie très proche du manuscrit originel).
- 15e siècle (11): Bruges, Grand Séminaire, 127/5 (*Chronicon Aldenburgensis monasterii majus*; vers 1458, or. Oudenburg); Bruxelles, Bibliothèque Royale, 7978-7979 (*Compendium historiae universalis* par Aegidius de Roya; vers 1480, abbaye des Dunes), 18064-18069 (*Chronique de Floreffe*; vers 1462-1465) et 18179-18180 (*Chronodromon* de Jean Brandon; troisième quart du quinzième siècle; or. abbaye de Saint Pierre à Gand); Londres, British Library, Additional Manuscripts, 30033 (*Chronicon Sancti Bertini* par Jean d'Ypres; copié en 1456 pour l'abbé de Saint-Pierre à Gand); Montpellier, Bibliothèque de l'Université, Faculté de Médecine, 375 (*Compendium historiae universalis* par Aegidius de Roya; vers 1464, probablement offert à l'abbé de Cîteaux par l'abbé des Dunes); Paris, Bibliothèque Nationale, Manuscrits Latins, 4867 (*Chronique* de Sigebert de Gembloux; origine incertaine mais probablement monastique) et 5995 (*Annales Hannoniae* par Jacques de Guise; même remarque); Saint-Omer, Bibliothèque Municipale, 739 (olim 630) (*Chronicon Sancti Bertini* par Jean d'Ypres; copié en 1405 par un moine de Saint-Bertin) et 740 (même texte; copié en 1437); Vienne, Österreichische Nationalbibliothek, Series Nova 12710 (olim Familien-Fideicommiss-Bibliothek, 9365) (*Historiologium Brabantinorum* par Johannes Giellemans; vers 1486-1487, or. Rouge-Cloître).

2. *Manuscrits provenant de milieux non monastiques ou incertains*

- 12e siècle (2): Cambrai, Bibliothèque Municipale, 965 (olim 863) (*Chronique* de Sigebert de Gembloux) et Paris, Bibliothèque Nationale, Manuscrits Latins, 14624 (olim Saint-Victor 238) (même texte, provenant de la bibliothèque de Henri de France).
- 13e siècle (1): Paris, Biblothèque Nationale, Manuscrits Latins, 8865 (*Historia succincta regum Francorum* d'André de Marchiennes (NaSo A053); troisième quart du 13e siècle, diocèse de Cambrai, peut-être Cambron).
- 15e siècle (5): Bruxelles, Bibliothèque Royale, II 1169 (*Chronodromon* par Jean Brandon (NaSo J187); après 1480, de la bibliothèque de Nicholas de Ruystre, évêque d'Arras entre 1501 et 1509); La Haye, Rijksmuseum Meermanno-Westreenianum, 10 A 21 (*Compendium historiae universalis* par Aegidius de Roya; circa 1464, de la collection de David de Bourgogne), Paris, Bibliothèque de l'Arsenal, 922 (même texte); Paris, Bibliothèque nationale, 4931A (*Chronicon de pontificibus et de imperatoribus* par Pierre d'Herentals (NaSo P022); première moitié du 15e siècle); Rouen, Bibliothèque Municipale, 1131 (olim U11) (*Chronique* de Sigebert de Gembloux, premier quart du 15e siècle).

3. *Manuscrits contenant de l'historiographie illustrés dans les sections non historiques*

- 9ᵉ siècle (1): Monza, Bibliotheca Capitolare, f-9/176 (*Annales Lobienses* (NaSo A076)).
- 11ᵉ siècle (1): Gand, Bibliothèque de l'Université, 224 (*Ratio fundationis seu aedificationis Blandiniensis coenobii* (NaSo F033)).
- 12ᵉ siècle (2): Douai, Bibliothèque Municipale, 170 (*Annales Marchianenses* (NaSo A077)) et Valenciennes, Bibliothèque Municipale, 406 (olim 388) (*De lite abbatiarum Elnonensis et Hasnoniensis anno 1055-1091* (NaSo D017), or. probablement Saint-Amand).
- 13ᵉ siècle (1): Bruxelles, Bibliothèque Royale, II 1515 (*Cantatorium* (NaSo L012), or. probablement Saint-Hubert).
- 14ᵉ siècle (1): Bruxelles, Bibliothèque Royale, 4459-4470 (*Gesta abbatum Villariensium* (NaSo C010, F022 et J179)).
- 15ᵉ siècle (2): Bruges, Bibliothèque de la Ville, 441 (*De insidiis regis Francorum in domum Burgundicam*, or. Les Dunes) et Vienne, Nationalbibliothek, Series Nova, 12708-12709 (olim Familien-Fideicommiss-Bibliothek, 9364) (*Chronicon Affligemense* (NaSo C014) et les *Gesta abbatum Villariensium*; or. Rouge-Cloître).

Initiale historiée dans la *Chronique* de Sigebert de Gembloux,
Aulne-Sur-Sambre, début du 13e siècle.
(Bruxelles, Bibliothèque Royale, II 1055bis, f. 1v).
© Bibliothèque Royale, Bruxelles

UNE ICONOGRAPHIE DE L'HISTORIOGRAPHIE MONASTIQUE 267

La destruction de l'abbaye bénédictine à Tournai en 882.
Miniature dans le *Tractatus quartus* de Gilles li Muisis, Tournai, vers 1353.
(Bruxelles, Bibliothèque Royale, 13076-13077, f. 56r).
© Bibliothèque Royale, Bruxelles

Fondation de l'église d'Oudenburg par Conon d'Eine et sa femme Hasecca, le comte de Flandre et divers prominents ecclésiastiques.
Chronicon Aldenburgense monasterii majus, Oudenburg, vers 1458.
(Bruges, Grand Séminaire, 127/5, f. LXIIIr).
© Grand Séminaire, Bruges

UNE ICONOGRAPHIE DE L'HISTORIOGRAPHIE MONASTIQUE 269

Miniature dans la *Chronique de Floreffe* du Norbertin Simon, Floreffe, vers 1462-1465
(© Bibliothèque Royale, Bruxelles, 18064-18069, f. 191v).

ANNEX

Jeroen DEPLOIGE

THE DATABASE NARRATIVE SOURCES FROM THE MEDIEVAL LOW COUNTRIES

A Short Introduction
Followed by the *User's Guide*[1]

The Internet-database *The Narrative Sources from the Medieval Low Countries*, commonly known as *Narrative Sources*, was first published in January 1997 and constituted the result of a research project in which the universities of Ghent and Leuven had been collaborating since 1986.[2] Up to 2001, the geographical scope of *Narrative Sources* was restricted to the medieval Southern Low Countries. Scholars of the medieval Northern Low Countries could rely upon the very succesful printed inventory of sources published by M. Carasso-Kok in 1981.[3] However, from 2000 onwards, a team of Dutch medievalists at the University of Groningen updated this standard work and the results of this endeavor have also been integrated into the Flemish database.[4] *Narrative Sources* thus became a database covering the whole of the medieval Low Countries. Updates of *Narrative Sources* are released at least once a year. The 3.3 version, launched in June 2004, constitutes the eighth update of the original database of 1997.

---

1. J. Deploige is postdoctoral Research Fellow of the Fund for Scientific Research – Flanders (Belgium).
2. See the Introduction by Ludo Milis in this volume. For a history of the project: V. Lambert, 'Potthast, Pirenne en de anderen: historici repertoriëren historici', in: L. Milis, V. Lambert en A. Kelders (eds.), *Verhalende Bronnen. Repertoriëring, editie en commercialisering*, Studia Historica Gandensia. Publicaties van de Opleiding Geschiedenis van de Universiteit Gent, 283 (Ghent, 1996), p. 17.
3. M. Carasso-Kok, *Repertorium van verhalende historische bronnen uit de middeleeuwen: heiligenlevens, annalen, kronieken en andere in Nederland geschreven verhalende bronnen* (The Haye, 1981).
4. See also the chapter by Renée Nip in this volume.

The main difference between *Narrative Sources* and other inventories of primary sources – such as the *Repertorium Fontium Historiae Medii Aevi* – is of course its medium of publication.[5] *Narrative Sources* is not a traditionally printed survey of primary sources, alphabetically arranged and supplied with an index. *Narrative Sources* is only available as a free online-database. The database-software used to publish *Narrative Sources* is SilverPlatter-software. SilverPlatter – now part of Ovid Technologies – is mainly known for its bibliographic databases such as the *MLA*-bibliography, *Sociofile*, *Medline*, the *Catalogue of the Belgian Scientific Libraries* etc. *Narrative Sources* is hosted on the webserver of the Ghent University Library but is also accessible from a special *Narrative Sources*-website, providing extra tools and information.[6]

At this moment, *Narrative Sources* contains 2141 source-descriptions. That number may still increase, as the hagiographical texts from the Southern Low Countries are still very underrepresented and as the sources from East-Friesland and the northern Rhineland still need to be incorporated by the Groningen team. As can be noted from the attached example, every primary source described in the database is treated in a record containing 23 fields of information. Every fieldname in *Narrative Sources* is displayed by a two-character abbreviation, which also has to be used in the database search syntax. It is possible however to display the long fieldnames as well by using the *Change display options*-button. The information in *Narrative Sources* is primarily given in Dutch, and, for the most important fields, in English as well. Fields for which our information is still lacking, are marked with two asterisks.

---

5. *Repertorium fontium historiae Medii Aevi*. Primum ab Augusto Potthast digestum, nunc cura collegii historicorum e pluribus nationibus emendatum et auctum (Roma, 1962- ...).

6. See: http://www.narrative-sources.be. Narrative Sources can also be consulted on the website of the Ghent University Library: http://www.lib.ugent.be. The database is listed there under the sections E- sources.

Example of a Narrative Sources-record

ID Identification Number
NL0054
TY Type
Hagiografie (Hagiography, Hagiographie)
LA Language
Latijn (Latin)
AU Author
Sibrandus
ST Status of the Author
OPraem., abt van het klooster Mariëngaarde bij Hallum (1230-1238).—
OPraem., abbot of the abbey of Mariengaarde near Hallum (1230-1238)
TI Title
Vita Fretheryci
IC Incipit
Prol.: Venerabilibus dilectis in Christo ancillis Dei...— Corpus: Recolende memorie Frethericus ortus Frisia, de villa que Hallum dicitur...
EX Explicit
...cui est honor et gloria in sanctis suis per infinita secula seculorum. Amen.
SI Size
<**>
CE Century
13
RG Region: Diocese and Principality
Dioc. Utrecht
RE Redaction: Place, Date, Patron and Dedication
Het klooster Mariëngaarde, c.1230. De vita is opgedragen aan Gerthrud van Driesem, eertijds priorin van Bethlehem, en Bernild. De tekst is overgeleverd in een laat-middeleeuws afschrift. Dit Brusselse handschrift bevat ook levensbeschrijvingen van vier latere abten van het Hallumer klooster: de Vita Siardi en de Vita Sibrandi, Iarici, Etelgeri (NL0143-144), naast een Vita Norberti, een Vita Hermanni Joseph (Steinfeld) en een korte kloostergeschiedenis (Carasso-Kok no 284). De Vita Fretheryci wordt in dit handschrift gevolgd door een berijmd gebed op Fretherycus en een acrostichon dat de naam van de kopiist Paulus Gisberti aanreikt.— The abbey of Mariengaarde, c. 1230. The Life is dedicated to Gerthrud van Driesem, prioress of the convent of Bethlehem, and Bernild. The Brussels manuscript contains also Lives of four later abbots, Siardus and, Sibrandus, Iaricus and Etelgerus (NL0143-144), the Life of S. Norbert, the Life of Hermannus Joseph (Steinfeld) and a short history of the monastery of Mariengaarde (Carasso-Kok no 284).
AB Abstract
Fretherycus (Frederik), zoon van Dodo en Swithberga, werd in het Friese Hallum geboren. Zijn vader overleed jong en zijn moeder zorgde ervoor dat hij een goede opleiding genoot. Hij studeerde in Munster en na zijn priesterwijding werd hij pastoor in Hallum. Na de dood van zijn moeder vroeg hij

de bisschop van Utrecht om kanunnik te worden en hem toe te staan een kloostergemeenschap te stichten. Ter voorbereiding verbleef hij eerst enige tijd in het klooster Mariënweerd aan de Linge. In 1163 bouwde hij bij Hallum een kapel ter ere van Maria en Sint Jan de Evangelist. De toeloop van mannen en vrouwen tot de nieuwe stichting was zo groot dat hij al spoedig besloot de vrouwen elders onder te brengen, in een huis dat hij Bethlehem noemde. Ten slotte bewerkstelligde Frederik dat de abt van het praemonstratenzerklooster te Steinfeld de paterniteit over zijn stichtingen op zich nam. Na zijn dood vonden er door zijn toedoen wonderen plaats.— Fretherycus (Frederik), son of Dodo en Swithberga, was born in Hallum (Friesland). He studied in Munster and became a priest in Hallum. After a preparation in the monastery of Marienweerd on the river Linge, he built in Hallum a chapel dedicated to Our Lady and St John the evangelist and with admission of the bishop of Utrecht he founded a religious house. Soon, he decided to house the women seperately in the nunnery of Bethlehem.

CO Context
Fretherycus (Frederik) was de stichter en eerste abt (1163-1175) van het klooster Mariëngaarde bij Hallum.— Fretherycus (Frederik) was the founder and first abbot (1163-1175) of the monastery Mariëngaarde near Hallum.

MS Manuscripts
BRUSSEL, KB: 6717-6721, f. 28v-51r (1497). Uit het klooster Mariëngaarde bij Hallum. Kopiist: frater Paulus Gisberti, afkomstig uit het Vlaamse St. Winoksbergen, supprior en bibliothecaris in Mariëngaarde.— cfr. LEEUWARDEN, Bibliotheek Fries Genootschap 31A (1617) 15-30.

ED Editions
A. W. WYBRANDS, Gesta abbatum Orti Sancte Marie. Gedenkschriften van de abdij Mariëngaarde in Friesland. Naar het te Brussel bewaarde handschrift uitgegeven met inleiding, aantekeningen en register (Leeuwarden 1879) 1-74.— H.TH.M. LAMBOOIJ, J.A. MOL ed. en vert. m.m.v. M. GUMBERT-HEPP en P.N. NOOMEN, Vitae Abbatum Orti Sancte Marie. Vijf abtenlevens van het klooster Mariëngaarde in Friesland (Hilversum, Leeuwarden 2001) 132-240.

TL Translations
E. BRUNA, Het leven van den zaligen Frederik van Hallum (Leeuwarden 1947). Frisia Catholica 10.— J. DOUMA,'It libben fen Frederik (Vita Fretherici)', in: Yn ús eigen tael 16 (1924) en 17 (1925) passim.— H.TH.M. LAMBOOIJ, J.A. MOL ed. en vert. m.m.v. M. GUMBERT-HEPP en P.N. NOOMEN, Vitae Abbatum Orti Sancte Marie. Vijf abtenlevens van het klooster Mariëngaarde in Friesland (Hilversum, Leeuwarden 2001) 133-241.

SC Sources
<**>

IF Influence
Vita Frederici (NL0055).— Sibrandus Leo, Vita et res gestae abbatum horti Divae Virginis, seu Mariengard, apud Frisios (NL0146).

LI Literature
CARASSO-KOK no 28.— BHL 3149.— MULLER, Lijst, 80-81.— REPERTORIUM FONTIUM IV, 738. CHEVALIER, Répertoire Bio-bibliographie I, 1602, 4235. POST, Kerkgeschiedenis I, 242; II, 243.—

WATERBOLK, in: Geschiedenis van Friesland, 639-642. WATTENBACH, Geschichtsquellen II (6de druk) 431.— ROMEIN, Geschiedschrijving, 66-69.— BRUCH, Supplement, 23.— BRUCH, Friese kronieken, 8.— A. W. WYBRANDS ed., XVII-XVIII.— A. W. WYBRANDS, De abdij Bloemhof te Wittewierum in de dertiende eeuw. Bijdragen tot de geschiedenis van kerk en beschaving in Nederland (Amsterdam 1883) 13-25 (Verh. Kon. Ak. van Wetenschappen, afd. Letterk. 15; fotograf. herdr. Groningen 1969).— G. VAN DEN ELSEN, Leven van den Zaligen Fredericus van Hallum. Stichter der abdij Mariëngaard in Friesland (Oosterhout (1893)) 7-12.— M. KLINKENBORG, 'Einige Bemerkungen zur Überlieferung der Gesta abbatum Orti S. Marie', in: Emder Jahrbuch 12 (1897) 151-158.— N. BACKMUND, Die mittelalterlichen Geschichtsschreiber des Prämonstratenserordens (Averbode 1972, diss. München) 156-168 Bibliotheca Analectorum Praemonstratensium 10.— D.A. WUMKES ed., Sibrandus Leo's Abtenlevens der Friesche kloosters Mariëngaard en Lidlum (Bolsward 1929) xx-xxi.— K. KOCH, E. HEGEL, Die Vita des Prämonstratensers Hermann Joseph von Steinfeld: ein Beitrag zur Hagiographie und zur Frömmigkeitsgeschichte des Hochmittelalters (Keulen 1958).— N. BACKMUND, 'Frédéric de Mariengaarde', DHGE 19 (Parijs 1977) 1169.— J.J. KALMA, Frederik van Hallum, dromer en doener (c.1125-3 maart 1175) (Leeuwarden 1978).— B.DE GAIFFIER, 'Un thème hagiographique: mer ou fleuve traversé sur un manteau', AB 99 (1981) 5-15.— J.A. MOL, De Friese Huizen van de Duitse Orde. Nes, Steenkerk en Schoten en hun plaats in het middeleeuwsw Friese kloosterlandschap (Leeuwarden 1991) 49-51.— H. PLATELLE, 'Le ministère pastoral dans une paroisse de Frise au XIIe siècle d'après la vie de Frédéric de Hallum (1175), prêtre séculier, puis chanoine prémontré', in: Le clerc séculier au Moyen Age (Parijs 1993) 81-99.— H. OLDENHOF in: P.J. MARGRY, C. CASPERS eds., Bedevaartplaatsen in Nederland 1 (Amsterdam, Hilversum 1997) 417-421.— D.E.H. DE BOER, 'Mirakels mooi. Groningers en wonderen in de dertiende tot vijftiende eeuw', in: id. e.a. ed., Het Noorden in het midden (Assen 1998) 206.— H.Th.M. LAMBOOIJ, 'Hagiografie in een Fries klooster', in: S. VAN DE PERRE ed., Omgang met norbertijner heiligen. Achtergronden en vormgeving van de heiligenverering in de orde van Prémontré (Brussel 1998) 31-50.— K. HEENE, 'Ad sanguinis effusionem', Queeste 6 (1999) 1-22.— LAMBOOIJ, MOL ed. 35-43.

DS Desiderata
<**>
NA Name of the Contributor
RN
UD Update Code
20030310

The figure below depicts the standard search screen that is used by all SilverPlatter-databases. This standard screen displays different tools to facilitate search requests. There are special boxes to specify the field in which you want to search or to limit your search to sources of a specific language. However, search possibilities in *Narrative Sources* are far more numerous when the user simply falls back on the general search box on the left, while using – and eventually combining – of course the different search operators. To retrieve a word in a specific field, the operator "*in*" is required, followed by the two-character-fieldname. To find all the works written by Cistercians, "*socist in st*" has to be entered. To execute more sophisticated search techniques in *Narrative Sources*, one can use the boolean operators *and*, *or*, *not*, *with*, *near* and in the numeric century-field also <, <=, >, >= and ...-.... A question mark and an asterisk can be used as a wildcard or truncation marker. Typing "*crusade**" thus results in *crusade* as well as in *crusades*.

Every word contained in a record of *Narrative Sources* is indexed and can be searched. Most of the fields, as for instance the author-field, are indexed in a so called free-text index. But some fields, containing relatively few possible values, are indexed separately. Among these limit fields are the type-field, the language-field and the century-field. Retrieving terms or values in these fields thus requires a specific search syntax, which specifies the specific limit field that has to be searched, e.g. "*french in la*". In limit fields, the operator "=" can be used as well, e.g. "*ty=annals*". It becomes clear in the case of limit fields that the abovementioned tools on the standard SilverPlatter screen designed to facilitate certain search requests are rather restricting: limit fields are not listed in the "field"-box on the right side of the screen. Thus searching in these limit fields is only possible by using and typing the "*in*" or "=" search syntax.

The Narrative Sources-search screen

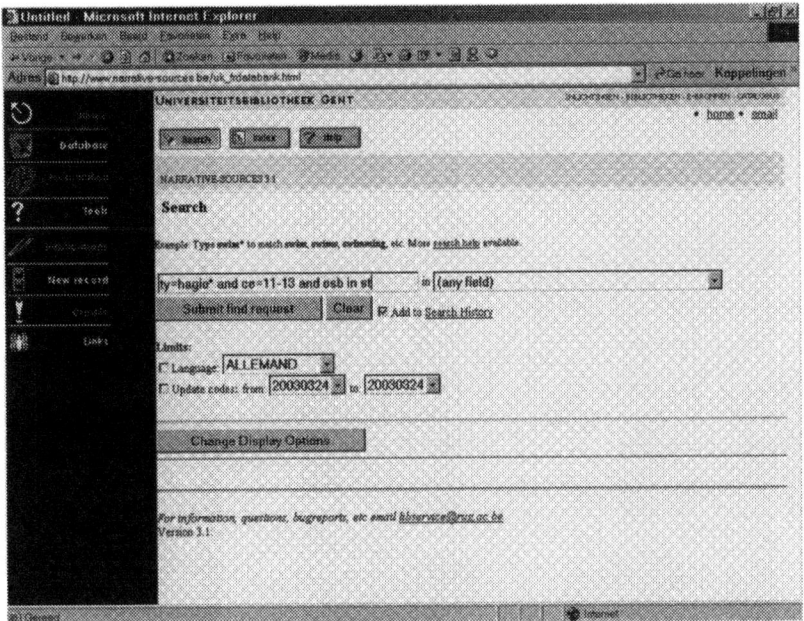

The most fascinating quality of *Narrative Sources*, especially compared to traditional printed inventories, is of course the possibility of combining different search requests and of developing sophisticated search strategies. An example: suppose one is looking for thirteenth-century French poetry related to the town of Arras. This requires the following search request: "*(atrecht or arras) and ty=poems and ce=13 and la=french*". In the 3.3 version of *Narrative Sources*, 13 records match this search. Combined searches can be typed in on one search line, as is shown in the search request in the figure above. The request "*ty=hagio* and ce=11-13 and osb in st*" – which looks for all hagiographical sources written by Benedictine monks between the eleventh and the thirteenth century – will yield 176 results in the 3.3 version.

SilverPlatter software makes it possible to print, download or e-mail search results. SilverPlatter databases always contain two different Help-files. The first one is a general helpfile concerning the use of SilverPlatter software. The other one is a user's guide to the specific database. *Narrative Sources* also contains such a specific guide in French, English and

Dutch.[7] Hereafter follows the printed English *User's guide* to *Narrative Sources* version 3.3.

---

7. The trilingual electronic version of this *User's Guide* can be consulted and downloaded on the database website http://www.narrative-sources.be. It has also been published as a separate booklet: J. Deploige, *Narrative Sources. User's Guide. Gebruikersgids. Guide de l'utilisateur. Vs. 3.1*, Gent-Leuven-Groningen 2003. This booklet can be ordered for free from Werner Verbeke, KULeuven Instituut voor Middeleeuwse Studies, Blijde-Inkomststraat 21, B-3000 Leuven, Belgium (werner.verbeke@arts.kuleuven.ac.be).

NARRATIVE SOURCES

The Narrative Sources from the Medieval Low Countries
De Verhalende Bronnen uit de middeleeuwse Nederlanden
Les sources narratives des Pays-Bas médiévaux

Universiteit Gent – Katholieke Universiteit Leuven –
Rijksuniversiteit Groningen

1996-2004

Scientific committee

Ludo MILIS
Werner VERBEKE
Jean GOOSSENS
Renée NIP
Dick DE BOER

Computerization

Jeroen DEPLOIGE
Herbert VAN DE SOMPEL

http://www.narrative-sources.be

Information copyright: Vakgroep Middeleeuwse Geschiedenis, Universiteit Gent, Blandijnberg 2, B-9000 Gent, Belgium – Instituut voor Middeleeuwse Studies, Katholieke Universiteit Leuven, Blijde-Inkomststraat 21, B-3000 Leuven, Belgium – Afdeling Geschiedenis, Rijksuniversiteit Groningen, Oude Kijk in 't Jatstraat 26, PB 716, NL-9700 AS Groningen, The Netherlands.

Software and Database Structure copyright: SilverPlatter International, Inc (since 2001 part of Ovid Technologies Inc.).

This non-commercial database may be used for research purposes only. The user may not publish, reproduce, reprint, broadcast, or otherwise make available or sell any material contained in the said database whether in hardcopy, electronically transmitted or any other form, and whether for commercial, educational or other purpose, other than for its own internal purposes. Users of the information should acknowledge its origin in their publications.

User's Guide
Version 3.3

Guide Index

Introduction to *Narrative Sources*	383
Fields in *Narrative Sources*	285
Limit Fields	295
Search Examples	296
Stopwords in *Narrative Sources*	296
Using the Index to Find an Author	297
Combining Searches	297
Truncation and Wildcards	297
Correspondence and Submission of New Records	298

INTRODUCTION TO *NARRATIVE SOURCES*

The aim of *Narrative Sources* is to give an exhaustive and critical survey of all the narrative sources originating from the medieval Low Countries. It is intended to cover all texts in prose or verse written in order to describe the past in a narrative way: annals, chronicles, letters, diaries, poems, saint's lives, genealogies etc.

Narrative Sources includes the information contained in M. Carasso-Kok's *Repertorium van de verhalende historische bronnen uit de Middeleeuwen* (The Hague, 1981) but its scope is larger. It does not duplicate L. Genicot and P. Tombeur's *Index scriptorum operumque Latino-Belgicorum Medii Aevi* (Brussels, 1973-1979) either. Other types of information are given and, moreover, the whole of the Middle Ages is covered. Contrary to the criteria of both Carasso-Kok (for the present-day Netherlands) and Genicot and Tombeur (for present-day Belgium), this survey is not limited to the present borders of Belgium and the Netherlands. It covers also those areas which belonged, historically speaking, to the Low Countries but are part now of France (French-Flanders, French-Hainault) or Germany (eastern Friesland, northern Rhineland). It also includes Liège, which was not, historically speaking, a part of the Low Countries. Chronologically the Middle Ages are considered as the period between 500 and 1550.

A survey of this type is never finished or definitive. We therefore consider an electronic database, available on the Internet, to be the most adequate way to publish the information, so that new data can continuously be added, and the existing data be adapted and corrected and thus kept up-to-date. At this stage, *Narrative Sources* contains 2141 records. We hope to increase this number, not only by new research within our existing project-structure, but also by new record submissions from the users of this database (see our Contact-address). Updates of *Narrative Sources* appear once a year.

This database is realised thanks to grants of the Flemish Fund for Scientific Research (FWO-Vlaanderen) and of the Netherlands Organization for Scientific Research (NWO) and with the kind permission of SilverPlatter International Inc.

Fields in *Narrative Sources*

Records in *Narrative Sources* are divided into the following fields. Highlighted fields are limit fields.

AB	Abstract
AU	Author
CE	**Century**
CO	Context
DS	Desiderata
ED	Editions
EX	Explicit
IC	Incipit
ID	**Identification Number**
IF	Influence
LA	**Language**
LI	Literature
MS	Manuscripts
NA	**Name of the Contributor**
RE	Redaction: Place, Date, Patron and Dedication
RG	Region: Diocese and Principality
SC	Sources
SI	Size
ST	Status of the Author
TI	Title
TL	Translations
TY	**Type**
UD	**Update Code**

* The information contained in the LA and the TY fields is in English as well as in Dutch and in French. The information contained in the ST, the RG, the RE, the AB and the CO fields is in English and in Dutch. The other fields can easily be consulted without special familiarity with Dutch.

Fields that are, fore some reason, not (yet) filled in, contain the symbol <**>.

There is also a special subset of fields, Citation (CITN), which consists of the ID, AU, TI, CE and RG fields. Use the Citation to display, print, or save only these fields for a set of records.

AB Abstract

Note: this field contains English information.

fourth crusade in ab

The AB field contains a brief description of the content of the narrative source.

AU Author

galbertus-brugensis in au
galbertus* in au
jacob-van-maerlant in au
maerlant in au
anon-mon-stabulensis in au
stabulensis in au

The AU field indicates the author(s) of the narrative source. Each author is listed first name first, followed by a hyphen and the last name or the geographical origin. The name of the author is always written in the language which he used to write his narrative source. Orthographic variants in the name of the authors are added between brackets in the AU field.

Anonymous authors are marked as 'anon.', with addition of the notion 'mon.' or 'can.' (in the cases a monk or a canon is considered to be the author), and, if relevant, with addition of their geographical origin.

If you are uncertain of an author's name, use truncation or look up the name in the Index.

CE Century

A limit field

12 in ce
ce=12

The CE field indicates the century (or centuries) in which the narrative source was written.

You can search the CE field with the following operators, as well as with **in** and =:

< Less than,
   such as *ce<13*

> Greater than,
   such as *ce>8*

<= Less than or equal to,
   such as *ce<=12*

>= Greater than or equal to,
   such as *ce>=14*

- Within a range,
   such as *ce=6-9*

CO Context

Note: this field contains English information.

veneration in co

The CO field contains general information about the historical context in which the narrative source was written. The CO field is not systematically filled in.

DS Desiderata

kritische uitgave in ds

The DS field indicates the desiderata in the research and gives suggestions for further research. However, the DS field is not systematically filled in.

ED Editions

pirenne in ed
mgh in ed

The ED field contains bibliographical information on the editions of the narrative source. Titles of journals are abbreviated according to the conventions of the *Revue d'histoire ecclésiastique* (Leuven, since 1900).

EX Explicit

nihil curius unquam habuit in ex

The EX field contains the 'explicit' of the narrative source.

IC Incipit

affin que li grant fait d'armes in ic

The IC field contains the 'incipit' of the narrative source. For some narrative sources, a distinction is made between the incipit of the prologue and the incipit of the corpus.

ID Identification Number

A limit field

C023 in id
id=NL0216

Each record in *Narrative Sources* is assigned a unique Identification Number. This allows to retrieve a specific record at any time or to refer to specific records in publications.

IF Influence

spiegel historiael in if
vincentius bellovacensis in if

The IF field indicates the influence of the narrative source on later works and authors.

LA Language

A limit field

Note: this field contains English information.

latin in la
la=french

The LA field indicates the language(s) in which the narrative source is written. You can search for one (or more) of the following languages:

Dutch
French
Frisian
German
Italian
Latin
Spanish

LI Literature

simons in li

The LI field contains literature on the narrative source and on its author(s). The surveys contained in this field are not exhaustive but should give the main and most recent references. Titles of journals are abbreviated according to the conventions of the *Revue d'histoire ecclésiastique* (Leuven, since 1900).

MS Manuscripts

gent in ms

The MS field contains information on the manuscripts preserving the narrative source. In some cases, the MS field refers to surveys in critical editions.

NA Name of the Contributor

A limit field

jd in na
na=mg

The NA field contains the initials of the contributor who is responsible for the redaction of each separate record. The contributors of *Narrative Sources* 3.3 are:

AK	Ann KELDERS - Ghent University
ALVB	Anne-Laure VAN BRUAENE - Ghent University
BB	Bea BLOKHUIS - University of Groningen
EB	Eric BOUSMAR - Facultés Universitaires Saint Louis, Brussels
FVT	Filip VAN TRICHT - Ghent University
IB	István BEJCZY - University of Nijmegen
IR	Inge ROOSENS - Ghent University
JA	Janick APPELMANS - Catholic University of Leuven
JH	Jelma HOEKSTRA - University of Groningen
JD	Jeroen DEPLOIGE - Ghent University
JVS	Jan VAN SCHAFTINGEN - Catholic University of Leuven
KDR	Karla DE ROEST - University of Groningen
LM	Ludo MILIS - Ghent University
MDR	Martine DE REU - Ghent University
MG	Marit GYPEN - Catholic University of Leuven
PJDG	Pieter-Jan DE GRIECK - Catholic University of Leuven
RN	Renée NIP - University of Groningen
SB	Stijn BOSSUYT - Catholic University of Leuven
SF	Suzan FOLKERTS - University of Groningen
SV	Steven VANDERPUTTEN - Ghent University
VL	Véronique LAMBERT - Ghent University
WV	Werner VERBEKE - Catholic University of Leuven

RE Redaction: Place, Date, Patron and Dedication

Note: this field contains English information.

brabant in re
1099 in re
robertus de craenwic in re

The RE field contains information on the redaction of the narrative source. The following items are treated (in this order): place of redaction, date of redaction, person who commissioned the narrative source, person to whom it was dedicated. An unknown place of redaction is marked as 's.l.'; an unknown date of redaction is marked as 's.d.'.

RG Region: Diocese and Principality

Note: this field contains English information.

dioc cambrai in rg
holland in rg

The RG field indicates the region in which the narrative source was written. First, the diocese is specified (preceded by the abbreviation 'dioc'.), then the Principality (e.g. County of Flanders). Note that the frontiers of the dioceses of the Low Countries did never change during the Middle Ages. This was of course not the case for the political frontiers.

SC Sources

speculum historiale in sc
horatius in sc

The SC field contains information on the sources used by the author(s) of the narrative source.

SI Size

10264 woorden in si

The SI field indicates the size of the narrative source in order to give an idea of its length: the number of words, the number of verses, the number of folios...

ST Status of the author

Note: this field contains English information.

sint-pietersabdij in st
opraem in st

The ST field contains biographical information on the author of the narrative source. Special attention is paid to the religious orders to which the authors belonged. The abbreviations of the religious orders follow the conventions of *Lexikon für Theologie und Kirche*, I (Freiburg, 1957), pp. 12*-15*:

CSA	Augustinian Canons
OCarm	Carmelite Friars
OCart	Carthusians
OFM	Franciscan Friars
OMel	Knights Hospitallers
OP	Dominican Friars
OPraem	Premonstratensian Canons
OSB	Benedictine Monks
OSCr	Crutched Friars
OTemp	Templars
SOCist	Cistercian Monks

TI Title

vita sanctae christinae mirabilis in ti
miracula in ti

The TI field contains the title of the narrative source, given in the language in which it is written. Titles that are not original or posterior to the original redaction are between brackets. Variant titles are given as well.

TL Translations

nederlands in tl
demyttenaere in tl

The TL field contains information on translations of the narrative source. Medieval translations as well as modern translations are indicated.

TY Type

A limit field

Note: this field contains English information.

hagiography in ty
ty=annals

The TY field indicates the type of the narrative source. The typology of this database mainly follows L. Genicot's *Typologie des Sources du Moyen Age Occidental*, fasc. 1, *Introduction* (Turnhout, 1972). It also considers a few types strictly speaking not narrative, but occasionally containing narrative historical information. The TY field includes the following:

Annals
Chronicles
Circumstantial-literature
Correspondence
Diaries-Memoirs
Encyclopedia
Exempla
Fiction
Genealogies
Hagiography
Historical-notes
Histories-Gesta
History-of-literature
Lists
Memorial-books
Necrologia-Obituaria

Pamphlets-Treaties
Poems
Sermons
Travel-stories

UD Update Code

A limit field

19960311 in ud
ud=20020823

The UD field indicates year, month and day of the latest update of the record.

CITN Citation

The Citation is a subset of fields consisting of the following fields:

Identification Number (ID)
Author (AU)
Title (TI)
Century (CE)
Region: Diocese and Principality (RG)

The Citation serves as an easy way to display, print, or save only these fields for a set of records.

Limit Fields

The limit fields listed below are specially indexed fields that have relatively few possible values. They allow to limit searches to records of a particular characteristic, such as type or language of the narrative source.

Identification Number (ID)
Century (CE)
Language (LA)
Type (TY)

You can search these fields with **in** or =. For example, to retrieve narrative sources written in French, type:

french in la or *la=french*

In addition to **in** and =, the following operators may be used with the CE field:

< less than,
such as *ce<13*

> greater than,
such as **ce>8**

<= less than or equal to,
such as *ce<=12*

>= greater than or equal to,
such as *ce>=14*

- within a range,
such as *ce=6-9*

Search Examples

The following examples demonstrate how to search Narrative Sources. These examples are not exhaustive, but do illustrate several search techniques. It is important to note that, although all examples are given in lowercase, this database is not case-sensitive; whether your search terms are entered in upper- or lower-case, the same records will be retrieved.

Example 1
Suppose you want to find narrative sources about the Burgundian court written in French.

1. Search for *b??rg??n**. Use the wildcard and truncation symbols to get various spellings including "bourgogn*" and "burgun*".

2. Combine the results with a search for court by entering *and court*.

3. Limit the results to French narrative sources only by entering *and french in la*.

Example 2
Suppose you want to find hagiographic narrative sources about miracles written between the 13th and the 15th century.

1. Search for **mira***.

2. Combine the results with a search for hagiographic narrative sources by entering *and ty=hagiography*. Searching in the Type (TY) field ensures that you limit your search to narrative sources of that type.

3. Limit the results to narrative sources written between the 13th and the 15th century by entering *and ce=13-15*.

Stopwords in *Narrative Sources*

Words of little intrinsic meaning that appear too frequently to be useful in searching text are known as "stopwords". You cannot search for the following stopwords by themselves, but you can include them within phrases:

and
en
et
in
niet
of
or
ou
voor

Using the Index to Find an Author

To locate an author, look up the first name in the Index. A segment of the Index beginning with the author's first name will be listed; included are all variations of the name that appear in the database. For example, if you look up *aegidius*, you will find "aegidius", "aegidius-aureaevallensis", "aegidius-carlerius" and others. Select and search for the appropriate variations and you will retrieve all narrative sources written by that author.

Alternatively, you can search for an author in the Author (AU) field.

Combining Searches

Beginning a search request with an operator (**and, not, or, with, near,** or **in**) automatically combines that request with the previous one.

For instance, if the search you just completed is *fourth crusade*, searching for *and baldwin* will give you the same results as if you search for *fourth crusade and baldwin*. Similarly, the completed search *sigebertus gemblacensis* followed by the search *in au* is the same as *sigebertus gemblacensis in au*.

Truncation and Wildcards

You can use the truncation symbol (*) as a substitute for any string of zero or more characters in your search term. For example, the search *mira** retrieves any record containing "mirakel", "mirakels", "mirakelboek", "miracula", "miraculorum", "miracles" etc.

You can use the wildcard symbol (?) as a substitute for one character or none. For example, the search *vla?nderen* retrieves records containing "vlaanderen" or "vlaenderen".

The truncation and wildcard symbols can be used anywhere in your search term, except as the first character.

Correspondence and Submission of New Records

Suggestions, additions, remarks or questions of any kind are always welcome. Users are invited to submit new records that will be integrated in the next version of *Narrative Sources*. Their contribution will be acknowledged. Record submissions should follow the field-structure of this database but can be in any language. All correspondence should be mailed to the following address:

Jeroen Deploige
Vakgroep Middeleeuwse Geschiedenis
Blandijnberg 2
B-9000 Ghent
Belgium
tel.: +32/9/264.40.21
fax: +32/9/264.41.82
e-mail: Jeroen.Deploige@UGent.be

INDEX LIBRORUM MANU SCRIPTORUM

Boulogne-sur-Mer
Bibliothèque municipale
   146 A: 254, 263

Brugge
Grootseminarie
   127/5: 260, 264, 268
Stadsbibliotheek
   425: 202
   441: 265

Bruxelles/Brussel
Bibliothèque royale Albert Ier - Koninklijke Bibliotheek Albert I
   837-845: 11
   2057-63: 94
   4459-4470: 265
   5764: 51
   7978-79: 964
   8146-9: 202
   8181: 202
   11974-11985: 201
   13076-7: 143, 145, 256, 257, 264, 267
   13524: 194, 195
   13525-26: 202
   18064-69: 261, 262, 264, 268
   18179-80: 264
   II 480: 190, 199
   II 1055bis: 254, 264, 266
   II 1169: 264
   II 1515: 265
   IV 119: 143, 145, 158, 256, 257, 264

Cambrai
Bibliothèque municipale
   965: 264

Den Haag
Rijksmuseum Meermanno-Westreenianum
   10 A 21: 264

Douai
Bibliothèque municipale
   170: 265
   798: 47, 52, 53
   850: 42

Gent
Universiteitsbibliotheek
   224: 265
   542: 107-108

Kortrijk
Stadsbibliotheek
Fonds Goethals-Vercruysse, Ms 135:
   142, 145, 256, 257, 264

London
British Library
   Add. 30033: 259, 264
   Sloane 1772: 94

Montpellier
Bibliothèque interuniversitaire, Section Médicine
   375: 264

Monza
Biblioteca Capitolare
   f-9/176: 265

Ophain
Archives Bois-Seigneur-Isaac
   34: 182-192

Oxford
Exeter College
   158: 103, 105

Paris
Bibliothèque de l'Arsenal
   922: 264
Bibliothèque Nationale de France
   lat. 4867: 264

lat. 4931 A: 264
lat. 5373A: 96, 97, 99
lat. 5390: 31
lat. 5406: 93
lat. 5407: 93
lat. 5995: 264
lat. 8865: 264
lat. 14194: 169
lat. 14624: 264
nouv. acq. lat. 1543: 254, 263
Bibliothèque Sainte-Geneviève
   240: 94

Rouen
Bibliothèque municipale
   1131 (olim U11): 264

Saint-Omer
Bibliothèque municipale
   739 (olim 630): 259, 264
   740: 259, 264
   1489: 259

Tournai
Archives de l'État
   Cartulaire 89bis: 114
   Cartulaire 91: 114

Utrecht
Universiteitsbibliotheek
   391: 13

Valenciennes
Bibliothèque municipale
   406 (olim 388): 265
   768-770 (olim 578): 258, 264

Vaticano, Città del
Biblioteca Apostolica Vaticana
   Vat. lat. 4015: 96, 99, 101
   Vat. lat. 4016: 96
   Vat. lat. 4017: 96
   Vat. lat. 4019: 95-97

Wien
Österreichische Nationalbibliothek
   12816: 203
   13708: 109
   Ser. n. 12708-9: 265, 196-198
   Ser. n. 12710: 260

INDEX NOMINUM

Aantekeningen uit Albergen: 10
Aantekeningen uit Galilea Minor: 10
Abaelardus, Petrus: 27
Acardus, abbot of Arrouaise: 82, 84
Adeliza of Louvain, queen: 21, 34-36
Adrianus de Budt
   Continuatio Chronodromis Brandonis et Bekae: 46
   Chronicon Flandriae: 46, 50, 51
Adso Dervensis, abbot of Montier-en-Der: 29-31
Aegidius Aureaevallensis (Gilles d'Orval): 49, 165, 168
   Gesta episcoporum Leodiensium: 165
Aegidius Breedeyck: 187, 188, 201, 203
Aegidius de Roya
   Compendium historiae universalis: 258, 264
Aegidius Li Muisis: vide Gilles Li Muisis
Affligem: 36, 43, 151, 166-180
Alanus ab Insulis (Alain de Lille): 176
Alardus de Bourgella: 153
Alardus de Ghelier: 203
Albert ter Achter, Life of -: 12
Albertus Magnus: 95
Alcuinus
   Vita S. Willibrordi: 5
Aldegundis, abbess of Maubeuge: 56-75
Aldetrudis, abbess of Maubeuge 56, 58, 59, 61, 63-69, 75
Alençon: 25
Alice of Brabant: 165
Altfridus
   Vita Liudgeri: 7
Amalberga, saint: 11
Amand (Leven van Sinte -): vide Gillis de Wevel
Amandus, saint: 39, 107-137

Amandus de Castello (Amand du Chastel))
   Vita Odonis episcopi Cameracensis: 77
Anchin: 44, 46, 87
Andreas Marchianensis (Marchiennes)
   Chronicon Marchianense: 42
   Continuatio Aquicinctina Sigeberti Gemblacensis: 46
   Historia succincta de gestis et successione regum Francorum: 54, 264
Andres: 87
Annales Cameracenses: 40, 42
Annales Gandenses: 46
Annales Laubienses: 46
Annales Lobienses: 41, 265
Annales Marchianenses: 265
Annales S. Jacobi Leodiensis: 44, 45
Anselmus S. Lamberti Leodiensis canonicus
   Gesta episcoporum Leodiensium: 165
Ansoaldis, abbess of Maubeuge: 73, 74
Antichrist: 29-31
Antwerp: 173,174
Arnoldus Beeltsens
   Chronica domus virginis Mariae in Herne: 51
Arnulfus, archdeacon of Thérouanne: 82
Arnulfus, bishop of Metz: 127, 128
Arnulfus, bishop of Soissons: 77, 127, 128, 261
Arras: 80-83, 86, 88, 89, 264
Asse: 168
Atropos, goddess: 33
Auchy: 86, 87
Audomarus, saint 259
Augustinus Hipponensis: 29, 32, 54, 232

Aulne-sur-Sambre: 254, 255, 264, 266

Baisy: 169
Balduinus I of Jerusalem: 169
Balduinus V, count of Flanders: 82
Balduinus VII, count of Flanders: 47
Barbara, martyr: 13, 14
Barlaam et Josaphat: 118-126, 135
Basse-Wavre: 169
Barthelemy, Reclus de Molliens: 159
Battle Abbey: 34, 36
Baudouin de Sebourc (Roman de -): 137
Bavo, saint: 118, 136
Bellingen: 178
Benedeit
　Voyage de Saint Brendan: 35
Benedictus I, pope: 236
Benedictus Casinensis: 157
Benoît de Sainte-Maure
　Roman de Troie: 246
Berardo Apillaterre, notary: 98
Bergues-Saint-Winnoc: 86, 87
Bernardus, abbot of Watten: 84
Bernardus Claraevallensis: 164
Bernardus Guidonis
　Sanctorale: 93, 94
Bernold of Watten: 83
Bertila, saint: 57, 59
Bertinus, abbot of Saint-Bertin (Saint-Omer): 259
Blomberg: 186
Bois-Seigneur-Isaac: 182-204
Bonaventura: 175
Boudewijn: vide Balduinus
Boulogne-sur-Mer: 23, 86, 87, 165, 169, 171
Bourbourg: 86, 87
Bourges: 97
Brabant, duchy of -: 163-180
Brendan, Voyage of Saint - : 35
Brevis relatio de Guillelmo nobillissimo comite Normannorum: 34
Bruges: 24, 107, 137
Bruille: 146
Brussels: 169, 172, 186, 187
Burchardus, bishop of Worms: 25, 26, 33

Buzelinus, Johannes: 127

Caesar, Caius Julius: 32
Calais: 148, 150
Cambron: 264
Carolus Magnus: 169, 173, 200
Cassel: 147
Celestinus I, pope: 236
Charlemagne: vide Carolus Magnus
Charles VII, king of France: 7
Charles, duke of Lotharingia: 170
Charles le Bon, count of Flanders: 24, 81
Chocques: 86, 87
Christina Mirabilis, mystic: 178
Chrodegangus, bishop of Metz: 62
Chronica de origine ducum Brabantiae: 170-174
Chronica monasterii Guatinensis: 43, 44
Chronica monasterii Villariensis: 43
Chronicon Affligemense: 265
Chronicon Aldenburgensis monasterii maius: 264, 268
Chronicon genealogicum Nivellense: 166
Chronicon monasterii Aldenburgensis: 50
Chronicon S. Huberti Andaginensis: 265
Chronicon Vormoselense: 86
Chronyke van Nederlant: 51
Clarembold of Senlis: 83
Clemens IV, pope: 95
Clemens VI, pope
　Collationes: 94
Clementia, countess of Flanders: 82, 86
Clotho, goddess: 33
Collectanea ad historiam Devotionis Modernis: 11, 12
Cologne: 186
Cono of Preneste, abbot of Arrouaise: 83, 84
Constance of Lincolnshire: 35
Constantinus I, emperor: 126-131, 236, 237
Cornelius Aurelius
　Divisiekroniek: 5, 7

Cornelius Menghers de Zantfliet
   Chronicon: 50
Cousolre: 60, 74
Crosses: 97

Dagobert I, king: 128
Damme: 109
Dares Phrygius
   De excidio Troiae historia: 246, 247
David of Bourgogne, bishop of Utrecht: 264
David the Scot: 35
De antiquitate urbis Tornacensis: 45
De Balduino VII comite Flandrensi: 47
De fundatione abbatiae Ninivensis: 42
De fundatione et lapsu monasterii Lobiensis: 40
De inchoatione monasterii Sancti Andree iuxta Brugis: 42
De insidiis regis Francorum in domum Burgundicam: 265
De institutione sanctimonialium Aquis-granensis: 62
De lite abbatiarum Elnonensis et Hasnoniensis: 265
De scriptoribus ecclesiasticis: vide Henricus Bruxellensis
Dentelin: 56
Deventer: 203
Die alder excellenste cronycke van Brabant: 174

Edith, queen of England: 26
Edith of Hereford: 99-106
Edmondus de Dynter: 174
Edward, king of England: 26
Egbert ter Beek, Life of -: 12
Eleanor of Aquitaine: 36
Emma of Rouen: 26
Engelbertus Admontensis (Engelbert of Admont)
   De miraculis Christi: 91, 95
Epistola contra eos qui dicunt cronicas inanes seu inutiles: 38, 47-49, 51, 53
Epitaphium Balduini VII comitis Flandriae: 47

Eusebius of Caesarea: 47
Eustach of Boulogne: 169
Eva Crispin: 23
Evantius: 110, 112, 113
Eversham: 87
Evrard de Béthune: 177
Exordium seu fundatio monasterii Affligemensis: 43, 172

Fécamp: 31, 32
Floreffe: 46, 261-264, 269
Florens Radewijns: 197
Folcuinus: 259
   Gesta abbatum Sithiensium: 40, 41, 43,
Forest: 177
Franco, abbot of Affligem: 176, 177
Frasnes: 169
Fundatio monasterii Aquicinctini: 44
Fundatio monasterii Arroasiensis: 42, 51
Fundatio monasterii Sancti Nicolai de Pratis Tornacensis: 43
Furnes: 86, 87

Gallus: 110, 112, 113
Galterius, archidiaconus Tervanensis (Walter of Thérouanne / Gautier de Thérouanne): 82
   Vita Johannis episcopi Teruanensis: 77-90
   Vita Karoli comitis: 81, 87
Gaspar Ofhuys: 190, 192, 196, 198, 199
   De benefactoribus: 198
   De originale cenobii Rubee Vallis in Zonia: 198
   De onere missarum: 198
Geert Grote: 12, 197, 200, 203
Geffrei Gaimar: 35
Gembloux: 171, 208, 222, 226
Genappe: 169
Genealogia comitum Buloniensium: 165, 167
Genealogia ducum Brabantiae: 165, 166, 169-171, 173, 179, 180
Gennadius Massiliensis: 175
Gerard of Cambrai: 82, 84, 172

Gerard of Ham, abbot: 84
Gerard of Lo, abbot: 84
Gerard of Louvain: 177
Gerard of Muro: 159
Gerard of Ypres, abbot of Saint-Martin: 84, 85
Gerard Suggerode
  Chronicon: 10
Gerberga, queen of France: 28, 29, 31
Gerberga of Brabant: 167
Gertrudis, abbess of Nivelles: 57, 166, 167, 170
Gervasius, saint: 11
Gesta Fresonum: 10
Gesta sanctorum Villariensium: 265
Gesta Silvestri: 126-131, 135, 136
Ghent: 39, 40, 49, 86, 186, 190, 191, 258-260, 264, 265
Ghislenus, saint: 57, 58, 75
Gilbert Foliot: 33, 34
Gilbert of Hereford: 100, 101
Gilles Li Muisis (Aegidius Li Muisis): 140-162, 255-259, 264, 257
  Abbatum memoria: 143
  C'est des curés et des capelains: 159
  C'est des estas de tous prélas: 151
  Ch'est de l'estat: 143, 156
  Ch'est des maintiens des homme et chou qu'il doivent faire: 158
  Ch'est li complainte des dames: 158
  Che sont les médidations: 150, 151, 159
  Chronicon: 144, 147, 148, 150
  Des estas de tous gens seculiers: 152, 157
  Ch'est li complainte des compagnons: 150, 151, 158
  Li Maintiens des monnes: 156, 157, 161
  Tractatus primus: 142, 144, 145, 160
  Tractatus secundus: 141, 142, 155, 156, 160
  Tractatus tertius: 141-155, 158, 159
  Tractatus quartus: 141-143, 145, 149-153, 155, 158-160, 267

Gilles of Orval: vide Aegidius Aureaevallensis
Gillis Breedeyck: vide Aegidius Breedeyk
Gillis de Wevel
  Leven van Sinte Amand: 107-137
Giovanni da Signa: 106
Gislebertus, abbot of Ename: 169
Godefridus, bishop of Amiens: 78, 84
Godefridus I, duke of Brabant: 168, 172
Godefridus II, duke of Brabant: 171, 172
Godefridus III, duke of Brabant: 169
Godefroid de Bouillon: 168, 169, 172
Godefroid of Anjou: 23
Godelieve of Gistel, saint: 261
Godeschalcus, abbot of Affligem: 169
Godfried: vide Godefridus
Gozelinus, dean of Thérouanne: 87
Grand-Bigard: 177
Gregorius Magnus (Gregory I the Great, pope): 31, 114-118, 178
  Dialogi: 115, 135, 136
  Homiliae: 114-115
Groenendaal (Viridisvallis): 51, 182, 189, 192, 200, 203
Gudula, saint: 167, 170, 172
Guerric of Saint-Quentin: 177
Guibertus Novigentensis (Guibert de Nogent): 25
Guibert de Tournai: 177
Guillaume I, count of Namur: 187, 198
Guillaume de Châtillon: 176
Guillaume de Jumièges: 23
Guillaume de Lorris
  (Le) Roman de la Rose: 159
Guillaume de Machaut: 151
Guillaume de Saint-Thierry: 47
Guillaume Durand, bishop of Mende: 95
Guillelmus (William of Volpiano), abbot of Fécamp: 31
Guillelmus Gemeticensis (William of Jumièges)
  Gesta Normanorum Ducum: 23
Guillelmus Malmesberiensis (William of Malmesbury): 25

Guînes: 86, 87
Gunnor, countess of Normandy: 26

Ham: 170
Hamme: 170
Hariulfus Aldenburgensis (Hariulf of Oudenburg): 77
Hasnon: 265
Hautmont: 56, 254, 263
Helena, saint: 237-239, 242
Hendrik: vide Henricus/Henry
Hennen van Merchtenen: 174
Henri de France, bishop of Rheims: 264
Henricus V, emperor: 23
Henricus I, duke of Brabant: 168
Henricus III, duke of Brabant: 165, 167
Henricus IV, duke of Brabant: 165
Henricus Bruxellensis, monk of Affligem: 175-178
   De viris illustribus: 178-180
Henricus Gandavensis (Henry of Ghent): 175
Henricus Pomerius (Hendrik Utenbogaerde): 202
   Liber de origine monasterii Viridisvallis: 51, 189, 197
Henry I, king of England: 21, 23, 33-36
Henry II of Verdun: 168
Henry de Schorne: 95
Herbert, archdeacon of Thérouanne: 82
Herbert of Voormezele: 84
Hereford: 95-106
Herent: 182
Herigerus Lobiensis
   Gesta episcoporum Leodiensium: 165
Herimannus Tornacensis (Herman of Tournai): 35
   Liber de restauratione monasterii Sancti Martini Tornacensis: 43
Herleva of Normandy: 25
Herne (Hérinnes-lez-Enghien): 51
Hesdin: 87
Hieronymus, saint: 175, 179

Hildebertus Lavardinensis (of Lavardin): 34
Henricus de Merica (Hendrik van der Heyden)
   Historia compendiosa de cladibus Leodiensium: 46
Hildefonsus Toletanus: 175
Historia monasterii Hasnoniensis: 42
Historia monasterii Viconiensis: 40
Historia sanguinis miraculosi de Busco Domini Isaac: 195
Historiae Tornacenses: 45
Homer: 246
Honorius III, pope: 98
Honorius Augustodunensis: 175
Hucbaldus Elnonensis (Hucbald of Saint-Amand)
   Vita Rictrudis: 68, 70, 71
Hugo a Sancto Victore: 176
Hugo Floriacensis:
   Historia Ecclesiastica: 53, 49
Hugo, archbishop of Lyon: 84
Hugo, bishop of Rouen: 84
Hystorie ende mirakelen vanden heilighen bloede van Boschysaac: 193, 194

Ida, abbess of Nivelles: 166, 169
Ida of Boulogne: 169
Innocentius III, pope: 94, 104, 105
Innocentius IV, pope: 98
Innocentius V, pope: 175
Inventio crucis-legend: 238, 239, 241, 242
Iohannes Amoury: 192
Iohannes Rooms: 192
Irmgard of Limbourg: 171
Isidorus Hispalensis: 175
Ittre: 189
Iudocus Rogerii: 192
Ivo Carnotensis, bishop of Chartres: 83, 84

Jacob van Maerlant
   Der naturen bloeme: 245, 246
   Scolastica (Rijmbijbel): 128-132
   Spiegel Historiael: 109-137, 173
   Ystorie van Troyen: 245-248

Jacobus de Vitriaco: 47, 176
  Historia Jherosolimitana abbreviata: 47
Jacobus de Voragine
  Legenda aurea: 14, 114, 118, 238, 242
Jacques de Guise
  Annales Hannoniae: 258, 264
Jacques Muevin: 144, 145
Jan I, count of Holland: 232, 233
Jan I, duke of Brabant: 165, 167, 170, 172
Jan II, count of Holland: 232, 233
Jan II, duke of Brabant: 170, 172
Jan of Hattem, Life of -: 12
Jan van Boendale
  Brabantsche Yeesten: 172-174
  Der Leken Spieghel: 234, 235, 243-245, 248
Jan van Ruusbroec: 182, 189, 200
Jaquemon Bochet
  Tiaudelet: 159
Jargeau: 97
Jason: 246
Jean II le Bon, king of France: 149
Jean de le Mote: 151
Jean de Meung
  (Le) Roman de la Rose: 159
Jean d'Abbeville: 176
Jean d'Outremeuse
  Ly Mireur des histors: 112
Jean Li Muisis: 150
Jean Wallegrape: 145
Jeanne, duchess of Brabant: 187, 200, 201
Jeanne Laboyson de Crosses: 97-99, 102-106
Jerome, saint: 175, 179
Jerusalem: 194, 238, 260
Jever: 5
Jocio, monk: 260
Jocundus
  Vita Servatii: 7
Joes van Dormael: 44
Johannes, abbot of Fécamp: 31
Johannes, bishop of Thérouanne: 77-80
Johannes Ammonius: 51
Johannes Bellens: 190-192

Johannes Brando
  Chronodromon: 50, 264
Johannes de Beka: 3
Johannes de Busco: 185, 189, 190, 192, 193, 203
Johannes de Loos
  Chronicon: 50
Johannes de Thielrode
  Chronicon Sancti Bavonis: 49
Johannes Diaconus
  Vita S. Gregorii: 114
Johannes Gielemans: 196-199, 202
  Hagiologium Brabantinorum: 199, 200
  Historiologium Brabantinorum: 260, 264
  Historia de miraculosa revelatione venerabilis Sacramenti in civitate Bruxellensi: 186
  Novale Sanctorum: 198, 199, 201
  Primordiale monasterii Rubee Vallis: 198, 202
  Tractatulus de origine monasterii Semptem Fontium: 198
Johannes Hagen: 186
Johannes Iperius
  Chronicon Sancti Bertini: 50, 259, 263, 264
Johannes le Familieur: vide Johannes de Busco
John of Worchester: 21
John Pecham: 101
Josaphat: 118-120
Josina Des Plancques: 191
Judas: 239
Julianus Cenomannensis (Le Mans), saint: 134-136
Julianus hospitator, saint: 134

Karel ende Elegast: 248, 249
Koksijde: vide Ten Duinen

Lachesis, goddess: 33
Lambert of Thérouanne: 81
Lambert of Utrecht: 83
Lambertus, bishop of Arras: 84
Lambertus, abbot of Saint-Bertin: 83, 84, 86, 90

Landry: 56, 58, 59
Le Bec: 21, 23, 32
Lescot, Hubert: 196
Liafwinus, saint: 11
Lidwina of Schiedam: 185
Lietbertus, bishop of Cambrai: 77
Lille: 82
Limbourg: 171
Lisiardus, bishop of Soissons: 77
Liudgerus
    Vita s. Gregorii: 5, 7
Liutgert of Buderick, Life of -: 12
Lo: 86, 87
Lobbes: 40, 41, 63, 167, 265
Lodewijk van Velthem: 110
Lotharingia: 180
Louis I the Pious: 62
Louis IV, king of France: 28
Louis IX, king of France: 94, 95
Louis XI, king of France: 7
Louis d'Anjou, bishop of Toulouse: 94
Louis de Nevers, count of Flanders: 147
Louvain: 171, 172, 180, 186
Loyset Liédet: 200, 260
Lucas d'Eyck, monk of Floreffe: 261, 262
Lutgart of Tongres, mystic: 178

Maastricht: 114, 128
Madelbertus, saint: 56, 58, 59, 61, 68-70, 75
Madelgarius, saint: 56
Manasses, archbishop of Rheims: 84
Marbais: 164
Marcel Voet
    Liber fundationis: 51
Marchiennes: 44, 47, 49
Margaret of Antioch, saint: 132-134, 136
Marie de France: 168
Marie d'Oignies, mystic: 179
Marie van Mostroel: 194, 195
Maroilles: 167
Martelinus, Marcus: 202
Martinus of Tours, saint: 11, 110-114
Mathieu de Haudion: 154
Matilda I of Germany: 2, 21, 23, 28, 31, 33, 34, 36

Matilda, duchess of Normandy: 30-33
Matilda II of Normandy: 33, 35
Matilda, abbess of Quedlinburg: 28
Maubeuge: 56-75, 167
Melis Stoke
    Rijmkroniek: 232-234
Melle: 188, 193, 203
Meltis Castellum: 56
Merchtem: 87
Milo Crispin: 23
Milo Elnonensis (of Saint-Amand): 108, 118
Mons: 56, 59, 60, 167
Mont-Saint-Eloi: 88, 89
Moorsel: 167, 170
Mora: 33

Nachor: 118-125
Namur: 164
Neithart Bulst: 31
Nicholas of Tolentino: 98
Nicolaus Ambianensis (of Amiens)
    De sancto Godefrido episcopo Ambianensi: 78
Nicolaus Cusanus: 186
Nicolaus de Cruce: 192
Nicolaus Ruterius (de Ruystre), bishop of Arras: 264
Nieuwlicht (Nova Lux): 13
Nijmegen: 171
Ninus, Assyrian king: 254, 255
Nivelles: 166-168, 170, 189, 190, 104
Nonnenbossche: 87

Odo, bishop of Cambrai: 77, 84, 171, 176
Odo of Châteauroux, cardinal: 95, 99
Oignies: 190
Ophain: vide Bois-Seigneur-Isaac
Ordericus Vitalis: 21, 25
Otto I of Germany: 28
Oudenburg: 50, 128, 260, 261, 264, 268,
Ovidius Naso, Publius: 246

Paschalis II, pope: 79, 85
Peter de Minci, bishop of Chartres: 95
Peter Hoorn: 12

Peter of Tarantaise (Innocent V, pope): 175
Petrus I, abbot of Marchiennes: 47
Petrus Cantor (Peter the Chanter): 177
Petrus Comestor
Historia scolastica: 128
Petrus de Alliaco (Pierre d'Ailly): 186, 187, 197, 198, 203
Petrus de Moussein: 153
Petrus de Thimo: 174
Petrus Impens: 203
Petrus Floreffiensis (Petrus de Herentals)
Chronicon de pontificibus et de imperatoribus: 264
Philip Berruyer, archbishop of Bourges: 95-99
Philip Utenbroeke: 109, 110, 118-131
Philippe II Auguste, king of France: 146, 168
Philippe IV le Bel, king of France 148
Philippe VI, king of France: 147
Philippe de Thaon: 36
Bestiaire: 36
Livre de Sibyl: 36
Philippe de Vitri: 151
Philippe le Bon, duke of Bourgogne: 193
Philippe of Bergamo: 176
Philippus de Eleemosyna (Philippe of Aumône): 108
Pierart dou Tielt: 141, 256
Pierre Courauld, abbot of Ghent: 259
Pierre Li Muisis: 149, 150
Pippin of Landen: 166, 167
Poleticum Marceniensis cenobii: 45
Pontanus, Ambrosius: 201, 202
Compendium historiale: 201
Gazophylacium: 201
Ponthieu: 35
Priamus: 165, 173

Quintinus, martyr: 60, 73

Radbodus, bishop of Utrecht: 10, 11, 17
Radulphus Cameracensis (Rodulph of Cambrai)
Vita S. Lietberti: 75

Radulphus Glaber: 31
Radulphus Trudonensis (Rodulph of Sint-Truiden)
Gesta abbatum Trudonensium: 44, 45, 50
Rainerus Sancti Jacobi Leodiensis prior
Annales Sancti Jacobi Leodiensis: 42, 44, 45
Rainoldus, archbishop of Rheims: 79
Rainout of Gelre: 171
Ralph Baldock, bishop of London: 95
Ralph Bocking: 94
Ratio fundationis seu aedificationis Blandiniensis coenobii: 39, 40, 265
Reading Abbey: 21, 36
Regnier V, count of Hainaut: 73
Regula S. Benedicti: 43, 62, 64, 66, 68, 74, 161, 168
Reiner d'Aubigny: 36
Renerus Snoyus (Reiner Snoy)
De rebus Batavicis: 5
Richard, bishop of Chichester: 94, 99
Richard of Arrouaise: 84
Rijmgenealogie van Brabant: 173
Rijmkroniek van Brabant: 173
Robert Curthose: 30
Robert d'Arras: 83
Robertus I, count of Flanders: 82
Robertus, archbishop of Rouen: 25, 26
Robertus de Beton, bishop of Hereford: 101
Robertus de Marzy, bishop of Nevers: 95
Robertus de Torineo: 23, 34, 35
Rocamadour: 98, 99
Rodulfus: vide Radulphus
Roland van den Dorpe
Die alder excellenste cronycke van Brabant: 174
Rolland, abbot of Hasnon: 42
(Le) Roman de Baudouin de Sebourc: 137
Rome: 189, 194, 236, 237
Rouge Cloître (Rooklooster): 182, 190, 192, 196-200, 202, 260, 261, 264, 265
Roussiaus li Kos: 153

Rudolf Dier of Muiden: 12
Ruisseauville: 86, 87

Saint-Amand-les-Eaux: 127, 265
Saint-André-lez-Bruges: 42, 43
Saint-Ghislain: 167
Saint-Gilles-du-Gard: 98, 99
Saint-Hubert: 265
Saint-Omer: 80, 86, 87, 90, 254, 258-261, 263
Saint-Trond (Sint-Truiden): 50, 75
Samer: 87
Satan: 113
Scheut: 51
Seghelijn van Jherusalem: 236-243, 246-249
Segher Diengotgaf: 245
Semiramis: 25, 26
Seneca, Lucius Annaeus: 136
Septfontaines: vide Zevenborren
Sibyl: 29-32, 36
Sigebertus Gemblacensis (Sigebert of Gembloux) : 42, 47, 167, 169, 175, 179, 180, 254
   Chronicon: 263, 264, 266
   Chronographia: 171, 173
Signy: 51
Silvester I, pope: 126-131
Silvinus, saint: 259
Simon de Floreffe
   Chronique rimée de Floreffe: 46, 261-264, 269
Simon of Affligem: 178
Simon of Tournai: 176, 177
Simon Sithiensis, abbot of Saint-Bertin
   Gesta abbatum Sithiensium: 78, 80, 82-84, 86-90
Soignies: 56, 59
Statius, Publius Papinius: 136, 246
Stephan of Grandmont: 93
Stephanus, protomartyr: 97, 99
Stephanus de Liciaco
   De revelatione beati Stephani: 93
Stephanus Predare: 192
Stephen, king of England: 36
Stigand, archbishop of Canterbury: 26
Suitbertus, saint: 11

Sulpicius Severus
   Dialogi: 110-114
   Vita S. Martini: 135, 136
Swansea: 101

Ten Duinen: 86, 258, 264, 265
Testamentum Aldegundis: 66, 67, 72, 73
Thérouanne: 77-90
Thierry de Saint-Hubert: 73, 74
Thomas, bishop of Hereford: 95, 96, 99-101, 103, 105
Thomas Aquinas: 93-95
Thomas Basin: 7
Thomas Cantimpratensis (Thomas de Cantimpré): 177, 178
   Bonum universale de apibus: 164
Thomas a Kempis
   Dialogus noviciorum: 197, 198, 202
Thomas of Saint Omer: 101
Tournai: 43, 45, 140-162, 177, 255-8, 264, 267
Tours: 113
Trubert: 218, 219

Urbanus II, pope: 83

Van der Hecken, Aegidius
   Cathalogus fratrum: 201
   Memoriale benefactorum: 201
Veranus, saint: 97-99
Verdun: 172
Vergilius Maro, Publius: 29, 32, 33
Versus de Unibove: 206-229
Vieux Monastère: 90
Villers: 43, 164, 265
Vincentius, martyr: 57-58, 61
Vincentius Bellovacensis (Vincent de Beauvais)
   Speculum historiale: 109, 110, 113, 114, 119-122, 126, 159, 260
Vincentius Stoop: 192
Vita Amandi: vide Milo Elnonensis, Philippus de Eleemosyna
Visio Tnugdali: 107
Vita Aldetrudis: 63-70, 71, 74
Vita Aldegundis prima: 59, 60, 63-65, 68

Vita Aldegundis altera: 65-72
Vita Aldegundis tertia: 71-74
Vita Aldegundis quarta: 73, 74
Vita Aldegundis quinta: 73, 74
Vita Amandi: 108, 110, 113, 128, 134, 135
Vita Gertrudis tripartita: 167
Vita Madelbertae: 68-74
Vita Norberti: 51
Vita Philippi archiepiscopi Biturcensis: 99
Vita Rictrudis: vide Hucbaldus
Vita Theodorici abbatis Andaginensis: 73, 74
Voet, Marcel: 51
Voormezele: 84, 86, 87
Voyage of Saint Brendan: 35
Vriesche Aentyckeninge: 10

Walbertus, saint: 57, 59
Waldetrudis, saint: 56-61, 64, 68, 167
Walo, bishop of Paris: 84
Walram IV of Limbourg: 171
Walter, archdeacon of Thérouanne: vide Galterius Tervanensis
Warnestun: 87
Watten: 43, 44, 87, 90
Waudru: vide Waldetrudis

Wazemmes: 127
Wiaert, Johannes Baptista: 202
Wilhelmus Catthem: 201
Willem van Affligem: 177, 178
William I, the Conqueror: 25, 32, 34, 36
William Adelin: 21, 34
William Cragh: 101, 105
William d'Aubigny: 36
William de Montfort: 101
William of Festa: 95
William of Jumièges: 23
William of Malmesbury: 25
William of Poitiers: 32
Wistanton: 102
Witgerus
 Genealogia Arnulfi comitis Flandriae: 51, 164

Ypres: 84, 86, 87
Ysentrude of Mekeren, Life of -: 12
Ysona: 238
Yves of Tréguier: 94

Zevenborren (Septfontaines): 182, 187, 188, 198, 200, 201
Zweder of Boecholt
 Passionale: 13

www.ingramcontent.com/pod-product-compliance
Ingram Content Group UK Ltd.
Pitfield, Milton Keynes, MK11 3LW, UK
UKHW021836140426
5217IPUK00021B/1489